T0285209

EMPIRE OF DEBT

Third Edition

EMPIRE OF DEBT

We Came, We Saw, We Borrowed

Third Edition

ADDISON WIGGIN

WILLIAM BONNER

WILEY

Copyright © 2024 by Addison Wiggin and William Bonner. All rights reserved.

Published by John Wiley & Sons, Inc., Hoboken, New Jersey.
Published simultaneously in Canada.

No part of this publication may be reproduced, stored in a retrieval system, or transmitted in any form or by any means, electronic, mechanical, photocopying, recording, scanning, or otherwise, except as permitted under Section 107 or 108 of the 1976 United States Copyright Act, without either the prior written permission of the Publisher, or authorization through payment of the appropriate per-copy fee to the Copyright Clearance Center, Inc., 222 Rosewood Drive, Danvers, MA 01923, (978) 750-8400, fax (978) 750-4470, or on the web at www.copyright.com. Requests to the Publisher for permission should be addressed to the Permissions Department, John Wiley & Sons, Inc., 111 River Street, Hoboken, NJ 07030, (201) 748-6011, fax (201) 748-6008, or online at http://www.wiley.com/go/permission.

Trademarks: Wiley and the Wiley logo are trademarks or registered trademarks of John Wiley & Sons, Inc. and/or its affiliates in the United States and other countries and may not be used without written permission. All other trademarks are the property of their respective owners. John Wiley & Sons, Inc. is not associated with any product or vendor mentioned in this book.

Limit of Liability/Disclaimer of Warranty: While the publisher and author have used their best efforts in preparing this book, they make no representations or warranties with respect to the accuracy or completeness of the contents of this book and specifically disclaim any implied warranties of merchantability or fitness for a particular purpose. No warranty may be created or extended by sales representatives or written sales materials. The advice and strategies contained herein may not be suitable for your situation. You should consult with a professional where appropriate. Further, readers should be aware that websites listed in this work may have changed or disappeared between when this work was written and when it is read. Neither the publisher nor authors shall be liable for any loss of profit or any other commercial damages, including but not limited to special, incidental, consequential, or other damages.

For general information on our other products and services or for technical support, please contact our Customer Care Department within the United States at (800) 762-2974, outside the United States at (317) 572-3993 or fax (317) 572-4002.

Wiley also publishes its books in a variety of electronic formats. Some content that appears in print may not be available in electronic formats. For more information about Wiley products, visit our web site at www.wiley.com.

Library of Congress Cataloging-in-Publication Data is Available:

ISBN 9781394174676 (Cloth)
ISBN 9781394201969 (ePDF)
ISBN 9781394201976 (ePub)

Cover Design: Mark O'Dell
Cover Images: © John Baggaley/Getty Images | © Michael Orso/Getty Images
Author Photos: Courtesy of the Authors

SKY10069991_032024

CONTENTS

INTRODUCTION

THE BUBBLE EMPIRE, REDUX

The will of Zeus is moving toward its end.

—*The Iliad*

What a strange delight! You are reading an updated version of a book we wrote nearly 20 years ago. Here, we have a chance to explain away our errors . . . and take another swing at the pitch.

Back then, in 2006, we argued that the United States had become, unmistakably, an empire. And that empires are expensive and dangerous. All of them eventually come to an end. And when you finance an empire with debt—our argument was—the end would come sooner rather than later.

That line of thinking still seems correct. The big difference between then and now is largely a matter of tense. Then, it was future. Now it is present. And looking at the big picture, the remarkable thing is how far the empire of debt has already declined. The empire owed "only" $5 trillion in 1999. Now, the total is $34 trillion . . . and rapidly rising. Annual interest was projected by Bloomberg to cross $1 trillion in 2024.[1]

And for what?

The US has been slipping in the international ratings for at least 20 years . . . and by some measures, for more than 50 years. The US share of world GDP, for example, has been cut in half, from about 40% in 1960 to a little more than half that, 24%, today.[2] In the same period of time China has risen from 4% to 18% of global output.

In the meantime, America's share of prison inmates has risen. With nearly 2 million people in jail, no other country comes close. China and Russia, said to be "repressive" regimes, actually leave many more of their citizens at liberty than the US. China has more than three times as many people as the US, but fewer prisoners behind bars. Statistically, you're more likely to be locked up in America than in any other advanced country, a percentage close to Cuba and El Salvador. Neither China nor Russia even make the top 10.[3]

And Americans, alone among people in developed nations, are living shorter lives. The US is now in 59th place, after China, Kuwait, and Albania, in average life expectancy.[4]

We were right about the direction. And right about the general trend. We were right to anticipate the real estate collapse of 2008, the rise in debt, the decline in US solvency, and a coming financial crisis.

Beyond that, we certainly had no idea that Donald Trump—a person with no "conservative" attachments—would become a Republican president. Nor could we imagine that a virus would cause the shutdown of much of the world economy. Nor that the aforementioned Republican president would go on the biggest spending spree of all time, trying to offset the foregone GDP output with completely fictitious money printed up by the Fed.

But we were right about another major thing we saw coming: inflation. "When the howls from consumers and voters grow loud enough," we wrote, "the Fed will panic. In desperation, [the Fed chairman] will point south, to Argentina. 'There . . . that is our way out,' he will say."

That event, which will determine the character of US economic life, probably for an entire generation, is still ahead. And now, dead ahead.

But let us return to our introduction, as we left it, 17 years ago . . .

Many years ago, when the United States was still a modest republic, US presidents were available to almost anyone who wanted to shoot them. Thomas Jefferson went for a walk down Pennsylvania Avenue, alone, and spoke to anyone who came up to him. John Adams used to swim naked in the Potomac. A woman reporter got him to talk to her by sitting on his clothes and refusing to budge.

But now anyone who wants to see the president must have a background check and pass through a metal detector. The White House staff must approve reporters before they are allowed into press conferences. And when the US head of state travels, he does so in imperial style; he moves around protected by hundreds of praetorian guards, sharpshooters on rooftops, and thousands of local centurions. A report circulated around the internet stemming from an article written in advance of a state visit President Ohama planned to Mumbai in November 2010. *The Press Trust of India* was quoted as saying that Obama's trip to India would "cost $200 million per day for security and living arrangements, among other things. The story claimed that the president would be accompanied by about 3,000 people, including Secret Service agents, government officials and journalists, and will stay at the Taj Mahal Hotel—the scene of a 2008 terrorist attack."

Later that day, Rush Limbaugh picked up the story and added some detail on his radio show that Obama's entourage would book "five hundred seven rooms at the Taj Mahal," and be composed of 40 airplanes, repeating the $200 million a day claim. The *Washington Times* Obama would "spend enough to bankrupt a small nation." In England, the *Economic Times* and *The Daily Mail* claimed Obama would book the entire 570-room Taj Mahal Hotel for the trip.

Of course, the White House denied the rumors. FactCheck.org further debunked the claims noting the White House does not publish costs of presidential trips for security reasons. FactCheck.org then offered this helpful fact: According to the Government Accountability Office, President Clinton's "trips to Africa, Chile and China in 1998 cost at least $42.8 million, $10.5 million and $18.8 million, respectively—not counting the still-classified cost of providing Secret Service protection. In Africa, Clinton was accompanied by about 1,300 individuals—not including members of the Secret Service—representing the White House, the Department of Defense and other federal agencies. The president visited six countries in 12 days, which means the trip cost $3.6 million per day."[5]

Today, the president cavalcades around Washington in an armored Cadillac. The limousine is fitted with bulletproof windows, equally sturdy tires, and a self-contained ventilation system to ward off a biological or chemical attack.

The Secret Service—the agency charged with preserving the president among the living—employs over 7,000 people: 3,600 special agents, 1,600 uniformed division officers, and more than 2,000 other specialized administrative, professional, and technical wonks.[6]

Everywhere the president goes, his security is handled—by thousands of guards and aides, secure compounds, and carefully orchestrated movements.

In late 2003, when Bush deigned to visit the British Isles, an additional 5,000 British police officers were deployed to the streets of London to protect him. Parks and streets were shut down. Snipers were visible on the royal rooftop.[7] After Bush's stay at Buckingham Palace in London, the Queen was horrified by the damage done to the Palace grounds. They were left looking like the parking lot at a Walmart two-for-one sale.[8]

That was 20 years ago. Since then, it has only gotten worse. When we passed through Dublin in summer 2023, for example, we noticed not just Air Force One on the runway but also Air Force Two. And dozens of black vans. Joe Biden had come to town, bringing the praetorian guard with him.

THE THEME OF THIS BOOK IN A NUTSHELL

Watching the news is a bit like watching a bad opera. You can tell from all the shrieking that something very important is supposed to be happening, but you don't quite know what it is. What you're missing is the plot.

Let us begin by noticing that this is a comic opera that seems as though it might veer into tragedy at any moment. The characters on stage are familiar to us—consumers, economists, politicians, investors, and businesspeople. They are the same hustlers, clowns, rubes, and dumbbells that we always see before us. But in today's performance they are doing something extraordinary: They are some of the richest people on the planet, but they have come to rely on the savings of the world's poorest people just to pay their bills. They routinely spend more than they make—and think they can continue doing so indefinitely. They go deeper and deeper in debt, believing they will never have to settle up. They buy houses and then mortgage them out— room by room, until they have almost nothing left. They invade foreign countries in the belief that they are spreading freedom and democracy, and depend on printing press money to pay for it. They run trillion-dollar deficits, routinely, giving almost no thought to who will eventually pay . . . or how.

But people come to believe whatever they must believe when they must believe it. All these conceits and illusions that we find so amusing come not from thinking, but from circumstances. As they say on Wall Street, "markets make opinions," not the other way around. The circumstance that makes sense of this strange performance is that the United States is an empire—whether we like it or not. It must play a well-known role on the world stage, just as you and I must play our roles, not because we have thought our way to them, but simply because of who we are, where we are, and when we are there. Primitive people play primitive roles. They are no less intelligent than the rest of us, but they would be out of character if they began doing calculus. They have their parts to play just as we do. Sophisticated people play sophisticated roles. They are no smarter than anyone else, but you still don't expect them to wear bones through their noses. We, citizens of today's great empire, have our roles to play, too, and the empire itself, must do what an empire must do. Fish gotta swim. Birds gotta fly. Empires gotta be empires.

Institutions have a way of evolving over time—after a few years, they no longer resemble the originals. The United States in the first quarter of the 21st century was no more like the America of 1776 than the Vatican under the Borgia popes was like Christianity at the time of the Last Supper, or Microsoft in 2024 is like the company Bill Gates started in his garage.

Still, while the institutions evolve, the ideas and theories about them tend to remain fixed; it is as if people hadn't noticed. In America, all the restraints, inhibitions, and modesty of the Old Republic have been blown away by the prevailing winds of the new empire. In their place has emerged a vainglorious system of conceit, deceit, debt, and delusion.

The United States Constitution is almost exactly the same document with exactly the same words it had when it was written, but the words that used to bind and chafe have been turned into soft elastic. The government that couldn't do so many things—for they were forbidden by the Constitution—can now do anything it wants. The executive has all the power he needs to do practically anything. Donald Trump, aided and abetted by go-along state governors, confined adult citizens to their homes. Joe Biden tells them with whom they can do business. And Congress goes along, like a simpleminded stooge, insisting only that the spoils be spread around. The whole process works so well that a member of Congress has to be found in bed "with a dead girl or a live boy" before he risks losing public office.[9]

US businesses are still nominally capitalistic. But a recent press item reports that General Motors will never be able to compete unless it ditches its crushing healthcare costs. Why does it not just cut the costs? It seems to lack either the nerve or the right, but the journalist proposed a solution: nationalize healthcare! Meanwhile, CEO pay has soared to 344 times the average worker in 2022, up from a 21:1 ratio in 1965.[10] Stockholders, whose money was being squandered, barely said a word. They were still under the illusion that the companies were working for them. They had not noticed that the whole capitalist system had been trussed up with so many chains, wires, red tape, and complications, it no longer functioned like the freewheeling, moneymaking corporations of the 19th century. Meanwhile, corporations in China—a communist country—had their hands and feet free to eat our lunches and kick our derrieres.

Back in the homeland, the entire economy has come to depend on artifice, fantasy, and debt. Americans (including their government) consume more than they earn. The difference shows up in two deficits—one in trade and one in the federal budget. Both rely on a "funny money" system in which the Fed is able to print money and lend it out to preferred customers at preferential rates. That's the exorbitant privilege of being the imperial front-runner. You provide money; the rest of the world pays you for it.

But these ironies, contradictions, and paradoxes hardly disturb the sleep of the imperial race. They permit themselves to believe so many absurd things that they will now believe anything. In fall 2001, people in Des Moines and Duluth were buying duct tape to protect themselves from terrorist "sleeper cells ready to attack the Midwest." In fall 2004, they believed the Chinese were manipulating their currency by pegging it to the dollar for nearly 10 years! By 2007, they thought they could "take out" equity from their houses as if they had an ATM in their own bedroom. And then, in 2020, they believed they could shut down almost the entire economy (to protect themselves from a virus that was no threat to the vast majority of them) and replace real output with "stimmie checks," drawn on the US Treasury, which was already deeply in deficit.[11]

Like Alice, they were expected to believe six impossible things before breakfast and another half dozen before tea: Real estate never goes down! You can get rich by spending! Savings don't matter! Deficits don't matter! Let them sweat, *we'll* think!

We can't help but wonder how it will turn out.

In this book, we turn once again to the dusty pages of history. We find ourselves often tracing the footsteps of the West's greatest empire—Rome—searching for clues. In Rome, too, the institutions evolved and degraded faster than people's ideas about them. Romans remembered their Old Republic with its rules and customs. They still thought that was the way the system was supposed to work long after a new system of *consuetudo fraudium*—habitual cheating—had taken hold.

Rome's system of imperial finance was far more solid than America's. Rome made its empire pay by exacting a tribute of about 10% of output from its vassal states. There were few illusions about how the system worked. Rome brought the benefits of *pax Romana,* and subject peoples were expected to pay for it. Most paid without much prompting. In fact, the cost of running the empire was greatly reduced by the cooperation of citizens and subjects. Local notables, who benefited from imperial rule, but who were not directly on the emperor's payroll, performed many costly functions. Many functions were "privatized," says Ramsay MacMullen in his *Corruption and the Decline of Rome.*

This was accomplished in a variety of ways. Many officials, and even the soldiers stationed in periphery areas, used their positions to extort money out of the locals. In this way, the cost of administration and protection was pushed more directly onto the private sector.

Commoda was the word given to this practice, which apparently became more and more widespread as the empire aged.

MacMullen recalls a typical event:

> From Milan, a certain Palladius, tribune and notary, left for Carthage in 367. He was charged with investigating accusations of criminal negligence—"if you don't pay me, I won't help you"—brought against Romanus, military commandant in Africa. Because of Romanus's inaction, the area around Tripoli had suffered attacks by local tribes, without defense from the empire. But the accused was ready for the inquisitor, and when Palladius arrived unexpectedly at military headquarters in the African capital—carrying the officers' pay—he was offered . . . under the table . . . a considerable bribe. Palladius . . . accepted it. But he continued his investigations, accompanied by two of the local notables whose complaints had launched the inquiry. He prepared his report to the emperor, telling him that the charges against Romanus were confirmed. But the latter threatened to reveal the bribes he had accepted. So Palladius reported to the emperor that the accusations were pure inventions. Romanus was safe. The emperor ordered that the two accusers' tongues be torn out.[12]

As time went on, the empire came to resemble less and less the Old Republic that had given it birth. The old virtues were replaced with new vices. Gradually, the troops on the frontier had to depend more and more on their own devices for their support. They had to take up agriculture. "The effectiveness of the troops was diminished as they became part-time farmers," says MacMullen.

Gradually, the empire had fewer and fewer reliable troops. In Trajan's time, the emperor could count on hundreds of thousands of soldiers for his campaigns in Dacia. But by the fourth century, battles were fought with only a few thousand. By the fifth century, these few troops could no longer hold off the barbarians.

The corruption of the empire was complete.

If you deny that the United States is now an empire, you are as big a fool as we were. For a very long time we resisted the concept. We did not want the United States to be an empire. We thought it was a political choice. We liked the old republic of Jefferson, Washington, the US Constitution . . . the humble nation of hard money and small government; we didn't want to give it up. We thought that if the United States acted as though it were an empire it was making an error.

What morons we were. We missed the point completely. It didn't matter what we wanted. There was no more choice in the matter than a caterpillar has a choice about whether to become a butterfly.

This was an important insight for us. Until then, all of the blustering and slapstick pratfalls on stage seemed like "mistakes." Why would the United States run such huge trade deficits, we wondered? It was obviously a bad idea; the nation was ruining itself. And why would it launch an invasion of Iraq or begin a war on terror—both of which were almost certain to be costly blunders? Why would it add $30 trillion (est.) to its national debt, in the first quarter of the 21st century? Why would it commit another $80 billion to keep a war going in the Ukraine? And billions more for a slaughter in Gaza? It was as if the United States wanted to destroy itself—first by bankrupting its economy, and second by creating enemies all over the globe.

Then, we realized, that of course, that is exactly what it must do.

We repeat: People come to believe what they need to believe when they need to believe it. America is an empire; its people must think like imperialists. In order to fulfill their mission, the homeland citizens have to become what George Orwell called "hollow, posing dummies."[13] An imperial people must believe that they deserve to be the imperial power—that is, they must believe they have the right to tell other people what to do. In order to do so, they must believe what isn't true—that their own culture, society, economy, political system, or they themselves are superior to others. It is a vain conceit, but it is so bright and so big it exercises a kind of gravitational pull over the entire society. Soon, it has set in motion a whole system of shiny vanities and illusions as distant from the truth as Pluto and as bizarre as Saturn. Americans believe they can get rich by spending someone else's money. They believe that foreign countries actually want to be invaded and taken over. They believe they can run up debt forever, and that their debt-laden houses are as good as money in the bank. That is what makes the study of contemporary economics so entertaining. We sit and laugh, like a divorce lawyer looking at photos of a rich man in flagrante delicto; we know there's money to be made.

Things that are unusual usually return to normal. If they did not, there would be no "normal" to return to. That is why stocks that are cheap become more expensive. Stocks that are too expensive become cheap. Houses usually go up at a rate roughly equal to the rate of inflation, income, or GDP growth—no more. So do other asset prices—stocks and bonds, for example. They are linked together by economic necessity. The average house must be affordable by the average household; otherwise, who will buy them? And the average corporation can only make its money by selling to the average consumer, who relies on an average income. GDP roughly tracks the buying power of the typical family. Capital values do not usually stray very far from the incomes that nourish them. So, if they get out of whack, you'd expect them to get back into whack before too long.

And yet, in the 21st century, capital values and GDP got seriously out of whack. How and when they get back into whack is our subject.

But GDP and asset values aren't the only things that need correction. An empire itself is a rare thing. It is normal, but unusual. Nature abhors a monopoly. An empire is a monopoly on force. Nature will tolerate it for a while, but sooner or later, the imperial people must revert to being normal people, and the preposterous beliefs that the imperial people cherish also must pass away. They must go up to a kind of humbug heaven, where absurd ideas and idle flatteries strut around while the gods point, snicker, and roll around on the floor clutching their stomachs as if the humor of it was going to kill them.

The dollar is an extraordinary thing too. Do you know what the long- term mean value of paper currency is? Well, it is zero. That is what the average paper currency is worth most of the time, and it is the black hole into which all paper currencies in the past have gone. There could be something magical about the dollar that makes it unlike any paper currency in the past—that is, something that makes it non-mean reverting. But if anyone knows what that magical quality is, they are not working on this book. As near as we can tell, the dollar is no different from any of the planet's hundreds of other now-defunct currencies.

For the last hundred years, the dollar has lost value faster than the decline of the Roman-era Denarius after the reign of Nero. This is not surprising. Roman coins had silver or gold in them. In order to make the coins less valuable, they had to reduce the precious metal content.

People didn't like it. The dollar, by contrast, contains no precious metal. Not even any base metal. It is just paper. It has no inherent value. There is nothing to take out, because there was never anything there in the first place. Over time, the dollar is almost certain to revert to its real value—which is as empty as deep space.

In the big picture of things, it is also unusual for one civilized nation to earn far more per capita than another. In the thousands of years of history, some groups were poor . . . others were rich. But extreme differences had a way of working themselves out—by trade, war, pestilence, and degeneracy. By the year 1700, a man in India, China, Arabie, or Europe had about the same standard of living, which was not very high anywhere. But along came the industrial revolution, which threw incomes out of balance and changed the way people think. Europe stole a march on the rest of the world's industries, with huge gains in output coming in a relatively short period of time. Soon, Europeans were the world's leading imperialists, convinced that they had its best economic system, its finest scholars, its highest morals, and its most splendiferous armies.

But if the world works the way we think it does, you can expect the incomes of Europeans—and their US cousins—to revert to their historic means. The process could take several generations. It could stall. There could be countertrends. But there is no reason to think a man's labor is inherently worth more in France than in Bangladesh, or that a plumber with stars and stripes on his overalls should earn more than one with a crescent moon.

If there is a mean, things will regress to it. We predicted, in the first edition of this book, 17 years ago that "you can expect, relatively speaking, Asian incomes to rise and US incomes to fall." That is of course, just what has happened. In this century, both India and China have seen substantial income gains for most of their people; in America there is some dispute about the numbers, but if there has been any income growth at all it has been slight.

Just to introduce a gloomy remark, we note that we are personally and individually regressing to the mean. The mean for a human being is death—or nonexistence. A person walks the earth for only three-score and ten, as it says in the Bible. The rest of the time, he is only a potential person or a former person. For millions of years, he is either in the future or in the grave.

You, dear reader, are enjoying that ever-so-brief period of exaggeration of hyperbole, of extraordinary, mean-busting unusualness we call *life*. It is not for us to know the time or place when it comes to an end. But like all mean-reverting phenomena, only a fool would bet against it. (For our own part, we do not seek immortality, but we wouldn't be too upset if it found us.)

Until recently betting against the end is just what most Americans were doing. They were borrowing and spending as if there were no tomorrow; their government still is. And if they'd only looked at the patterns of the past, they would have seen that borrowing and spending doesn't make you rich. Tomorrow always comes—at least it always has up until now—and you have to pay your debts.

Over time, prices go up and down. Many other things ebb and flow as well, boom and bust or bloom and wither. All of these phenomena go through predictable cycles that can be roughly modeled. Analysts study the cycles to try to figure out where we are currently located in the habitual pattern. It is often frustrating work, because the patterns are rarely quite as regular and well-defined in the present as they appear to have been in the past.

People come to think what they must think when they must think it. They are bullish near the end of a bull market; they are bearish near the end of the bear market. If it were otherwise, the market could never fully express itself. If investors grew suddenly cautious while nearing an epic bull market peak, they would sell their stocks, and the peak would never be reached. Or suppose that after several years of soaring house prices homeowners came to believe that housing prices would fall? How could you have a proper housing bubble? How can you have a rip-roaring party without anyone getting drunk, in other words? How can people make fools of themselves if they are unwilling to get up on the tables and dance?

These are deep philosophical questions. But they help us recognize where we may be in the cycle. As prices reach a loony excess, peoples' ideas grow loony, too. Ergo, the loonier the ideas, the more likely it is that a turning point is near; the wilder the party, the more likely someone will call the gendarmes.

We also suspect that attitudes evolve similarly in an imperial cycle, during which a country's economic, financial, and military power runs up over several generations and then declines. At the peak, the imperial people come to believe that their system is superior, that their values are universal, and that their way of life will inevitably dominate the entire world.

Readers will recognize these attitudes in a famous article by Francis Fukuyama, written after the fall of the Soviet Union, in which he suggested that the world may have reached the "End of History."[14] It was the end of history because the US system had triumphed—no improvement seemed possible. Fukayama's idea was not original. Hegel and Marxist intellectuals had proposed the same thing more than 100 years earlier. With the victory of the proletariat, no further advance could be made. History had to stop.

Hegel stopped ticking. Marx died, too. History continued.

But when people feel they are on top of the world, they begin to take things for granted that they previously took for absurd. Subconsciously, they come to believe what imperial people always seem to believe—that their society is so superior, that the rest of the world longs to be just like them or is inevitably drawn to become like them, whether they like it or not. That was the premise behind the billions of dollars Americans invested in China, for example. A few years earlier, if someone had suggested that they invest in a communist country, they would have thought the person mad. By 2000, China was still run by veterans of various "great leaps forward," but Americans were convinced that they were all leaping to become just like us—capitalists and democrats at heart! So vain are we that we can't imagine anyone wanting to be anything else.

And, of course, the invasion of Iraq was based on the same sort of thinking: that even the grubby desert tribes wanted to be just like us. All we had to do was to get the dictator off their backs and the men would start building shopping malls and the women would all start dressing like Britney Spears.

Those are the sort of delusions you get at the top of an imperial cycle. By our reckoning, the end of the 1990s was the peak. It's been mostly downhill—by almost any measure—ever since.

Culture, political systems, and economies are never as universal and eternal as we think. Instead, everything evolves. Even in Europe, our closest cousins do not share our US attitudes. In the United States, we all seek to maximize our incomes. We work long hours. We start enterprises. We invest. In Europe, they aim to maximize their leisure, their security, and the quality of their lives. They spend more time talking about how to cook the bacon than they do about how to bring it home.

France once had a European Empire that reached from Spain to Moscow. Later, it had a worldwide empire, with subject countries and colonies in Africa, the West Indies, and the South Pacific. From the time of Richelieu to the time of Leon Blum, France had one of the most powerful armies on earth. Even at the beginning of World War II, France had the largest army in Europe—on paper. But there never was a cycle that didn't want to turn. And the imperial cycle turns along with the rest of them. For many generations, the French believed they had the finest culture, the best schools, the most advanced scientists, and the most dynamic builders in the world. France saw its mission as bringing the benefits of its civilization—of vin rouge and the Rights of Man—to the rest of the globe.

Now it's our turn. It is we Americans who think we have the best culture, the best economy, the best government, and the best army the world has ever seen. Every president tells us so, even one who ran on a promise of trying to restore our greatness (admitting that it had slipped away). Now, it is we Americans who have the burden of the *mission civilisatrice*. It is our duty to bring freedom and democracy to this tattered old ball; our president said so.

How did America become an empire? We don't recall the question ever coming up. There was never a debate on the subject. There was never a national referendum. No presidential candidate ever suggested it. Nobody ever said, "Hey, let's be an empire!" People do not choose to have an empire; it chooses them. Gradually and unconsciously, their thoughts, beliefs, and institutions are refashioned to the imperial agenda.

Although there has been no discussion of whether America should be an empire, there has been much public clucking on the specific points of the imperial agenda. Should we attack Iran or Iraq? Russia? China? Should we have national identity cards? Should we suspend the Bill of Rights in order to combat terrorists more effectively? At least, let us do away with the First Amendment so we can stop people from spreading "disinformation" about us.

Many people wondered, including your authors, what was the point of the war against Iraq. The country had no part in terrorist attacks. Au contraire, Saddam's Iraq was a bulwark of secular pragmatism in an area unsettled by religious fanaticism. It was the religious fanatics who posed a danger, said the papers, not the ruthless dictators who suppressed them. Others wondered if an attack on Iraq would make the world safer or more dangerous. Or if the United States had committed enough troops to get the job done.

But the big question had already been settled without ever having been raised. Why should Americans care what happened in the Middle East? Or, later, on the Eurasian steppes? Or, in the Levant? Or anywhere else? Did the Swiss wonder what kind of government Iraq should have? Did the Swiss try to make the rest of the world more like Switzerland, or allow themselves the vain fantasy of imagining that everyone on the planet secretly yearned to yodel?

Although no one noticed, the imperial weed put down roots deep in the soil of North America. By the early 21st century, hardly anything else grew; it had completely crowded out the delicate flowers planted by the Founding Fathers. The debate surrounding the invasion of Iraq was an imperial debate—about means and methods, not about right and wrong or national interest. No one from either major political party bothered to suggest that the United States should mind its own business. Both parties recognized that Iraq was not a matter of national interest—it was a matter of imperial interest. No business, nowhere, was too small or too remote not to be of interest to the empire. From its military bases all over the globe, and its sensors orbiting the planet, the US imperium watched everyone, everywhere, all the time. By the year 2000, at the height of its power and the apogee of its conceit, no sparrow fell anywhere in the world without triggering a monitoring device in the Pentagon.

This marked what may be the peak of a trend that began more than 100 years ago. Just about the turn of the 20th century, the United States became the world's largest economy—and its fastest growing one. Near the same time, Theodore Roosevelt began riding rough over small, poor nations. America's fat proto-imperialists rarely saw a fight they didn't want to get into. It was at his urging (he had threatened to raise his own army to do the job) that Wilson announced his readiness to join the war in Europe in 1917. Wilson said he was doing it to "make the world safe for democracy." This is the stated goal of nearly all US foreign policy ever since: to improve the planet with more democracy. Of course, almost all empire builders think they are improving the planet. Even Alexander the Great thought he was doing it a favor by spreading Greek culture.

But when Wilson sent troops to Europe, people wondered then what the real point was. America had no interest in the war and no particular reason to favor one side over the other. But there, too, they missed the point. America was quickly becoming an empire. Empires are almost always at war—for their role is to "make the world safe."

President Truman clarified the imperial modus operandi when he sent the United States into battle in Korea with no declaration of war. He didn't even tell Congress until after the army was engaged and Americans were dying. Then, President Johnson followed up with another war in a far-off place that made no difference to Americans—Vietnam. What was the point? The Swiss army was nowhere to be found. And where were the Belgians? Even the French had given up on Vietnam a decade before. But more than 3 million US soldiers went to Vietnam and many came back flat. And for what? Just another war on the periphery of the empire. None of these engagements made any sense for a humble nation that minded its own business. None would have made any sense for America until the first Roosevelt administration; but once the nation had become an empire—with a homeland and wide-ranging interests beyond it— almost all wars seemed appropriate.

Another landmark in the history of the US empire came on August 15, 1971. That was the day that Richard Nixon severed the link between the imperial currency and gold. Thitherto, empire or no, the United States had to settle its debts like other nations—in a currency it couldn't manufacture. Henceforth, the way was clear for a vast increase in empire spending and debt.

Thus we arrive at the real problem for the US empire. It has by far the strongest military in the world. Protected by two vast oceans, it has no reason to fear an invasion. But an empire needs enemies. If it has none that are up to the challenge, it must find other threats. All empires must pass away. All must find a way to destroy themselves. America found debt.

The traditional method of empire finance is so simple even a Mongol barbarian could master it. Nations are conquered and forced to pay tribute. The homeland is supposed to make a profit; it is supposed to grow richer compared to the vassal states. But here, America fell victim of its own scam. Pretending to make the world a better place, the United States could not very well require the poor nations it conquered to pay up.

This was not a problem in the early days. Until the mid-1980s, US industries were so robust they were able to take advantage of the *pax dollarium* to expand sales, jobs, and profits. But in the 1970s, the US trade balance turned negative. By the year Alan Greenspan took over at the Fed, foreigners owned more US assets than Americans owned foreign ones. US factories had grown old and expensive. US workers were paid too much. The new "funny money" reduced investment in the US; it made it too easy to buy from overseas. US businesspeople invested too little in training and new capital equipment. The whole nation developed an attitude more in harmony with an empire on the decline than one that was still rising. The imperial people chose to spend rather than to save, and to hallucinate, rather than think hard. They demanded bread and circuses at home; let the Mexicans sweat.

Empires are thought by many to be good things. They expand the area in which trade can take place. In modern parlance, they allow for increased "globalization." Generally, globalization is good for everyone. It permits people to specialize in what they do best, producing more and better things at lower costs. But it is more beneficial to some than to others. There are three billion people in Asia. And almost every one of them is willing to work for a fraction of the average US wage.

Globalization and artificially low interest rates in America allowed Asian industries to flourish. But every dollar in revenue to an Asian exporter was a dollar less to US-based manufacturers. This was neither good nor bad, but it had consequences.

Things happen that no one particularly wants or especially encourages, and the average person goes along with whatever humbug is popular—with no real idea where it leads or why they favor it.

Each person plays the role given to them; everyone believes what they need to believe to play the part.

Alan Greenspan was famously against paper money that was not backed by gold when he was a libertarian intellectual. When he became a government functionary, his views conveniently changed. He came to believe what he had to believe in order to be the head of the US empire's central bank: the Federal Reserve. The empire needed almost unlimited amounts of credit to carry out its foreign wars, while making bread and circuses available at home. Alan Greenspan, followed by Ben Bernanke, Janet Yellen, and Jerome Powell, made sure it got it.

Institutions play their roles, too. One grows; another decays. One is young and dynamic while another is old and decrepit. One has to die to make way for the new one to take its place. One has to ruin itself so that another may flourish.

Americans could have cut their military budget by 75% and still have had the biggest, most advanced army in the world. They could have trimmed their household spending by half, and still lived well. They could have driven less in smaller cars; they could have ceased mortgaging their houses; they could have "made do" with last year's clothes and yesterday's laptop; but how could they ruin themselves if they put on the brakes before getting to where they are going?

You never know where you are in the cycle until it is too late to do anything about it. For all we know, we could be facing merely a temporary pullback in what is still a long-term bullish period for the US empire. Not likely, but who knows?

The theory we have been teasing out is that politics and markets follow similar cyclical patterns—boom, bust, bubble, and bamboozle. A handful of companies usually take a dominant position in the market; sometimes a single one does. So do a few countries dominate world politics . . . *empires* they are called. The difference between a regular nation and an empire is profound. A regular nation—such as Belgium or Bulgaria—tends its own affairs. An empire looks outward, taking on its shoulders the fate of much of the world. An empire is like a bull market. It grows, it develops; often it passes into a bubble phase, when people come to believe the most absurd things.

We don't know what stage the US empire has reached, but we look around and see so many degenerate and absurd things, we guess: We must be nearer the end than the beginning.

How will it end? What will happen next? We don't know, but we note that people do not give up their self-serving conceits and illusions readily. They hold on to them as long as possible. "America still has the greatest, most dynamic economy on earth," they tell themselves, even as the nation loses money (its income is less than its expenses). This kind of madness is hard not to like; it is like an aging person who thinks they become more fetching with each passing year. The gap between perception and reality grows wider every day, until finally, the mirror cracks.

But the glass has now fractured; the spell has been broken. When the US inflation rate rose over 9% in 2022, the Fed could no longer provide such free-and-easy credit. More money-printing would result in higher consumer prices. The voters wouldn't like it.

And yet, with $95 trillion of domestic debt—government, corporate, and household—how could Americans afford higher interest rates. All of a sudden, they were squeezed between higher prices and higher interest rates. The empire had become too expensive.

Long-suffering readers will find our outlook familiar. We provided a foretaste of it many years ago in another book with Addison Wiggin called *Financial Reckoning Day* (Wiley, 2003). We thought then that the tech bubble would blow up, resulting in a long, soft slow slump, à la Japan. We were wrong. Instead of a real slump, the United States had a nine-month phony recession (in which consumer debt actually expanded) followed by a huge, though largely phony, boom. The boom ended in two key milestones. First, the bond market hit an all-time high in July 2020, with the yield on the 2-year US Treasury at 0.11%. And then, the stock market reached its peak in December 2021, with the Dow over 36,000. Since then, the Dow has (as of this writing) recovered, but only in nominal terms. Adjusted for inflation, investors are still down about 17% from the top.

These turnarounds, if they hold (which, we think they will), doom the empire. Not to an imminent death but to further acts of absurdity and self-destruction.

Read on!

PART I

IMPERIA ABSURDUM

Look back over the past with its changing empires that rose and fell and you can foresee the changing future, too.

—Marcus Aurelius

CHAPTER 1

DEAD MEN TALKING

One of the nicest things about Europe's cities is that they are so full of dead people. In Paris, the cemeteries are so packed that the corpses are laid down like bricks, stacked one atop the other. Occasionally the bones are dug up and stored in underground ossuaries that are turned into tourist attractions. Thousands and thousands of skulls are on display in the catacombs; millions more must be spread all over the city.

In Venice, a dead man gets—or used to get—a send-off so gloriously sentimental he could hardly wait to die. There is barely room within the city walls for the living and none at all for the dead. Cadavers were loaded onto a magnificently morbid floating mariah—a richly decorated funeral gondola, painted in bright black with gold angels on her bow and stern. Then, as if crossing the river Styx, the boat was rowed across the lagoon to the island of San Michele by four gondoliers in black outfits with gold trim.

How US versifiers must have envied one of their own, Ezra Pound, when he took his last gondola ride in such fabulous style in 1972. And then, what luck! The former classical scholar, poet, and admirer of Benito Mussolini got one of the last empty holes on the cemetery island. Today, when Venetians reach room temperature, the best they can hope for is a damp spot on the mainland.

We do not hasten to join the dead, but we seek their counsel. When corpses whisper, we listen.

"Been there. Done that," they often seem to say.

Reading Margaret Wilson Oliphant's history of the dead dukes, or *doges*, in her classic book, *The Makers of Venice, Doges, Conquerors, Painters and Men of Letters*,[1] we felt as though someone should have sent a copy to George W. Bush. "Read this. Spare yourself some trouble," the author might have written on the accompanying note. But who reads anything but emails and blog posts in the Capital City? Who reads at all? In the United States if it isn't on the evening news, it didn't happen. Ancient history is something that happened last week.

Too bad. For practically all the most preposterous ideas that emanate from the feverish swamps of the Potomac were tried out in the feverish swamps of Venice, hundreds of years ago.

LESSONS OF THE FOURTH CRUSADE

"Democracy! Empire! Freedom! Nation building!" The ideas are cast into the murky lagoon of human affairs as if the words were clarifying magic. Suddenly, wrong is as distinct from right as day from night. Good from bad . . . success from failure . . . how clearly we see things in the crystal waters of our own delusions!

The United States congratulates itself as being the finest democracy the world has ever seen, but the system for ruling Venice eight centuries ago was also democratic. People voted for people who voted for other people, who then voted for yet more people who elected the doge. The whole idea was to allow ordinary people to believe that they ran the nation, while real authority remained in the hands of a few families—the Bushes, Kennedys, Gores, Clintons, Obamas, and Rockefellers of 13th-century Venice.

"So easy is it to deceive the multitude," says Oliphant. "The sovereignty of Venice, under whatever system carried on, had always been in the hands of a certain number of families, who kept their place with almost dynastic regularity undisturbed by any intruders from below—the system of the *Consiglio Maggiore* was still professed to be a representative system of the widest kind; and it would seem at the first glance as if all honest men who were *da bene* and respected by their fellows must one time or other have been secure of gaining admission to that popular parliament."[2]

To Oliphant's dictum on the multitude, we add a corollary: It is even easier to deceive oneself. Today, rare are the Americans who are not victims of their own scams. They mortgaged their homes and thought they were getting richer. They bought Wall Street's products as though they were gambling in Las Vegas and believed they were as clever as Warren Buffett. They went to the polling stations in November 2020 and believed they were selecting the government they wanted, when the choice had already been reduced to two men of the same class, same age, same schooling, same wealth, same secret club, same society, with barely distinguishable ideas on how things should be run. Just who should run them. As emotional as voters get about the contents of this laptop or that estimate of another's net worth, astute readers will already be aware there is little distinction between Joe Biden and Donald Trump. Still voters get uppity about both. Families are broken apart for support of one or the other candidate. Holiday dinners ruined. College campuses savaged.

Meanwhile, in Washington, DC, the United States House and Senate meet in the same solemn deceit as the *Consiglio Maggiore*— pretending to do the public's business. Down the street, America's own set of doges, take up where the Venetian doge Enrico Dandolo left off: trying to hustle the East.

Making a very long story short, at the beginning of the 13th century, as at the beginning of the first quarter of the 21st, many people saw a clash of civilizations coming and sharpened their swords. They were, then as now, the same civilizations, clashing in about the same part of the world—the Middle East.

What was different back in the age of the Crusades was that the effort to make the world a better place (at least in this episode) was being prodded forward by the French, who were then an expanding, imperial power. St. Louis (King Louis IX) went on two crusades with a French army and failed both times.

Oliphant's history tells of the arrival of six French knights in shining armor, who strode into San Marcos Piazza to ask the doge for help. They were putting together an alliance of civilized Western armies to reconquer Jerusalem, they explained—in the same spirit as King Louis centuries before.

They brought out all the usual arguments. But the Venetians were not so much convinced by the French as they convinced themselves. They were, they said to themselves (just as Madeleine Albright would repeat centuries later), the "indispensable nation." Without them, the effort would fail; therefore, they must act. Yes, they could still fail, they acknowledged, but look what they had to gain! For not only would they be doing good, but they stood to do well, too—implanting trading posts and ports along the way.

And so a fleet of 50 galleys was assembled and set off, the old doge leading the way. Finding their French allies a bit worse for wear and tear, the Venetians proposed a new deal: Instead of attacking the infidels forthwith, they would warm up with an assault on Zara, a town on the Dalmatian coast that had recently rebelled against its Venetian masters.

The French protested. They had come to make war against the enemies of Christ, not against other Christians. But because they needed the Venetians' support, they had no choice.

In five days, the city of Zara surrendered; its defenses were no match for the armies in front of them. And so the city was sacked and the booty divided up. Soon after came a letter from Pope Innocent III, who wondered why they were killing fellow Christians; it was the pagans they were meant to be killing, he reminded them. He commanded them to leave Zara and proceed to Syria, "neither turning to the right hand nor to the left."

The pope's letters greatly troubled the pious French, but the Venetians seemed undisturbed. They ignored the letters and remained in Zara until a new comic opportunity presented itself.

This time Constantinople was the unfortunate target. A young prince from that city had come to them, asking support for a mission at once as audacious as it was absurd. His father had been blinded and thrown in a dungeon; the capital of Eastern Christendom was in the hands of men who must have been ancestors of Saddam Hussein— evil usurpers, dictators whom the people detested. If the Venetians would come to his aid, he promised, they would be rewarded generously. More than that, he and his father would return the entire Eastern Empire back to the one true church of St. Peter in Rome.

The Venetians couldn't resist. In April 1204, they set sail for Bosporus Strait. And in a great battle that must have been an undertaker's dream, they took the city. Historian Edward Gibbon describes the scene:

> The soldiers who leaped from the galleys on shore immediately ascended their scaling ladders, while the large ships, advancing more slowly in the intervals and lowering a drawbridge, opened a way through the air from their masts to the rampart. In the midst of the conflict the doge's venerable and conspicuous form stood aloft in complete armor on the prow of his galley. The great standard of St. Mark was displayed before him; his threats, promises and exhortations urged the diligence of the rowers; this vessel was the first that struck; and Dandolo [the doge] was the first warrior on shore. The nations admired the magnanimity of the blind old man. . . .[3]

It proved, however, that the young prince on whose stories and promises the campaign was launched had been a bit frugal with the truth. Like the intelligence services' warnings of weapons of mass destruction in Iraq, his depiction of the circumstances prevailing in Constantinople at the time was inaccurate. Much of it seemed fanciful.

Though the initial conquest was fairly easy and glorious, subsequent events were less so. The local population rose up against the invaders. The city had to be retaken; this time, the battle was bloodier, and thousands of innocent citizens were put to the sword.

As near as historians can tell, the Venetians earned no lasting gain or benefit. Dandolo died in 1205, never having set foot in his homeland again. As for his compatriots, what was left of them eventually returned to Venice.

"But there still remains in Venice," adds Oliphant, "one striking evidence of the splendid, disastrous expedition, the unexampled conquests and victories yet dismal end, of what is called the Fourth Crusade. And that is the four great bronze horses, curious, inappropriate bizarre ornaments that stand above the doorways of San Marco. This was the blind doge's lasting piece of spoil."[4]

"Been there. Done that," whispers the old doge.

THE TYRANNY OF THE LIVING

Who cares? Each generation needs to be there to do that, too. Though happy to turn on an electric light invented by a dead man, the living—in love, war, and finance—believe nothing they haven't seen with their own eyes, except when they want to.

"Avoid foreign entanglements," cautioned the father of the country. But corpses have no voice and no vote, neither in markets nor in politics. Before launching "shock and awe" in Iraq and declaring "mission accomplished" on the deck of an aircraft carrier, George W. Bush was undoubtedly better informed than George Washington. He may have neither the wisdom of a Washington nor the brain, but at least he had a pulse. And the military to wield globally. Once the "war on terror" was declared, there was little further reflection. It was a given, the United States was the "indispensable nation." Too bad if we had to borrow the money to fight the forever wars.

Few people complain about this tyranny of the living. Most accept it as a fact of life. They would not want people to be excluded from the pleasures of life because of an accident of birth. But they are perfectly happy to have the oldest and wisest of our citizens systematically barred from the polling stations and the trading floors by the accident of death. The departed shut up forever, leaving behind them their car keys, their stocks, and their voter registrations—that is all there is to it. Goodbye and good riddance. It is as if they had learned nothing useful, noticed nothing, and had no ideas that might be worth preserving; as if each generation were smarter than the one that preceded it and every son's thoughts improved on those of his father.

Oh, progress! Thou art forever making things better, aren't thou? Throw out the sacred books—what are they, but the thoughts of dead imbeciles? Forget the old rules, old tales, old traditions and habits of old generations, old-timers' superstitions, the old fuddy-duddies' doubts! We are the cleverest humans who have ever lived, right?

Maybe. But if we could convene a council from the spirit world and invite the dead to have their say, what would the corpses tell us?

Veni et vidi. Gaze on the dead, and learn their secrets.

No one seems to care about dead people. No stockbrokers ask for their business. No politicians pander for their votes. No one cares what they think or what they may have learned before they shucked their mortal shell. They get no respect, just a quick send-off, and then they are on their own.

What did the old-timers know of war? Of politics? Of love? Of money? If only we could ask!

Years ago, investors wanted more from a stock than just the hope that someone might come along who was willing to pay more for it. They wanted a stock that paid a dividend out of earnings. When they heard about a stock, they asked, "How much does it pay?" That was what investing was all about.

But by the 1990s, the old-timers on Wall Street had almost all died off. Stock buyers no longer cared how much the company earned or how large a dividend it paid. All they cared about was that some greater fool would come along and take the stock off their hands at a higher price. And the fools rushed in. And now the market is full of greater and greater fools who think the stock market is there to make them rich. What would the old-timers think of them?

And what would our dead ancestors think of our mortgages? Most of them had small mortgages, if any at all, on their homes. And if they had them, they couldn't wait to get rid of them. (Even our own parents held little parties to celebrate finally paying off the mortgage on the family home.) What would our forebears think if they were to learn that the richest generation in US history has mortgaged a greater share of its homes than any in history? What would they have thought of the no-money-down mortgages, minimum payment plans, and negative amortization schedules that led to the financial crisis in 2008, only to kick off a decade of zero-interest-rate policies and open market operations to bail out unwitting speculators?

And what would the old-timers think of our government debt? The unpaid liabilities and obligations, expressed as though they had to be paid today, come to about $104 trillion, depending on the source you choose to believe.

And what do the generations of Republicans, now in their graves, who believed so strongly in balanced budgets, limited government, low taxes, and peace for so many years, think of the recent *republicano* in the White House, who proposed the most unbalanced budgets in history?

And what about the millions of dead Americans who immigrated to the United States to find freedom; what do they think of the country now? They came believing that if they minded their own business, they would be left alone to do what they wanted. But now, every pettifogging Pecksniff with a government service rating is on their grandchildren's case.

And what about those millions of dead people who scrimped and saved—who got by on almost nothing—so their children and grandchildren might live free, prosperous, and independent lives? What would they think of their descendants, so deep in debt and so dependent on Asian lenders that they can barely pass a Chinese restaurant without bending over and kissing the pavement?

Each generation seems to think it is the first to stand upright, that its mothers and fathers walked on four legs and howled at the moon! Even when the living feign admiration for the same fallen forebear, it is usually without paying the least attention to what the poor schmuck actually said or knew. The dead leave us their memoirs, their gospels, their histories, and their constitutions—for what is a constitution but a pact with the dead?—and we ignore them. We seem to believe that all that they suffered, all they went through, all the mistakes they made, hold no more interest for us than a comment by a sunstruck contestant in a TV survival show: "This is . . . like . . . weird. . . ."

WISDOM OF THE FOUNDING FATHERS

A dead man, Edmund Randolph of Virginia, attended the Constitutional Convention in Philadelphia in 1789. He explained why America needed a constitution: "The general object was to produce a cure for the evils under which the United States labored; that in tracing these evils to their origins, every man had found it in the turbulence and follies of democracy."[5]

Another dead man, James Madison, made it even clearer: "Democracies," he wrote, "have ever been spectacles of turbulence and contention; have ever been found incompatible with personal security or the rights of property; and have in general been as short in their lives as they have been violent in their death."[6]

So, we leave you "a Republic, if you can keep it," added Ben Franklin.[7]

Well, we couldn't keep it. Now, we have a curious empire, with a constitution as flexible as its money. Everybody gets a vote in this new democratic Valhalla. Every fool and miscreant gets to have an opinion. Only the dead are left out. Excluded. Ignored. Forgotten.

It is as if only the living had opinions worth hearing, as if only the here and now counted for anything; as if the small, arrogant oligarchy of those who happen to be walking around had all the answers; as if the present generation had found the ultimate truth and reached the end of history.

Your authors have never killed anyone, but we read the obituaries with approval and interest. We look for the distilled wisdom of saint and sinner alike. The trouble with the news is that it is impossible to know what is important when you must rely solely on the judgment of people who happen to be breathing. The living can imagine no problems more urgent than the ones they confront right now, and no opportunities greater than the ones right in front of them. We prefer the obituaries.

THE SECOND REICH

Germany's Third Reich is infamous. But what happened to the Second Reich? History never repeats itself perfectly. But what else can we study but history? The past may be imperfectly understood, but it is the only reference we have. Why not take a look at it? Why not shake the dust off a dead person and get their opinion? Why not venture into the land of the dead to ask some questions?

"The state's need of money increased rapidly," writes a dead man, Bresciani-Turoni, describing the scene in Germany in the 1920s. "Private banks, besieged by their clients, found it impossible to meet the demand for money."[8]

As the situation heated up in summer 1923, there were some old-timers who gave advice: "Less," they said.

But officials were in roughly the same situation as Jerome Powell and Joe Biden today. "More," they said. They feared the economy might fall into trouble unless they made more cash and credit available. The Powell Fed has paid lip service to curbing credit. The government itself pays no attention. "More," they say again.

One finance minister, named Helferrich, in Germany's Weimar Republic, explained:

> To follow the good counsel of stopping the printing of notes would mean—as long as the causes which are upsetting the German exchange continue to operate—refusing to give economic life to the circulating medium necessary for transactions, payments of salaries and wages, and so on, it would mean that in a very short time the entire public, and above all the Reich, could no longer pay merchants, employees, or workers. In a few weeks, besides the printing of notes, factories, mines, railways and post office, national and local governments, in short, all national and economic life would be stopped.[9]

When an economy comes to depend on more and more credit, it must get more and more of it or that economy will come to a stop. A person who has borrowed heavily to finance a lifestyle they cannot afford must continue borrowing to keep up appearances. Or else they must stop. In market manias, love, politics, or war, people rarely stop until they are forced to.

In 1921, a dollar would buy 276 marks. By August 1923, it would buy 5 million of them. Middle-class savers were wiped out.

If only we could roust Herr Helferrich from his eternal sleep! We have some questions we would like to put to his wormy cadaver. (And here, we think not of praising the dead, but of tormenting them.) What fun it would be to show him what his policies—the same, by and large, as are now put forward by Janet Yellen and Joe Biden—provoked. How gratifying it would be to see the little guy squirm under an intense interrogation: What was he thinking, after all? Why did he think that more of the dreadful printing-press money would undo the harm that had already been done by too much? Bresciani-Turoni continues:

> The inflation retarded the crisis for some time, but this broke out later, throwing millions out of employment. At first inflation stimulated production . . . but later . . . it annihilated thrift; it made reform of the national budget impossible for years; it obstructed

the solution of the Reparations question; it destroyed incalculable moral and intellectual values. It provoked a serious revolution in social classes, a few people accumulating wealth and forming a class of usurpers of national property, whilst millions of individuals were thrown into poverty. It was a distressing preoccupation and constant torment of innumerable families; it poisoned the German people by spreading among all classes the spirit of speculation and by diverting them from proper and regular work, and it was the cause of incessant political and moral disturbance. It is indeed easy enough to understand why the record of the sad years 1919–1923 always weighs like a nightmare on the German people.[10]

Surely some special corner of hell is reserved for central bankers. Ben Strong. John Law. They are probably all down there. Maybe Charles Ponzi is with them. What do they do down there? Play cards, perhaps.

Helferrich must be there too—roasting. For when he undermined the Germans' faith in their system, their money, and their culture, did he not also pave the way to hell for millions of his fellow countrymen?

If only we could talk to them! Didn't they sacrifice their souls, and do they not now writhe in eternal torment? And for what? Why should God make a moral example out of them if no one pays attention?

Every central banker in the world has taken the devil's bait, creating money, out of thin air, as if no one were looking. As if it had not been tried before. As if they could get away with it and people really could get something for nothing! And yet, they all seem unable to do anything different—even with the threat of scorching their fat derrieres in the afterlife.

SECRETS OF THE NEAR DEAD

If the dead have secrets, what about those who are almost dead?

We read an interview with Sir John Templeton before he died. The great old man said he thought shares and houses in America were too expensive and that the United States was cruising for trouble with its trade deficit and US federal deficit. He said he anticipated a long bear market in shares, falling residential real estate prices, and a serious slump in the economy. Implicitly, he advised investors to hold cash.[11]

The person who wrote the article then asked local analysts and stockbrokers what they thought of Templeton's opinion. One challenged Templeton's competence, saying that because of his advanced age (Templeton was 92), he might be "out of touch" with current thinking. Templeton was not even dead yet, and already they were shoveling the mud on his face. But being out of touch is precisely what made his opinions valuable.

We like old things. Old buildings. Old ideas. Old trees. Old rules. Old investors. The older the investor, the more confidence we have in him. He has seen good times and bad times. He has seen bulls and bears.

People who have been around for a long time have had an opportunity to see several cycles. An American born after 1960, however, barely came of age when the 1982 to 2002 boom began. Until recently they never saw a sustained bear market or a period when the nation was downcast or desperate. Barely have they still, apart from the financial panic of 2008, which the Federal Reserve and Treasury made sure didn't last long, by extending more credit and printing more money.

Templeton was a young man when Wall Street crashed in 1929. He was an adult in the Great Depression. He recalled the dark days of World War II, when it looked as though the allies might lose. During his life span, there were booms and busts, mass murders, the worst wars in history, famines, hyperinflation, and national bankruptcies. Dozens of currencies and at least five empires had gone defunct. Dozens of coups and revolutions had taken place. Ideologies had come and gone. Thousands of banks and businesses had gone bust. Prominent careers had been ruined and reputations lost.

A man who has seen so much and still has his wits about him is a great treasure. If he is still solvent, that is even better. Somehow, he must have avoided the bad ideas, bad investments, and bad advice.

Innovations are like genetic mutations. Most of them are mistakes. Most fail. Old people tend to reject new ideas, new styles, and new things. This is not simply because these dogs are too old to learn new tricks. What the oldsters know—from experience—is that the new tricks are probably not worth learning. What we have around us are only the innovations that succeeded. Companies, products, ideas, governments, clubs, styles—all that we see are the successful ones. The unsuccessful innovations—thousands and thousands of them—all disappeared.

Even wildly successful innovations, such as heavier-than-air flight, are not successful for everyone. Warren Buffett estimates that if you had owned the entire airline industry from the moment after Orville and Wilbur made the first flight, right up to the day the Concorde made its last flight, you scarcely would have made a dime. Many other industries are the same. There are companies quoted on Wall Street that make money in those industries. But they are the survivors. Many others failed long ago.

Nassim Nicholas Taleb explains it in his book, *Fooled by Randomness:*

> Mathematically, progress means that some new information is better than past information, not that the average of new information will supplant past information, which means that it is optimal for someone, when in doubt, to systematically reject the new idea, information, or method . . . .
>
> The Saturday newspaper lists dozens of new patents of such items that can revolutionize our lives. People tend to infer that because some inventions have revolutionized our lives that inventions are good to endorse and we should favour the new over the old. I take the opposite view. The opportunity cost of missing a "new new thing" like the airplane and the automobile is minuscule compared to the toxicity of all the garbage one has to go through to get to these jewels (assuming these have brought some improvement to our lives, which I frequently doubt).[12]

A young man has access to information. With the internet, he can get all he wants. What he lacks is the "high-proof" distilled information—the wisdom—that comes with age.

Taleb continues, "A preference for distilled thinking implies favoring old investors and traders, that is, investors who have been exposed to markets the longest, a matter that is counter to the Wall Street practice of preferring those that have been the most profitable and preferring the younger whenever possible. . . ."[13]

Testing the proposition using a mathematical model, Taleb "found a significant advantage in selecting aged traders, using, as a selection criterion, their cumulative years of experience rather than their absolute success (conditional on their having survived without blowing up)."[14]

Distilled information tends to be expressed as moral interdictions. Don't steal. Don't lie. Don't buy expensive stocks or sell cheap ones. Don't expect to get something for nothing. Don't neglect your spouse. Don't forget St. Patrick's day. Don't spend too much. Don't eat too fast. Don't drink before 6 p.m. Don't mess around with the boss's wife. Each don't represents lessons learned by previous generations. For every don't, there must be a million sorry souls burning in hell.

Undistilled information, however, is nothing more than noise— newspaper headlines, TV babble, cocktail chatter, the latest innovation, the latest business secret, the latest fashion. It is public information, backed by no real experience or private insights. It is not useless. It is worse than useless, for it misleads people into thinking they know something.

DEAD PRESIDENTS

David M. Walker, former Comptroller General of the United States, with whom we later made a documentary movie called *I.O.U.S.A*, clarified America's debt situation as early as 2004. The federal government's gross debt—the accumulation of its annual deficits—was about $7 trillion last September, which works out to about $24,000 for every man, woman, and child in the country. But that number excluded items like the gap between the government's Social Security and Medicare commitments and the money put aside to pay for them. At the time, with these items factored in, the burden for every American already rose to well over $100,000.[15] In the film we traveled with Mr. Walker touring the country as he tried to alert business leaders, local politicians, and civic groups what a dreadful path the country had set itself on. David had broken his address into four deficits the nation faced at the time: savings, trade, budget and the biggie: leadership.

We add to Walker's lament: As we will see, $7 trillion was chicken feed.[16] The real debt was far higher. Plus, one out of every four dollars spent by the federal government was borrowed. And for every dollar that came in the door from income taxes, the feds borrowed another 80 cents. Economists used to worry about the government using up the nation's savings. But Americans had no more savings to use. Still, the nation that couldn't save a dime set out to save the entire planet. In the next four years, the official US debt would grow nearly 50%. And then, in an effort to bail out the entire world economy after the pandemic, US deficits would soar over $1.7 trillion per year in 2023.[17]

Meanwhile, the private sector already had immense debts. In 2005, for every $19 Americans earned, they spent $20. This difference was recorded in the trade deficit figures, measuring the speed at which Americans raced down the road to ruin. Top speed in 2005 was $58.3 billion. That was the figure for January 2005 when the nation was clocked overspending at a rate of almost $2 billion per day. It was the difference between what Americans sold to foreigners in the month of January and what they bought from them. It was a negative number. On a chart of the nation's accounts, it would be in red. Or in brackets. Or preceded by a minus sign.[18]

Back then, if it were divided among the nation's families, it would come to about $600 for each one. This represents only a single month's trade deficit, so we should multiply it by 12 to get the measure of damage on an annual basis: $7,200 per family per year. Compared with the average family's income, it is such a big number that we wondered if we had done the arithmetic correctly. On a macroeconomic scale, the shortfall was rising to 6% of GDP.[19]

Nearly two decades later, in October 2023, little had changed. The trade deficit for that autumn month was still clipping along at a negative $63 billion.[20]

What a quaint project the documentary now seems in retrospect. In the early months of 2024, the unfunded liabilities have ballooned year-over-year to $212,421,900,000,000. That's over $212 trillion. And it's moving higher so fast, it's even difficult to round to the nearest $100 million. Every citizen's share of this unfunded liabilities in 2024 are approaching $700,000.[21]

In 2010, following the policy response to the financial panic of 2008, a curious shift in the average families balance sheet took place.

The Federal Reserve slashed interest rates to zero. Consumers took the bait. In just two weeks, between March 17, 2010, and March 31 of the same year, consumer loans—composed of credit cards and other revolving credit at all commercial banks—more than doubled from $313 billion to $647 billion while the national savings rate hovered about 6%.[22] Following the pandemic the diverging trends got far more pronounced. By January 2024, consumer loans had nearly doubled again to $1.04 trillion while the savings rate had sunk below 4%.[23] Not surprising really. The first serious period of rising interests in over a decade caused consumers to both spend down savings and take on more debt in order to maintain their lifestyle.

In the old days of the gold standard, the nation on the plus side of this exchange would pile up its excess foreign currency and take it to the other nation's central bank. Gold was the common reference and an uncommon restraint. It was real money. If a nation ran out of gold, it ran out of money. It could no longer borrow. It could no longer run trade deficits, because when the foreign currencies were presented to it, it would have no means of settling up. It would have to declare bankruptcy, which happened from time to time.

But it had been 34 years since the United States settled its overseas obligations in gold. Since then, it has found it far easier to offer US dollar–denominated Treasury bonds. Remarkably, the foreigners accepted them as if they were as good as gold. More remarkably, for most of that time the bonds were not only as good as gold—they were better. Gold fell in price for two decades following Ronald Reagan's first presidential election. Overseas central bankers took the Treasury bonds and felt grateful, even lucky, to have them.

The United States was just too lucky. It could spend without really paying. It could borrow without ever really paying back. It could dig itself into such a deep hole of debt, it could find no easy way out.

Among the noisy headlines of 2005 was the remarkable information that China—a Third World nation—lent over $300 billion per year. The trend continued, topping out at $1.3 trillion in 2012, and remaining consistently above $1 trillion for another decade. By 2023, the Middle Kingdom seemed to have come to their senses (a little). Chinese purchases of US treasuries had dropped to an annual rate of $770 billion.[24] Without Chinese support, the dollar would have collapsed, bond yields soared, and the US economy would have been in a prolonged recession, if not a depression.

Where did the money come from? The Chinese got the dead presidents from selling products to live Americans, who seemed ready to consume anything that came their way. First, the dollars came rolling off US printing presses, then they made their way into the hands of Chinese and other manufacturers, and finally, they returned to their birthplace as loans.

At the turn of the 21st century, China and Japan combined were fast becoming America's "company store," to whom we owed our standard of living and maybe even our soul. By August 2023, two central banks—Japan and China—held more than $2 trillion worth of US Treasury bonds. On their willingness to save and to recycle savings into US Treasury bonds stood the US consumer economy. A single word from either central bank could send the US economy into a severe slump: *sell*.[25]

Markets make opinions.

Thus began an even more remarkable curiosity: The United States began accusing the Chinese of manipulating their currency to maintain the trade advantage. The latter already sold to United States more goods and services than the United States sold to it, by a ratio of 5 to 1. The unfair distortion, policymakers in Washington argued, was due to China pegging its own currency to the dollar. In spring 2005, the exchange was called *manipulation*; the United States demanded that China revalue by 10%.

But, one wondered, how were the Chinese manipulating the yuan? By fixing it to the imperial currency! Oh, that was clever, wily, diabolical. The Chinese insisted on maintaining their 10-year-old policy of pegging the yuan to the dollar. The United States counted on a steady devaluation of its money. It bought from overseas and paid in dollars. Then, in effect, it printed up more dollars to replace those it had shipped overseas. The resulting inflation of the currency—reflected in the increase in prices of oil, gold, and other internationally traded goods—was a form of imperial tribute. It was America's only way of making the empire pay. As the dollar went down, the trillions of dollars held in foreign accounts became less valuable. An "exorbitant privilege," said Charles de Gaulle.[26]

But the Chinese refused to play along. As the dollar went down, so did their yuan. Instead of raising prices on Chinese goods and lowering the value of Chinese dollar holdings relative to its own currency, everything remained even. The Chinese weren't paying their tribute.

Americans were indignant. A Senate committee said it would rewrite the law of the land to make what the Chinese were doing qualify as currency manipulation. Bush administration officials gave the Chinese a deadline to shape up. In summer 2005, the Chinese finally announced that they were giving up the dollar peg, or at least widening "the channel" a little. But the problem was never caused by China.

An entire US generation had grown up being told that it could spend its way to prosperity. In the early years of the 21st century, Treasury Secretaries Snow, Paulson, and Geithner, and Federal Reserve Chairs Greenspan, Bernanke, and Yellen all still believed it. Debt was no problem, they said. Spend, spend, spend. The illusion of prosperity was only magnified and distorted more in the decade following the global financial crisis in 2008. By the time Federal Reserve Chairman Jerome Powell was tasked with raising interest rates to battle the worst inflation in a generation in 2022, a whole generation of investors and consumers came to believe money was virtually free and would remain that way owing to the magical black box hidden somewhere on the East Coast between Washington and Wall Street. Savers had all but given up getting any stable returns from their actual savings. Whether they liked it or not, savers were incentivized to speculate alongside the institutional traders toiling away behind glass and steel in lower Manhattan.

US spending created a boom in China, where the average person works in a sweatshop, lives in a hovel, and saves 25% of their earnings. Americans had come to believe there was something unfair about China's trade practices, that they must be stealing jobs with a distorted currency, instead of competing for them fair and square.

Meanwhile, in the United States, the average person lived in a house they couldn't pay for, drove a car they couldn't afford, and waited for the next shipment from Hong Kong for distractions they couldn't resist. They saved nothing and believed the Chinese would lend them money forever, on the same terms.

That this could go on forever hardly seemed worth pointing out. The world created in the *pax dollarium* era had to end. Then the dead could cluck, "I told you so."

Today, as we reconsider arguments we made initially in 2005, the numbers are simply staggering. Here's a fund activity. Go to https://www.usdebtclock.org/ and watch as the debt mounts. As we write, the national debt is quickly approaching $35 trillion. The annual deficit itself is consistently above $1.8 trillion. According to real-time stats, the average taxpayer owes $259,949. The national debt is 122% of the nation's gross national output. That ratio of debt to output is up more than double from the 54% when we started this project in 2005.

There are many reasons why politicians and civic voices simply ignore these numbers. None of them conservative or thoughtful. "Reagan proved the debt doesn't matter," Dick Cheney said, and by that he meant it doesn't matter because voters will never punish politicians at the ballot box for promising to spend more money.[27] When we were making *I.O.U.S.A.* the refrain we heard from luminaries like Warren Buffet and Alan Greenspan was the national debt is no problem because "we'll grow our way out of this."

Well, now, years have passed, the debt has mounted to a percentage perilously close to impeding the nation's ability to grow its economy at all. That is, except by adding more debt.

Lather. Rinse. Repeat.

CHAPTER 2

EMPIRES OF DIRT

Long is the historical record of empires. Short is the list of common elements. There are "good" empires. And bad ones. There are ones in which the imperialists get rich and others in which they become very poor. There are some in which the imperium functions with the brute elegance of a guillotine; in others, the complexities and subtleties baffle historians. But among all the empires that have come and gone, the US imperium stands out as the most absurd.

The absurdity arises at the most basic level. Seeking to deceive, the Ivy League Alexanders and the Plain State Caesars deceived themselves more than anyone. From the very beginning, they knew not what business they were in.

We can enjoy a superior chuckle at the screwball humbug of it. Historians of the future are likely to get cramps from laughing. But economists—when they finally come to their senses and realize what is happening—are the ones who will revel in the biggest joke. The only reason they are not palsied with mirth already is that they have missed the punch line. This is the funniest and most preposterous scheme of imperial finance the world has ever seen; when they finally get it, they will laugh till it hurts.

At the risk of spoiling a great joke, we will explain it. The typical program for imperial finance is simple. The imperial power, the imperium, provides—at its own initiative—a public good; it extends security and order. In return, the groups that benefit pay tribute. The imperium should not merely break even; it should make a profit. Living standards in the homeland should rise, compared with those in vassal states. Even the Austro-Hungarians got that right, as a trip to Vienna will easily confirm. The city got rich in the 19th century.

America provides a *pax dollarium* for nearly the entire world. But the US does not take direct tribute from its vassal states and dependent territories for providing this service. Instead, it borrows from them. Living standards rise in the United States. But they are rising on borrowed money, not on stolen money. The big difference is that America's vassal states can stop lending at any time. If they care to, they can even dump their current loans on the open market, destroying the US dollar and forcing interest rates so high that a recession—or depression—is practically guaranteed. What is worse, the longer the present system continues, the worse off Americans are.

The closer you look at it, the larger the absurdity becomes. In the first half of 2005, Americans got poorer, not richer—at the rate of $80 million per hour. Their system of imperial finance was impoverishing them. Even that is not the worst of it, because it also reduced their ability to compete in the modern economic world. While they were providing a public good—at a loss—their competitors were saving money, building capital and expertise, setting up factories, and taking market share away from them. Each year, Asians produce more of what Americans buy, and Americans produce less of what anyone buys.

Products leave Asia for North America. Money leaves North America for Asia. The money comes back to America within days. America's economists breathe easy. What is there to worry about, they ask, as long as it comes back to us. "It is a form of tribute," they claim; the empire works. But it works in a perverse way. The money that comes back is not the same as the money that left. It has been transformed: It goes out as an asset and comes back as a liability.

THE HUNS ARE COMING!

For many centuries, Europeans had nightmares. Periodically, barbarian invaders from the East came in waves from the steppes of Eurasia.

Celtic tribes pushed out or exterminated whoever was there before them. Then, new groups came after them. Mounted on horseback, they came fast and hard. They so terrified the more settled communities that the tribes picked up and pushed to the West. Germanic tribes eventually pushed the Celts to the far corners of Europe and later sacked Rome.

The Huns were barbarians. They were ruthless, cunning, fearless, and reported to be invincible in battle. What chance was there against them?

In market terms, this was a good time to be "short" Europe. A fund manager might say that they chose to "underweight" the Old World. It was a time when the expansion of the previous period was likely to be corrected. There would be wailing people and gnashing of teeth. It was a time when fear and despair would likely dominate. It was a sell signal for the growth of civilization and commerce, which tend to go hand in hand like a prisoner with his police escort.

Politics and war are not zero-sum games. For every winner there is not a loser. Nor is a dollar gained for every dollar that is lost. Instead, the destruction of war and the costs of politics make them net losing propositions always. Most people lose. Wealth disappears. As a whole, people are poorer.

But, as in a bear market, some people gain from war. Those who win the war feel like winners, even though they may be poorer and many of their comrades may be dead. A few contractors and speculators actually make money on war.

The barbarian invasions of Europe had their bright side. The barbarians were in their expansion phase—their bull market stage—with rising expectations and positive, bullish hopes. They were getting something, not for nothing, but for next to nothing. What was the effort of killing a man compared with the wealth it brought the killer? A small investment. A trifle really, and an enjoyable one for many people. But conquest was not without risk. There are no completely free lunches, even for thieves and murderers. The Huns took a risk. On the upside were booty, women, slaves—and the pure exhilaration of battle and the prestige of conquest. On the downside, they might be defeated and killed.

The Huns might have been a sell signal for civilization, but they were a buy signal for their own fortunes, their status, their group, their empire, and their genes. It was a time to be "long" politics: There is a time to plant, to reap, and to trade with others peaceably. And there is a time for force, for taking what you want without paying for it and for killing anyone who gets in your way, for the Hunnish invasions meant rape, not for sweet talk and courtship. They meant theft, looting, and pillage, not further elaboration of property rights or the division of labor. Things got simpler, more brutal, mean, and nasty; lives were shortened. It was not a time to be in the insurance business.

What caused the periodic invasions no one knows. Perhaps good weather out on the plains produced population explosions that caused the nomads to expand. Perhaps bad weather caused famine that sent hungry mouths in search of someone else's meat and grain. Historians don't know. But fear of the barbarians from the steppes has been a chronic theme of Western history—particularly among the Teutonic tribes that were most exposed to them.

THE GREAT KHAN

Perhaps the most successful empire builder of all time was a leader of one of these periods of barbarian expansion—Genghis Khan. Since the time of the Romans, it has been fashionable to put a civilized mask on your face when you put the imperial purple on your back. You are bringing religion to the heathen. You are bringing civilization to the indigenes. You are bringing culture, education, and technology. Even Alexander the Great thought he was doing the world a favor. Conquerors do not like to admit—even to themselves—that their instincts are no different from those of barbarians. They have better table manners. But they are subject to the same urges as Genghis or Attila. Bloodlust, prestige, power, status— who can deny that it would be a thrill to conquer a whole city or an entire nation? But empire builders typically put on the imperial purple like a set of angel's wings, leap off the balcony, and come down with a thud.

Genghis Khan needed no mask. The man showed his face as it really was. He united the Mongolian tribes in about 1129 and beginning with a series of attacks on northern China, he embarked on a spectacular epic of mass slaughter and rapine from which two empires were derived. One of them, the Ottoman Empire, lasted until the end of World War I. The Mongol hordes overran northern China, Tibet, Persia, nearly all of central Asia and the Caucasus, Korea, Burma, Vietnam, Anatolia, and much of Russia. They attacked India and eventually, in 1526, Babar, one of Genghis Khan's descendants, set himself up as emperor of the place. In China, too, Genghis's descendants founded the Yuan dynasty, which ruled until nearly the 15th century.

All empires have to pay, in one way or another. The Mongols made theirs pay in the most elemental, and probably most satisfying, way. From an evolutionary point of view, all human activity has a single purpose—to propagate one's genes. A man tries to get rich or get elected to demonstrate that he is the sort of fellow a woman would want to mate with; he will produce offspring as capable as he is; and he has the resources to take care of them. In this sense, history records no more spectacular success than the great Genghis Khan.

At one point, Genghis was told by his generals that the sweetest pleasure in life was falconry. "No," the empire builder is said to have replied, "You are mistaken. Man's greatest good fortune is to chase and defeat his enemy, seize his total possessions, leave his married women weeping and wailing, ride his gelding and use the bodies of his women as a nightshirt and support."[1] Genghis was so successful that a recent DNA study of 2,123 men from across Asia permitted scientists to estimate that he may have as many as 16 million male descendants spread out from Manchuria to Afghanistan.[2]

Genghis made the empire pay in another way, too. He imposed a rough income tax tribute on all his subject peoples. The rate was only 10%—considerably less barbaric than today's rates.

Now that Mongolia is free from Soviet rule, its citizens are beginning to take a renewed interest in the man so many of them can trace as an ancestor. "Within this rapidly changing world, Genghis Khan, if we acknowledge him without bias, can serve as a moral anchor. He can be Mongolia's root, its source of certainty at a time when many things are uncertain."[3]

We quote that passage from the *Harvard Asia Pacific Review* merely to embarrass Professor Tsetsenbileg, of the Mongolian Academy of Sciences, who said it. Genghis Khan may be popular in Mongolia, but it just raises questions about the Mongolians.

"All who surrender will be spared; whoever does not surrender but opposes with struggle and dissension, shall be annihilated,"[4] said Genghis before attacking the ancient cities of Bukhara and Samarkand. It has been estimated that his campaigns killed as many as 40 million people based on census data of the times:

> Genghis Khan preferred to offer opponents the chance to submit to his rule without a fight, but was merciless if he encountered any resistance. Genghis Khan's conquests were characterized by wholesale destruction on unprecedented scale and radically changed the demographics in Asia. According to the works of Iranian historian Rashid al-Din, Mongols killed over 70,000 people in Merv and more than a million in Nishapur. China suffered a drastic decline in population. Before the Mongol invasion, China had about 100 million inhabitants; after the complete conquest in 1279, the census in 1300 showed it to have roughly 60 million people. How many of these deaths were attributable directly to Genghis and his forces is unclear.[5]

But those were also the days when a man lied to exaggerate his murders, rather than cover them up. Genghis Khan was proud of killing people. In a way, he should have been; he did it so well.

But how could so few have done so much to so many? The entire population of Mongolia could not have exceeded about 200,000 persons. Military historians argue that it was largely because the Mongols were so bloodthirsty, so merciless, so fanatical, so fast, and so lethal that they were hard to stop. They were superb horsemen, frequently without infantry support, who were able to move more quickly than their more sedentary enemies much like panzer divisions in World War II. Their *ghazi* was a forerunner of today's *jihad*. Their composite bows were like today's Kalashnikovs (a Russian-made rifle that can fire bullets continuously). And they had a sophisticated system of communications that included semaphore-like information exchange on the battlefield and a pony express relay of "arrow riders" shooting across the prairies. With these advantages, they took what they wanted and killed everyone who got in their way.

It was not a very polite way to run an empire, but it worked.

Genghis died in 1227. His son Ogedei was elected to succeed him. Those who think democracy deters state violence do not bother to talk to the dead: Mussolini, Hitler, and Ogedei Khan all won office, at least in part, thanks to the ballot box. After his election victory, Ogedei Khan continued his father's expansion. He pushed farther into northeastern Asia and conquered Korea and northern China. By the time of his sudden death in 1,241, his armies were on the frontier of Egypt and present-day Poland. But democracy cut them off. Mongol law required that the new Khan be chosen by a new vote of Genghis's descendants. Were it not for this interruption, the Mongol armies might have pushed beyond the Rhine and thrown Europe into a new Dark Age. As it turned out, by the time the Mongols had chosen a new leader—Genghis's grandson, Mongka—the momentum in Europe had been lost.

In 1257, the Mongols turned toward Baghdad. Hulagu, another grandson of Genghis, demanded that the caliph of Baghdad, al-Muta'sim, receive him as his sovereign, just as he had done with the Seljuk Turks when they swept over the area. But the caliph of Baghdad was the 37th of the Abbasid dynasty and leader of Muslims throughout the Middle East. He believed that his people would come to his aid against the infidel. They did not, and Hulagu marched on Baghdad with an army of hundreds of thousands of cavalry, wiping out the old Assassin fortress at Alamut on his way.

The caliph realized his mistake. He offered Hulagu the title of *Sultan*. Hulagu's name would be given at Friday prayers in all the mosques of Baghdad, he added. Later, the caliph went in person to see Hulagu. This time, he said his citizens would lay down their arms if the Mongols would spare their lives. But as soon as their swords and bows had been collected, the Muslim fighters were exterminated. Then the Mongols went to work on the civilians. Eighty thousand men, women, and children were massacred. The caliph was strangled.

The only people not killed in Baghdad were the Christians. Mongka Khan's mother was a Nestorian Christian. At one point, perhaps at her urging, the Mongols sent emissaries to the King of the Franks, who was then fighting their mutual enemies—the Muslims—in the Holy Lands. The Mongols offered to turn to Christ, but his suggestion seems to have been ignored so he turned East, instead of West. Mongka Khan died just as his armies were about to attack Cairo. The next Khan, Kublai, moved the Mongol court to Beijing and founded the Yuan dynasty.

Something about the Baghdad area must attract empire builders the way a beehive attracts bears. Only a few miles away is the site of ancient Ctesiphon—a city that was taken and retaken at least 36 times before it was finally destroyed after the Saracens took it in AD 637. The Romans took the place five times, three times in the second century alone. Before that, the Hittites, Akkadians, Persians, Parthians, Sassanids, Macedonians, and countless others had already left their sandal prints between the Tigris and Euphrates.

Emperor Trajan captured Ctesiphon in AD 116 and made it part of Rome. The next year, Hadrian gave it back to the Parthians in a peace settlement. In 164, it was again taken, by Roman general Avidius Cassius, but later abandoned. Then, Septimus Severus finally made the campaigns pay when he took the city in 197. He sold as many as 100,000 of the city's citizens into slavery.

A hundred years later, the city was again in the news. Emperor Galerius was defeated outside the city walls by an army of Persians. In 296, he sought a rematch and this time won the city, which he traded for Armenia. Much later, in 627, Heraclius, took the city. The Western Empire was already history, but Heraclius ruled briefly from Constantinople. He gave up the city soon after its capture. Ten years later, it fell to the Saracens and was soon in ruins. A British army was defeated by Ottoman forces in 1915, but regained title to the city in the Treaty of Versailles. Later, the British readily let go of Baghdad, after they realized how expensive it was to hold on to the place. It gained its independence along with other British imperial possessions in 1921. More recently, the city was once again taken by US forces.

WHERE HAVE ALL THE DEAD EMPIRES GONE?

Of all the silly things people said toward the end of the 20th century, perhaps the silliest came out of the mouth of Francis Fukuyama. The man was so infatuated by the apparent success of the US imperium, he believed the "end of history" might have arrived. What is the history of this tattered ball but the record of the rise and fall of civilizations, of governments, of battles and heroes? But so perfect in Fukuyama's eyes was the new US empire, he thought it had risen beyond the tug of gravity. So solidly launched was the rocket of democratic capitalism that he could not imagine that it would ever fall to earth. Nor could he fathom how anything could ever compete with it or take its place.[6]

Fukuyama did not seem to appreciate how history works. Politics, like markets and love affairs, often throws up periods of relative contentment, as well as sour periods of despair and bubbles of temporary insanity. If they last for more than a generation, people think they are permanent. In the case of bubbles, people believe that some new era has arrived and that things will never be as they were before. Bubble markets—such as the tech bubble in the late 1990s or the residential property bubble in certain areas of the United States in 2004 and 2005—come along from time to time. People take leave of their senses. They are willing to buy things at twice, three times, ten times prices they would have judged too high just a few years before. In the famous tulip bubble in Holland from 1634 to 1637, people paid up to 5,000 guilders for a single tulip bulb. In the South Sea bubble in England, in 1711, speculators paid up to 1,000 pounds for stocks that were reduced to nothing by the latter half of 1720. In the Japanese bubble of the late 1980s, investors paid such high prices for real estate in downtown Tokyo that the grounds of the Imperial Palace were said to be worth more than the entire state of California.

Investors pay extravagant prices because they are convinced that something fundamental has changed and that they will never again have an opportunity to buy at current prices, no matter how high they have become. They believe the world will never be the same, that the rules that govern human activity have been altered or suspended.

"Markets make opinions," the old-timers say. It is an expression we return to several times in this book. As prices rise, people invent explanations for why they have gone up and they will continue. In the case of the tech bubble of the late 1990s, they told themselves that new developments in electronic communications had completely changed the ancient relationships. Thanks to computer-driven devices and the internet, material progress was about to accelerate. Assets were about to get much more valuable. It did not bother them that the two propositions were contradictory. A society in which the future comes faster should logically depreciate the present more quickly. Factories, means of production, and capital assets should be expected to become obsolete sooner and thus should be worth less, not more. But no one thinks very hard when markets are rising. This is true of the real estate bubble on both coasts in 2004 and 2005. Houses in Southern California were increasing in value at four times the rate of gross domestic product growth and an infinitely great multiple of real income growth—which was negative. It made no sense, but who mentioned it? Prices were rising; investors had no trouble coming up with reasons. It was a new era, they said; property would never again be worth what it used to be.

In politics, too, there are bubbles—times when the horizon is so clear and cloudless, people begin to think it will never rain again. The old principles—the wisdom of the dead and the virtues that brought them to where they are—no longer matter. It is a new era. They are the imperial power, the hegemon, the cock of the walk. They are on top of the world and are looking for reasons they will be there forever. But the reason comes to them readily. They look in the mirror, and there it is. Instead of their own faces, however, they see only the dull, puerile masks they have put on. It is as if they all have become candidates for president; they are "hollow dummies," to use Orwell's expression—vain imposters, pretending to be something even dimmer and less interesting than they actually are. They look in the mirror and think they see a race so clever, virtuous, sturdy, and industrious that they deserve to be on top of the world. Surely, they have created something that can never be matched. All of history has been marching toward this perfection. Time has stopped. History has come to an end; there is no need for any more of it. In 1989, US democratic imperialism triumphed unmistakably against its adversary—the Evil Empire. The Good Empire was the last one standing. God had shined his light on us and would never turn it off.

Many people said many dumb things in the 20th century. Usually, they were only mistakes or lies. When Neville Chamberlain said we would have "peace in our time," he was making a prediction. He was wrong. But if you hung everyone who guessed wrong about the future, the lampposts and traffic lights of Wall Street would be full of bodies. And when Adolf Hitler said Germany needed *lebensraum*, he was merely covering up his desire for conquest by putting on a mask. But when, after the Berlin Wall fell and Francis Fukuyama declared the end of history, he must have made the gods chuckle. Here was a reflection so vain and imbecilic, it practically cracked mirrors.

It was as if Fukuyama never actually read any history. Empires are living things. They are born; they must die, too. No one conquers without eventually being conquered. No bubble expands without eventually blowing up. There are no exceptions. All empires die. Here, for amusement, we look at the gravestones (see Table 2.1). Only one, and that one of relatively recent naissance, still lives. But the grave and the tombstone are there, waiting for it.

Fukuyama's concept was that the desire for power, glory, conquest, revenge—all the dark forces of destruction and regression—had

Table 2.1 **Empires Throughout History**

• Abyssinian Empire (1270–1974)	• Haitian Empire (1804–1806)
• Achaemenid Empire (*commonly known as the Persian Empire*) (c. 550–330 BC)	• Hittite Empire (c. 1460–1180 BC)
• Akkadian Empire (c. 2350–2150 BC)	• Holy Roman Empire (843–1806)
• American Empire (1917–)	• Inca Empire (1438–1533)
• Arabian Empire (c. 630–1258)	• Ilkhanate Empire (c. 1256–1338)
• Assyrian Empire (c. 900–612 BC)	• Japanese Empire (1871–1945)
• Athenian Empire (c. 500–300 BC)	• Khmer Empire (802–1462)
• Austro-Hungarian Empire (1867–1918)	• Kongo Empire (c. 1230–1665)
• Austrian Empire (1804–1867)	• Korean Empire (1897–1910)
• Aztec Empire (1375–1521)	• Macedonian Empire (c. 338 BC– 309 BC)
• Brazilian Empire (1822–1889)	• Mexican Empire (1822–1823, 1864–1867)
• British Empire (c. 1583–) De jure	• Mogul Empire (1526–1857)
• British Raj (1858–1947) (Imperial: 1877–1947)	• Mongol Empire (1206–1294)
• Byzantine Empire (395–1453)	• Old Babylonian Empire (c. 1900–1600 BC)
• Central African Empire (1977–1979)	• Ottoman Empire (1281–1923)
• Chinese Empire (221 BC–1912)	• Persian Empire (c. 648 BC –330 BC)
• Dutch colonial empire (1627–1814)	• Portuguese Empire (1495–1975)
• Egyptian Empire (1550–1070 BC)	• Roman Empire (31 BC–AD 476)
• First French Empire (1804–1815)	• Russian Empire (1721–1917)
• Second French Empire (1853–1871)	• Sassanian Empire (224– 651)
• French colonial empire (c. 1605–1960s)	• Seleucid Empire (323–60 BC)
• German Empire (1871–1918)	• Seljuk Empire (c. 1037–1194 AD)
• German colonial empire (1884–1918)	• Spanish Empire (1492–1975)
• German Third Reich (1933–1945)	• Swedish Empire (1561–1878)
• Golden Horde (1378–1502)	• Timurid Empire (1401–1505)
• Greater East Asia Co-Prosperity Sphere (1940–1945)	• Ur III Empire (c. 2100–2000 BC)
	• Vijayanagara Empire (c. 1350–1700)

disappeared. They had been replaced by an evolving civilization of consensual, democratic government and market-driven material progress, led by an enlightened US imperium. This is what America offered the world—peace and prosperity. But even a casual look at the historical record would show that neither empires nor democracy are any guarantee of peace or prosperity.

For proof that empires are hardly peaceful places, we turn to the history of Rome. And here we offer readers a history of the rise and fall of the world's greatest empire as brief as the latest Italian underpants.

THE ROMAN EMPIRE

In the eighth century BC, Rome was nothing more than a collection of villages along the Tiber, inhabited by several tribes, principally Latin, Sabine, and Etruscan. Gradually, these Romans grew in numbers and power and went to war with almost everyone. They were already constructing an empire before the fifth century BC. In a celebrated early incident, perhaps only legendary, they invited their neighbors, the Sabines, to a feast and then stole their women. The Sabine men were not happy; they took offense and nursed a grudge. But there was hardly a tribe, kingdom, or empire in Europe, North Africa, or the Middle East with whom the Romans did not pick a fight. After the Sabine war, there were wars against the Albii, Etruscans, Volcii, Carthaginians, Etruscans again, the Latin League (and this is only a partial list), the Volsquii, Equii, Veieii, Gauls, Samnites, more Gauls, Epirians, Carthaginians again, and more Gauls, Macedonians, Syrians, Macedonians again, slaves in Sicily, Parthians— and even Romans in the civil wars. And we have not even arrived at Caesar's wars against the Gauls in 58 to 51 BC. Roman history has another 500 years of wars to go!

The civil wars in the first century BC put an end to the Republic. Then, Caesar crossed the Rubicon, and it was a new era in Rome. It was as if Tommy Franks had decided to move his army to Washington, DC, and make a regime change of his own. Some people would object, of course (the liberal papers would howl), but most people wouldn't care.

In ancient Rome, as in modern Washington, people chose their ideas the same way they chose their clothes—they wanted something that not only did the job but also was fashionable. And at the time, it was à la mode for emperors and individuals alike to pretend they lived in a free republic that honored citizens' rights. But in practice, the government, and its leader, could get away with almost anything. And what they seemed to like doing was going out and making war against everyone they thought they could beat. That is what empires do.

Back then, war was a paying proposition. When Emperor Trajan took Ctesiphon (near modern Baghdad), he captured 100,000 people who were sold into slavery. When Augustus took Egypt, he used the Nile's wheat harvest to feed the growing population of rabble in Rome.

But although some people came out ahead, in the aggregate, wars then—as now—were negative gain enterprises. And as the empire grew, the costs also mounted, to the point where both became grotesque and insupportable.

Octavian, under the name Augustus, was installed in 27 BC. The Romans used only pure gold and silver coins, but Augustus needed more money to finance his wars and domestic improvements. There were no government printing presses capable of running off a batch of $100s in a few seconds. Nor was there a global bond market, from which he could raise billions in loans overnight. All he could do was to order the government-owned mines in Spain and France to work overtime. Around the clock, miners dug out the precious metals. The money supply rose. As the supply of something rises relative to the supply of something else, the value of the former declines relative to the latter. Thus, prices rose in Rome as more money chased the same quantity of consumer goods. Between the day Augustus came to power and the day Jesus Christ was born—a period of 27 years—consumer prices nearly doubled. Augustus, or his advisors, realized the problem. They cut back the money supply and prices stabilized.

Rome wasn't built in a day, nor was its money destroyed overnight. In AD 64, in Nero's reign, the aureus was reduced by 10% of its weight. Thereafter, whenever the Romans needed more money to finance their wars, their public improvements, their social welfare services and circuses, and their trade deficits, they reduced the metal content of the coins. By the time Odoacer deposed the last emperor in 476, the silver denarius contained only 0.02% silver.

THE INVINCIBLE ARMADA

The impulse to build up an empire seems to be as strong as the impulse to tear one down. To the question, when does a country aim for empire?, comes the answer: whenever it can.

Every country in Europe has at one time or another reached for the imperial purple. Portugal and Spain discovered and conquered vast jungles, swamps, and pampas, and built empires for themselves. For Spain, the conquests were extremely profitable after they found huge quantities of gold and silver. But nothing ruins a nation faster than easy money. The money supply grew larger with every ship's return from the New World. People felt rich, but prices soon soared. Worse, the easy money from the new territories undermined honest industry. In the bubble economy of the early 16th century, Spain developed a trade deficit similar to that of the United States today. People took their money and bought goods from abroad. By the time the New World mines petered out, the Spanish were bankrupt. The Spanish government defaulted on its loans in 1557, 1575, 1607, 1627, and 1647. Not only was the damage severe, it was long-lasting. The Iberian Peninsula became the "sick man of Europe" and remained on bed rest until the 1980s.

If empires are to endure, they must pay. But if they pay too well, success ruins the homeland.

In summer 1588, the Invincible Armada of King Philip II of Spain headed toward the Low Countries. You and I, dear reader, can spot the error already. Philip would have done better to call his fleet the *Almost Invincible Armada*, or perhaps even better, the *Best Little Armada We Could Put Together at the Time*. Calling an armada *invincible* is like calling a WorldCom *unbeatable;* it is a challenge to the gods and an invitation to destruction.

The armada's mission was simple, but not easy—to pick up soldiers in the Netherlands and transport them to England. It had been 500 years since anyone had attempted an invasion of England.

The last assault, led by William, Duke of Normandy, had been a big success. Philip was ready to have a go at it again.

The reasons for the campaign were not so simple. In the jargon of today, he might have labeled his effort a *War on Terror*, for English pirates had been terrorizing Spanish shipping for years. The pirates were not necessarily sponsored by the English crown. But they, literally, found safe harbor in English ports, similar to the way al-Qaida found Afghanistan hospitable.

Of course, there was more to it. Religion played a part. Just as George Bush's War on Terror had a subtext of religion, so did Philip of Spain's campaign against England. Henry VIII of England had rejected the authority of the pope and set himself up as head of the Church of England. When his daughter, Elizabeth, ordered the execution of her Catholic rival, Mary Queen of Scots, Philip (who had been king of England 30 years prior, when he was married to Mary I) thought the time had come for action.

By 1588, Spain had become a powerful empire—with colonies in the New World that had made them rich. Money poured into Spanish coffers during the 16th century—the country imported it the way the United States imports big-screen televisions—giving little in return. What a magnificent system of imperial finance. Ships went west with soldiers and came back with gold and silver. It was almost as good as America's system. In 2005, ships went west from Long Beach and Seattle almost empty. They came back full to the gunwales with Asian-made goods. And like America's system, Spain's trade was almost too good to be true.

Anything that must come to an end must come to an end somehow. Great empires look for ways to destroy themselves. They usually have little trouble finding them. In 1588, Spain found the English fleet—and the North Sea.

History records the Battle of Gravelines as one of the world's most important naval engagements. The Spanish ships were trapped against the Flemish coast. The Spanish commander, the Duke of Medina, decided to use a portion of his fleet to hold off the English, while the rest made their way to open water.[7]

The English engaged the defending Spanish ships with a 10-to-1 numerical advantage. Soon, three of the huge Spanish galleons were sunk, with 600 Spaniards killed and more than 800 others wounded. "The decks ran with their blood," said eyewitness accounts.[8]

Most of the English ships, having done their work and run out of ammunition, sought their ports. The Spanish, badly battered and realizing their cause was doomed, decided they could not fight their way back through the Channel. Instead, they sailed north intending to make their way around Scotland (though they had neglected to bring maps of the area) and thence back to Spain by the open Atlantic.

What the English began, the gods finished. On September 18, 1588, the Spaniards ran into one of the worst storms ever to smash into Scotland. In high seas off Cape Wrath, the Invincible Armada proved vincible; it broke up. Some ships sank; others ran out of food and water. In an effort to keep the leaky vessels above water, sailors manned the buckets day and night, but many soon ran out of energy or died of scurvy, dysentery, and fever.

The sun was never supposed to set on Philip's Spanish empire. But it sank along with the armada in 1588. Financially, Spanish fortunes had begun taking on water long before.

"The mines of Brazil were the ruin of Portugal, as those of Mexico and Peru had been of Spain; all manufacture fell into insane contempt . . . ," explained Alfred Thayer Mahan in his opus, *The Influence of Sea Power upon History, 1660–1783.* "The tendency to trade, involving of necessity the production of something to trade with, is the national characteristic most important to the development of sea power."[9]

Prices rose sharply in the 16th century. As a result of the increase in the money supply caused by the gold and silver shipped in from the colonies, prices in all of Europe went up 400%. Then, when the mines and robberies eased off after 1580, the inflationary boom was over. A long depression began on the Iberian Peninsula. The Spanish and Portuguese were victims of their own good fortune.

CHAPTER 3

HOW EMPIRES WORK

Nothing is born but from another living thing. No empire ever arose without some link to its predecessors. But the system of imperial finance in the United States bears little resemblance to its immediate predecessor, the British Empire. There are no colonies from which we buy raw materials at discount prices. And there are few US factories for turning raw materials into salable products. Nor does the US imperium bear much likeness to the imperial finance systems of the Germans, the Austro-Hungarians, the Romans, the Greeks, or the Mongols. But there is a slight family resemblance in the Spanish colonial empire.

Ships went to the New World from Spanish and Portuguese ports armed with soldiers, provisions, and colonial administrators. They came back laden with gold and silver. Gold and silver was real money. It could not be easily replicated, counterfeited, or called into being with the stroke of a keyboard. Still, the increase in money—with no corresponding increase in productive output—was fatal to the Iberians. They spent without really earning. They consumed without producing. When the flow of easy money stopped, they found that real money had made them really poor, not rich.

America's impoverishment is even more ridiculous. She is sustained by foreign wealth, but without real money. It is merely paper money without the paper—electronic registration of units of paper money. It is a mirage—a chimeric representation of something that doesn't exist anywhere. For every additional dollar the US Treasury calls into being, there is no extra dollar of savings, no extra dollar of profit, not even the paper dollar itself. At least the gold taken from Latin America is still around today and is still valuable. The dollars created by the Treasury are likely to disappear completely.

The United States entered the empire business in the late 19th century. She was able to straighten herself out for a few years but the lure of it later became irresistible. Between 1917 and 1971, the country was transformed from a simple republic that mostly minded its own business to a grandiose empire with imagined interests and real troops nearly everywhere.

In normal places at normal times, people go about their normal lives earning a living the best they can. But an empire changes the way people think. The common householders turn away from their humble house and their spouse and begin to think about the fair world beyond their kith, kin, and ken. They look outward and see how much better the world could be if they and their fellow citizens could run it their way. They see that they must play a greater role in global affairs, that they must walk on the world stage, not as a bit player, but as the main character—the hero. They must play the lead role.

Instead of sticking to their looms, fields, and factories, the imperial citizens begin to appreciate the financial logic of empire: They enjoy the loot that comes from the far edges of the imperial system. Gradually, they neglect their own commerce and depend on their subordinates, lackeys, and subject peoples to support them. While administrative commands, fashions, and proclamations flow from the center of the empire to the extremities, there also is an important flow in the other direction. Rome brought in its wheat from Egypt (Romans needed bread), its gladiators from the Balkans (Romans wanted circuses), its soldiers from Gaul, and its money from foreign treasuries and tax collectors from Judea to Britannia.

A modest republic pays its own way. In 1952, nearly 90% of the federal government's borrowings came from domestic investors. Americans saved their money and used some of it to support the programs of the Eisenhower administration. But the maturing empire of 2005 depended on a global debt market and the savings of foreigners. From less than 5% of Treasury bonds in overseas hands in 1952, the total approached 45%, while the percentage of lending coming from domestic sources had been cut in half.

Americans still grow their own wheat, but the trucks to move it may be manufactured in Europe or Asia, and the pans it cooks in are probably made in China. They get their electronic paraphernalia from Taiwan, clothes from Malaysia, and automobiles from Japan. They get scientists from India and classical musicians from Korea. And money comes from all over the Eastern Periphery to keep it all going.

THE HISTORY OF EMPIRES

Reading the history of empires, we learn that the central power tends to weaken as the periphery states grow stronger. Eventually, the subordinate states get tired of supporting the imperium. They stop paying tribute and show up at the gates of Rome.

France and England built their own empires in the 18th and 19th centuries. Napoleon's conquests took less than a dozen years to complete, but the empire collapsed even faster. By the end of the 19th century, all that was left of the French empire were a few islands no one could find on a map and some godforsaken colonies in Africa that the French would soon regret ever having laid eyes on. Almost all were lost, forgotten, or surrendered by the 1960s with nothing much to show for them except what you find in the Louvre—and a population of African immigrants who now weigh heavily on France's social welfare budget.

England's empire was much grander, stretched further, and left more debris when it broke up. But the end result was about the same: The pound was degraded and the British were nearly bankrupt.

Germany lost its overseas colonies after World War I. It then created another empire—by conquest—in the late 1930s and early 1940s. The enterprise ran into Russia's empire in the East—resulting in history's largest and bloodiest land battles. In the end, thanks partly to US intervention on the side of the Russians, the German empire was destroyed. The Russians' empire collapsed under its own weight 44 years later.

While the Romans were still kicking Sabine derrieres, Athens was already a mini-empire. By 431 BC, Athens had become an empire, with subject states throughout the Aegean. In that year, on some pretext not worth recalling, the first Peloponnesian War began between Sparta and Athens and its allies.

Pericles decided that the best offense was a good defense. He brought the Athenians within the city's walls hoping that the enemy would exhaust itself in futile attacks.

But bubonic plague broke out in the besieged city and killed a quarter of the population—including Pericles. Thence, a nephew of Pericles, Alcibiades, stirred the Athenians to an offensive campaign. A great armada was assembled to attack Syracuse, a city in Sicily allied with Athens's foes.

The campaign was a complete disaster. The armada was destroyed and the army sold into slavery. Sensing a shift in the wind, other Greek city-states broke with Athens and went over to Sparta. In 405 BC, the remaining ships in the Athenian fleet were captured at the battle of Aegospotami. Not long after, Athens's walls were breached and the city became a vassal state to Sparta.

The Athenian empire was replaced by the Spartan empire, which was eventually supplanted by the Macedonian empire, which then became the empire of Alexander. When Alexander died in 323 BC, his empire died with him. The next great chapter of imperial history was written by the Romans, who defeated what was left of the Greeks at the Battle of Pydna in 168 BC.

One empire died. Another was born. Nature can't bear a vacuum and abhors a monopoly. A world without an empire is a world with a hole in it. An empire fills the empty spot. But Nature is a fickle mistress. No sooner has an empire been born than Nature hardens her face against it. An empire has a monopoly on the use of force, or attempts to have one. An empire claims for itself the exclusive right to use preemptive force against any power that may pose a challenge. Nature tolerates it for a while. But she nurtures rivals and encourages competitors. Sooner or later, they find their opportunity.

Athens ran the first recorded empire in the West. America runs the current one; it took over from Britain after World War I. For the first eight decades, Americans denied any imperial role or purple ambitions. But by the early 21st century, they were warming up to empire. In March 2004, the *New York Times* reported that it was now respectable to describe the United States as an empire. "Today," said the

New York Times, "America is no mere superpower or hegemon, but a full blown empire in the Roman and British sense."

"No country has been as dominant culturally, economically, technologically and militarily in the history of the world since the Roman Empire,"[1] added the columnist in the same paper.

Robert Kaplan's book, *Warrior Politics: Why Leadership Demands a Pagan Ethos*, gave this assessment: "Our future leaders could do worse than be praised for their tenacity, their penetrating intellects and their ability to bring prosperity to distant parts of the world under America's soft imperial influence. The more successful our foreign policy, the more leverage Americans will have in the world. Thus, the more likely that future historians will look back on the twenty-first century United States as an empire as well as a republic, however different from that of Roman and every other empire throughout history."[2]

The June 11, 2005, edition of the *International Herald Tribune* ran Roger Cohen's "Globalist" column, which contained this remark: "'We guarantee the security of the world, protect our allies, keep critical sea lanes open and lead the war on terror,' said Max Boot of the imperial burden. '. . . the Pax Americana in Asia, as in Europe, has been conducive to a half-century of growth, peace and prosperity.'"[3]

Paul Kennedy went further, pointing out that the imbalance is even greater than in the Roman era. "The Roman Empire stretched further afield," he notes, "but there was another great empire in Persia and a larger one in China."[4]

America had no rivals, he said. Militarily, China was no real competition; it was just another country on America's hit list.

Even after 227 years, America's stock continued to rise. That it had gotten high enough to vex Nature worried no one. That it might decline troubled no one's sleep. That being an empire is not necessarily an unadulterated blessing bothered neither the president nor his ministers.

The modest republic of 1776 had become the great power of 2005 with pretensions to empire that could no longer be denied. That its citizens will not be freer was understood and accepted. But would they be richer under an empire than they would have been under a humble republic? Would they be safer? Would they be happier?

If so, pity the poor Swiss. In their mountain fastnesses, they had only themselves to boss around; only their own pastures, lakes, and peaks to amuse their eyes; and only their own industries to provide employment and sustenance. And their poor armed forces! Imagine the boredom, the tedious waiting for someone to attack. What glory is there in defense? Oh, for a foreign adventure! Thanks to their colonial empire, the sun never set on the British. After the Napoleonic Wars, as many as a quarter of the world's population lived under British rule. Meanwhile, the sun set every single day on the Swiss Federation. But that didn't stop the Swiss franc from rising, almost daily, against the British pound. In 1815, a British pound could have been exchanged for 13 Swiss francs and a half-pound of cheese. Today, a pound brings you only 1.6 Swiss francs. And forget the cheese.

While the British economy grew sluggish in the 20th century, the Swiss economy boomed. By the end of the century, gross domestic product (GDP) per person in Britain was only about $20,000. The Swiss, meanwhile, were producing $28,550 in GDP per capita.

But the poor yodelers never got the glory of empire. They never got to admire themselves on maps or in headlines. What Swiss president gets to send troops to remote hellholes, join a peace-keeping mission, or fight terrorists? How often do the Swiss get to cheer on their heroes and mourn their dead? Who even knows who the president of Switzerland is? Who cares? While Americans get to make a public spectacle of themselves, the Swiss have to make do with private life.

The Swiss have to mind their own business and watch the Sturm und Drang of the world pass them by. But would the Swiss really be better off if they, too, had an empire to run?

The available evidence from history is mixed and anecdotal. If the past is any guide, early military successes are inevitably followed by humiliating defeats. Financial progress is nearly always trailed by national bankruptcy and the destruction of the currency. And the good sense of a decent people is soon replaced by a malign megalomania that brings the whole population to complete ruin.

But who cares? It is not for us to know the future or to prescribe it. Instead, we get out our field glasses and prepare to watch the spectacle.

BACK TO THE FUTURE

A great empire is to the world of geopolitics what a great bubble is to the world of economics. It is attractive at the outset, but a catastrophe eventually. We know of no exceptions.

After the battle of Pydna, Rome became the leading empire of the Western world. (We continue our simplified narrative to show how things worked out.)

Augustus died in AD 14, leaving the empire in the hands of his stepson, Tiberius, who had married Augustus's free-and-easy daughter, Julia. Tiberius clipped the coinage (reduced the precious metal content). This, and other prudent policies, greatly increased the amount of money in the treasury. By the time he was assassinated in AD 37, there were 700 million denarii in the treasury—far more than there had been at the time of Augustus's death.

Tiberius handed off the imperial purple to Caligula, who quickly spent all the savings and more. Rome suffered a series of mad and lavish rulers. To confiscate the money of wealthy Roman families, Caligula would falsely accuse them of plotting against him. He was succeeded by Claudius who, in turn, gave way to Nero. By this time, Rome was deeply in debt and running large trade deficits with its periphery states—similar to the condition of the United States today. Nero took the time-honored expedient of clipping the coins even more. In AD 64, he proclaimed that henceforth the aureus would be 10% lighter in weight. So, whereas in the past, 41 aurei had been minted from one pound of gold, the ratio now become 45 aurei to a pound.

Nero was deposed in AD 68. But the precedent was set. Maintaining order throughout the empire was expensive. Rome became dependent on imported capital, imported soldiers, and imported goods—just as America is today. But Rome had its own version of a central bank. Each new emergency was met with more phony cash just as it is today. By the time the barbarians sacked Rome, the currency, the denarius, still bore the ancient form with the images of dead emperors pressed on it. But the value had been taken out; the currency had lost 99.98% of its value. Although this seems like a dreadful rate of inflation, it is not really as bad as the current US example. In less than 100 years, the US dollar has lost 95% of its value. If this rate continues for just another 150 years, the dollar will do in half the time what took the denarius almost 500 years.

Thomas Cahill describes the last days of Rome in his book, *How the Irish Saved Civilization:*

> . . . the changing character of the native population, brought about through unremarked pressures on porous borders; the creation of an increasingly unwieldy and rigid bureaucracy, whose own survival becomes its overriding goal; the despising of the military and the avoidance of its service by established families, while its offices present unprecedented opportunity for marginal men to whom its ranks had once been closed; the lip service paid to values long dead; the pretense that we still are what we once were; the increasing concentrations of the populace into richer and poorer by way of a corrupt tax system, and the desperation that inevitably follows; the aggrandizement of executive power at the expense of the legislature; ineffectual legislation promulgated with great show; the moral vocation of the man at the top to maintain order at all costs, while growing blind to the cruel dilemmas of ordinary life . . .

Cahill continues:

> . . . these are all themes with which our world is familiar, nor are they the God-given property of any party or political point of view, even though we often act as if they were. At least, the emperor could not heap his economic burdens on posterity by creating long-term public debt, for floating capital had not yet been conceptualized. The only kinds of wealth worth speaking of were the fruits of the earth.[5]

Finally, the cost so weakened the empire that the barbarians were at the gate. "The thicker the grass, the more easily scythed," said Alaric, king of the Visigoths from ad 395 to 410. He was speaking to the Roman envoys sent to shoo him away.[6]

The Roman envoys had just told him that if he and his filthy band of barbarian buddies didn't go away, they would unleash legions of Roman warriors to crush him. They then asked him what it would take for him to turn around and go. He replied that his men would like to comb the city, take all the gold and silver plus everything else valuable that could be moved, plus all the barbarian slaves.

And what, said the envoys, would that leave us Romans? Replied Alaric, "your lives."[7]

Empires, like bubble markets, end up where they began. Rome began as a town on the Tiber, with sheep grazing on the hills. A bull market in Roman property lasted about 1,000 years—from 700 BC to about AD 300, when temples, monuments, and villas crowded the Palatine. Then, a bear market began that lasted at least another 1,000 years.

As late as the 18th century, Rome was once again a city on the Tiber with sheep grazing on the hillsides, amid broken marble columns and immense brick walls. They had been built for a reason, but no one could recall why.

IN PRAISE OF EMPIRES

It is said that empires provide an expanse of law and order under which trade, commerce, investment, and profit taking can flourish. Here, we will spot the empire builders and their apologists a point or two. Even the Mongol reign of terror was said to have permitted an uptick in trade. And why not? The imperialists levied a tribute on output. They had an interest in economic growth. Why shouldn't they make sure bills were paid and property was safe?

One of the leading proponents of the US empire is a man named Deepak Lal, who wrote a book entitled *In Praise of Empires*. "The Roman empire had through its Pax brought unprecedented prosperity to the inhabitants of the Mediterranean littoral for nearly a millennium," Lal writes.[8] He believes that empires are good things, because people are materially better off under imperial rule than other forms of government. We have no intention of trying to prove him wrong. The economic record is not complete enough to prove anything. How fat and happy might the residents of the Mediterranean littoral have been if the Romans had stayed in Rome? We don't know. Nor do we know much about the relative growth rates of groups not under Roman rule. So we cannot prove anything, except that Lal can't either. And for that we need to call only one witness to the stand, Lal himself.

In the 500 years preceding World War II, when the economic picture is more visible, the Holy Roman Empire—which, as Voltaire remarked, was neither holy, nor Roman, nor a real empire—was extinguished. In its place rose various sovereign nation-states, often with imperial ambitions and bubble-like excesses, but none able to assert itself over much of Europe or for very long. Europe, in other words, was nonimperial. China, India, and Anatolia/the Middle East, by contrast, were still run by the vestiges of the Mongol Empire and its successors. Which civilization was most successful economically? We have no figures for the Ottoman Empire, but the 500 years in China produced a net decline in GDP per person. In India, the rate of increase was negligible according to the figures that Lal presents; all the growth that there was came after the Mogul Empire had been replaced by the British. It wasn't imperial rule that gave the place a shot in the arm; it was British investment and know-how.

Lal makes the point decisively and then proceeds to ignore it: "By creating order over a large economic space, empires have inevitably generated Smithian [as in Adam Smith's *Wealth of Nations*] growth. But given limited technological progress (except for the exceptional period under Sung China), Promethean intensive growth remains a European miracle of the anarchical system of nation-states established after the breakdown of the Roman empire."[9]

Actually, there are other instances of Promethean growth (e.g., Japan, Hong Kong, and Singapore after World War II).[10] From 1992 to 2013, China was said to be growing at or above 8% per year, including over 14% in 1992 and 2007 respectively.[11] Russia and India were growing too, at 5% and 7% respectively.[12] It could be argued that their growth was largely thanks to the shade provided by the Americans' imperial protection. But then you have to wonder why other places, similarly protected, enjoyed no such growth. You also have to wonder how other places, such as Switzerland and the Scandinavian countries got to be the wealthiest places in the world when they enjoyed no more imperial benefits than anywhere else and were largely indifferent to the imperial system. You also have to wonder how it is possible for China to register such high growth rates in the 1990s and 2000s when it is the very thing from which the US imperium offers protection. Apparently, an empire may increase growth rates even for its enemies.

The logic of Lal's "praise of empires" is no different from saying he likes chocolate cake. It is purely a matter of personal taste, nothing more. All we actually know about economic growth is that empire is neither a necessary nor a sufficient condition for it.

Empires come and go often, like stock markets. When they shoot up quickly, they generally fall sharply, too. And when they take centuries to build—as with the Romans—it takes centuries to take them back to where they began. By using carrier pigeons, the Mamelukes could have speedy news of all who come and go by sea or land, and thus escape surprise because they live without defenses and have neither walls nor fortresses. What finally destroyed the Mongols was the plague, which they picked up in the Far East, and gunpowder, which they also encountered in China. The first so reduced their numbers in the 14th and 15th centuries that they abandoned not only many of their conquests but also much of their own steppes; some of the best pastureland in Asia was effectively returned to nature. The second ended their attacks on more civilized people—who could now blow them out of the saddle. Their descendants in the Mogul Empire in India and the Ottoman Empire in Turkey were largely absorbed into the cultures where they had inserted themselves. And by the 17th and 18th centuries, the Mongols were once again tending herds of horses in the lonely and inhospitable wastes of Mongolia. By the 19th and 20th centuries, they were paying their own tribute to Russian and Chinese empire builders.

Since the days of the great Khans, empires have become much more entertaining. This is not because they are less lethal; it is because they are much more delusional. They cannot bear the barbaric clarity of Genghis's imperial ambitions. They cannot put on the purple without putting on the masks. After a while their faces take the shape of the mask itself. Rather than follow their atavistic urges and give honest voice to their primitive instincts, they feel obliged to provide reasons that are often fatal to the believers and their victims, but hilarious to the distant observer.

Modern imperialists, like their distant ancestors, lust after the usual things—prestige, power, money, status—all proxies, perhaps, for genetic disbursement. These were the same urges that enticed the Khans and the Caesars. But today's imperialists feel ashamed to admit it. So, they pretend all manner of selfless and world-improving motives, every one of which is either an obvious fraud or a monumental bamboozle. But that is what makes the whole thing so much more amusing and enter-taining than either a modest republic or a primitive empire: Modern empire builders are such quacks and popinjays that they practically sprout tail feathers and grow webbed feet.

The gist of the modern empire builders' creed is that they have a duty to make the world a better place, and they can only do it by telling other people what to do. It is inconceivable to them that others might have their own ideas of what a better world would be like. Or that their own plans are nothing more than their own vain tastes and prejudices. It is as if they burst in on their neighbors to tell them what they were going to do on the weekend; it wouldn't bother them at all that their neighbors had their own plans. Their ideas are more important!

The charm in this is not in watching the empire builders make a mess of things, which they invariably do—usually a bloody mess. The charm is in the elaborate lies and imbecilities they spin to cover up what they are doing. Their real purpose is no different from those of any Mongol, Greek, or Roman—to feel important, to rule the world and boss other people around, to puff out their chest and pin medals on it, to have power over people and feel superior toward them. The logic of it is inescapable: They feel superior because they rule them. And why do they rule them? Because they are superior!

Since the days of Alexander, empire builders have developed elab-orate and heroically absurd proofs for why they are superior. They have before them the evidence of their achievements; they have their neighbors under their heel and not the other way around. Fooled by the randomness of historical events, they look for a reason that explains their superiority and justifies their own rule.

Many are the daffy explanations and spurious proofs offered. Typically, a group believes it is given its right to rule directly from God. Jehovah delivered to the Jews title to the land of milk and honey. It didn't matter to them that there were other people who claimed title, too. "Slay them all," says their God. "And woe to you if you let any of them get away." The Jews thought they had a special covenant with God. But historians will search in vain for an imperial race whose gods opposed them. No matter what vile mischief they take up, people believe they have the gods' approval.

The European colonial empires in the New World, Africa, and Asia were justified on every imaginable pretext. The Spanish thought they had a duty to Christianize the heathen. The English saw their duty in bringing the benefits of Victorian morals and virtues, including clothing, to the naked savages:

> Take up the White man's burden—
> Send forth the best ye breed—
> Go, bind your sons to exile
> To serve your captives' need[13]
> 　　　　　　　—Rudyard Kipling

The French, meanwhile, thought the natives should learn to like baguettes and French poets. Their culture was so superior, it was said, they wanted to share it with everyone. They were all successors to Cicero, who maintained that only under Roman imperial rule could civilization flourish.

It was obvious to them all that Europeans were superior to other peoples. Was it a matter of race? Religion? Culture? At one time or another, they put forward each of these hypotheses—sometimes all of them. Europeans were a superior race; therefore, they had evolved superior forms of religion, government, and culture.

And what accounted for their racial superiority? No delusion was too preposterous. When the Romans were on top of the world, they thought their mild climate must be responsible for creating the world's best humans. Two millennia later, when the center of empire had shifted to northern Europe, the rigors of European winters were credited with stiffening upper lips, backbones, and virtues. English ladies, traveling in the tropics, wore long-sleeved shirts and carried parasols, for fear that too much of the tropical sun might cause them to "go native."

The effect of all this self-deception is to turn the imperialists into a race of fools. They have to believe what isn't true—that they are, personally and collectively, better than the people they boss around. Constant dissembling has a corrosive effect on brains and a numbing effect on souls. European imperialists wondered if the Africans, East Indians, and Asians were fully human; often, they treated their subjects as though they thought they were not.

AUSTRO-HUNGARIANS

The impulse to imperial power is always the same, but there are many types of imperium. From the pure simplicity of the Mongols to the incomprehensible complexity of the Austro-Hungarians, you could make a go of almost any kind of empire. Whereas the Mongols got their empire by force, the Austro-Hungarian Empire (1867–1918), also known as the *dual monarchy*, came into being largely because they couldn't think of anything better to do with it. Even its formal name—The Kingdoms and Lands Represented in the Imperial Council and the Lands of the Holy Hungarian Crown (of Stephen)— was a pileup of words on the information highway. Then, as now, no one knew how the empire worked—including the people who supposedly ran it.

But that it was an empire, we have no doubt. "A basic, consensus definition would be that an empire is a large political body which rules over territories outside its original borders," explains Stephen Howe in *Empire*.[14] Austro-Hungary ruled over the Kingdom of Bohemia, the Kingdom of Dalmatia, the Kingdom of Galicia and Lodomeria, the Archduchy of Austria, the Duchy of Bukowina, the Duchy of Carinthia, the Duchy of Carniola, the Duchy of Salzburg, the Duchy of Upper Silesia and Lower Silesia, the Duchy of Styria, the Margraviate of Moravia, the Princely County of Tyrol (including the Land of Vorarlberg), the Coastal Land (including the Princely County of Gorizia and Gradisca, the City of Trieste, and the Margraviate of Istria).

And this was just on the Austrian side. On the Hungarian side were all the many obnoxious, quarreling peoples of central Europe and the Balkans—the Slovaks, Bohemians, Moravians, Italians, Poles, Ukrainians, Serbs, Albanians, Macedonians, Croats, Bosnians, Herzegovinians, Montegrans, Czechs, Magyars, and many others.

Each of these territories had its own language and customs. Many detested each other. All were jealous of power and how it was used. And at the top were some of the weakest and most confused and conflicted administrators who ever lived. Each had several layers of loyalties: to his own nation; his own class; his own religion; his own family, region, culture, and linguistic group; and his own aristocracy. How could you hope to govern such an empire?

The beauty of it was that you couldn't. There were two separate parliaments and two separate prime ministers along with a collection of archdukes of various talents and responsibilities. In theory, the one royal house—the Habsburgs—had absolute power over the central administration—particularly the military. In practice, they could do little or nothing; they had no money. Occasionally a forceful edict would issue from the government, such as the April 5, 1897, proclamation from the Austrian prime minister, Kasimir Felix Graf von Badeni, that permitted the use of the Czech language, along with German, in Bohemia. The ordinance caused so much trouble that poor Badeni was tossed out and Czech was more suppressed than before. Henceforth, Czech newspapers would have to be printed in German!

Despite these annoyances, the empire was a modest success. It was largely peaceful and prosperous. Between 1870 and 1913, GDP per capita rose at an annual rate of 1.45%, which was faster than the rate in Britain or France, and almost as fast as in Germany.

But the imperial family had a bad habit of attracting trouble. Emperor Franz Josef's only son died under circumstances that are still considered mysterious. His brother had the bad judgment to meddle in the affairs of Mexico and died in front of a firing squad. And, finally, his nephew and heir, the Archduke Franz Ferdinand, had the misfortune to visit Sarajevo in 1914 at the very moment when Bosnian nationalists were gunning for him; he even wore a hat with a huge ostrich plume so they would be sure not to miss.

THE MAKING OF AN EMPIRE

When did Rome become an empire? Historians look for a particular moment, even a natural, physical boundary—such as when Caesar crossed the Rubicon—to mark the end of one period and the beginning of the next. No such simple marker exists, however, between empire and other forms of government. Nor does any precise boundary exist between democracy and, say, theocracy or dictatorship. Governments are categorized artificially and often arbitrarily on the basis of theories—usually fraudulent ones. It is often said that democracies depend on the consent of the governed, whereas dictatorships and monarchies do not. A moment's reflection, even by a professor of government, would reveal the lie. All systems of government depend on some measure of complicity.

"Given the very small number and insignificant presence of imperial agents and municipal officials to insure obedience to the state," explains Ramsay MacMullen in his *Corruption and the Decline of Rome*, "millionaires, magnates, and other local notables of all sorts must have cooperated, and from their own free will."[15] It doesn't matter whether you call a political society free, a democracy, a dictatorship, or an empire, it always involves a great amount of collusion and cooperation on the part of the population.

"[Imperial] administrators occupied only a minor place in the system. The emperor had only a handful of agents, whose means of reaching the people were few and rudimentary. The police were practically nonexistent. There were neither social workers nor prosecutors,"[16] MacMullen continues.

The people who actually ran things "had no official function, or if they had one, they had no need of it to make themselves heard. A huge number of decisions were taken each day and throughout the empire that conformed to their own desires more than to the law, the emperor, or his representatives. What's more, these decisions were those that counted, those that concerned property, movement, career choices, success on the farm, commerce or banking; sometimes even a person's physical safety."[17]

In business, as in empire, vast, complex, informal systems work largely on the basis of trust. People trust others to do more or less what they expect. The emperor could no more control what was done in Judea or Gaul than we can control what goes into our hamburgers. Still, we trust there is nothing too unsavory in them.

In the Roman Empire, order was transmitted through an extended web of personal connections, family ties, official functions, traditions, habits, and accepted ideas and procedures so that what happened was more or less what everyone expected. The emperor trusted not only his own functionaries to do what they were supposed to do but also the local big shots with no official post or authority. The lowest slaves responded to their overseer, who responded to their master, who responded to their landlord, who responded to their patron, who responded to their *potentiores, consuls, proconsuls*, *proteuntes*, *praetors*, and *quaestors*, on up the chain of command to the emperor himself.

Even prisons function with the cooperation and complicity of the convicts. In the Soviet gulag system, for example, a group of people—soldiers conscripted and sent to Siberia against their will—policed one group of prisoners who in turn policed a less fortunate group. Supposedly, the entire Soviet Union functioned as a vast slave society, in which everyone was told what to do and no one had any choice in the matter. But how could it be? If they were all in chains, who held the keys? And why did the jailers suddenly undo the locks in 1989?

We do not argue that the Soviet system was not wretched, but only that the border between its wretchedness and the misery inflicted by other systems of political organization is not nearly as well marked as we have been told. Always and everywhere, nuances and particularities trump the theories.

Dictators cannot rule a country on their own. They need the help of minions and executioners, soldiers and administrators, tax collectors, and spies. Depending on the size of the country, they might have millions of people all with a stake in their rule. Likewise, what monarch really ruled alone? Even the Sun King, Louis XIV, depended on a whole solar system . . . no, a galaxy . . . of supporters, agents, and factota. He had a vast web of private interests to which he was either beholden, in league, or at odds with: the clergy, the aristocracy, the bourgeoisie, the moneylenders, the armed forces, the tax farmers. There is no discreet line between empire and republic, or any other form of government for that matter. But that doesn't mean there is no difference. Sailing from the Caribbean to the North Atlantic, a voyager crosses no white line. Still, the weather in the two places is hardly the same.

A nation may have elections and yet not be a genuine democracy. It may have a king, but not be a genuine monarchy. It may even call itself an empire—such as the Central African Empire, which bullied several tribes in West Africa—but that doesn't mean it is one.

There is plenty of room for fraud and interpretation in political institutions, just as there is in the rest of life. Julius Caesar was accused of being a dictator. He was cut down by the old guard, who wanted to preserve the republic. But Rome had taken the path of empire long before Caesar was born. Like the United States today, it had troops spread far beyond the homeland. For five centuries, the Romans had been imposing themselves, first in what is now Italy and then the Cisalpine region, the Greek Isles, the coast of Anatolia, and down through the Middle East. Caesar himself made his reputation in his wars against the Gauls—people far from Rome who spoke a different language, with different customs, different traditions, different institutions, and different ideas about how things should be done. Caesar believed he was bringing the benefits of Romanization, which to him was one and the same as bringing civilization itself.

Octavian, Caesar's heir, did not call himself emperor or announce that henceforth Rome would be an empire. He did not need to. The term *imperator* meant "general." He was already an imperator. Nor was he particularly eager to stir up resentment among the republican partisans. He had seen what had happened to his uncle. Let the empire evolve; just don't mention it. Speaking to the senate, he was careful to play to the old sentiments: "And now I give back the Republic into your keeping. The laws, the troops, the treasury, the provinces are all restored to you. May you guard them worthily."[18]

But the old Republic existed only in their dreams and imaginations. No matter what they said, Rome was an empire. The senators crowned him Augustus, and forgot the old constitution.

"People do not easily change, but love their own ancient customs," wrote Aristotle in his *Politics*. "And it is by small degrees only that one thing takes the place of another; so that the ancient laws will remain, while the power will be in the hands of those who have brought about a revolution in the state."[19] The revolution in Rome took centuries. In America, it took only 58 years (1913–1971). In both cases, most people hardly noticed. The changes were gradual and, generally, agreeable.

A republic, a monarchy, or even a dictatorship is a relatively modest undertaking. Its scope is limited, and controlled by leading citizens either through their influence on the autocrat or by shaping public opinion. An empire, however, steps onto the world stage and plays a role that is beyond the control of the citizens. Private life becomes auxiliary, moving to a supporting role while the grand public spectacle plays itself out. In the United States Constitution, it is expressly stated that the people are sovereign, not the government. Ultimately, what people want in their private lives is what is supposed to matter. But the idea passed away when the US Republic died and the empire was born. By 1960, John Kennedy was able to lecture voters to "ask not what the country can do for you; ask what you can do for your country." Suddenly, the government that was created by, for, and of the people was way out in front of them. They found themselves servants to it, no longer its masters.

They could, of course, still write letters to the editor and still vote, but the force of these expressions had gone out of them. The form had barely changed, but the meaning of it had turned around, like a word that had come to mean the opposite of what it once signified. Virtually, for example, once meant "truly." People would promise to be there "virtually" at noon. Over time, meaning follows practice; virtually slipped to mean not truly, almost, nearly, or sort of. So did the United States Congress come to be what it now is, something not-quite-what-it-was-meant-to-be.

Another important event of the revolution in US politics occurred on June 25, 1950. That is the day on which Harry Truman involved the United States in a war in Korea without authorization from Congress. The Constitution clearly states that the people's representatives alone have the power to determine when the nation's blood and treasure should be put at risk. But on that date, Truman sent US troops to kill and die, without even informing Congress. Even though this happened while Congress was in session, members of the people's assemblies found out about it from reading the newspapers. For a week, Congress had little idea of what was going on, until the commander-in-chief decided to tell them.

As you might expect, a few members of Congress were cheesed off. But the majority went along. Like the senate in Rome, they had eaten of the imperial fruit and liked the taste of it. US forces had to react quickly, they were told. It was a "new era" in warfare, they believed. There was no time for discussion. Meanwhile, the Korean War went on for another 37 months—you would think that they might have found time to talk about it.

What had happened was not that the rest of the world had changed so much, but that America had changed. Truman's doctrine—that the United States would intervene anywhere in the world where it felt its interests were threatened—was not the doctrine of Monroe or Jefferson. It was an imperial doctrine. By then, the nation's focus had shifted away from the private desires and opinions of citizens, as expressed through their elected representatives, to the world outside America's borders. What the people thought no longer really counted for much. Public opinion was important, but it was merely part of the imperial burden—something to be carried around, manipulated, and managed. To that end, even in 1951, a huge propaganda apparatus was already set up—with confidential briefings, press leaks, public relations specialists, and enormous printing and publishing arms. Even then, the executive branch was spinning the news to appeal to the marginal voter.

They hardly had to bother. The average American reacted just as the average Roman had reacted. When the purple was hoisted, he stood up and saluted. It made him feel like a big shot. If Americans were bossing people around in Asia or the Middle East, it made him feel more important. His homeland team was winning all over the world. And if it did not always seem to be on the winning side, he knew he must support his troops and stand behind their commander-in-chief. No one wants to carp and criticize when soldiers take the field. It is unpatriotic. So, keep the soldiers in the field all the time!

Although there is no precise DNA test that separates an empire from an ordinary country, there are certain telltale characteristics. A regular country has only its own territory. An empire has a "homeland" and various territorial interests beyond it. It may have subordinate states, protectorates, colonies, satellites, or other client states over whom it exercises a substantial authority. Sometimes it is not even mentioned; but the clients know that if they get out of line, the imperium will come down on them. Typically, the people in the homeland feel superior to the people in the periphery areas. As described, they develop reasons and explanations for their superiority, which are then used to justify further imperial expansion.

THE US EMPIRE

America took its first awkward steps toward empire at the end of the 19th century, with Theodore Roosevelt intervening in various diarrhea countries for forgettable reasons and with regrettable results.

Later, in April 1917, Woodrow Wilson took off at a trot with the Rough Rider still breathing down his neck. He urged Congress to declare war on a distant country with which it had no real beef and in which it had no genuine interest.

Twenty-three years later, the United States was in another major war. Few would argue that World War II was a case of needless intervention, because the US fleet was attacked at Pearl Harbor. Still, had America wanted to stay out of it, she could have done so. Pearl Harbor was attacked because the US Navy posed a threat to Japanese imperial ambitions. If the United States had not displayed imperial ambitions of her own and had no satellite state in the Philippines, she would have presented no danger to the Japanese imperial forces. Nor was there any particular reason to go to war against Germany. Though allied to Japan, there was no question of Germany intervening in the Pacific War.

After World War II, America stepped up the pace, engaging in 111 military actions between 1945 and 2005.

Today, the US military divides the world into four regional commands, each given initials—PAC, EUR, CENT, and SOUTH. Each region has its own commander-in-chief, who is like a proconsul of the Roman Empire. US military bases can be found in 120 different countries, with strike forces ready to light out for almost any place on the planet at a moment's notice.

There is also a vast army of functionaries, intermediaries, consultants, advisors, scientists, engineers, contractors, and busybodies spread all over the globe. Trained in US universities, on the payroll of either the US government or oft-linked US companies, these people provide a class of administrators to keep the imperial money and papers moving.

The work of these people was revealed in a marvelous book by John Perkins called *Confessions of an Economic Hit Man*. A supervisor explained to him:

> There were two primary objectives of my work, First I was to justify huge international loans that would funnel money back to MAIN [the consulting firm for whom he labored] and other U.S. companies (such as Bechtel, Halliburton, Stone & Webster, and Brown & Root) through massive engineering and construction projects. Second, I would work

to bankrupt the countries that received those loans (after they had paid MAIN and other U.S. contractors, of course) so that they would be forever beholden to their creditors and so they would present easy targets when we needed favors, including military bases, UN votes, or access to oil and other natural resources.

"Who can doubt that there is an American empire?" wrote Arthur Schlesinger Jr. "an informal empire, not colonial in polity, but still richly equipped with imperial paraphernalia: troops, ships, planes, bases, proconsuls, local collaborators, all spread around the luckless planet."[20]

America had mixed and confusing sentiments about empire from the get-go. Its founders were schooled in the history of Rome and determined to avoid what they saw as her mistakes. But at the same time, they couldn't help but lust for the grandeur of it. They longed for the imperial purple, perhaps, from the very beginning.

William Drayton, chief justice of the highest court in South Carolina, wrote in 1776:

> Empires have their zenith—and their declension and dissolution. . . . The British period is from the year 1758, when they victoriously pursued their Enemies into every Quarter of the Globe. . . . The Almighty . . . has made the choice of the present generation to erect the American Empire . . . and thus has suddenly arisen in the World, a new Empire, styled the United States of America. An Empire that as soon as started into Existence, attracts the attention of the Rest of the Universe; and bids fair by the blessing of God, to be the most glorious of any upon Record.[21]

John Quincy Adams, however, cautioned that although "she might become the dictatress of the world: she would be no longer ruler of her own spirit."[22] More than two centuries later, her spirit has run wild. She has soldiers garrisoned all over the world. She has interests in places few Americans have ever heard of and fewer still care about. There is no corner or dead-end street in the world that is not somehow patrolled by US forces. As of April 24, 2023, America has spent more in the prior year on defense than all the rest of the world combined.[23]

Already, readers must be asking themselves questions: The United States is the world's only superpower; since the capitulation of the

Soviet Union, it has no enemies capable of inflicting serious damage; what is the country defending herself against? But that is just the point. The imperial spirit has gotten the best of the political class. The country no longer plays a role that it can understand and control. Now, it is an imperial power; and must read from the imperial script.

Following its promise, the US military must provide security for the entire world. Its legal system must establish the public good of law and order. Its banks must provide the financial structure for markets around the globe. Someone has to do it. Who else could, but America? It is her turn to wear the purple, whether she wants to do so or not. Thus, did she become dictatress of the world, but no longer ruler of her own spirit—or her own finances.

We stop a moment to reflect. The urge to empire is as irresistible as a free lunch. The male of the species cannot pass up a chance to strut around feeling superior. Scarlet tunics and ostrich feathers have gone out of style, but the people who wore them are the same as those who sacked Rome with Alaric, laid waste to Albi with the Duke de Montfort, and entered Baghdad with the Third Army. The uniforms change, but people are the same grasping, vaunting, humbugging persons they always have been.

There is nothing quite so amusing as watching other people make fools of themselves. That is what makes history so entertaining. And what makes the history of empires particularly entertaining is watching the great emperors: the Napoleons, Alexanders, Caesars, Attilas, and Adolfs—with all their pretensions and sordid butchers—put on the red tunics and burnished helmets, mount their white chargers, and ride right into a stone wall.

While leaders make fools of themselves, the mass is tanned by the reflected glory of empire. The common person's chin grows stronger as they admire the stalwart troops. Their chests swell with every victory. They grow so tall they almost hit their head at the top of doorjambs. We literary economists, however, can barely suppress a laugh. It is obvious that the poor person has become delusional, but no one appreciates our saying so. Still, we also feel superior, for we cannot help but notice what numbskulls they are.

Evolutionary biologists reduce the whole impulse to empire to nothing more than genes and math. After people have enough to eat, their genes—and by command, their thoughts and emotions—want nothing more than to spread themselves as widely as possible. Genes are only interested in replication, according to the hypothesis. All the trappings of wealth and power—including the urge to lord it over others—are merely proxies and substitutes for sexual attractiveness. A great ruler conquers a city much for the same reason a middle-aged lawyer buys an expensive sports car, a peacock spreads his tail feathers, or a moral philosopher writes a popular book. It indicates to females that he has good genes. The entertainment comes in when the great ruler is defeated and hung from a meat hook, when the peacock is taken by a fox, and when the red sports car gets the boot. (The prospect of finding this book on the remainder table is not entertaining!)

President Wilson got America's self-deception off to a running start early in the 20th century: "I believe that God planted in us visions of liberty," he said, seeking the Democratic nomination in 1912, "that we are chosen and prominently chosen to show the way to the nations of the world how they shall walk in the path of liberty."[24]

So worthy was the mission that there seemed no need to figure out how to pay for it. If God had set us on the trail of empire, He could jolly well figure out how to pay for it. Neither then, nor now, have Americans bothered to understand how the business of empire works. They think they are doing the world a favor. That deception alone would not be so grave, but they totally miss the point: Nearly every imperial power has claimed to act for the good of others, but they all found a way to make it pay. When it stops paying, they are out of business.

Like the Mafia, the United States runs a protection business. Under the protection of the imperial pax dollarium, trade and commerce can flourish. People get rich. They should be grateful and happy to pay for the service. The imperial power must charge for that service; otherwise, what would be the point?

But America has so cleverly deceived itself that it believes it gets its immediate tribute from global commerce and its thanks in heaven. We have no way of knowing what awaits it in heaven, but we look around and notice that the tribute America gets is so perverse that we're glad she does not get more. Instead of getting paid for providing protection, the United States is on the receiving end of loans from its tributary states and trading partners. The whole idea is mad and preposterous. An imperial power is supposed to control lesser states and exploit them for its own selfish ends. Of course, it does not admit it. Truthfulness is as much a disappointment in politics as it is in poker. The idea is to pretend to do good, while you do well. In America's absurd version, she does badly for herself and good for others. That is the theme of this book: to call America an imperial power is flattery. In her bizarre version of empire, it is the subordinate powers that control her. They can stop paying tribute whenever they want.

"Will China be setting U.S. rates?" asked an article in a May 2005 edition of the *International Herald Tribune*.[25] The writer, Floyd Norris, had noticed the perverse logic of US imperial finance. What he hadn't realized was that China was already setting US interest rates. By the end of 2004, China owned $120 billion of US Treasury obligations—or 10% of the total in foreign hands, which itself was 25% of the total outstanding.[26] Had it not bought those bonds, or had it decided to sell them, there would have been significantly less demand for US debt. Or, looked at from a more traditional perspective, there would have been fewer people willing to lend to the United States. Either way, the almost certain result of Chinese lending was to lower the price of lent money, that is, to lower interest rates. Thanks to Asian lending, the United States was able to drop its interest rates below the rate of inflation and keep them there for 22 months.[27]

"The way things work now," Norris explained, "China sells to the world most everything the world wants. China then uses the dollars it receives to buy Treasury securities. That helps to hold down U.S. interest rates and stimulates consumer spending, enabling Americans to buy more from China."[28]

This put China in a commanding position. As Americans spent, China built its productive capacity. China got rich, selling gewgaws, electronic knickknacks, and assorted consumer goods. The imperial consumers, however, got poorer. In 2004, alone, wealth equivalent to 1% of the value of all the assets in the United States passed out of Americans' hands.

The idea of imperial finance is that the central, imperial power gets rich at its vassals' expense. America found a way to do it in reverse; it grew poorer, relatively and absolutely, every day. GDP growth during the five years—2000 to 2005—averaged only 4.4% per annum in nominal terms.[29] Meanwhile, net operating losses—the difference between what she earned on overseas sales and what she spent on imports far outpaced GDP, growing in 2004 by 24%.[30] And the cost of maintaining her imperial role—the military budget—was 3.3% of GDP.[31] The whole thing was a losing proposition. America had found a way to make empire pay—but only for its rivals and enemies.

To make matters worse, the periphery powers, which were supposed to be subordinate, were capable of ruining the central imperium. If the Chinese and other major holders of US Treasury bonds were to sell, there would be hell to pay in the United States. Interest rates would rise. The housing boom would turn into a housing bust. The imperium would have to beg its subordinate states for more credit.

"The U.S. suffers from . . . structural deficits that will limit the effectiveness and duration of its crypto-imperial role in the world," explains Niall Ferguson. "The first is the nation's growing dependence on foreign capital to finance excessive private and public consumption. It is difficult to recall any empire that has long endured after becoming so dependent on lending from abroad."[32]

What kind of odd empire is this? We have had a long line of US leaders strutting across the world stage—the buffoonish Theodore Roosevelt, the weaselly Wilson, the other Roosevelt, Truman, Kennedy, Johnson, Reagan, Bush (both of them)—but none of them seems to have understood how to make an empire pay.

One of the most riveting features is the remarkable way the masses rush not only to their own ruin but also to the elimination of the institutions they claim to cherish. In America, they claim to love freedom but at the first imperial trumpet blow—the war to make the world safe for democracy, the Cold War to contain the red menace, or the War on Terror—they line up to get registered, inspected, searched, probed, approved, and certified. There seems to be no violation of their liberty so great that they would protest nor any violation of anyone else's that they wouldn't applaud, and no expenditure of funds so extravagant that they would bother to ask questions. In 1989, America's post–World War II rival empire—the Soviet Union—threw in the towel. Not only had it had enough of military competition with the United States but also, in one of the great turnarounds of history, it simply renounced its whole ideology. It was almost as if the Jews had tossed aside the Torah, thrown off their yarmulkes, and decided to become Rosicrucians or Jehovah's Witnesses. But even more astonishing was what happened next. For the first time in 16 centuries, and perhaps the first time in history, the world faced almost no serious military crisis. America had no military competition. No serious threats. There were no nations on earth who could do serious damage to the United States. That did not mean that Americans were guaranteed safe. In addition to the harm they did to each other, they might be kidnapped or killed by any number of freelance gangs or revolutionary groups. But the US government had no reason to worry. No nation posed a worthy challenge. So what happened in America? Military expenditures rose!

The absurdity can be illustrated by the United States' attack on Iraq. Like so many imperial powers before it, US forces took Baghdad. But where was the payoff? Were slaves sold? Was oil stolen? Were women carried off, or at least violated on location? Was Iraq made to pay tribute? No. America seems to have missed the whole point. It invaded Iraq and now pays tribute to the Iraqis! It sends in engineers, medical people, food, contractors, administrators—at a cost of $1 billion per week—to try to keep the Iraqis from disliking them. They would be a lot better off, financially, if the Iraqis had beaten them off. But Americans have worn the mask of their good intentions for so long, their faces have grown in to it. They look in the mirror and see an imperialist who wants only good things for the world—democracy, freedom, harmony. They are all set to ban cigarettes and require seat belts all over the world.

They think they can be a "good" empire—killing people neither for glory nor for money, but to make the world a better place.

We have to rub our eyes and shake our heads to believe it.

CHAPTER 4

AS WE GO MARCHING

The Germans occupy a special place in world history. "Give a German a gun and he heads for France," was a common expression in the past century. "The Hun is either at your throat or at your feet" was another.

People wondered what it was about the Germans that had made them so ready to go to war and so willing to go along with ghastly deeds on a national scale. Was it something in their blood, in their culture, or in their water?

Now, of course, the Huns have been tamed and have become pacifists. America urged them to join the war against Iraq, but they demurred; they have had their fill of war. And so the question is more puzzling than ever. Has their blood changed? Their culture? Or their economy?

A marvelous little book by John T. Flynn, *As We Go Marching*,[1] was written during World War II and provides some insights. Flynn argues that fascism had no particular connection to the Germans themselves nor was there anything in the Teuton spirit that made them especially susceptible. Instead, he points out that the creed was largely developed by an Italian opportunist, Benito Mussolini. It was the hefty Italian who figured out the main parts—including the glorious theatrical elements. The Germans merely added their own corruptions and attached a peculiarly vicious policy of persecuting, and later exterminating, Jews.

But it is Flynn's description of the economic circumstances in Italy in the late 19th and early 20th centuries—the fertile soil in which fascism took root and flourished—that caught our attention. Italy went to war against Turkey in September 1911. The war was over 12 months later and soon forgotten by everyone. But the impulse that drove the Italians to war in the first place was the focus of Flynn's attention: "The vengeance of the Italian spirit on Fate was not appeased. Instead, it whetted the appetite for glory. And once more glory did its work on the budget. But once more, peace—dreadful and realistic peace, the bill collector, heavy with her old problems—was back in Rome. The deficits were larger. The debt was greater, and the various economic planners were more relentless than ever in their determination to subject the capitalist system to control.[2]

Perhaps they should have lowered interest rates. Or pressured China to raise its currency. Any policy initiative, no matter how pathetic, could be considered. As Flynn puts it: "Out of Italy [as out of America currently] had gone definitely any important party committed to the theory that the economic system should be free."[3]

Italy had dug herself into a deep hole of debt. Between 1859— when the centralized Italian state came into being—and 1925, the government ran deficits more than twice as often as it ran surpluses. Politicians, who depended on giving away other people's money, found themselves with little left to give away.

"All the old evils were growing in malignance," writes Flynn. "The national debt was rising ominously. The army, navy, and social services were absorbing half the revenues of the nation. Italy was the most heavily taxed nation in proportion to her wealth in Europe."[4]

Of course, there followed many episodes of financial *risorgimento* and many pledges to put the books in order. None of them stuck for long. Italian politicians were soon making promises again.

When grand promises must be fulfilled, debt creeps higher and so does the resistance of taxpayers and lenders, especially from conservative groups. "Hence it becomes increasingly difficult to go on spending in the presence of persisting deficits and rising debt," writes Flynn. "Some form of spending must be found that will command the support of conservative groups. Political leaders, embarrassed by their subsidies to the poor, soon learned that one of the easiest ways to spend money is on military establishments and armaments, because it commands the support of the groups most opposed to spending."[5]

Military spending gives an economy the false impression of growth and prosperity. People are put to work building expensive military hardware.

Assembly lines roll and smokestacks smoke. Plus, the spending goes into the domestic economy. Americans, for example, may buy their gewgaws from China, but their tanks are homemade.

Military adventures not only seem to stimulate the domestic economy; they also goose up popular support for government. Soon, "it was a time for greatness . . . ," as Flynn describes the approach of war. War, Giovanni Papini raved, was "the great anvil of fire and blood on which strong peoples are hammered."[6]

There was a time when kings, princes, and emperors ruled the world. Back then, the people knew their place. But in this new, modern world, it became necessary for rulers to appease the masses with various programs designed to fool them into obedience. Armed with ballots, everything seemed possible.

Jose Ortega y Gasset describes the scene: "Whereas in past time life for the average man meant finding all around him difficulties, dangers, want, limitations of his destiny, dependence, the new world appears as a sphere of practically limitless possibilities, safe and independent of anyone . . . and if the traditional sentiment whispered: 'To live is to feel oneself limited, and therefore to have to count with that which limits us,' the newest voice shouts: 'To live is to meet with no limitation whatever and, consequently, nothing is impossible, nothing is dangerous. . . .'"[7]

He might have been describing the mindset of the contemporary US investor, who sees no limit to stock prices and no risk anywhere. And so he was—70 years ahead of his time.

Voting cannot really increase the masses' well-being. It brings no more hogs to market, builds no more gadgets, improves no meals, nor does it increase the efficiency of the internal combustion engine. But the masses will believe anything; and after Bismarck and Garibaldi came to believe that this new world of assemblies, parliaments, and election fraud offered a better world, it then became the job of politicians to find a way to appeal to these fantasies. This they did, in 19th-century Italy as in 21st century America, by borrowing money—thus creating the illusion of spending power out of thin air.

From 1859 to 1925, the Italian government ran deficits over 46 years. In only 20 years was the budget balanced. The lire was not a reserve currency; Italian politicos had to do the best they could. But the debts continued and led to war. Not because anyone in particular wanted war or debt for that matter. It was just that one was an evolutionary consequence of the other and both were consequences of the natural urges of democratic society.

> Out of the condition of Italian society sprang certain streams of opinion and of desire that governments acted on and people accepted or at least surrendered to with little resistance, even though they may have not approved or even understood them. Bewildered statesmen turned to government debt as a device for creating purchasing power. No one approved it in principle. But there was no effective resistance because people demanded the fruits it brought. Another was the ever-growing reliance of social-welfare measures to mitigate the privations of the indigent, the unemployed, the sick, the aged. The instruments of debt and spending became standard equipment of politicians. And this need for spending opened the door to an easy surrender to the elements most interested in militarism and its handmaiden, imperialism.[8]

Whenever the debts threatened to overwhelm the nation, inventive politicians found new enemies to distract the people and quiet opponents. "If the country had no natural enemy to be cultivated, then an enemy had to be invented," wrote Flynn.[9]

Following the war with Turkey, World War I provided fresh diversions. But after the war, the debts mounted even higher. The prewar debt was 15 billion lire. When the war ended it was four times as much. But after the war came new promises: an old-age pension system, unemployment insurance, a national healthcare plan. The deficit reached 11 billion lire in 1919, then rose to 17 billion in 1921. How could the debts possibly be paid? Was there any way out, people wondered?

It was at this point that a scoundrel worthy of the crisis arrived on the scene and proceeded to make things worse. Benito Mussolini was the man for the job—energetic, opportunistic—with no scruples or fixed positions to hamper his movements. Mussolini, like Roosevelt,

Bush, and practically every politician elected to any office in the entire 20th century, denounced the loose spending policies of his predecessors and then spent even more. He decried the unbalanced budgets that had brought Italy to the brink of ruin and then piled new debt on the heavy end of the scale. Taking office in 1921, he found himself with a debt of 93 billion lire. By 1923, the *New York Times* estimated that his debt had risen to 405 billion lire, with a deficit for the year of 83 billion lire.

"Spending had become a settled part of the policy of fascism to create national income," concluded Flynn, "except that the fascist state spent on a scale unimaginable to the old premiers."[10]

"We were able to give a new turn to financial policy," explained an Italian pamphlet from the period, "which aimed at improving the public services and at the same time securing a more effective action on the part of the state in promoting and facilitating national progress."[11]

The policy ended in disaster. Spending on domestic programs shifted to spending on military ones. Soon, Italy was at war again. In blood, steel, shame, disgrace, and financial ruin, it settled its accounts.

The romantic lure of empire—the political pull of military spending, the economic delusion, the polished brass and boots—it was all too much to resist. Despite a disastrous experience in World War I, even the fun-loving Italians were soon marching around in jackboots and getting out maps of Abyssinia under Mussolini's new leadership.

Mussolini was the perfect fascist. Like America's leading neoconservatives, he was really a leftist who saw an opportunity. And also like America's neoconservatives, he was an admirer of Machiavelli, who believed that the ruler "must presuppose that all men are evil and that they are always going to act according to the wickedness of their spirits."[12] And further to exploit the evil qualities in their nature whenever suitable occasion offers.

Even Americans were impressed. "He is something new and vital in the sluggish old veins of European politics," said Sol Bloom, then chairman of the House Foreign Relations Committee in 1926. "It will be a great thing not only for Italy but for all of us if he succeeds."[13]

In investments, as in war, an early defeat is often more rewarding than a later one. Fortunately for the Italians, the African campaign was a fiasco. In a few years, Mussolini was hanging from a meat hook and Italians went back to making shoes, handbags, and pasta.

MILITARY ADVENTURISM

A characteristic of all empires is an elevation of the military caste. The essential business of empire builders is providing security for parts of the world beyond their own homeland—whether the subject nations want it or not. That is a military exercise. Over time, other forms of business and commerce are neglected. But military might rests on economic might.

People are generally blockheads when it comes to military adventures. Built into their genes is not only the desire to lord it over their neighbors but also a deep distrust of anyone who fails to do their duty when the nation is at war. That is one of the things that make empires so attractive. Once underway, they meet with little domestic resistance. As time goes by, not only do other forms of business drop by the wayside, so do other domestic concerns. Everything gets sacrificed to the war gods—even the liberties for which they are meant to be fighting.

All that is needed is a war. For that, US imperialists have been blessed twice. First, in 1950, began the war against the Evil Empire. It was a nearly perfect military engagement; it threatened every life in America in a tangible, but not immediate, way. Billions of dollars would have to be spent to protect the nation. Everybody and everything must be available for confiscation, should the need arise. Even money that did not exist—the wealth that future generations had not yet earned—seemed a small price to pay to meet the danger right in front of them.

The *New York Times* of October 31, 1951, noticed the change:

> . . . the Korean War has brought a great and probably long-lasting change in our history and our way of life . . . forcing us to adopt measures which are changing the whole American scene and our relations with the rest of the world. . . . We have embarked on a partial mobilization for which about a hundred billion dollars have been already made available. We have been compelled to activate and expand our alliances at an ultimate cost of some twenty-five billion dollars, to press for rearmament of our former enemies and to scatter our own forces at military bases throughout the world. Finally, we have

been forced not only to retain but to expand the draft and to press for a system of universal military training which will affect the lives of a whole generation. The productive effort and the tax burden resulting from these measures are changing the economic pattern of the land.

What is not so clearly understood, here or abroad, is that these are no temporary measures for a temporary emergency but rather the beginning of a wholly new military status for the United States, which seems certain to be with us for a long time to come.[14]

As long as the empire lasts.

On the other side of this vast mobilization was another imperial power doing its own mobilizing—and for similar reasons. Both were in the protection racket. Both benefited—in an imperial sense—from the rivalry. But the Soviet Union's economy had been so wrecked by its economists and central planners, it couldn't keep up.

By the 1980s, it was no longer a worthy adversary. By 1989, the Soviets came to their senses and got out of the empire business and dropped tax rates 41% across-the-board.[15] And then, went on their way.

During the period of the Cold War—from 1950 to 1989, including the hot periods in Korea and Vietnam—the United States spent a total of $5 trillion protecting the free world from the Evil Empire. Much, or all of that spending had to be borrowed first. The national debt kicked off the Cold War in 1950 with a post–World War II debt of $257 billion. It crossed the Cold War finish line in 1989 over $3 trillion in the whole.[16] If it had not spent a dime, the outcome might have been exactly the same—but we cannot know that. What we do know is the US imperial role was already expensive. But who was counting?

After the collapse of the Soviet empire, only one empire was still standing. But it left this US empire in an awkward position. It was in the business of providing protection, but from whom? How could it justify high rates of taxation? How could it continue to employ its military men? For a few years—during the Clinton administration—the nation hesitated. But by 2004, the Pentagon budget was nearly 20% greater than it was in 1989.

Fortunately for the imperialists, on September 11, 2001, a small group of Muslim terrorists managed one of the most daring and successful attacks in history. With resources no greater than that which would leave a chemical trace in the United States, terrorists hijacked commercial airliners and flew them into landmark buildings in New York. The event was seen on television around the world. Within hours, George W. Bush announced a new war—against terrorism. This was an absurd stretch, too. Never before had a war been declared against a tactic. It was as if he had gone to war against naval blockades or fighting on Sunday. Every other empire made war on its enemies or its friends. The Bush administration was making war on no one in particular, and everyone in general. Every fighting force uses terror at one time or another. Besides, *terror* could be defined almost any way you wanted, and is only unacceptable so long as it remains unsuccessful. A terrorist who succeeds gets to have tea with the Queen of England, as did Menachim Begin.

But none of these issues seemed to matter. In the homeland, scarcely anyone complained.

"We are no longer able to choose between peace and war. We have embraced perpetual war. We are no longer able to choose the time, the circumstance or the battlefield."[17] You may think that this is a quotation from a journalist after September 11, 2001. Actually, it is a quote from Garet Garrett, writing about the Cold War in 1952. The comment works for the entire period, just as it would have worked for the Romans almost anytime during their 900-year empire. Or for the Mongols or even the British.

Garrett leaves us another interesting quote from the period:

"Talk of imminent threat to our national security through the application of external force is pure nonsense," said General Douglas MacArthur. "Indeed it is a part of the general pattern of misguided policy that our country is now geared to an arms economy which was bred in an artificially induced psychosis of war hysteria and nurtured upon an incessant propaganda of fear. While such an economy may produce a sense of seeming prosperity for the moment, it rests on an illusionary foundation of complete unreliability and renders among our political leaders almost a greater fear of peace than is their fear of war."[18]

Was he speaking in 1952 or 2002?
Senator Flanders elaborated in 1951:

Fear is felt and spread by the Department of Defense in the
Pentagon. In part, the spreading of it is purposeful. Faced with
what seem to be enormous armed forces aimed against us, we can
scarcely expect the Department of Defense to do other than keep
the people in a state of fear so that they will be prepared without
limit to furnish men and munitions. . . . Another center from which
fear is spread is the State Department. Our diplomacy has gone
on the defensive. The real dependences of the State Department is
in arms, armies and allies. There is no confidence left in anything
except force. The fearfulness of the Pentagon and that of the State
Department complement and reinforce each other.[19]

"Senator Flanders missed the point," says Garrett. "Empire must
put its faith in arms. Fear at last assumes the phase of a patriotic
obsession. It is stronger than any political party."[20]

Neither Flanders nor MacArthur recognized what business
America had gotten itself into.

As the imperium moves toward a military footing, civil institutions sink. Senators still debate the merits of particular items of
legislation and still sneak pork-barrel projects into military authoriza-
tions, but more and more, they become idle windbags rather than real
legislators. Even when they see clearly the drift of the continent, they
are powerless to stop it. Garet Garrett mentioned the case of Senator
Taft discussing the expenses of the Korean War in March 1950.

"I do not know how long this program is going to continue. . . .
We simply cannot keep the country in readiness to fight an all-out
war unless we are willing to turn our country into a garrison state
and abandon all the ideals of freedom upon which this nation has
been erected."[21]

Still, Senator Taft was not going to stand in the way of empire. He
voted for the appropriations bill.

Fifty-five years later, the people's representatives don't even want
to take up the most important issues. Maybe they are too hot to handle. Or maybe, somehow, they know that the important issues are
beyond them. It is as if some instinct directs people to doing Nature's
own work. Nature will not tolerate an imperial monopoly forever.
The empire must find a way to exterminate itself. No one wants to

stand in its way. The two most important public issues of the early 21st century were the growth of debt in the United States, both public and private, and the stretch of US military resources around the world. Each of these matters had the potential to ruin the imperium itself and gave rise to vital questions. Why are we meddling all over the world? And, how are we going to pay for all the promises we've made? Every publicly elected official should have posed these questions. But almost none did.

Even in 2001, on the matter of war, the United States Constitution was the same as it had been since 1789. "The Congress shall have the power to declare war," it still says. It does not say the president has the power. Nor the secretary of the Treasury or the postmaster general. It says Congress. We cannot imagine a graver, more serious act than a declaration of war. We assume that it is just that sort of weight on their shoulders and their conscience that a member of Congress is paid to carry. But when the time came to consider a declaration of war against the lawful government of Afghanistan and then Iraq, out of 98 members of the Senate, not a single one voted against the use of military force in Iraq, and none asked for a declaration of war.

Similarly in matters of domestic policy, Congress becomes more and more marginalized as the work of empire goes forward. Not that it particularly matters. There is nothing necessarily better about a decision made by an elected group of hacks than one made by a dictator, an appointee, or a monarch. We only point out that as empires develop, power develops at the center, around the executive, and radiates outward. The pre-empire forms are still there. But they become meaningless. Executives can do what they like, for they control the business end of the state: the military.

To the extent that it promoted economic progress and prosperity, the Roman Empire did so by establishing public order and otherwise letting people get on with their business. Tax rates probably averaged only about 5% of GDP, even lower than the tribute demanded by the Mongols. But as the imperial bureaucracy develops, it has a tendency to clog up the plumbing of commerce with increasingly detailed controls. One measure causes a backup, which, in turn, provokes remediation by functionaries. Another measure is laid on, which causes even a worse backup. Eventually, people are up to their knees.

This is what happened in Rome. After clipping the coins in the period from Nero to Diocletian, inflation seemed out of control. There were more and more coins. It took more of them to buy the same things every year. Finally, Emperor Diocletian announced his Edict of Prices to stop inflation. Prices for everything—including wages—were controlled. The result, as can be imagined, was even worse disaster.

By the time of the Nixon administration, the water was rising in America, too. We mention it here not to explore the plumbing but the constitutional system. There is nothing in the United States Constitution allowing a president to fix prices as though he were a Roman emperor. But that is exactly what Richard Nixon did. The measure was desperate, illegal, and so ill-advised as to be financially suicidal. But who opposed it? A few old fuddy-duddies in his own party put up a fight, but most members of Congress seemed not to care.

PART II

DEAD PRESIDENTS

The road to hell is paved with good intentions.

—Anonymous proverb

CHAPTER 5

THE ROAD TO HELL

We are dogged by dead men. Down the street from our old office in Paris was the site of the world's first central bank, put up by John Law, before he was forced to hightail it out of town. Around the corner from our new office is the Crillon Hotel, where Franklin Roosevelt, then an assistant secretary of the US Navy, dined in high style while pretending to get the lowdown on the doughboys in the trenches. In the next war, Ernest Hemingway claimed to have liberated the bar at the Crillon from the Nazis as they left for the Rhine.

But it is back in Baltimore, Maryland, where the ghosts haunt us most. In our very own office, according to the local history buffs, Woodrow Wilson got together with the US ambassador to Belgium, Theodore Marburg, and ginned up one of the grandest wish lists of all time—the League of Nations.

An honest, upright man has no place in national politics. A man with his wits about him is too modest for the role. He suffers greatness as a sort of hypocrisy. He has no better idea of how the nation should be led than anyone else—and he knows it.

Dissembling wears him down until he is shouldered out of the way by bolder liars and abject stoneheads. The former will say whatever the voters want to hear—and then go on with disastrous projects. The latter have no plans or fixed ideas of any sort; they merely shake hands and blabber whatever cockamamy nonsense comes into their heads. The former never make good presidents. The latter often do.

THE BEST PRESIDENTS

Many of the best US presidents—such as Garfield, Harding, and Arthur—are rarely even mentioned. Lincoln, Wilson, and Theodore Roosevelt, however, are routinely described as national heroes. Nobody really knows which president was good for the nation and which was bad. We would have to know what would have happened if the man in the Oval Office had done something different. Would the nation be better off if Lincoln had not slaughtered so many Southerners? Would world history have been worse if Wilson had not meddled in World War I? We can't know the answers; we can only guess. But the historians who guess about such matters have a disturbing tilt—not toward mediocrity, but toward imbecility. Like crooked butchers, they advertise our biggest mutton brains as prime beef—and push their thumbs down on the scales of history to give them extra weight. Those they select as great are merely those who have given them the most meat—those who have made the biggest public spectacles of themselves.

Most historians rate Lincoln, Wilson, and Franklin Roosevelt as our greatest presidents. But all of them might just as well have been charged with dereliction, gross incompetence, and treason. For at one time or another, each of them betrayed the Constitution, got the country into a war that probably could have been avoided, and practically bankrupted the nation.

The presumption that underlies the popular opinion is that presidents face challenges. They are rated on how well they face up to them. But the biggest challenge a president will face is no different from that faced by a Louis or a Charles—merely staying out of the way. People have their own challenges, their own plans, and their own private lives to lead. The last thing they need is a president who wants to improve the world. Every supposed improvement costs citizens dearly. If it is a bridge, it is they who must pay for it, whether it is needed or not. If it is a law forbidding this or regulating that, it is their activities that are interdicted. If it is a war, it is they who must die. Every step toward phony public do-goodism comes at the expense of genuine private improvements.

That is why a president who does nothing is a treasure. William Henry Harrison was a model national leader. Rare in a president, he did what he promised to do. He told voters that he would "under no circumstances" serve more than a single term. He made good on his promise in the most conclusive way. The poor man caught pneumonia giving his inaugural address. He was dead within 31 days of taking the oath of office.

James A. Garfield was another great leader. He took office in March 1881. The man was a marvel and could write Latin with one hand and Greek with the other—at the same time. He was shot in July and died three months later. "He didn't have time to accomplish his plans," say the standard histories. Thank God.

Millard Fillmore was one of America's greatest presidents. He did little—other than try to preserve peace in the period leading up to the War Between the States. Preserving peace was an achievement, but instead of giving the man credit, historians hold up the humbug, Abraham Lincoln, for praise. The United States has never suffered more harm than on Lincoln's watch. Still, it is the Lincoln Memorial to which crowds of agitators and malcontents repair, not the Fillmore Memorial. As far as we know, no monument exists to Fillmore, who not only kept the peace but also installed the first system of running water in the White House—giving the place its first bathtub. Fillmore was a modest man. Oxford University offered him an honorary degree. But Fillmore couldn't read Latin. He refused the diploma, saying he didn't want a degree he couldn't read.

If Fillmore couldn't read Latin, Andrew Johnson was lucky to be able to read at all. He never went to any kind of school; his wife taught him to read. He is often held up as an example of a failed presidency. Instead, he seems to have made one of the best deals for the American people ever—buying Alaska from Russia for $7.2 million. Who has added so much since? Who has actually made the nation richer, rather than poorer? Johnson did the nation a great service. Still, he gets little respect and practically no thanks.

But our favorite president is Warren Gamaliel Harding.

In his hit book, *Blink*,[1] Malcolm Gladwell tells how Harry Daugherty (a leader of the Republican Party in Ohio) met Warren

Harding in 1899 in the back garden of the Globe Hotel in Richwood, Ohio, where both were having their shoes shined.

Daugherty blinked and thought he saw a man who could be president.

Journalist Mark Sullivan described the moment:

> Harding was worth looking at. He was at the time about 35 years old. His head, features, shoulders and torso had a size that attracted attention, their proportions to each other made an effect, which in any male at any place would justify more than the term handsome. In later years, when he came to be known beyond his local world, the word "Roman" was occasionally used in descriptions of him. As he stepped down from the stand, his legs bore out the striking and agreeable proportions of his body; and his lightness on his feet, his erectness, his easy bearing, added to the impression of physical grace and virility. His suppleness, combined with his bigness of frame, and his large, wide-set rather glowing eyes, his very black hair, and bronze complexion gave him some of the handsomeness of an Indian. His courtesy as he surrendered his seat to the other customer suggested genuine friendliness toward all mankind. His voice was noticeably resonant, masculine, and warm. His pleasure in the attentions of the bootblack's whisk reflected a consciousness about clothes unusual in a small-town man. His manner as he bestowed a tip suggested generous good-nature, a wish to give pleasure, based on physical well-being and sincere kindliness of heart.[2]

Not only did Harding have the looks and the presence, he also had the bad-boy image. Gladwell writes, "Not especially intelligent. Liked to play poker and to drink . . . and most of all, chase women; his sexual appetites were the stuff of legend."[3]

As he rose from one office to the next, he "never distinguished himself." His speeches were vacuous. He had few ideas, and those that he had were probably bad ones. Still, when Daugherty arranged for Harding to speak to the 1916 Republican National Convention, he guessed what might happen.

"There is a man who looks like he should be president," the onlookers would say. Later that day, in the smoke-filled rooms of the Blackstone Hotel in Chicago, the power brokers realized they had a problem. Whom could they find that none of them would object to? Well, there was Harding!

"Harding became President Harding [in 1921]," writes Gladwell. "He served two years before dying unexpectedly of a stroke. He was, most historians agree, one of the worst presidents in American history."[4]

On the surface, he sounds like one of the best. We have never heard of anyone being arrested and charged under the "Harding Act." We have never seen a building in Washington, or anywhere else, named the *Harding Building*. We know of no wars the man caused. We recall no government programs he set in motion.

As far as we know, the nation and everyone in it were no better off the day Warren Harding stepped into office than they were the day he was carried out of it.

Harding was a decent man of reasonable talents. He held poker games in the White House twice a week. And whenever he got a chance, he sneaked away to a burlesque show. These pastimes seemed enough for the man; they helped him bear up in his eminent role and kept him from wanting to do anything. Another saving grace was that the president neither thought nor spoke clearly enough for anyone to figure out what he was talking about. He couldn't rally the troops and get them behind his ideas; he had none. And even if he tried, they wouldn't understand him.

H. L. Mencken preserved a bit of what he called *Gamalielese*, just to hold it up to ridicule: "I would like government to do all it can to mitigate, then, in understanding in mutuality of interest, in concern for the common good, our tasks will be solved."[5]

The sentence is so idiotic and meaningless, it could have come from the mouth of George W. Bush. But the crowds seemed to like the way he delivered it. He said it with such solid conviction, it "was like a blacksmith bringing down a hammer on an egg,"[6] says Mencken.

Harding was so full of such thunderous twaddle that he stormed into office . . . and then drizzled away until he died. Bravo! Well done.

WILSON CROSSES THE RUBICON

Harding, Arthur, Fillmore—unlike the clumsy giants who left their deep footprints in the earth along Pennsylvania Avenue and trod on practically everyone who got in their way—these midgets managed to make their way through the nation's highest office leaving hardly a trace. That is, they left the country alone.

You will find their pictures on no "dead presidents," that is, on none of the nation's currency. Nor will you find their profiles chiseled on the towering rocks of the Dakota hills. Instead, there you find blowhards such as Theodore Roosevelt and saintly frauds such as Abraham Lincoln. But in the crowded field of contestants for America's worst president, one man stands out. As a world improver, his stature is world class. He was humorless, immodest, and self-righteous.

Woodrow Wilson was the worst kind of politician—he wouldn't lie and couldn't be bought. He was so full of good intentions he could practically pave the road to hell by himself.

Between the beginning of the 20th century and the end of World War II, the United States became the world's richest, most advanced, and most powerful nation in history. More people owed more money to America than had ever owed money to any nation anywhere. More people viewed America favorably than ever had viewed any country before. Americans stood astride the globe, a well-meaning and able colossus.

But there never was a silver lining without a cloud wrapped around it. America was too fortunate for her own good. Now, just six decades later, the country is the world's biggest debtor. It is the world's biggest consumer—the "world's mouth." It is the world's most aggressive and meddling military power. No country on earth is so godforsaken as to escape America's notice nor too poor to lend it money. The United States had been the freest country on earth. Now, it has more people locked up in jail than any other country (some of whom it tortures) and employs a huge army of busybodies and snitches who all determined that no commercial act between consenting adults will take place without the explicit approval of a half dozen major bureaucracies.

We pause a moment and wonder how we got where we are. Surely, some terrible crime has been committed. We go to the scene to look for evidence. There, we find a few samples and take them over to the lab. And what do we find? The DNA samples are those of Thomas Woodrow Wilson.

We do not blame the man. Or hold him uniquely responsible. His protégé at the Navy Department, Franklin Roosevelt, was an eager accomplice. Lyndon Johnson drove the getaway car. Ronald Reagan, Alan Greenspan, and George W. Bush joined the gang later. But Wilson was the mastermind. It was he who decided to "improve" the US system of government. It was he who also decided to improve much of the world. It was as if he thought all the generations of Americans that preceded him—and all the peoples of the world outside US borders—were a bunch of nincompoops. He and, apparently, he alone was blessed with the ability to see just what the entire world needed. And thus he undertook to change the US Constitution in the most fundamental ways and to reorder the system of international relations that had evolved over thousands of years.

"The spirit of liberty is the spirit which is not too sure that it is right," said Judge Learned Hand in 1944.[7] Such modesty never bothered America's 28th president.

"A mentally ill, pitiless, mythomaniac, . . . who believed himself in direct communication with God, guided by an intelligent power outside of himself. . . ."[8] Thus did the father of modern psychoanalysis describe Woodrow Wilson. But Freud's judgment of the man was too generous. Wilson was a self-satisfied, sanctimonious delusional bungler who practically single-handedly transformed the country into a mocking shell of what it was supposed to be.

We begin our inspection with a quotation attributed to Wilson after his presidential election victory: "Remember that God ordained that I should be the next president of the United States. Neither you nor any other mortal or mortals could have prevented this."[9]

Is there any doubt that Wilson was mad? He claimed to be a Democrat. Later, he claimed to want to make the world "safe for democracy." But right here, we see he believed in divine providence to decide leadership issues. He had not been elected by the people; he had been chosen by God. Why then, bother to have elections at all?

We also pause to wonder how the former college professor could have known God's mind. We have tried ourselves, many times. Does God intend stock prices to rise, we ask ourselves? Will God let this plane land safely, we wondered recently? Where the hell did God let us leave the car keys? But though we have given the matter a good faith try, we have never mastered it.

Surely, Woodrow must have supped with the gods. Perhaps he had God's ear or even his throat. For the man could look into the future as easily as we can look into an empty beer stein. He knew not only that he was destined to become president, but that he could build a world even better than the one God had given him—by looking into the future and improving it before it happened and by replacing the private goals and hopes of millions of people with those of his own.

How did he know that the world would be a better place if a Federal Reserve System were set up to control the nation's money? How did he know that Mexico would be a worse country and a worse friend to the United States—if it had General Huerta at its head, instead of Wilson's man, Carranza? What made him think that his own judgment about what sort of government Mexicans should have was better than that of the Mexicans themselves? What made him think that a democracy was superior to a constitutional monarchy or that World War I would end better if Americans got involved in it?

In his April 2, 1917, speech, in which he urged the nation to war, Wilson noted that the Russians had always been "democratic at heart." "[W]onderful, and heartening things . . . have been happening with the last few weeks in Russia,"[10] he continued. What had been happening was the beginning of the uprising that would later become the Bolshevik Revolution. First, the moderates took over from the Tsar. But the Kerensky government kept Russia in the war. Germany, meanwhile, feared America's entry in the war on the enemy's side. She desperately needed to stabilize the Eastern Front so she could turn her attention to the renewed threat in the West. Her technique was as clever as it was disastrous. She found a windy revolutionary named Lenin who had been exiled from Russia many years before. He was bankrolled, put on a train, and sent back into Russia with the express purpose of making trouble. The trouble he made was the Bolshevik Revolution, which knocked Russia out of the war, just as the Germans had hoped.

Wilson had no clue. He had no way of knowing what would happen anywhere. He was guessing, just like everyone else, and almost always guessing wrong. Many readers will rush to judgment. "He made a mistake," they will say. Or, "How could anyone know that the Russian Revolution would be followed by one of the most cruel and absurd episodes of bad government in the entire sordid, history of the planet?" Because it is impossible to know, they will add, "You just have to do your best. . . . Besides, you have to take action!"

The prejudice for action in public affairs is a constant. And a constant disappointment.

Of course, Wilson could not know what would happen. It was vain to think otherwise. But Wilson did think otherwise and was determined to edit history before it was written—in Haiti, in Mexico, in Nicaragua and then, when the stakes were bigger, in Europe. He even sent troops to Russia to try to beat back the Bolsheviks. But this was typical of Wilson. He seemed to want to intervene everywhere.

THE HALLS OF MONTEZUMA

Americans were perfectly happy with the government of Porfirio D'az in Mexico. But then, the malcontents in Mexico began causing trouble because the most important industries in the country were owned by non-Mexicans. In economic terms it barely matters what passports capitalists carry, but politicians prefer to have locals own local industries so that they will be closer to hand to lean on. Beyond that, the Mexicans found foreign ownership a useful spoon with which to stir up the mobs. A new president, Francisco Madero, came in after Porfirio was overthrown in 1910. He immediately went to work trying to dispossess the foreigners—many of whom were Americans.

"Give us a dictator we can trust," the dispossessed said to then-president Taft. In February 1913, Madero was overthrown and murdered by General Victoriano Huerta. The new US president, Wilson, did not like the latest regime in Mexico and refused to recognize it. Instead, he backed the opposition movement, led by Venustiano Carranza and his Constitutionalist party. Wilson said he was following a policy of "watchful waiting," but he must have gotten tired of watching after a while. On April 21, 1914, he decided to act. He ordered the bombardment of Vera Cruz. Blowing up another country's city is not an ambiguous act. It is a decisive act of war. The United States Constitution specifically says that Congress, and only Congress, has the power to declare war. But Wilson couldn't wait.

The Mexican "crisis" pot had been on a low boil for months. Foreign ships lay off the coast of several Mexican ports awaiting trouble. An incident in Tampico, where a group of American sailors was detained by Mexican troops, turned up the heat. The sailors were released shortly, with apologies. But Wilson rarely let an opportunity for mishap pass unmolested. He demanded that the Huerta government hoist the US flag over Tampico and give a 21-gun salute to atone for the insult. Huerta would have rather jumped naked into an alligator pond. He refused.

Wilson brought up his marines. But Tampico had no decent place to land them; Vera Cruz was substituted. The proximate reason for Wilson's attack on Vera Cruz was the approach of a German ship, said to have arms aboard for the Mexican government. Mexico was not at war with the United States. The United States was not at war with Germany. No one was at war with anyone. Mexico could buy its arms from whatever country it wanted. Wilson's intervention was fantastic, almost unbelievable.

In the battle of Vera Cruz, 90 Americans died and more than 300 Mexicans. What they died for, no one knew. Wilson's military meddling quickly produced the exact opposite result than the one he had expected. His man, Carranza, was so appalled he joined forces with his adversary, uniting the entire country against the United States and demanding the removal of US troops. The Mexican government severed diplomatic relations with the United States and prepared to seize assets of US nationals. Now, the two nations were on the verge of real war. And for what? Mr. Wilson had never met either General Huerta or Mr. Carranza, nor as far as we know, had he ever set foot in Mexico, eaten a single taco, or swallowed a single shot of tequila. Yet, the US president thought he knew best who should be head of state south of the Rio Grande.

The whole affair ended as preposterously and pathetically as it began. The war in Europe began and Wilson's wife died. The president no longer had the time or energy to build a better world in Mexico. After a bit of negotiation, Wilson typed up a press release: "Both General Carranza and the Convention at Aguascalientes having given the assurances and guarantees we requested, it is the purpose of the Administration to withdraw the troops of the United

States from Vera Cruz on Monday, the twenty-third of November. All the persons there for whose personal safety this Government had made itself responsible have now left the city. The priests and nuns who had taken refuge there and for whose safety fears were entertained are on their way to this country."[11]

But the Wilsonian intervention was not over. After the settlement of the Vera Cruz incident, Wilson backed a rival to Carranza—a colorful character named Francisco "Pancho" Villa, who once owned a chain of butcher shops. Villa must have been an early role model for Che Guevara. He loved publicity and was accused of staging battles only to get his name in the paper. Hollywood adored him. If there had been a T-shirt industry in 1916, his picture would have been on millions of them. But Villa was not only comic, he was lethal. On January 10, 1916, his men attacked a group of US mining engineers who had been invited to the area to revive abandoned mines at Santa Ysabel. Villa murdered 18 of them. Then on March 9, he grew more provocative. His men crossed the border to attack a small garrison in Columbus, New Mexico. The town was burned and 17 Americans were killed in the raid. Before you could say *ay, chihuahua,* people all over the United States were foaming at the mouth, eager for war. Once again, Wilson gave up watchful waiting and appointed General John J. ("Black Jack") Pershing to bring him the head of Pancho Villa—dead or alive. This, too, was a failure. Despite the call-up of a punitive force of 12,000 soldiers, Pancho always seemed to get away. "Villa is everywhere, but Villa is nowhere," Pershing told Wilson.

Pershing chased Villa for nine months. He was called home by Wilson two months before the president announced his plans for a new intervention, this time a major league operation. But Villa did not get away for long. He was ambushed several years later and killed.

From humbug, to farce, to disaster, Wilson had written the script for nearly all America's imperial military adventures. The effect of Wilson's interventions in Latin America (he had troops in Nicaragua, Haiti, and the Dominican Republic, as well as Mexico) was the opposite of what he had hoped for. Instead of increasing friends of the United States in the region, the number of her sworn enemies multiplied. For the next two generations, the expression, "Yanqui go home" was as familiar as frijoles in many Latin American countries.

THE GREAT WAR

He had a "self-regarding arrogance and smugness, masquerading as righteousness," says historian Paul Johnson of Woodrow Wilson, "which was always there and which grew with the exercise of power." Like all the great empire builders, Wilson was so sure he was making things better he had no need for the polite constraints of bourgeois society, simple truth, or constitutional government. Wilson had "a passion for interpreting great events to the world," he told his first wife. He wanted to "inspire a great movement of opinion."[12] It was not enough to boss around the hidalgos of Latin America; Wilson had an even greater ambition, to lord it over the Europeans, too. Economically, the nation was already on top of the world—US gross domestic product surpassed England's in 1910. Just as every young buck wants to challenge the old bulls, here was America's turn to assert itself militarily among the world's major powers. In answer to the question, why did the United States begin meddling in foreign affairs in the 20th century, and not before, comes the easy answer: because it could.

On April 2, 1917, Thomas Woodrow Wilson stood before a joint session of Congress and dazzled the assembly with a torrent of rhetorical air. He had hardly to say a word. The animals were already snorting and pawing the ground. The European powers had locked horns. Now, it was America's chance to join the battle and Wilson's chance to become alpha male of the entire world.

"We must put excited feeling away," said the president, and then launched into one of the greatest mob-inciting declarations ever delivered. Wilson was urging Congress to declare war against Germany. The Huns, he said, were governed by a "selfish and autocratic power."[13] What they had done to justify trying to kill them was a matter of great dispute. Robert "Fighting Bob" La Follette, senator from Wisconsin, thought they hadn't done much of anything. They were accused of bayoneting babies and cutting off the arms of boys in Belgium. But when a group of US journalists went on a fact-finding

The Road to Hell   113

mission to get to the truth of the matter, they could find no evidence of it. Clarence Darrow, the lawyer who later made a monkey out of William Jennings Bryan in the Scopes Trial, said he would offer a $1,000 reward to anyone who came forward whose arm had been cut off by the Germans. A thousand dollars was a lot of money back then (this was when the Fed had barely settled down to work), equal to about $20,000 today. Still, no one claimed the money.

The Germans had also sunk a few ships. But there was a war going on in Europe. Germany tried to impose a blockade of English ports with the only weapon it had, submarines. You took a risk trying to sail into England, especially if your ship was carrying ammunition; everyone knew it. The English were blockading German ports, too. The difference was that the English had a bigger navy and were better at it. There was nothing new about naval blockades. Lincoln had blockaded the South during the War Between the States.

It was a long and complicated story. In retrospect, the United States would almost certainly have been better off by staying out of it. Senator Robert La Follette thought so at the time. He told anyone who would listen that the struggle in Europe was best understood as a political and commercial rivalry. The Germans were challenging the English everywhere. The German economy was growing faster. Although Germany industrialized much later than England, she went about it with typical German thoroughness and energy. Output increased more than 600% from 1855 to 1913. Whereas Britain's empire seemed to be peaking out, the Germans were building new factories and developing new markets. As late as 1870, Britain was responsible for a third of the entire world's manufacturing. By 1910, her percentage had fallen in half; Germany and America both produced more. In Africa, German colonialists were menacing English territories; twice in the years running up to World War I, a crisis in Africa brought the major powers close to war. In Europe, German manufacturers were taking market share from their English competitors. On the high seas, the German Navy was becoming a bigger and bigger threat to the Royal Navy. And so, the English and the Germans were finally having it out. Leave them to it, said Fighting Bob La Follette.

But Woodrow Wilson had his own ideas. "Civilization itself" seemed in the balance, he told the politicians. "We shall fight for the things we have always carried in our hearts—for democracy, for the right of those who submit to authority to have a voice in their own governments, for the rights and liberties of small nations [he did not mention Mexico, Haiti, or Nicaragua], for a universal dominion of right by such a concert of free peoples as shall bring peace and safety to all nations and make the world itself at last free."[14]

When he finished his speech, most of the members of Congress rose to their feet and cheered. Tears streamed down many faces. At last, the United States was going to war! Two million people had already died in the war. For what reason, no one quite knew. Wilson had to resort to bombast and balderdash to try to explain it. It had been just another foolish European war until then—the very sort of war the Founding Fathers had urged their descendants to avoid. Don't go forth looking for "monsters to slay," said Adams. But now the happy moment had come. Now, the United States was ready. Wilson had found a monster. Hallelujah!

Until this date, the war in Europe was just another war in Europe. Not the first, and not the last. As recently as 1870, France and Germany had gone at it. France had attacked. Germany counterattacked so brilliantly, she was able to encircle Paris and lay siege to the city.

The United States felt no desire to enter the Franco-Prussian War. She was still hobbling around on crutches from her own War Between the States. And when the war of 1870 was over, the French were forced to pay reparations. But the money paid over to the Germans was quickly recycled back to the French, from whom the Germans bought goods and services. Losing the war turned out to be as good as winning it; France boomed and Germany, too. Apart from that conflict, Europe had enjoyed an entire century of peace and prosperity. The upper brain might have thought—well done, we will hold a steady course. But down in the limbic system, primitive urges were swelling. After such a long period of peace, war might be refreshing. After such a long period of prosperity, they heard the wild call of debt, destruction, and insolvency.

On June 28, 1914, the archduke Franz Ferdinand, of the Austro-Hungarian Empire, and his wife were shot and killed by a malcontent named Gavrilo Princip. No one in America particularly cared. For all it mattered out on the prairie, they would have had the duke stuffed and used as a parlor ornament. Few people had any idea why the Europeans were at war. They had been warned by the Founding Fathers to mind their own business. America had the most dynamic economy in the world; Americans had plenty of business to mind. To sensible people in the United States, minding your own business still seemed like the best foreign policy.

But the editorial pages fulminated with reasons to get into the fight. Nationalism, economic competition, militarism, secret treaties, lofty ideals, low-down secret deals, treachery, rivalry—the answers flew out of the frontal lobe like plastic bags out of a welfare high-rise. Pretty soon, they were hanging from every tree and electric pole.

Even today, you could go from one end of the country to the other asking historians why the United States decided to enter the war or why it entered on the side of England and France instead of on the side of Germany and Austria. You would get plenty of answers, but not a single reason that comes close to justifying the deaths of nearly half a million Americans. You would not, because they don't exist.

Princip was like a character from a Chekov play says historian A.J.P. Taylor. Except that he didn't miss. Did it make sense to sacrifice half a million Americans because Princip hit his mark? Had he been a worse shot, would the war ever have begun? Is that the real reason the war began?[15] Princip's marksmanship did not so much trigger the war as allow it to commence. None of the major powers really wanted war—not in the sense that they expected any benefit from it. None was prepared for it. And yet, none was very good at stopping it. All of a sudden, troops were being mobilized throughout the Balkans. German Kaiser Wilhelm II was alarmed and tried to stop it. On July 30, at 2:55 a.m., he sent an urgent telegram to the German ambassador in Vienna: Try mediation, he told the diplomats.

Then, as now, nobody really knew anything. Britain, France, Austria-Hungary, Russia, Germany—all repeatedly misread each other's intentions, miscalculated the effect of their own actions, and completely misunderstood what they were getting themselves into. Many people in Europe at the time had been influenced by the writings of Norman Angell, who believed that war was practically impossible. Angell made a good argument. Modern economies are based on trade, commerce, and manufacture. Wealth no longer rested on land—which could be seized—but on factories, railroads, capital, and business relationships. War destroys capital and stifles economic activity. Therefore, people would not make war; it would be too costly, illogical, and unreasonable.

Norman Angell's book, *The Great Illusion,* was translated into several languages and received high praise from many quarters. One of its most visible admirers was Viscount Esher, chairman of the War Committee in England. Lord Esher gave lectures on the new idea at Cambridge and the Sorbonne. He told listeners that "new economic factors clearly prove the inanity of aggressive wars." No one would make war, said he, because it would cause such "commercial disaster, financial ruin and individual suffering" that people would naturally turn away from it. The whole idea of modern warfare, he explained, was "so pregnant with restraining influences" that war must soon be a thing of the past.[16]

There was also the argument that technology inhibits war. At the beginning of the 20th century, Winston Churchill said, "Humanity was informed that it could make machines that would fly through the air. . . .

"The whole prospect and outlook of mankind grew immeasurably larger, and the multiplication of ideas also proceeded at an incredible rate. . . .

"While he nursed the illusion of growing mastery and exulted in his new trappings, he became the sport and presently the victim of tides and currents, of whirlpools and tornadoes amid which he was far more helpless than he had been for a long time."[17]

Not long after the turn of the new century, Orville and Wilbur Wright demonstrated that the promise of air transportation was real. On the windswept banks of North Carolina, for the first time in history, an airplane got off the ground and completed a controlled flight.

The promise was fulfilled. Airplanes worked. Three decades after the birth of airplanes, they were over Churchill's wartime bunker in London, dropping explosives on the city.

"We took it almost for granted that science would confer continual boons and blessings upon us," Churchill explained. But it "was not accompanied by any noticeable advance in the stature of man, either in his mental faculties or his moral character. His brain got no better, but it buzzed the more. . . ."[18]

Others expected advances in civilization had made war passé. Freud explained this sentiment in the spring of 1915:

> We were prepared to find that wars between the primitive and civilized peoples, between the races who are divided by the color of their skin—wars, even, against and among the nationalities of Europe whose civilization is little developed or has been lost—would occupy mankind for some time to come. But we permitted ourselves other hopes. We had expected the great world-dominating nations of the white race upon whom the leadership of the human species has fallen, who were known to have world-wide interests as their concern, to whose creative powers were due not only our technical advances toward the control of nature but the artistic and scientific standards of civilization—we had expected these peoples to succeed in discovering another way of settling misunderstandings and conflicts of interest. . . .[19]

Only two of the major combatants in World War I, the United States and France, were democracies, more or less officially. But all of them were headed in that direction. In every country, there were parliaments and popular assemblies. Votes were taken. Public opinions were registered. Newspapers shouted out the current prejudices and delivered the latest misinformation. Heads of state hesitated. Autocrats consulted their ministers and advisors. Nowhere in Europe were there any real absolute monarchs. The press, the church, the assemblies, the trade unions, the aristocrats, the bourgeoisie, the industrialists, the bankers, and moneylenders—all had a hearing.

After Wilson declared it a "war to make the world safe for democracy," people began to wonder if democracy itself might have prevented the war. Wilson said as much. "Self-governing nations do not fill their neighbor states with spies," said the chief executive, not quite anticipating the CIA. Nor do they begin "cunningly contrived plans of deception or aggression . . . ," he added.[20]

Kerensky, the moderate revolutionary in Russia, declared that democracies never made war on one another. The idea was widely believed at the time, even in America, where two democracies—the North and South—had battered themselves for four years in North America's bloodiest war ever: the War Between the States. Nor did anyone bother to wonder why it was that, before their very noses, the worst war in history was taking place between nations that may not have been complete democracies, but were, nevertheless, more democratic than any in history.

Even today, people still believe that democracies are more peaceful than other forms of government. The United States of America maintains that her form of democracy is so important to the peace and prosperity of the world, she not only invites other nations to join her, she insists. And yet the point has hardly ever been seriously addressed and never proven.

What we do know is that since democracy has become widespread, there has been little letup in the incidence of war and probably an increase in its violence. Unlike the subjects of a tyrant or a monarch, the citizens of a democratic regime are more fully and readily engaged in wartime. When people feel threatened, or feel that they have a stake in the conflict, they are more inclined to devote their energy and resources to victory. Popular newspapers and television work them up to violence easily. Give them the right line of guff and they are prepared to hand over their wallets as well as their lives. France was able to finance 83.5% of its wartime expenditures by borrowing. Offering national defense bonds in small denominations, France succeeded, says Hew Strachan, in "mobilizing the wealth of the public."[21]

George Orwell wondered how England could ever triumph over Germany in World War II because socialism was so much better at marshaling the resources of a people in wartime. What he didn't realize was that in wartime, England and America quickly took on many of the attributes of a socialist society such as rationing, censorship, economic planning, and price controls. He also didn't realize that it is not merely the percentage of a society's output that the state is able to grab that counts; what also matters is the total gross amount to grab from. Both of these points were to become critical to the development of global politics in the 20th century.

Approaching the subject from another angle, we ask ourselves, If democracy was such a good idea, why did people put up with other forms of government for so many hundreds of years? We turn to the dead and ask the question. The answer we get is that most never considered it. Those who did thought democracy a bad system of government.

The Greeks invented it. But their democracy was nothing like our definition of the word. Even America's founders had a deep mistrust of popular democracy. "Democracies," James Madison wrote in the *Federalist Papers*, "have ever been found incompatible with personal security, or the rights of property, and have been as short in their lives as they have been violent in their deaths." Alexander Hamilton wrote, "Real liberty is never found in despotism or in the extremes of democracy." Samuel Adams wrote, "Democracy never lasts long. It soon wastes, exhausts and murders itself."[22] Thomas Jefferson believed that "the majority, oppressing an individual, is guilty of a crime, abuses its strength . . . and breaks up the foundations of society."[23] After the Revolutionary War was over, the crafter of the Declaration of Independence also argued that "an elective despotism was not the government we fought for."[24] In the republic they designed and anticipated, few people voted. And then, only for one chamber of the national government: the House of Representatives. The Senate was chosen by the states.

If it was so apparent that US-style democracy was the best system of government ever invented, why didn't the Chinese pick it up? Why did the Chinese never try it in over 4,000 years of civilized community? Surely someone must have thought of it. And how can we be so sure that it really is the best form of government? Isn't it an insult to our ancestors? To the hundreds of generations who never thought of it, or never tried it? And what about all the smart people in all the other countries of the world from the moment people first stood up on two legs to the day before yesterday—why did they so rarely experiment with such a gloriously successful form of government, which, as we all know, not only promotes peace and prosperity but also lifts people up and ennobles them into the most perfect beings who ever walked the earth?

We have an answer to propose. Democracy is not really God's choice. It is not really a universal constant; it is not perfect for all people at all times. It is merely an evolutionary development—like a business suit or rap music—sometimes suitable for some people. What has made democracy triumph in the modern world is probably that it is better than monarchy or dictatorship at taking resources from citizens, but rarely takes too much. Totalitarian regimes, such as the Soviet Union, could take nearly all the resources their citizens produced, but it was still not enough to compete with the smaller percentages taken from more democratic regimes. It is also worth noting that democracy has evolved spectacularly over the past 200 years, and especially since Woodrow Wilson redefined it. The US system of the 21st century has no more in common with the system set up by the Founding Fathers than, say, a new Mercedes-Maybach has with a Tin Lizzie.

In the Great War, almost all the innovations and advances that were thought to prevent war actually made it longer and more brutal—including democracy.

Interlocking treaties were said to prevent any one nation from going to war; instead, the system brought in more combatants. Modern methods of production were supposed to make war too economically destructive; instead, they brought more weapons with greater killing power to the battlefield. Booming economies had the wealth to spend far more on war than ever before and to sustain the spending for a longer period of time. Medieval armies could only take the field for a few months. After that, they were exhausted. It was also rare for them to make war in bad weather; they simply didn't have the means to stay at it. Even in modern wars, intensely bad weather puts an end to the fighting, as it did every winter in the Wehrmacht's campaigns in Russia. Modern technology, modern transportation, and modern methods of production all helped put more resources at the warriors' disposal. So did modern democracy. The awakened and awakening democracies in all the major war makers in World War I brought far more popular participation to the war effort—more money, more resources, more soldiers. And all these factors contributed toward keeping nations at war for a much longer period.

But even with all these things, the ability of Germany, Austria-Hungary, Russia, England, and France to sustain a war was still far more limited than one might have thought. Especially in the matter of finance.

Spending in the war exceeded everyone's expectations. After Germany defeated France in 1871, it used the money it received from France in settlement to create a war chest of 120 million marks held in the Julius Tower at Spandau. On the eve of World War I, the amount was doubled to 240 million gold marks, along with an additional 120 million in silver. It seemed like a lot of money. Yet, in 1913, the Reichsbank figured that mobilization alone (to say nothing of wartime losses) would cost 1,800 million marks. Actual expenditure August 1914 was 2,047 million marks. And the war had hardly begun. During the war, Germany's annual expenditure averaged 45,700 million marks, a sum 200 times greater than the entire contents of the war chest. And the war continued for four years. The situation on the Entente side was little different. The war cost far more than expected and needed not only the support of the citizenry but also of the world's largest democracy—the United States.

No one can know for sure what might have happened. But it seems very likely that without US financial and matériel support, the Great War would have ended much sooner.

The democratization of the war extended it in another way, as well. The rulers of Britain, Germany, and Russia were all related. Wilhelm II of Germany and George V of England were both grandsons of Queen Victoria. Tsar Nicholas II of Russia was married to their cousin. Nicholas was the cousin of George V through his mother, the Dowager Empress Marie. Before the war, Wilhelm tried to bring Russia into common cause with Germany, sending him a series of letters addressed to "Nicky," from "Willy." Both Willy and Nicky, we soon find, were prepared to make war on each other if need be. But neither they, nor their cousin George V, would do so to such an extent as to endanger their empires, their positions, or destroy the royal houses of Europe. It was precisely because their powers had been weakened that the war continued and expanded to such an extent that two out of three of them not only lost their thrones, their royal houses were extinguished completely. We can't know, but we can imagine, that if democracy and Woodrow Wilson had not transformed the war into a bigger event, Willy might have written to Nicky and Georgy and called the whole thing off. But it was too late for that. This was a war between peoples, not royal houses. It was already a largely democratic war, in other words, even before Wilson stuck his nose in it.

The progressive left steadfastly maintained that growing socialism would also make war impossible. Pacifism had always been a major headline in the socialist agenda. They saw war as a by-product of capitalist competition and bourgeois nationalism. Both would be eliminated, "come the revolution." But when push came to shove, socialists in all countries started swinging. The Kerensky government in Russia, after the Tsar's arrest, decided to stay in the war. It called on citizens to fight: "Peasants and workers, all who desire the happiness and welfare of Russia, . . . harden your spirits, collect all forces, and when you have defended the country, liberate it."[25]

Later, in World War II, after Russia had been completely liberated, Stalin found that he, too, had to call on atavistic national sentiments to rally the country behind him. After years of purges, starvation, gulags, and Communist claptrap, the Russians were no longer willing to fight for socialist ideology. But they would still fight for the Motherland.

Both Russia and Germany (and Italy, too) took soft, well-intentioned intellectuals of socialism and put them in uniform. The transformation was a huge success. As an evolutionary strain, National Socialism was much more robust and aggressive than the dreamy, internationalist idealism of the Second International. Here again, the results were just the opposite of what had been expected. Instead of promoting peace, socialism became the most militaristic, warmongering creed on the planet.

Twenty years after World War I, the US government was still scratching its head—wondering how it ever got involved in such a pointless and costly exercise. A committee was set up in Congress to look into the matter. Two years later, the Nye Committee reported that between 1915 and April 1917, the United States loaned Germany $27 million ($470,000,000 adjusted for inflation in 2005 dollars). During that same period, US loans to Britain and its allies totaled $2.3 billion ($40,000,000,000 adjusted for inflation in 2005 dollars). The committee concluded that Americans had entered the war for commercial reasons and on the side of the Allies because it had 85 times as much money at stake.

At least the numbers made sense, from the Americans' point of view. What never quite made sense was why the Europeans went to war in the first place. Many unsatisfying books have been written on the subject. The problem is not that they are incorrect or are not useful explanations; they are reasons as good as any. It is just that they are not sufficient. Looking back nearly 100 years later, we can't see what people got so worked up about. It might just as well have been a religious war, a War of the Roses, or the crusade against the Albigensians.

War is rarely taken up with a cool head. And looking in the head for reasons is as futile as looking for dignity on television. A better place to look is in the heart. Once the mob's sentiment is roused for war, there is practically no stopping it. Mass emotions—whether in the stock market or in war—are infectious. In practically no time, the whole population clamors for uniforms and murder.

"My darling One and beautiful . . ." Winston Churchill began a letter to his wife on July 28, 1914. "Everything tends toward catastrophe, and collapse. I am interested, geared-up and happy."[26] What a rush of excitement swept through Europe in the summer of 1914. Something new. Something big. Something magnificent was underway.

"Strangers spoke to one another in the streets," wrote Stefan Zweig. The Austrian author was a Jew. Later, he would flee another mass movement, but this one, in 1914, he found to his tastes: "People who had avoided each other for years shook hands, everywhere one saw excited faces. Each individual experienced an exaltation of his ego, he was no longer the isolated person of former times, he had been incorporated into the mass, he was part of the people, and his person, his hitherto unnoticed person, had been given meaning."[27]

There's nothing like a good war to give meaning to empty lives.

"War is the health of the state," Bismarck had said.[28] The European states never felt better than at the beginning of World War I. The words of politicians were reported in all the papers. People who would otherwise have never been noticed by the masses were treated as though they were rock stars or sports heroes. Young men lined up to volunteer in the state's armies. Young women joined nursing associations, whose goals were not to take care of people, but to fix up the injured warriors so they could return to battle as quickly as possible. Mothers were honored for their willingness to sacrifice sons to the war effort. Even factory workers were encouraged to think of their work as noble, even glorious—for they were supplying the matériel that made the war possible. Suddenly, everyone had a job to do, an important job.

There was a sense that a war would be good for the spirit and maybe the soul. Poets longed for war to end the "opulence of peace." They saw themselves as suffering from bourgeois prosperity—growing pale, rotting at desks, growing effete over polite dinner conversation. "Today's man," wrote Dezso Kosztolanyi just after the war broke out, ". . . grown up in a hothouse, pale and sipping tea—greets this healthy brutality enthusiastically. Let the storm come and sweep out our salons."[29] Philosopher Max Scheler welcomed the war as "an almost metaphysical awakening from the empty existence of a leaden sleep."[30] Wyndham Lewis wrote that "killing somebody must be the greatest pleasure in existence: either like killing yourself without being interested by the instinct of self-preservation—or exterminating the instinct of self-preservation itself."[31]

While the intellectuals saw the war as "deadly enlivening," to use Rainer Rilke's phrase, the common people were titillated, too. Butchers and clerks went home in crisp new uniforms and wives fell in love with them all over again. Freud remarked that his libido had been mobilized for war.

The leaders had their own private joys and sorrows . . . and their own empty lives to fill. Wilson's first wife died in early 1914. German Chancellor Theobald von Bethmann-Hollweg's wife had died in May 1914. Would he have been so eager for war in July if she had still been alive in June? General Count Franz Conrad von Hotzendorf longed to be a war hero, it was said, so he could win the heart of his beloved Gina von Reininghaus, inconveniently married to someone else. And poor Kaiser Wilhelm; would he have been better at avoiding war if his mother had not rejected him? (The Kaiser had a withered arm, said to be the cause of his mother's coldness toward him.) Wilhelm was "not quite sane," in the judgment of more than one observer at the time. "The Kaiser is like a balloon," Bismarck had said of him. "If you don't hold onto the string you never know quite where he will be off to."[32]

Why look for the causes of such a preposterous war deep in the *-isms* that fill history books? The real causes are closer at hand—in the pompous twit of a pedant like Wilson or the bluster of Theodore Roosevelt or in Wilhelm's insecure strut and Bethmann-Hollweg's broken heart. They, and millions more, found the prospect of a short, sanitary war charmingly distracting.

WILSON'S WAR

America had no dog in the European fight. During his reelection battle of 1916, Woodrow Wilson correctly read the public mind. "He kept us out of war," was his campaign slogan.

But there was no glory in sitting on the sidelines. Wilson longed to get into it and imagined that he could transform the war—and the world that came out of it—in his own image. First, it would be a world war, not one confined to the Europeans. And, second, it would have a high-minded purpose: to free the world from tyranny. Never before had such a bloody enterprise been undertaken for what appeared to be such a high-minded reason.

The reasons were just fluff. The real reasons were the same sordid, complex instincts that always lure people to war and ruin. Even the dumbest species have their alphas and omegas—their lead dogs and their drones and mules.

"If it a fearful thing to lead this great peaceful people into war, into the most terrible and disastrous of all wars, civilization itself seeming to be in the balance. But the right is more precious than peace, and we shall fight for the things we have always carried in our hearts," said Wilson.

"To such a task we can dedicate our lives and our fortunes, everything that we are and everything that we have, with the pride of those who know that America is privileged to spend her blood and her might for the principles that gave her birth and happiness and the peace which she has treasured. God helping her, she can do no other."[33]

With this last whoosh of inflated language, the empty bubbles of Mr. Wilson's rhetoric practically exploded. Since the Gettysburg Address, no one in US history had said such a preposterous thing in public that wasn't followed by contemptuous laughter. But it was hardly the last time Americans were to hear such things. In 1961, President Kennedy offered another blank check to the forces of improvement: "We will pay any price, bear any burden, meet any hardship, support any friend, oppose any foe, in order to assure the survival and the success of liberty."[34]

(Science may be cumulative, but war, finance, and love operate in cycles. After 14 years of paying for the Vietnam War, Americans figured it was time to retrench. Richard Nixon addressed the sentiment of the time at his inauguration in 1973: "The time has passed when America will make every other nation's conflict our own, or make every other nation's future our responsibility, or presume to tell the people of other nations how to manage their own affairs."[35] Nixon was wrong. The time had not passed—it was hardly beginning.)

A cynic might dismiss Wilson's high-mindedness as pure claptrap. But it was more than that. The professor of government had managed to take an idea and turn it inside out. He now proposed to waste America's blood on what was practically the exact opposite of the "principles that gave America birth" and squander the happiness and peace she treasured in the process. The Founding Fathers couldn't have cared less about whether Germany or England won the war, to say nothing of the government structure in those countries. They almost certainly would have despised Wilson's busy-bodying. If they had been subject to the Espionage and Sedition Acts that Wilson put in place to stifle criticism, they probably would have revolted all over again.

Then, as now, critics hacked away at the limbs and branches of Wilson's war fever. What else could they do? They challenged the leafy reasons. None could get at the noxious roots.

After Wilson's speech, practically every member of Congress was on his feet. Amid yelps and war whoops, the world's greatest deliberative body convulsed with excitement. Finally, the war was on.

But there was one important exception: Senator Robert La Follette. A founder of the Progressive Party, La Follette was one of the reasons Woodrow Wilson was elected in the first place. The progressives split the Republican Party vote in two, leaving Wilson—the Democrat—with a 42% majority, and so he won on a fluke. La Follette represented Wisconsin, with a large German American population. But his resistance to war fever seemed to come from his own resources; he held to it longer than politically necessary. He argued against it so strongly that his colleagues thought he was committing political suicide. Many couldn't help but wonder: Is La Follette mad? According to some papers, he was a "Benedict Arnold." He was a "Judas Iscariot," said others. Students at the Massachusetts Institute of Technology burned him in effigy, and when La Follette left the Capitol after giving his spirited challenge to the war, another colleague handed him a rope.

But Fighting Bob was not easily bullied, not even after Senator Ollie James of Kentucky rushed at him with a gun in hand. Fortunately for the Wisconsin delegation, Senator Harry Lane of Oregon attacked James with a file and several other senators tackled him.

People were in no mood for question marks. The questions typically come later. In a bubble, or an empire, things that would seem preposterous and absurd under other circumstances—stocks at 200 times earnings, getting yourself killed for no apparent reason—become commonplace. Doubt and skepticism give way to fever.

"It is no time for criticism of the president, of the cabinet, of Congress. . . . It is time for one hundred percent Americanism," said the sage Senator William Squire Kenyon of Iowa.[36] He might have said that it was time to get drunk and dance naked around a fire. The leading politicians were ready for anything as long as it was hysterical. By this time, the superpatriots were out in force and cranked up to 150% Americanism. There were rumors that the Huns were stirring up an invasion from Mexico—with an army made up of Mexicans and "armed Negroes." In an exhibition game, baseball legend Ty Cobb beat up another player, Buck Herzog, yelling "German!" People who opposed the war were being accused of cowardice.

In Tulsa, Oklahoma, a crowd hauled a Bulgarian immigrant out of a bar and lynched him. They mistook him for a German. All over the country, people declared they hated Germans, though none knew why. People changed their names to avoid sounding too Teutonic. The *New York Tribune* carried a phony story about a German factory that had been converted to turn corpses into soap.[37] Nothing was too absurd.

Even after the war, the momentum of hatred took years to halt. The British continued their blockade of German ports and tightened it after the Armistice was declared. Thousands of Germans—especially children—starved to death. But so what? said Georges Clemenceau, the prime minister of France

There were 20 million too many Germans anyway, reasoned the French premier.[38]

Finally, at 4 p.m. on April 4, two days after the president's appeal for war, Senator La Follette took the floor of the Senate. Why should Congress get behind the president, he wanted to know. Wilson had been wrong about other things, mightn't he be wrong again?

What about the charge that Germany was sinking ships? Isn't that what nations at war are supposed to do? England had put on a blockade of Germany. Germany had retaliated with its own blockade. US ships could respect the blockades or not. But they shouldn't meekly consent to the English blockade of German ports while being indignant about Germany's blockade of England.

La Follette spoke for 2 hours and 45 minutes. He ended with tears streaming down his face, for he knew that his words were not enough. He might have been explaining to a pack of hounds why they should let the rabbit go. According to Gilson Gardner, it was "the best speech we will . . . ever hear." [39] But blood was up all over America already. It didn't matter what La Follette said. He was wasting his breath.

Much of what he said concerned who was at fault for the war. Wilson and the warmongers maintained it was Germany's fault. Germany had invaded poor little Belgium, whose neutrality was guaranteed by all the major combatants—including Germany. Yet, Belgium was not really neutral at all; she had signed a secret agreement with Britain.

Germany had started the war, said the Wilsonians. But on the evidence, the Huns no more wanted war than anyone else. The Kaiser himself had tried to stop it. The war began amid a flurry of troop mobilizations, ultimatums, and declarations of war on all sides. Who was really guilty of having begun the war? Who was the aggressor?

Albert Einstein signed a declaration asserting that Germany was innocent. It had not broken international law by invading Belgium, said the text. Nor had Germany committed atrocities against the civilian populations of France and Belgium. In fact, the declaration went on to say that the future of European civilization depended on a German victory. And practically every professor at every German university agreed.

Even old enemies admitted, after the fact, that Germany was no more to blame than anyone else. Lloyd George, Britain's former prime minister, began his memoirs in 1933 by stating that nobody wanted the Great War and nobody expected it. Instead, the nations of Europe merely "slithered over the brink."[40]

Now, America was preparing to slither over the brink, too. Only La Follette and a handful of skeptics stood in her way.

The president claimed that Germany's submarine blockade of England constituted a "war against all nations." Why then, La Follette, wanted to know, was the United States the only one that objected to it? All of Scandinavia, Latin America, Spain—all the world's nations were affected in exactly the same way. But not a single one of them even protested Germany's decision. Certainly, none of them saw the action as a declaration of war.

And then, there was the claim that Germany was under the heel of a "Prussian autocracy." So what, La Follette might have said. What business is it of ours how Germany governs herself? The Wisconsin senator guessed that the average German was more likely to back his government's war effort than Americans were to back Wilson's intervention in Germany's war. And if Wilson was sure of the contrary, let him prove it. Put the matter to a referendum.

But America's entry into what became World War I was never subjected to a popular vote. Democracy is all very well, as long as it takes you where you want to go. Besides, who would really trust the bumpkins to vote on something so important? Wilson knew what was best for everyone—US voters as well as Germans. With little more debate, the US Congress voted to back the president. Only one member, apart perhaps from La Follette, seems to have had any idea what was at stake. William J. Stone, of Missouri, told his colleagues: "I won't vote for this war because if we go into it, we will never again have this same old Republic."[41] The newspapers practically accused him of treason.

Stone was right, but that was the point of the war: to make the United States into an empire. Wilson was proposing to cross the Atlantic as Alexander had crossed the Hellespont and Caesar had crossed the Rubicon.

Every great public movement—and almost every empire—begins in deceit, develops into farce, and ends in disaster. Wilson's war was no different. The idea of making the world safe for democracy was pure humbug. The Europeans had been fighting for two years. If it was a fight for democracy, it came as news to them. After the fighting was over, the French and English laughed at Wilson and ignored his Fourteen Points whenever they conflicted with their own interests. "Mr. Wilson bores me with his Fourteen Points," said Clemenceau, puncturing the American's bubble, "Why, God Almighty only has ten."[42]

The US president was appalled and humiliated; he suffered a stroke and never recovered.

Was the world any safer for democracy at the end? Not on the evidence. Just the opposite; in the aftermath of the war, and Wilson's inept settlement, arose democracy's most aggressive and ruthless opponents—men who had ambitions to empire themselves and few scruples about how to achieve it.

ARMISTICE DAY

Finally, 18 months after the United States entered the war, it was over. In much of Europe, the end is still recalled. At 11 a.m. on the 11th day of the 11th month, bells toll in France. In Britain, everything goes silent. The remembrance is for all the millions of young men who began putting on uniforms in August 1914. These wet, furry balls were plucked from towns all over Europe, put on trains, and sent toward the fighting. Back home, mothers, fathers, and bar owners unrolled maps so they could follow the progress of the men and boys they loved and trace, with their fingers, the glory and gravity of war.

It was a war unlike any other the world had seen. Aging generals looked to the lessons of the US War Between the States or the Franco-Prussian War of 1870 for clues as to how the war might proceed. But there were no precedents for what was to happen. It was a new era in warfare.

People were already familiar with the promise of the machine age. They had seen it coming, developing, building for a long time. They had even changed the language they used to reflect this new understanding of how things worked. In his book, *Devil Take the Hindmost,* Edward Chancellor recalls how the railway investment mania had caused people to talk about "getting up steam" or "heading down the track" or "being on the right track."[43] All these new metaphors would have been mysteriously nonsensical prior to the Industrial Age. The new technology had changed the way people thought and the way they spoke.

World War I showed the world that the new paradigm had a deadly power beyond what anyone expected. At the outbreak of the war, German forces followed Alfred von Schlieffen's plan. They wheeled from the north and drove the French Army before them. Soon the French were retreating down the Marne Valley near Paris. And it looked as though the Germans would soon be victorious.

The German generals believed the French were broken. Encouraged, General von Kluck departed from the plan; instead of taking Paris, he decided to chase the French Army, retreating adjacent to the city, in hopes of destroying it completely. But there was something odd; there were relatively few prisoners. An army that is breaking up usually throws off lots of prisoners.

As it turned out, the French Army had not been beaten. It was retreating in good order. And when Galieni, the old French general, saw what was happening—German troops moving down the Marne only a few miles from Paris—he uttered the famous remark, "Gentlemen, they offer us their flank."

Galieni attacked, driving soldiers to the front line in Paris taxicabs. The Germans were beaten back and the war became a trench-war nightmare of machine guns, mustard gas, barbed wire, and artillery.

By the time the United States entered the war, the poet Rupert Brooke was already dead, and the life expectancy for a soldier on the front lines was just 21 days.

One by one, the people back at home got the telegrams, the letters. The church bells rang. The black cloth came out. And, one by one, the maps were rolled up. Fingers forgot the maps and clutched nervously at crosses and cigarettes. There was no glory left, just tears.

Another poet's mother got the sad news on Armistice Day. A telegram arrived informing the family that Wilfred Owen had been killed. Coming as it did on the day the war ended, the news must have brought more than just grief. "What was the point?" they must have wondered.

Wilfred Owen had wondered, too. His poetry mocked the glory of war. He described soldiers who had been gassed as "gargling" their way to death from "froth-corrupted lungs." Owen saw many men die; it was neither sweet nor glorious, he observed, but ghastly.

It doesn't seem quite right that so many people should have died for nothing. People can't stand the idea. It leaves a hole, a huge gap that the brain labors to fill. Otherwise, the deaths have no meaning. It is not enough to appreciate bravery and self-sacrifice for its own sake. It must make sense. So, bring out the humbug!

Canadian soldiers were among the best colonial troops, said the press report, and the most likely to be killed. If dying in war is sweet, the Newfoundlanders got the most cavities. One out of four of the 6,000 men of the Newfoundland Regiment never returned home. But "nothing matched the toll of the massacre at Beaumont-Hamel on the western front on July 1, 1916," reports the *Toronto Globe and Mail*. "About 800 Newfoundlanders charged out of their trenches into the teeth of German machine-gunfire. They had been told that the Germans would be weakened by intense bombardment, that the lethal strings of thick barbed wire strewn across no man's land would be gone and that another regiment would join them. None of it was true. The next morning, only 68 members of the regiment answered the roll call.

"One eyewitness said the Newfoundlanders advanced into the hail of bullets with their chins tucked into their necks, as they might weather an ocean storm."[44]

Then, the old lie swallowed them up, like a tempest.

In the small villages of France hardly a family was spared. Every small town has its monument in a central location to *Nos Heros . . . Mort Pour La France*. Often, the list of names seems longer than the present population. And still people wonder, what happened? We can turn to Wilson's bogus explanation or any one of hundreds. The capitalists are to blame! It's the Germans fault! If only European nations had been democracies! If only Princip had missed his mark!

But there is another way to understand the Great War: A bull market in death began in August 1914; it probably would have ended in 1916 or 1917 but for the fresh new resources of the United States. Wilson longed to give the war meaning by using it to turn America into a world-improving, hegemonic power. All he had to do, he thought, was to prevent an early settlement of the war giving him time to help the French and English win a total victory rather than a negotiated peace. Then, he believed, he would be the true victor. He could come to Europe like an archangel at a Catholic school picnic. He would walk across the Atlantic and impose his Fourteen Points on the world as if they were written on clay tablets and had been handed to him by God.

MAKING THE WORLD SAFE FOR DEMOCRACY

When Woodrow Wilson stood before Congress and asked for a declaration of war against Germany, the words came out of the advanced part of the brain. They were the nice, multisyllabic, Latinate words you would expect from a former professor of government. They were not simple, honest words, but greasy and meaningless ones, also just what you would expect. It was the kind of bosh you find on a typical high-minded editorial page. It was as if the president opened his mouth and brightly colored bubbles popped out. Airily . . . lightly . . . they floated above the crowds, who craned their necks upward in admiration and awe. They didn't seem to mind that the words were empty. They were gaudy; that was all that seemed to matter.

Wilson's talk of making the world safe for democracy was nothing more than gas. He was proposing to go into the war on the side of the English, who were at that very moment suppressing democracy all over the globe. The Irish, the Indians, the Egyptians—the US president didn't even mention them. Had the upper brain been allowed to do its work, surely it would have told him that if he wanted to make the world safe for democracy, he ought to ask some questions of the nation that held it in check. As a matter of logic he might just as well have entered the war on the side of Germany against England.

But buried deep in the president's sly brain were idealized pictures of the Magna Carta, the robes and wigs of English judges, high tea at the Savoy, Dickens and Thackeray—all the trappings of the English upper classes as they were imagined by a naive and admiring college professor from Princeton, New Jersey. The president, his advisors, his cabinet, and his leading allies had such bad cases of anglophilia, they practically stuttered and drooled. And when they stirred the mob with big words, the gaudy balloons they sent aloft meant nothing more than a signal that the fight had begun. The poor schmucks' blood was up already. All it took was a reason and they were ready to die.

A moment of real thought by firing a few synapses in the upper lateral prefrontal cortex would have shown what a losing proposition the European war would likely be. But whatever thinking was taking place was deeper down in the limbic system, not in the lateral prefrontal cortex.

Wilson had already made his decision. And the public, too, was soon engaged. The cannons were drawn up. Medals were polished. In no time at all, people were on their knees pledging all they had to the war effort, giving up their purses, their sons, and their integrity. Around the country, superpatriots were drilling holes through their walls so they could spy on neighbors with names like Bauer and Feldgenhauer. In Baltimore, a former mayor blew his brains out after being charged with being a German sympathizer. Anyone who dared to laugh or cry was soon doing penance or doing time.

War appeals to the limbic system like a new pair of shoes. The yahoos grow taller when war is announced. And when people walk, they take on a proud martial air. Looking around them, they see the bright shine of polished brass and of bombs exploding in air and they are drawn to them like sinners to the sparkling gates of hell. Politicians feel the need to explain it, to justify it, to dress it up in respectable clothes to hide the jackboots and to slosh on perfume to cover the stench of death. But the words mean nothing. When the sentiments in the limbic system are ready for it, the common people are as eager for war as they are for an extension of their line of credit.

World War I turned out to be a catastrophe as meaningless and senseless as Wilson's words. We look at it here because it marks the beginning of the US imperium. It helps explain today's world. Now, as then, the yahoos cheer a new group of "Wilsonian" officials. Once again, they think they are making the world safe for democracy. Once again, they believe that almost no price is too heavy for the benefits of the better world they imagine. And once again, they soften up the nation's heads and its money to pay for it.

But it is not the same world that we had in 1917. It is Wilson's world now, the world he helped to make. America is no longer the rising power; China is rising now. America is in Britain's World War I position, trying to hold on to its commercial edge against newer, more aggressive rivals. Americans are no longer lean and hungry for work and profit; now they are the fattest people on the planet and have grown used to living off the hard work of others. What used to pay for Americans were the virtues of hard work, thrift, self-discipline, and minding their own business. Americans were virtuous until Wilson took over. Since then, they have given up on what used to pay in favor of what seems to pay now—meddling, borrowing, and spending—overseas as well as at home.

In the private sphere, a delusional man is soon impoverished, friendless, powerless, and hopeless. All he can do at that point is run for public office, because in public life, foolish arguments have fewer and less immediate consequences. It is in public life, that people get carried away with reason. "History is an argument without end," said Pieter Geyl.[45]

One nation argues that it must dominate its neighbors because it needs "living room." Another says it has a manifest destiny to do so. One public leader says he must create a "co-prosperity sphere." Another says he will make the world safe for democracy. None of these flourishes are rooted in logic or reason, but in the rich, fetid loam of the heart.

Within every world improver and empire builder lurks a vain animal—displaying his tail feathers. And within every democratic assembly is a bunch of stags in rut, waiting for an opportunity to butt heads and make a public spectacle of themselves. For it is neither love nor money that makes the world go 'round—but vanity. Wilson had no particular love and not much money. King George V drew his measure as accurately as Freud, calling him "an entirely cold academic professor—an odious man."[46] But vanity he had in abundance.

PAYING FOR WAR

Nothing softens money up as fast as war. The shells pound it. The bullets puncture it. Armies march on it. And politicians and central bankers stretch it out to the point that it inevitably breaks. Nothing much has changed in the 110 years since the guns of August boomed across the Western Front in Europe.

In July 1914, all the major belligerents were on the gold standard—along with 44 other countries. The system was simple and effective. It had fostered an international financial climate so conducive to the growth of capital and trade that most of the West had never been more prosperous. Central banks of the various nations held gold in their coffers. The gold was used to back up the paper currencies. If a nation spent too much on external products, its currency flowed to foreign countries. It came back in payment for either goods or services supplied by the home country. In the event of an imbalance, that is to say, when a foreign nation found itself with more of the nation's currency than it could spend on goods and services from that nation, the resulting surplus currency was presented to the central bank to be replaced by gold. Every nation's imbalances were settled in the one thing that none of them could print or counterfeit: gold. If a nation ran a persistent trade deficit, it would find its gold pulled away. This would encourage the central bank to do something to protect it. Usually, interest rates rose, which had the effect of rewarding savings and discouraging the outflow of funds.

The system was neat. It was honest. Which made it ill-suited to the needs of war and empire builders. War, particularly, was distressingly expensive. Politicians noticed—as monarchs had long ago—that people might be enthralled by the cannon fire, but they hated to pay for it. Typically, according to R.S. Hamilton-Grace, who studied English war financing, about a 70% of the cost of war had to be covered by borrowing.[47]

Gold was famously uncooperative. It yielded neither to flattery nor to technology. You couldn't pretend it was worth more than it was. And you couldn't create more "out of thin air." Each ounce needed to be dug up out of the earth—at considerable expense. Increasing the money supply—no matter how glorious or worthwhile the cause—was a difficult thing to do. Central banks had only so much gold. If they wanted more, it had to come from somewhere. It had to be saved, put away, stored. The old expression "you can't get something for nothing" seemed to have been coined to describe the yellow metal. Every ounce of it represented an ounce of thrift, a pound of self-discipline, and a ton of forbearance. It represented money that had not been spent on new clothes, or guns, or food, or entertainment, lodging, tools, roads, or a million other potential uses. Gold was so hard to get that central banks were reluctant to let it go. Kings used to castrate the keepers of their royal mints if they let the gold slip away, either through chicanery or lack of attention. Central bankers were naturally careful with the stuff; caution was in their blood. They knew that if they issued too much paper—that is, if they allowed too many claims against their horde of gold—they risked having it taken from them.

However, war also was a serious matter. And central banks were asked to help finance the war. This difficult position was made even worse in 1914 when the threat of war caused a drop in stock prices—wiping out much of the liquidity that might be sopped up for wartime finance. The European nations needed to borrow vast amounts to cover the war expenses. But each additional unit of currency further reduced the gold cover or the ability of the borrowing nation to pay its debts with real money.

Readers will be quick to notice the parallels to the global financial system of 2005. The Europeans wanted to increase the consumption of war matériel. Now, Americans consume other things as if they were fighting for their lives. Cannons and bullets were not much different from big-screen TVs and automobiles; they were quickly used up with no economic progress to show for it. From 1914 to 1918, France and Britain needed US financing to conduct war beyond their means. Now, America turns to its principal suppliers in Asia and asks for credit. Without it, the United States cannot continue consuming at its present rate. In 1914, the world's most important supplier was the United States. France, Britain, and Russia (and to a much lesser extent, Germany, early in the war) had to turn to the United States for supplies. But since they consumed more than they earned, they put their gold reserves at risk. France dealt with this problem early on by simply going off the gold standard. Britain remained on the gold standard throughout the war, barely, but only by the grace of US creditors.

Fortunately for Britain, the United States did not force the issue. (Fortunately for America 90 years later, its major creditors in Asia do not seem to want to force the issue either—at least, not yet. Even without a gold standard, China and Japan could wreak havoc with the dollar any time they chose. For the moment, like America in 1914 to 1916, they are happy to take the orders and increase market share, knowing that their major customer cannot really afford to pay for all that they send her.)

As the war grew more and more grim, not only was the honest money of the gold standard abandoned by most belligerents but also the export of gold to settle accounts was expressly forbidden (under cover of fear that the gold would fall into enemy hands). Each nation began increasing its supply of money, issuing more paper currency, borrowing more and more money from foreign (mostly American) and domestic sources, and spending far beyond its means.

France was already heavily in debt when the war began, with a consolidated debt in July 1914 of 27,000 million francs, in arrears already by 967 million. Normally, the French assembly resisted—however weakly—plans to spend more money. But with war cries in their ears and the Huns at the Somme, the peoples' representatives got in the habit of merely rubber-stamping any request that came their way. They voted for credits of 22,804.5 million francs in 1915—an amount that rose every year, reaching 54,537.1 million in 1918. In practice, the government spent far more than the credits that had been voted, using special accounts that we might call "off budget" accounts similar to those used by the Bush administration to pay for the war in Iraq. In 1920, 30,000 million francs—an amount nearly equal to the nation's entire prewar debt—passed through the special accounts (see Figure 5.1).

When America entered the war, its expenditures outdid the other combatants, averaging $42.8 million per day from July 1917 until June 1919. Total federal expenditure rose 2,454% in the three years 1916 to 1919. The Federal Reserve issued more and more paper notes; the supply rose by 754% between March 1917 and December 1919. The overall money supply increased 60% between 1913 and 1918, while GDP increased only 13%. The government raised money partly by taxing people much more heavily and partly by borrowing

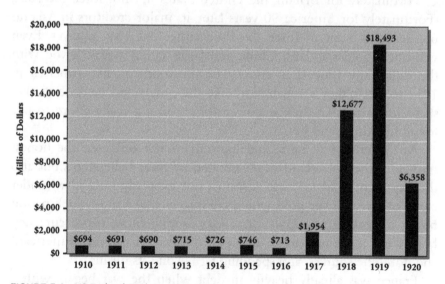

FIGURE 5.1 US Federal Outlays, 1910–1920

Woodrow Wilson is best remembered for his desire to "make the world safe for democracy." However, his involvement in World War I was costly. The one and only respect in which the war paid off was that it turned America into an empire.

Source: U.S. Government Publishing Office, Public Domain.

from them. Four "Liberty Loans" were floated during the war years. At the war's end, a "Victory Loan" was offered.

All of this borrowing, spending, and taxing left the world's major economies—especially those in Europe—very fragile. After the war was over, they all attempted to return to the prewar gold standard that had worked so well for so long. But they were like the farmers going out to plow their fields in northeastern France; they kept hitting unexploded bombs and blowing themselves up.

Wilson's meddling was disastrous from practically every point of view—except one. The war continued for another 18 months. Not a single major government in Europe survived in its prewar form. "In 1914, Europe was a single civilized community . . ." wrote A.J.P. Taylor, "A man could travel across the length and breadth of the Continent without a passport until he reached . . . Russia and the Ottoman empire. He could settle in a foreign country for work or leisure without legal formalities. . . . Every currency was as good as gold."[48] In 1919, European civilization was a wreck, out of which tough new menaces would be hammered—first in Russia, then in Italy and Germany. Nor did any currency buy as much at the end of the war as it did at the beginning. All the principal belligerents, with the exception of the United States, were forced off the gold standard. The one and only respect in which the war paid off was that it turned America into an empire.

And here we pick up the trail and follow the money that leads to America's empire of debt.

CHAPTER 6

A GREAT DEPRESSION

Readers of this book will scarcely have given any thought to the fact that they have never lived in the system of government argued for by Madison, Jay, and Hamilton in *The Federalist Papers*. "It may come as a shock. . . ," wrote John Flynn, "to be told that [you] have never experienced that kind of society which [our] ancestors knew as the American Republic. . . ." Flynn, the editor of the popular weekly, *The Saturday Evening Post*, had already come to this conclusion in 1955. In his book *The Decline of the American Republic*, Flynn observed that Americans needlessly "live in the war-torn, debt-ridden, tax-harried wreckage of a once imposing edifice of the free society which arose out of the American Revolution on the foundation of the U.S. Constitution."[1]

An empire needs a source of income sufficient to fund its military campaigns, regulatory regimes, and domestic schemes. It also needs a strong central authority to direct its ambitious new programs. In one short 12-month span, a year the writer Frank Chodorov calls the "Revolution of 1913," the empire got the tools it needed. That year—the same year European countries abandoned the gold standard in preparation for World War I—the old Republic ceased to exist.[2]

WHERE THE MONEY COMES FROM

America's current system of income tax is a 20th-century invention. Previous attempts at creating a national tax had failed or had been thrown out because they violated tenets of the Constitution deemed essential by the founders. In its first 100 years, the United States supported its federal government with a series of what we would today call "sin taxes" on whiskey, tobacco, and sugar. By 1817, all internal taxes were abolished by Congress, leaving only tariffs on imported goods as a means for supporting the government.

The first income tax that citizens of the young Republic were forced to endure came about because Congress had been asked to fund the War Between the States. In 1862, a tax on incomes between $600 and $10,000 was assessed at the rate of 3%, and the Internal Revenue Service (IRS) was created. The war was costing $1.75 million per day.[3] The government sold off land, borrowed heavily, enacted various fees, and increased excise taxes, but it simply wasn't enough. The income tax seemed like the only way to finance the war and service the country's then-staggering $505 million debt. That tax was promoted as a temporary wartime measure. Temporary it was. In 1872, after servicing the Reconstruction, Congress yanked the "temporary" tax.

But that was not the end of it. The income tax appealed to empire builders because it alone offered enough cash to finance the enterprise. But it had another appeal—to the larceny and envy in the hearts of ordinary citizens. Following a banking panic in 1893, Senator William Peffer of Kansas supported the progressive income tax in this way: "Wealth is accumulated in New York, and not because those men are more industrious than we are, not because they are wiser and better, but because they trade, because they buy and sell, because they deal in usury, because they reap in what they have never earned, because they take in and live off what other men earn. . . . The West and the South have made you people rich."[4]

That sentiment was puffed up by Nebraska's bellicose world-improver William Jennings Bryan, who argued against the "equal taxation" requirement in the Constitution, in favor of the current progressive one: "If New York and Massachusetts pay more tax under this law than other states, it will be because they have more taxable incomes within their borders. And why should not those sections pay most which enjoy most?"[5]

This logic is simple. People who are more productive should be forced to pay a bigger share of their common expenses. But this kind of logic had no place in a free republic where all people were supposedly created equal; if they were equal they could each carry their own share of the burden of central government. Under this new regime, people were no longer equal, but given differing loads to carry based on the whims of elected hacks.

With considerable foresight, one member of the House of Representatives predicted: "The imposition of the [income] tax will corrupt the people. It will bring in its train the spy and the informer. It will necessitate a swarm of officials with inquisitorial powers. It will be a step toward centralization. . . . It breaks another canon of taxation in that it is expensive in its collection and cannot be fairly imposed . . . and, finally, it is contrary to the traditions and principles of republican government."[6]

When the tax was again introduced in 1894, a challenge went to the US Supreme Court. In 1895, even among the cacophony of appeals in Congress to "soak the rich," the Supreme Court declared the bill unconstitutional in a 5-to-4 ruling. In writing the majority opinion, Justice Stephen J. Field quoted another case to support his conclusion: "As stated by counsel: 'There is no such thing in the theory of our national government as unlimited power of taxation in congress. There are limitations, as he justly observes, of its powers arising out of the essential nature of all free governments; there are reservations of individual rights, without which society could not exist, and which are respected by every government. The right of taxation is subject to these limitations.'"[7]

But when the winds of empire blew, the old yellowed paper of the US Constitution went flying. Following The Panic of 1907, President Theodore Roosevelt sided with a faction in the Democratic Party that wanted to amend the Constitution to allow a national income tax. In 1909, President Taft stated that he had "become convinced that a great majority of the people of this country are in favor of vesting the National Government with power to levy an income tax."[8]

Of course, politicians are always able and willing to argue that "the people" want a government to have more power. If the voters see a free lunch in the deal, they're for it. By 1913, just in time for Wilson's emergence on the world stage, the Sixteenth Amendment had been ratified by enough states to put the income tax into law. The Amendment states: "The Congress shall have power to lay and collect taxes on incomes, from whatever source derived, without apportionment among the several states, and without regard to any census or enumeration."[9]

It wasn't long before Congress exercised its new powers. Wilson even convened a special session of Congress to rush through the first tax law under the Sixteenth Amendment, in which earnings above $3,000 were subject to a 1% tax, gradually moving up to 7% on higher income levels.

With its rather modest rates, the original income tax was viewed as a benign inconvenience. As early as 1916, however, the top rate was more than doubled from 7% up to 15%. Then as cash was needed to send Pershing to France, the rate was hiked to a staggering 67% in 1917 and 77% by 1918. Even the low rates were raised. From their microscopic origin of only 1%, the rate settled into a "modest" 23% by the end of World War II. But by that time, the people of the old republic had grown to accept an income tax as a necessary evil. Now that the nation was an empire, it needed the money.

In our present era, the complexity of the Internal Revenue Code has created an army of specialized lawyers and accountants. Even attempts at reform are out of control. A "technical corrections" bill exceeds 900 pages of adjustments. In fact, by the beginning of the 21st century, the tax codes exceeded 7 million words, about nine times longer than the Bible; and the IRS was sending out about 8 billion pages of forms and instructions every year—at the cost of about 300,000 trees! In 2023, it has been estimated the average American spends 13 hours filling out annual tax forms. Multiplied by the number of known taxpayers in the nation (160 million), all this effort translates to about 2.1 trillion hours spent every year by individual Americans just complying with the tax rules. Our calculator strains trying to calculate the number.

From 1913 to 2024, the income tax has enabled, entitled, empowered, and engorged the federal government, states, and local governments, private enterprises, and millions of private citizens. Spending has grown by more than 13,592%. In 2024 the government "guestimate" is they will spend another $9.46 trillion, up another 10% from the post-pandemic year 2023.

The income tax gives the federal government a blank check to spend money, even money it does not yet have. The federal government lays a claim on all future economic activity of its citizens; its massive debts are a lien on the earnings of people who have not yet even drawn their first breaths. What's more, the income tax could be used as both an economic tool and as a political weapon. Tax rates could be manipulated, for example, to punish or reward favored political groups.

When the Constitution was ratified in 1789, the colonists in the New World believed they had won for themselves a measure of freedom and independence. "A republic, if you can keep it," Benjamin Franklin warned. But by the end of 1913, a scant 124 years later, Americans were happy to lose their republic; an empire was what they wanted.

AMERICAN CAESARS

But the income tax was only the beginning. If one of the defining features of empire is an open-ended source of funding, another is the shift of power away from the legislature in favor of the central executive. In 1913, a second amendment tipped the scales of authority toward Washington in a way hardly conceived of in the debates of the late 18th century. When the Founding Fathers set down the rules for how senators were to be elected, they anticipated a balance between states' rights and the central government.

In its original form, the Constitution reads: "The Senate of the United States shall be composed of two Senators from each State, chosen by the Legislature thereof, for six Years; and each Senator shall have one Vote. . . . And if Vacancies happen by Resignation, or otherwise, during the Recess of the *Legislature* of any State, the *Executive* thereof may make temporary Appointments until the next Meeting of the Legislature, which shall then fill such Vacancies." The emphasis on *Legislature* and *Executive* are ours.[10]

The founding fathers saw the indirect election of senators as a means for keeping a balance of power, enabling the states to exert control over the federal legislative branch. The Senate was perceived originally as serving two roles: "Keeping one eye on states' rights and interests, and the other wary eye on the executive branch, the federal courts, and the House of Representatives. It was contemplated that members of this body would be older, wiser, more experienced, and better qualified than members of the House and members of state legislatures. Appointed Senators were expected to be somewhat isolated from knee-jerk reactions to current public debates. They would answer for their political acts to state legislatures, and only indirectly to public mobs and voters."[11]

"The preservation of the states in a certain degree of agency is indispensable," stated John Dickinson, the Delaware delegate at the 1787 Constitutional Convention, "It will produce the collision between the different authorities that should be wished for in order to check each other."[12]

James Madison, primary architect of the US Constitution, noted that indirect elections would serve as "a defense to the people against their own temporary errors and delusions [and would] blend stability with liberty."[13]

Each state—acting through its own legislature—should have the right to direct its senators how to vote on issues and how to best represent the state's interests. But along came the great humbug, William Jennings Bryan (again). He maintained the Senate was controlled by corrupt state legislatures. Bryan, who tried to win the presidency three times (in 1896, 1900, and 1908), was described by C. H. Hoebeke, Fellow in Constitutional History at the Center for Constitutional Studies: "Secretary Bryan put his seal upon the reform that, in the expectations of those who had labored for it, would end the dominance of party "bosses" and the state "machines," stamp out the undue influence of special interests in the Senate, make it more responsive to the will of the people, and of course, eliminate, or greatly reduce, the execrable practice of spending large sums of money to get elected."[14]

The Seventeenth Amendment "improved" the original way that senators were picked by making the election system more democratic. Senators would now be elected by a direct vote of the people of each state. The senators would no longer have to answer to the legislature of their respective states, effectively making them citizens of Washington and answerable directly to the federal government. The ills of indirect democracy would thereby be cured . . . by more direct democracy.[15]

To the modern reader, the direct election of senators by popular vote might seem like a subtle footnote in the history of the nation. But as so often happens in the annals of world improvement, the cure was worse than the malady. Corruption and undue influence were not undone by the amendment; they were simply shifted to Washington. The states were reduced to vestiges of their former selves.

Taken together, the Sixteenth and Seventeenth Amendments greatly increased the power of the central government. The original constitutional system involved taxing power at the state level, with revenues submitted to the federal government for the funding of common needs (raising an army, protecting the coast, printing money). Since 1913, the process has been completely reversed. The federal government now collects most of the money from the income tax, and then doles out the revenue to the individual states, usually with many provisos, dictates, and commands attached. This allows the central government to exert great influence over state funding and in many areas not mentioned in the Constitution: highway speed limits, education, healthcare, medical matters, ownership of weapons, food and drug oversight, vaccines, police and law enforcement, libraries, the environment, business practices—the list is long and dreary. And now with Homeland Security and the Patriot Act, both enacted after the 9/11 attacks on the World Trade Center in New York City, the list is getting longer. In the fiscal year 2023, the Department of Homeland Security had 17 different subdivisions and a budget, allocated by Congress, of nearly $180 billion dollars.

NEW MONEY

A central bank, as the name implies, is intended as a national center for the control of currency in circulation. It referees the exchange of funds between states and their own banks, and manages debt, both domestically between banks and internationally between the host country and other governments. The republic, in the years leading up to 1913, had an uneasy relationship, at best, with the notion of a central bank.

Alexander Hamilton, first treasury secretary of the new nation, struggled with high debts from the Revolutionary War. He proposed a central bank to manage the war debt and to create a single currency. In 1791, Congress drafted a charter for the First Bank of the United States. But by 1811, the national emergency had subsided; Congress decided the bank no longer served any purpose, so it was closed.

As a consequence of closing the central bank, state banks flourished. They issued bank notes and the widespread debt-based exchange system went far beyond banking itself. The system grew like zucchini. Every location large enough to have "a church, a tavern, or a blacksmith shop was deemed a suitable place for setting up a bank," said John Kenneth Galbraith.[16] These banks issued notes, and even barbers and bartenders competed with banks in this respect.

But the delightful free-for-all banking situation couldn't last forever. Predictably, the War of 1812 ended with a large war debt and inflation rose to about 14% per year. President James Madison signed a new bill in 1816 creating the Second Bank of the United States— with the purpose of again managing debt caused by war.

By the end of the 1820s, a conflict had grown between the bank and President Andrew Jackson, who saw the system as a threat to the virtues of the republic. Jackson argued that the bank should be disbanded. Jackson prevailed, and the bank's charter was vetoed in 1832, with the Second Bank of the United States closing in 1836. The period that followed—1837 through 1862—is known as the era of "wildcat" banks; only state-chartered banks operated, limited to activities mandated by each state's laws.

The legal footing for the creation of currency is limited in the Constitution. Article 1, Section 8 permits Congress to coin money and regulate its value, and Section 10 denies the states the same right. But because any agreed-on medium serves the purpose that we associate with money (an exchange of value) there is no absolute ban on state banks issuing notes. Nor is there any reason a private individual cannot issue his own IOUs, for that matter.

At the beginning of the wildcat bank era, the Supreme Court ruled that state banks had the right to issue notes as media of exchange. When Michigan became a state in 1837, it allowed a bank to gain a charter if it met specific criteria, without also requiring permission from the state legislature. Banks came and went like nail salons. A study of 709 banks in four states found that between 1838 and 1863, half of the banks failed, and a third were not able to honor redemption of notes for gold or silver specie. Overall in the period, banks remained open only five years on average. Widely circulated bank notes—often not backed by reserves—replaced the national currency. States struggled with widespread counterfeiting, inflated note valuation, and the natural instability of the free market.

But the War Between the States brought the wildcat banking era to a crashing halt. The first National Banking Act of 1863 brought control over banking to the federal government once again. In addition to creating a uniform national banking system and a single national currency, the new law also provided a secondary market to the US Treasury to finance the growing debts of the Civil War. The change was gradual. By 1870, there were 1,638 national banks versus only 325 state banks. However, state banks continued to operate, having replaced the bank note system with a new concept: the checking account. By 1890, only about 10% of the US money supply was represented by currency. The rest was transacted primarily through the bank drafts customers used through their checking accounts.

Then, the same financial crises that induced national support for the income tax tipped the scales in favor of a permanent national banking system. The Wall Street Panic of 1907 was blamed for the worst depression in US history up to that time. Unemployment climbed to 20%. Dozens of banks failed. J. P. Morgan saved several New York banks by granting personal loans.

By 1910, Wall Street executives and Washington politicians saw an opportunity. They met at Jekyll Island off the coast of Georgia, in seclusion and secrecy, to discuss formation of a centralized monetary agency. Senator Nelson Aldrich met with executives of what is today known as Citibank; Morgan Bank; and Kuhn, Loeb Investment House. The so-called Aldrich Plan recommended the formation of 15 regional banks controlled by a national board. The banks would be allowed to make emergency loans to members and create a flexible currency, serving as the monetary arm of the federal government. Although the original plan was defeated in the House, the formula modeled what is now known as the Federal Reserve System.

The legislation, variously called the *Currency Bill* and the *Owen-Glass Act*, emerged as the Federal Reserve Act of 1913. It created a dozen regional Reserve Banks to be coordinated by a chairman who would be appointed by the president. Although the Constitution grants Congress the right to print money, under the Federal Reserve Act of 1913, Congress approved a plan to delegate this right to the Fed, which is not part of Congress. The US dollar is not issued by the US Treasury but by a privately owned organization, which also influences bank interest rates, the amount of currency in circulation, and even the levels of inflation in the United States. After months of testimony, debate, and over 3,000 pages of documentation of the hearings, the bill was passed and, on December 23, 1913, ratified and signed. For the first time, privately issued debt instruments (currency) would be issued by a private institution but guaranteed by the full faith and credit of the United States.

This last innovation—the establishment of the Federal Reserve System—plays a special role in shaping America's unique system of imperial finance, as we will see later.

A SAFETY NET

If 1913 was the year that set the stage for the empire, the 1930s were years of heavy plot development. Franklin Roosevelt's New Deal had many components but, more than anything else, it was organizing the government for its imperial tasks. In the Old Republic, the government was a referee between individuals and between states. Laws were rules of order that were intended to be relatively neutral. Relatively few laws were passed because most of what happened was thought to be out of the range of the rule makers.

But this idea of government changed radically in the 1930s. The government would no longer be accurately described as functioning solely as a law-making and law-enforcing body. This new government would make things better!

It is rarely talked about these days, but at the time the New Deal programs were being passed into law, most people believed they were intended to be temporary measures. At the very least, these programs were never thought to be the cornerstones of a long-term change in the homeland.

In 1935, when the Social Security Act was passed, the promise was that every American would have a secure, if minimal, retirement (if they beat the averages and outlived the retirement age of 65). The government, once and for all, would eliminate the common ailments related to old age—sickness, homelessness, disability, and poverty. This was a radical departure from US tradition. The New Deal created a permanent, paternal central government that has only grown more paternal and more centralized in the years since.

Franklin Roosevelt's plan for Social Security was a massive rethinking of the *state,* in the sense that the new system was much more than a simple safety net. It bound ordinary citizens to the federal government in a way that had not been imagined by the Founding Fathers. People came to rely on the state for their daily bread, and to take a much keener interest in the state itself. Traditional virtues—thrift, independence, self-reliance—were replaced with new virtues: political activism and gaming the system. In the second Roosevelt era, people came to expect the state to take care of things at home; later, they would come to expect the US government to build a better world outside the homeland, too.

While campaigning for presidency, Roosevelt had denounced Hoover as a spendthrift. The democratic platform during the campaign of 1932 called for, among other things, a drastic reduction of government spending by at least 25%, abolishing useless commissions and offices and requiring a budget balanced annually and a sound currency to be preserved at all hazards. But the country was in the throes of the Great Depression.

The causes of the Depression have been hotly debated. They go beyond the scope of this book. But the consequences of the economic setback were to spur the nation toward its imperial mission. After the crash of the stock market in 1929, and after the country had entered a deflationary depression in the 1930s, there was little that a man sitting in a chair at 16 Pennsylvania Avenue could do to avert the aftermath of the debt bubble. Soon Washington was flooded with do-gooders chomping at the bit to tell the president what to do. New books published as early as 1932 led the way. George Soule of

The New Republic penned the influential tract "A Planned Society." Stuart Chase penned another called "A New Deal." Before long, Roosevelt was awash in new ideas. With the new tools from 1913 in his hands, Roosevelt had the ability to turn screws and tighten values throughout the economy. How could he resist?

Among the ideas adopted was one pushed forward by a California physician named Francis Townsend in 1933. The Townsend Plan was designed to extinguish poverty forever. When it first hit the presses, Roosevelt was opposed. But its popularity caught on; two years later under pressure from the voters, Roosevelt introduced the Social Security Act. The organizers of the Townsend Plan became major critics of the government program, complaining that it did not provide enough assistance.

Following the establishment of the act's primary benefit, the old age insurance provision, Congress amended the law four years later to add survivors' insurance. Medicare benefits were added in 1965. By 2005, Social Security and Medicare took up 27% of the federal budget. While the program was relatively young, it was a novel idea and controversy surrounded the question of whether the program paid out enough based on the required payroll deductions people paid in. Little concern was given to whether it could remain solvent in the long term.

Other programs introduced as part of the original act included the Federal Unemployment Insurance Act, funded by a tax on employers' side of payroll, and Aid to Dependent Children, now called Aid to Families with Dependent Children. Social Security and its related legislation have expanded broadly beyond the biggest pieces: old age insurance and Medicare. The Act began institutionalization of a dual-track system, providing both old age insurance and related benefits, and the other designed to work with the states in a dollar-matching program for a vast network. Today, the overall program includes national minimum wage and child labor laws, federal disability insurance, Medicaid, public housing and rent entitlements, food stamps, and means-tested income assistance for the elderly and disabled. All these programs—outgrowths of Social Security—have expanded today to represent a large, complex, and expensive system of what the Romans called *panem et circensis*—bread and circuses (see Figure 6.1).

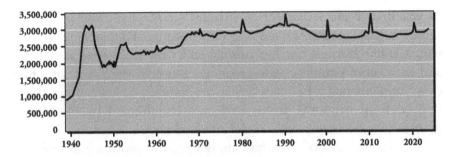

FIGURE 6.1 Number of Federal Government Employees 1936–2023

The government programs created in the 1930s have required an ever-increasing bureaucracy. All of these programs—outgrowths of Social Security—have expanded today to represent a large, complex, and expensive system of what the Romans called *panemet et circensis*—bread and circuses.
Source: U.S. Department of Labor, Public Domain.

PANEM ET CIRCENSIS

That the government should take responsibility for the needy, poor, and disabled is not a new idea at all. The Elizabethan Poor Laws were enacted in England in 1597. The individual duty to provide the "seven corporal works of mercy" predates the modern era. These seven were to feed the hungry, give drink to the thirsty, welcome the stranger, clothe the naked, visit the sick, visit the prisoner, and bury the dead. What is new is the idea that the state should serve as the primary caregiver.

The Elizabethan Poor Laws were based on the premise that the family was primarily responsible for providing help to anyone in need, especially within their own families. Elderly parents were to be cared for by younger family members. Beyond that, the churches were responsible for providing relief. In fact, the community parish was the basic unit of responsibility under the Elizabethan Poor Law system. By 1601, inconsistencies in the administration of relief, the growing problem of burglars and robbers—the "sturdy beggars" of the times—and the difficulty of dealing with those who took advantage of the system led to a consolidation of these poor laws.

The Tenth Amendment to the US Constitution declared, "The powers not delegated to the United States by the Constitution, nor prohibited by it to the states, are reserved to the states respectively, or to the people."[17] Although broad, the intent of this amendment is clear: The federal government of the old republic had never been intended to watch over the welfare of its citizens. Yet, the feds now administer more welfare programs than we can imagine. Remembering their names is like learning the logarithmic tables by heart—just as difficult and even more pointless. State programs, although they exist, are often only supplementary. In many instances, funding of state programs is derived from handouts determined and administered by the federal government, invariably with strings attached.

The robust mob of organizations, designed to provide jobs, training, and more, is mind-boggling. These groups included the Civil Works Administration, the Civilian Conservation Corps, the National Youth Administration, and the Works Progress Administration—all agencies of the federal government, all intended to provide services that "are reserved to the states respectively" as identified in the Tenth Amendment.

The largest volume of legislation, however, was passed during the first congressional session, known as the "Hundred Days" (from March 9 to June 16, 1933):

March 9	Emergency Banking Act (expanding federal banking oversight)
March 20	Economy Act (reorganization of federal salary levels and veterans' benefits)
March 22	Beer-Wine Revenue Act (created taxes on alcoholic beverages)
March 31	Civilian Conservation Corps Act (created work camps to train 250,000 men between ages of 18 and 25, and created the CCC).
May 12	Federal Emergency Relief Act (set up system to distribute $500 million to state and local agencies)
May 12	Agricultural Adjustment Act (created farm subsidies)
May 18	Tennessee Valley Authority Act (created authority to the federal government to build dams and power plants and to create the TVA)
May 27	Federal Securities Act (created new regulations in the securities industry and removed the United States from the gold standard)
June 6	National Employment System Act (created the U.S. Employment Service)
June 13	Home Owners Refinancing Act (created the Home Owners Loan Corporation to refinance nonagricultural home loans)
June 16	Glass-Steagall Banking Act (created banking reforms and established the Federal Bank Deposit Insurance Corporation, or FDIC)
June 16	Farm Credit Act (set up provisions to grant refinancing of existing farm loans)
June 16	Emergency Railroad Transportation Act (expanded federal regulation over railroads and transportation companies)
June 16	National Industrial Recovery Act (created the National Recovery Administration and the Public Works Administration)

STUFFING THE COURT

By the time the New Deal legislation had passed into law, a rift developed between President Roosevelt and the Supreme Court. In 1935, the justices—a majority of whom had been appointed by stodgy old Republican presidents—declared much of the New Deal agenda unconstitutional. That year, the Court threw out the Railroad Retirement Act of 1934, a law that had set up pension plans for railway workers. It also threw out one of the most significant pieces of the New Deal, the National Industrial Recovery Act of 1933. In 1936, the trend continued when the Court declared the Agricultural Adjustment Act of 1933 unconstitutional.

The Supreme Court was intended to have the last word for the judiciary branch. It was expected to be made up of wise old men, like a council of elders in more primitive societies. At the time, six of the nine judges were over 70. They were not dead, but they were old enough to know better than to go along with the president's ambitious new programs. Early in 1937, Roosevelt spoke with his advisors about a new draft bill that called for Supreme Court justices to retire at the age of 70. Under the proposed new rule, if they did not retire, the president would be able to appoint a new judge, increasing the number of justices on the Court to 15.

Roosevelt appealed directly to the masses during a Fireside Chat in March 1937. He explained his proposed new legislation and defined both the new imperial executive and its contempt for the wisdom of old age:

> The American people have learned from the depression. For in the last three national elections an overwhelming majority of them have voted a mandate that the Congress and the president begin the task of providing . . . protection [aka something for nothing]—not after long years of debate, but now. The courts, however, have cast doubts on the ability of the elected Congress to protect us against catastrophe by meeting squarely our modern social and economic conditions. . . . [S]ince the rise of the modern movement for social and economic progress through legislation, the court has more and more often and more and more boldly asserted a power to veto laws passed by the Congress and by state legislatures. . . . The court in addition

to the proper use of its judicial functions has improperly set itself up as a third house of the Congress—a super-legislature, as one of the justices has called it—reading into the Constitution words and implications which are not there, and which were never intended to be there.

What is my proposal? It is simply this: Whenever a judge or justice of any federal court has reached the age of 70 and does not avail himself of the opportunity to retire on a pension, a new member shall be appointed by the president then in office, with the approval, as required by the Constitution, of the Senate of the United States.[18]

Although retirement would not be mandatory as soon as a judge turned 70, the outcome of this proposal is apparent. As soon as a judge did reach that age, the president would certainly appoint a new member. The United States would have ended up with a younger, more obliging Court with a permanent membership of 15. Those bringing appeals forward to the Court would time their filings based on current age, time to age 70, and the president then in office. Even Roosevelt admitted this in a veiled threat to the Court, in the same address. He said "The number of judges to be appointed would depend wholly on the decision of present judges now over 70, or those who would subsequently reach the age of 70."[19]

Congress balked. After months of hearings on the bill, the Senate killed FDR's plan with a 70 to 20 vote. The proposal was sent back to committee and nothing came of it.

But the winds of empire continued to blow hard. Economists, philosophers, radicals, and other malcontents rolled into Washington like tumbleweeds, with plans for centralized control of the economy.

When Roosevelt entered office, having chided the Republicans before him for spending too much money, the federal debt, after 143 years, had grown to $19 billion. Roosevelt—in just four years—borrowed almost as much money as all the dead presidents who came before him. He and members of Congress at the time were disturbed about it, but ideas arise as they are needed. The big spenders needed an idea that would permit huge new levels of government debt. They soon found it: *A government, unlike an individual, can borrow and spend indefinitely without fear of bankruptcy.* A government borrows money from its citizens. Therefore, it owes that debt to its citizens. The debt is therefore owed by the people to themselves. And no matter how large the debt gets, the financial impact on the citizens and the government is negligible. On the subject of what would happen if that debt were owed to foreign bond holders, the Roosevelt era empire builders were less clear.

"The apostle of this sly philosophy was Dr. Alvin Hansen of Harvard," writes John T. Flynn, "When this small book, written by Dr. Hansen's disciples, appeared, the doctor was promptly brought to Washington and installed in the Federal Reserve Board as the economic philosopher of this new dispensation. . . . Now Roosevelt had a luminous guide through the chaos," observed Flynn, "The American economic system planned and directed from Washington and an endless flow of funds to spend, supplied by endless borrowing."[20]

TEN THOUSAND COMMANDMENTS

The Social Security system was considered to be a great improvement of the Roosevelt era. It was supposed to provide a cushion of cash for retired people—so they wouldn't have to eat dog food in their old age. But never was a shiny bell cast by world improvers without a big crack in it somewhere. Economist Martin Feldstein pointed out that if you could count on receiving payments from Social Security, you had less need to save. Fewer savings meant less money for the economy to invest in new industries. Less money invested meant lower productivity and wages. If the government had funded its Social Security system honestly, the missing private savings would have been replaced by public savings in the "Social Security Trust Fund." Instead, the system was unfunded. There were never any savings in the fund—just liabilities from other parts of the federal government. Social Security reduced the availability of capital and indirectly reduced capital investment. Like other taxes, Social Security made people poorer—by reducing the rate of economic growth.

There was also unemployment compensation to blame. When people could expect money even if they didn't work, many would choose to be unemployed, creating an obvious drag on the productive economy. All the hundreds of thousands of pettifogging rules, laws, and regulations acted on the economy like Velcro on a fuzz ball.

By the early 21st century the total cost of federal regulation of the economy was all but impossible to calculate. In an annual report called "Ten Thousand Commandments" published by both the Cato Institute and the Competitive Enterprise Institute, the author, Wayne Crews, "shines a light on the large and under-appreciated 'hidden tax' of America's regulatory state."[21]

The report makes some astounding assertions:

- The preliminary 2022 Federal Register page count of 80,756 is a 10% rise over 73,321 in 2021. Trump's 86,208 pages in 2020 is the second-highest count ever. However, Trump's rollbacks of rules—and historically, there were fewer final rules overall—also added pages to the register.
- By comparison, in 2017, Trump's first year, the Federal Register finished at 61,308 pages, the lowest count since 1993 and a 36% drop from President Barack Obama's 95,894 pages, which remains the highest-ever count.
- Since 1993, when the first edition of "Ten Thousand Commandments" was published, agencies have issued 118,315 final rules (not including guidance documents). Since the Federal Register first began itemizing final rules in 1976, 215,405 have been issued.
- Of 99,429 final rules issued since the Congressional Review Act passed in 1996 during the Clinton administration, just 20 rules have been revoked, including one guidance document.[22]

Bossing people around like this costs a lot of money. How much? By 2022 . . .

- Regulatory burdens of $1.939 trillion amount to nearly 7.4% of U.S. gross domestic product, which was $26.14 trillion in 2022.
- When regulatory costs are combined with federal outlays of $6.27 trillion, the federal government's share of the entire economy reaches 31.4%. State and local spending and regulation would add to these costs.
- If it were a country, US regulation would be the world's ninth-largest economy (not counting the United States itself), ranking behind Canada and ahead of South Korea.

- The hidden regulatory "tax" rivals individual income tax revenues, estimated at $2.263 trillion for 2022.
- Regulatory costs stand at nearly two-thirds the level of corporate pretax profits of $3.138 trillion (which have surged from $2.18 trillion). They greatly exceed estimated corporate income tax revenues of $382 billion.
- US households pay $14,514 annually on average in a hidden regulatory tax. This amount exceeds every item in the household budget except housing. A typical US household spends more on embedded regulation than on healthcare, food, transportation, entertainment, apparel, services, or savings.[23]

"More than a century into the rise of the federal Administrative State," reported *Forbes* magazine, "the largest government on earth still has no thorough map of itself when it comes to the least disciplined of its activities—its thousands of rules and regulations."[24]

The National Association of Manufacturers, *The Cost of Federal Regulation to the U.S. Economy, Manufacturing and Small Business* puts the "costs of regulatory compliance now stands at $3.079 trillion for 2022 (in 2023 dollars). That $3 trillion breaks down to $277,000 in average annual compliance costs for a typical U.S. firm." The report also estimates that "the cost per employee for the typical U.S. firm is almost $13,000. This cost of federal regulation in the typical U.S. firm equals 19% of payroll expenditures."[25]

Between them, the Revolution of 1913 and the New Deal set the stage for the nation's new role as an empire of debt. For over 100 years, throughout the 20th century and into the 21st, residents of Washington never looked back. Neither party has the desire nor the gumption to roll back the tide. Nor is there any support for limiting political influence through term limits, returning power to the state governments or balancing the national budget by legislative decree.

NECESSARY EVILS

Between the Great Depression and the commencement of what we've come to think of as the empires "forever wars" there was a global military conflagration known historically as World War II. It is, of course, not within the scope of this work to identify the distinct causes or historical events leading up to or defining the war itself. We will point out, however, that during the war the United States borrowed a significant amount of money to fund its own war effort. It also lent money to Great Britain and other countries fighting the Nazis in Europe. During the New Deal years of the depression US debt grew 50% from $22 billion in 1933 to $33 billion by 1937. The war years beginning in earnest for the United States in 1941 saw an explosion in US debt to $258 billion by 1945, mostly in the form of War Bonds.[26] The 1945 debt level was equal to 117% of the national GDP at the time a height not reached again until the pandemic years of 2020–2023. In 2021, national debt reached an all-time 134% of GDP, a level putting many economists on high alerts themselves.[27]

While the war spending was considered a necessary evil to defeat totalitarian regimes in Europe, Dwight D. "Ike" Eisenhower, supreme allied commander at the end of World War II and president of the United States from 1953 to 1961, identified and warned the nation about two more necessary evils in the United States that were birthed in execution of the war effort.

Following the war effort, Harry S. Truman, US president 1945–1953 began paying off the war debt. By the end of his tenure the debt had declined to 68% of GDP aided by an economic expansion enjoyed among all the victorious nations. Eisenhower continued the trend, nearly balancing the budget during each of the eight years of his presidency. The national debt continued to get paid off until 1974 when it reached a postwar low of 38%.[28]

Despite having been fiscally conservative during his presidency, Eisenhower famously warned in a farewell address he gave to the nation on January 17, 1961, of the large and growing influence of the "military-industrial complex" that had been radically mobilized to fight the war. "A vital element in keeping the peace is our military establishment," Eisenhower admitted. "Our arms must be might, ready for instant action, so that no potential aggressor may be tempted to risk his own destruction. . . . American makers of plowshares could, with time and as required, make swords as well. But now we can no longer risk emergency improvisation of national defense; we have been compelled to create a permanent armaments industry of vast proportions."[29]

The creation of a new and powerful arms industry he admitted was needed to sustain the peace following such a devastating global conflict. But it also created a standing military with global reach. "This conjunction of an immense military establishment and a large arms industry is new in the American experience," the 34th president lamented. "We must not fail to comprehend its grave implications. . . . In the councils of government, we must guard against the acquisition of unwarranted influence, whether sought or unsought, by the military-industrial complex. The potential for the disastrous rise of misplaced power exists and will persist."[30]

The West was already in the throes of the Cold War with the Soviet Union and its satellite protectorates in Europe and Asia. With those words, this American Caesar also foretold ongoing and ruinous episodes of military adventurism in Vietnam (1962–1975), Iraq (twice: 1990–1991 and 2003–2011), and the "graveyard of Empires," Afghanistan (2001–2021). Data collected by the Uppsala University in Sweden "identifies 285 distinct armed conflicts having taken place since 1946" not necessarily large enough to enjoy "war" status among historians.[31]

Eisenhower's second grave warning garners a lot less attention than his admonition regarding the defense industry and its concomitant legal counterparts in the imperial city. Ike also warned of a growing tech elite among the engineers and scientists employed by the military industrial complex. "Akin to," Eisenhower observed to the nation, "and largely responsible for the sweeping changes in our industrial-military posture, has been the technological revolution during recent decades. In this revolution, research has become central; it also becomes more formalized, complex, and costly. A steadily increasing share is conducted for, by, or at the direction of, the Federal government."[32]

Eisenhower worried, and increasingly so, that "because of the huge costs involved, a government contract becomes virtually a substitute for intellectual curiosity. For every old blackboard there are now hundreds of new electronic computers. The prospect of domination of the nation's scholars by Federal employment, project allocations, and the power of money is ever present and is gravely to be regarded."[33]

Yet with these warnings, Eisenhower remained hopeful in his fare-well, if only to mingle concerns over the "necessary evil" of the military industrial clients with those regarding the national balance sheet:

> It is the task of statesmanship to mold, to balance, and to integrate these and other forces, new and old, within the principles of our democratic system-ever aiming toward the supreme goals of our free society. . . . As we peer into society's future, we—you and I, and our government—must avoid the impulse to live only for today, plundering, for our own ease and convenience, the precious resources of tomorrow. We cannot mortgage the material assets of our grandchildren without risking the loss also of their political and spiritual heritage. We want democracy to survive for all generations to come, not to become the insolvent phantom of tomorrow.[34]

Perhaps the outgoing president underestimated the power of the purse in election politics and future employment beyond the years held in office. Or maybe he didn't foresee the rise of career politicians, residents of the empire's seat of power, that would come part and parcel with both military and technical dominance over the planet. These concerns achieve a whole new level of importance a half century later when the internet, itself a technological advance of the military, global communications, and social media begins to tear at the vestiges of honored institutions—free elections, free speech, freedom of movement, sound money—developed to maintain the old Republic.

Alas, the Republic envisioned by Franklin and the founding fathers only lasted 124 years.

CHAPTER 7

MCNAMARA'S WAR

We had a unique vantage point from our offices on the rue de la Verrerie in Paris early in the new century. From there we watched 9/11 unfold. And the War on Terror. A joke made its way around the internet following the train bombings in Madrid in March 2004: "In response to the terrorism events in Madrid, the French government announced a change in its alert status . . . from 'run' to 'hide.' If the threat worsens, the French may be forced to increase their level of security, declaring a move to 'surrender' or 'collaboration' status as events develop."

One of the many conceits Americans permitted themselves in their imperial position was that they bravely faced up to the world's terrorist menace, whereas others—most notably, the French—cowered in fear. But they mistook vanity for courage.

At about the same time, the editor of the *International Herald Tribune* received a letter in which the writer referred to a big problem in the presidential campaign of Democratic hopeful John Kerry. The poor man was worried about looking "too French," which would be a sign of "weakness" in the eyes of the lumpen voters.

We stopped still in our tracks. We held our breath. Anyone who had ever been in the same room with a history book couldn't help but know that French history is drenched in blood. When it came to butchering each other, what the French didn't know about it probably wasn't worth knowing. There were the wars with the Romans and with the English, and religious wars, wars between princes and between kingdoms, wars for no apparent reason whatsoever. Weakness? Cowardice? A group of Norman French fighters no bigger than a small-town police force invaded and captured all of England. Bonaparte took on all of Europe and almost beat them.

General Marbot records an incident in Napoleon's campaign against Russia in which a group of French soldiers was cut off from the main force, but was visible from the Emperor's command post. Realizing that they could not expect reinforcements, the brigade sent a message to Bonaparte: "We, who are about to die, salute you." They fought to the last man.

Then, there was the Battle of Camerone. Napoleon's nephew sent troops to Mexico in the 1860s. In the action surrounding the siege of Puebla, a group of 60 French foreign legionnaires was cut off and confronted by an army of 2,000 Mexicans. The Mexican commander asked for surrender. Instead, the French vowed to fight to the death. Trapped in an inn, the soldiers had nothing to eat or drink. Then, the Mexicans set the place on fire.

"In spite of the heat and smoke," explains a report on the internet, "the legionnaires resisted, but many of them were killed or injured. By five p.m. on April 30, 1863, only 12 men could still fight with 2nd Lieutenant Maudet. At this time, the Mexican colonel gathered his soldiers and told them what a disgrace it would be if they were unable to defeat such a small number of men. The Mexicans were about to give the general assault through the holes opened in the walls of the courtyard . . . [they] once again asked Lieutenant Maudet to surrender. Once again, Maudet scornfully refused."

The final charge was given. Soon, only five men were left around Maudet: Corporal Maine and legionnaires Catteau, Wensel, Constantin, and Leonard. Each had only one bullet left. In a corner of the courtyard, their backs against the wall, still facing the enemy, they fixed bayonets. When the signal was given, they opened fire and fought with their bayonets. Lieutenant Maudet and two legionnaires fell, mortally wounded. Maine and his two remaining companions were about to be slaughtered when a Mexican officer saved them. He shouted:

"Surrender!"
"We will, only if you promise to allow us to carry and care for our injured men and if you leave us our guns."
"Nothing can be refused to men like you," answered the officer.[1]

More recently, there was the Battle of Dien Bien Phu (May 7, 1954). Writer Graham Greene visited the French just before the shooting started. He found them well supplied—with 48,000 bottles of wine.

The French had a number of advantages similar to the advantages Americans would bring to bear in Vietnam 10 years later. They controlled the air. Using airpower, they brought in 15,000 soldiers and provisions to a remote airfield west of Hanoi. The idea was to install themselves there, disrupt General Giap's supplies, block his move into Laos, and bring him to a pitched battle in which superior French firepower would be decisive.

"A defeat can be borne from a victory," began the *Figaro's* 50-year look back on May 7, 2004. "In order to understand Dien Bien Phu, you have to remember Na-San. This battle, won by the French Army, explains the other ... and brought the whole thing to disaster. Eighteen months separated them. General Giap, commander of the Vietminh forces, used these 18 months to learn from his defeat. The French high commander, on the other hand, became more sure of himself than ever."[2]

At Na-San, the French established a base on a plateau. Giap attacked. The French were able to hold their ground while the Vietminh staggered away. In a single night, Giap lost 3,000 men. If the French were going to destroy themselves in Southeast Asia, they had to find a better way. They found it at Dien Bien Phu. The broad outlines of the battle were as follows: French parachutists took control of the airfield followed by 15,000 troops under Colonel Christian de Castries. The French dug trenches and set up bases, to which they gave women's names. Dien Bien Phu was not on a plateau, but in a depression, surrounded by hills covered in jungle.

If the Vietminh brought up heavy artillery, the French goose would be cooked. But neither de Castries nor the French high command thought Giap could do it. The surprise began on March 13, 1954. Giap's artillery threw off its camouflage and opened fire in the afternoon. A shell hit the French every six seconds, off and on, for the next 56 days. Then, Giap sent in waves of infantry. Camp "Gabrielle" was taken by the Vietminh and then retaken by the Legionnaires, before being abandoned to the enemy. "Beatrice" was lost after its commander was killed. "Anne-Marie" went down next.

The French held. But the Vietminh noose was getting tighter. On March 26, a plane managed to get off the ground with a cargo of wounded men. It was the last one. After that, the French lost control of the airfields. The only way to get supplies was to drop them from the sky; often they fell into the hands of the enemy. The French were cut off and doomed. Still, they held out hoping a diplomatic solution could be found. It did not come.

The weather turned against the French, says the *Figaro*. They fought in a blast furnace. Then came the rains and they were up to their knees in mud. Doctors operated standing up in it. On May 6, Giap ordered a general assault. "Dominique" and "Eliane" were quickly overrun. On May 7, the order was given to blow up the munitions. Colonel Piroth committed suicide. By 5:30 p.m., a cease-fire was sounded, though "Isabelle" held out until 1:00 a.m. the following day.

After the 56-day siege, French General de Castries radioed his superior in Hanoi, sounding Napoleonic: "I'm blowing up the installations. The ammunition dumps are already exploding. Au revoir."

"Well, then," came the reply, "au revoir, mon vieux."[3]

Thousands of French were captured. From the evidence, the Vietminh were not particularly mean to them, but indifferent. The victors had little to eat themselves, and hardly any medicine. The French, many of them wounded, died quickly. They were forced to march 500 to 600 kilometers; many didn't make it. Only about 3,900 of them ever returned to France. Still, the French should cheer. It was a small price to pay to "put an end to illusions," as the *Figaro* described it a half-century later.[4] General Giap should have been so lucky. Like many colonies, Vietnam had flourished under French administration. There were bars, brothels, and sidewalk cafés in Hanoi.

There were elegant hotels and well-dressed women, dignified beach houses near the ocean, and splendid plantation homes in the hills. People could do pretty much as they pleased. France was bringing civilization to the Indigenous peoples of Indochina. A fat lot of thanks they got for it. Ho Chi Minh learned French and went to Paris. Scarcely a year or two had passed, and he was printing up leaflets urging his countrymen to kick the French out.

Nguyen Sinh Cung, who would later change his name to Ho Chi Minh, was born on May 19, 1890. He was good at his studies, but he seemed to have an itch for world improvement from the get-go. The urge grew stronger, according to biographer William J. Duiker, when young Ho went to school. He had won a scholarship to the French-run National Academy in Hue. Coming in from the country, he was teased by other students, who thought he was a bumpkin. On one occasion when he lost his temper and slugged a fellow student, a teacher advised him to "channel his energy to more useful purposes such as the study of world affairs."[5]

Ooh la la! If only the teacher had suggested an anger management program instead, maybe the French would still be running the place. The Vietnamese never had it so good, before or after. Ho should have left well enough alone. But Vietnam's history in the 20th century is a history of people who should have left well enough alone. Old Ho couldn't keep his hands to himself. Then, after Ho took over at the end of World War II, the French should have left well enough alone. And when they washed up, the Americans should have left well enough alone. Time after time, the history of world improvement yields the same lesson: *Leave well enough alone.* And time after time, the world improvers ignore it; they always know better.

But we are getting ahead of our story. When Ho came of age, the gabby talk of independence was running through Europe's colonial possessions like an epidemic of bird flu. Locals who had been exposed to a little education were quickly infected and often succumbed. Ho Chi Minh was one of many thousands who got the bug. He had gone to Europe, where he heard Woodrow Wilson's airy song of freedom. It was just after World War I had ended. Paris had a habit of turning a young man's head. Ho's head swiveled around just like everyone else's. Soon, he had joined not only the Annamite Patriots league but also the communist party. Of all the world improvers of the time, the Bolsheviks had the biggest improvements in mind. Near the close of the war, against all odds, they took over the world's biggest country and were improving it mercilessly. The rest of the improvers looked on in admiration, and turned to Moscow for guidance and money. Ho was no exception.

Ho Chi Minh traveled widely, partly to see how the rest of the world worked, and partly to make contacts that would be useful in his campaign to liberate Indochina from the French. One trip took him to New York and Boston, where he claimed he worked as a cook's helper in the Parker House Hotel in Boston. He also said he once took a trip to the South, where he witnessed the lynching of blacks by the Ku Klux Klan. (Sounds improbable; the Klan did not exactly lynch someone every day. It is also hard to imagine a young man fresh off the boat from Vietnam standing around to watch the Klan at work; we imagine Ho would have felt like a lamb attending a wolves' picnic.) Ho spent much of the Great War years in London, working as a sous-chef under the celebrated culinary master, Auguste Escoffier at the Carlton Hotel. In this passage from Ho Chi Minh's biography, wherein he refers to himself as *Ba*, we see how close the world came to having another decent pastry chef instead of another indecent world improver:

> Each of us had to take turns in the clearing up. The waiters, after attending the customer, had to clear all the plates and send them by means of an electric lift to the kitchen. Then our job was to separate china and silver for cleaning. When it came to Ba's turn he was very careful. Instead of throwing out all the bits left over, which were often a quarter of a chicken or a huge piece of steak, and so on, Ba kept them clean and sent them back to the kitchen. Noticing this, Chef Escoffier asked Ba: "Why didn't you throw these remains into the rubbish as the others do? "
>
> "These things shouldn't be thrown away. You could give them to the poor."
>
> "My dear young friend, listen to me!" Chef Escoffier seemed to be pleased and said, smiling: "Leave your revolutionary ideas aside for a moment, and I will teach you the art of cooking, which will bring you a lot of money. Do you agree?"
>
> And Chef Escoffier did not leave Ba at the job of washing dishes but took him to the cake section, where he got higher wages. It was

indeed a great event in the kitchen for it was the first time the "kitchen king" had done that sort of thing.[6]

Alas, the smell of good works must have been more alluring then the *pain au chocolat*. The world lost a good pastry chef and gained a bad activist. Instead of bringing pleasure to a few hundred, or maybe a thousand, customers, the Annamite Wilson decided instead to launch himself into politics and begin a campaign that would bring misery and death to millions. In London, he warmed up with street demonstrations in favor of Irish independence and a variety of progressive causes. When he read Marx and other revolutionary *penseurs*, his head was turned so far his neck almost broke. Here were people with a grand theory of how the entire world could be improved. And here were people ready to help a skinny, poor young man take over a country.

Ho Chi Minh returned to Indochina, organized the Vietminh, and began the long campaign for independence. The struggle was neither easy nor short. If he was to be the *capo* of Vietnam, he had a number of other *capos* to bury first. First, he had the French to deal with. Then, the Japanese. Then, the Chinese. Then the Vietnamese nationalists. Then the French again. More Vietnamese. And, finally, the Americans. Before he was finished, he would have to bury nearly as many people as Alexander or Pol Pot.

Ho Chi Minh's brief visit to the United States had left him somewhat naive and puzzled about America. Ho had not kept up with Wilsonian improvements in the land of the free. When he addressed the crowd in Ba Dinh Square following the August Revolution of 1945, he spoke not of America as it was, but perhaps as it should have been. It was the America that existed before Wilson improved it. It was the America that minded its own business and had not yet taken the road to empire.

"All men are created equal," said Ho. "They are endowed by their creator with certain inalienable rights; among these are life, liberty, and the pursuit of happiness." This statement appeared in the Declaration of Independence of the United States of America in 1776. In a broader sense, it means: All the peoples on the earth are equal from birth, all the peoples have a right to live and to be happy and free.

The Declaration of the Rights of Man and the Citizen, made at the time of the French Revolution, in 1791, also states: "All men are born free and with equal rights, and must always remain free and have equal rights."

In this short speech, Ho extended a hand to two nations. One already had not just one empire, but several of them. It had been home to the Empire of the Franks, and then the Holy Roman Empire. Bonaparte made his own empire and his nephew revived it, briefly. The other nation, the United States of America, had been a modest republic only a few years before, but now had imperial responsibilities all over the globe. Ho didn't know it, but if he wanted to rule Indochina he would have to kick both their derrieres.

The August Revolution had been swift and relatively bloodless. On August 14, the Japanese surrendered. All of a sudden, there was an empty hole where an imperial power used to sit. The Japanese were laying down their guns. In Vietnam, they wanted to surrender, but didn't know to whom. French administrators were still in the prisons where the Japanese had put them. So were other allied troops. Chiang Kai Shek's Nationalist Chinese troops would soon be coming down from the north to oversee the Japanese departure. The French would soon be out of jail. Ho's Vietminh forces had to act fast. On the morning of August 25, 1945, his "defense units" swiftly seized government installations and enterprises all over Vietnam. Within hours, the country was under Vietminh control. Vo Nguyen Giap described the joyful scene in Ba Dinh Square, formerly known as Place Puginier:

Hanoi was bedecked with red bunting. A world of flags, lanterns and flowers. Fluttering red flags adorned the roofs, the trees and the lakes.

Streamers were hung across streets and roads, bearing slogans in Vietnamese, French, English, Chinese and Russian: "Viet Nam for the Vietnamese." "Down with French colonialism," "Independence or death," "Support the provisional government," "Support President Ho Chi Minh," "Welcome to the Allied mission," and so on.

Factories and shops, big and small, were closed down. Markets were deserted . . . the whole city, old and young, men and women, took to the streets. . . . Multicolored streams of people flowed to Ba Dinh Square from all directions.

Workers in white shirts and blue trousers came in ranks, full of strength and confidence. . . . Hundreds of thousands of peasants came from the city suburbs. People's militiamen carried quarter-staffs, swords or scimitars. Some even carried old-style bronze clubs and long-handles [sic] swords taken from the armories of temples. Among the women peasants in their festive dresses, some were clad in old-fashioned robes, yellow turbans and bright-green sashes . . .

Most lively were the children. . . . They marched in step with the whistle blows of their leaders, singing revolutionary songs.[7]

At that very moment, about 15,000 French people living in Hanoi, and 5,000 French prisoners still being held in Japanese internment camps, along with any number of Vietnamese nationalists, were all preparing to contest Ho's authority. But naive Ho called on his people to treat foreigners with tolerance and respect and looked to the United States for support. Surely the country that made wars of independence popular would back him up. Ho wrote several letters to the Truman administration asking for help. One requested food for starving people in the north of the country. In 1945, over a million people in Vietnam starved to death. Another letter praised the United States for its humanitarian ideals and asked for US support of the new government. None of the letters was answered.

Americans had come to see the world in a new way. They were an imperial power; they had to think like one. Winston Churchill, representing a declining empire, stood before a crowd in Fulton, Missouri, and said an "iron curtain" had come down separating one empire from another. There was now a "communist bloc" that threatened the "free world." Communism must be "contained," or it would take over the entire world. A new war had begun—the "Cold War."

Typically, the empire builders see the globe in simple-minded terms. It is the only way they can understand it; the only way they can justify their own vain and preposterous interventions. There was no iron curtain in Vietnam, just the same diaphanous fabric that was draped over the rest of the world. Ho Chi Minh explained it to a US official, Archimedes Patti, on September 30, 1945.

At the close of the conversation, Ho recounted to his visitor some of the key events in his life as a revolutionary. Conceding that many Americans viewed him as a "Moscow puppet," Ho denied that he was a communist in the US sense. Having repaid his debt to the Soviet Union with 15 years of party work (Ho had been an agent of the Comintern), he now considered himself a free agent. In recent months, he pointed out, the Democratic Republic of Vietnam had received more support from the United States than from the USSR. Why should it be indebted to Moscow?

As they parted, Ho Chi Minh asked his visitor to carry back a message that the Vietnamese people would always be grateful for the assistance they received from the United States and would long recall it as a friend and ally, and that the US struggle for independence would always serve as an example for Vietnam. A few weeks later, another departing US military officer carried a letter from Ho Chi Minh to President Truman. But the likelihood of any US assistance was rapidly dimming. Patti's activities had strengthened suspicions among US officials in China and the United States, and when his successor cabled Washington that Hanoi would welcome a US effort to mediate the dispute, Hanoi's offer and Ho's previous letters were ignored.

Americans were once again in no mood for modest restraint, ambiguity, or question marks. Senator Joseph McCarthy was readying his inquisition. Children were pledging allegiance to the flag and hiding under their desks in preparation for a nuclear attack. The enemy was at the gates. It was time for "100% Americanism."

Poor old Ho ought to have given up. In a matter of weeks, the French were on the loose and rebuilding their bases. There was an awkward period—a modus vivendi was worked out with the French. They were tolerated, but agreed not to impose themselves. On October 18, the French ship, *Dumont d'Urville,* sailed into Cam Ranh Bay with Ho aboard, back from a peace conference in Paris. But there was no peace. The French were becoming more and more insistent. They drove around in US-made jeeps and carried US-made arms. Ho began to wonder whose side the Americans were on.

Again, as in World War I, the United States seemed to pick its ally without much real thought. In Indochina, for the next quarter of a century, the world improvers would run into each other. Ho wanted to liberate the Annamites from the yoke of colonial rule. Other Vietnamese—Catholics, Buddhists, capitalists, traditional nationalists— wanted to liberate them from Ho. The French, meanwhile, didn't want to liberate them at all—but force them to be good subjects of France's reconstructed empire in the Far East. And America, what did America want? America didn't know exactly what she wanted. But she definitely wanted to throw her weight around.

Ho was duly elected in January 1946. As president of the country, it was not at all clear that he had to run in a district election, but he chose to do so, and won 98.4% of the vote. The French were about to nullify the vote and reimpose colonial rule. A moment's thought would suggest that the Americans would side with Ho, or at least stay out of it.

But if America could back the world's two largest colonial empires in World War I—and do so in the name of democracy—there was no effective limit to the hypocrisy of her foreign policy. Besides, once again, she looked up at those big, gaudy bubbles, those empty, floating words, and she was in a trance. This time they did not say anything about democracy. The mood had changed. This time the bubbles said "red menace."

The first Indochina war began on December 19, 1946, when the Vietminh blew up the municipal power station in Hanoi. It ended 89 months later, in defeat for the French at Dien Bien Phu in May 1954. Next it was the American's turn to meddle.

After the fall of Indochina, the French renounced their "civilizing mission" foreign policy. Now, it is the United States that claims to make the world a better place. But when it comes to blockheaded bellicosity and desperate courage, Americans have nothing to teach the French. In comparison to Napoleon's grand campaigns, America's early wars were piddling affairs. Its wars against the Mexicans and Spaniards were more sordid than glorious. Even its Revolutionary War was merely a minor engagement compared with the Napoleonic Wars, and only won because the French intervened at a crucial moment to pull Americans' chestnuts out of the fire. Here, we quote Charles W. Eliot's history, in which he describes how the patriots had fallen "into a condition of despondency from which nothing but the steadfastness of Washington and the Continental army and the aid from France saved them."[8]

In World War I, the French battered themselves against the Germans for two years—and suffered more casualties than America had in all its wars put together—before Pershing ever set foot in France. Again, in World War II, Americans waited until the combatants had been softened up before entering the war with an extraordinary advantage in fresh soldiers and almost unlimited supplies.

Americans have no history. Probably just as well. The French, however, have too much. Practically every street in Paris reminds them of a slaughter somewhere. On the Arc de Triomphe, Les Invalides, and dozens of other piles of stone, the names of towns in Germany, Spain, Italy, Poland, Russia, or North Africa are inscribed. Each one marks the deaths of thousands of French soldiers—gone early to their graves for who-remembers-what important national purpose. Every town in France, even the most remote and forlorn little burg, has at its center a pillar of granite or marble—with the names of the men whose bodies were torn to bits by flying lead or corroded by some battlefield disease. A whole race of orphans grew up after World War I and special seats on the subway were designated for those "mutilated in war" including thousands of *sans gueules*— men who had had their jaws blown away and yet survived, too horrible to look on.

The French have had enough of war—at least for now. Let them enjoy a well-earned cowardice.

McNAMARA'S WAR

On May 1, 1995, the world—or at least the part of it that happened to be gathered at the LBJ Library in Austin, Texas, witnessed a rare and remarkable thing. Robert S. McNamara was in tears. He had just explained how what he had done as Secretary of Defense during the years from 1961 to 1968 was "terribly, terribly wrong."

"War Criminal Says Sorry, Sobs" was how Alexander Cockburn described it in his column in *The Nation*, February 9, 2004. Heads of state, their ministers, and their generals get people killed often. Rarely do they apologize for it. If they're lucky, the war goes their way and they don't have to. If they are unlucky, they get strung up like Mussolini, or they shoot themselves like Hitler. Mr. McNamara didn't have to do either. The North Vietnamese never posed any real danger to the United States, so there was never much danger in bombing them—unless China or Russia got spooked and fired nuclear warheads toward North America. There was no way Ho and his men were ever going to seize Washington and put US leaders in the dock for war crimes. Nor did Mr. McNamara, Mr. Kennedy, Mr. Johnson, or any other of the vast cast of earnest incompetents who had a hand in the Vietnam affair ever volunteer for the front lines. If anyone was going to die, it wasn't going to be them. And it was not their money paying for it either.

Mr. McNamara was never really cut out to be an empire builder. He was too circumspect. The typical world improver goes to his grave believing he has done people a favor and is often bitter that they don't seem to appreciate it. In 1945 when Berlin was near starvation and being overrun by Soviet troops, the Führer complained about the ingratitude of the German people.

Wilson, too, felt abandoned and betrayed—first because Democrats wanted nothing to do with the brain-damaged president in the election of 1920, and second because in rejecting his League of Nations, Congress seemed to repudiate him and all he stood for.

"I beseech you in the bowels of Christ to consider that you may be wrong."[9] Oliver Cromwell's warning has no effect on real empire builders; you might as well caution sailors against getting drunk on shore leave. No matter what you say, they'll find a way to get themselves in trouble.

According to his memoirs, McNamara was always plagued by doubts. He seems a decent man, who had no business at the Department of Defense. He said so much himself. "I'm not qualified," he told President Kennedy when the job was offered to him. But he took the post, and over the next seven years, he proved it.

What is astonishing about McNamara's mea culpa is not his admission that he made a colossal error—though that is extraordinary in itself and places him in a superior category to most public officials—but his candid record of how life-and-death decisions are made by supposedly intelligent and responsible governments.

When McNamara took over the most lethal armed forces in the world, what preparation did he have? Did he know anything about war? Strategy? The history of combat? He had been a junior officer in World War II doing statistical analysis. Then, he had gone to work for the Ford Motor Company as an executive. Had he even read Sun Tzu or Clausewitz or Machiavelli, or Caesar or Bonaparte? Had he tried to learn a single thing from the millions of dead soldiers, the thousands of battles, the hundreds of wars? If so, he doesn't mention it.

"I entered the Pentagon with a limited grasp of military affairs and even less grasp of covert operations," he says.[10]

What about Vietnam? He knew nothing, zero, about the place. But then, as he points out, neither did Kennedy or National Security Advisor McGeorge Bundy, or military advisor General Maxwell Taylor. The only people in the Western world who knew anything about Vietnam were the French. And the US team decided to ignore the French; they were losers. By this time, the French were becoming cynical of military affairs. Every war they had been involved in since the time of Napoleon had gone bad, even those they won. By contrast, every war America had fought—at least since the War Between the States—had been a reasonable success. Americans were still bright eyed, full of energy, ambition, and "can do" spirit. Robert McNamara was one of the "brightest and best" of the lot—the kind of American who makes you proud to be one. He was a problem-solver, a doer, a take-charge guy, the youngest Secretary of Defense ever, badly in need of some Gallic cynicism. He was surrounded by people who were even bigger blockheads than he was. In their minds, they were stopping the advance of communism in Southeast Asia. Could they do so? Why would they want to do so? What would happen if they didn't? Even if they could do it, how should it be done? Could it be done in some other way that didn't involve killing people or spending a lot of money?

You would think that the brightest and best would have thoroughly chatted out such basic questions. Apparently not. There was plenty of discussion, but the major question was never really answered: What damned difference did it make? Instead, the whole team merely went from one gaff to the next, improvising as they went along. Many were the reasons given why Vietnam was important to America, but all were generalities or theories. If Vietnam fell, so would all of Southeast Asia, like a "row of dominoes," as Eisenhower had put it.[11] Even if that had been true, why did it matter to the United States of America what kind of governments ruled the region? As far as the US republic was concerned, it was of no interest whatever.

But in the new empire, any change of allegiance set off alarms. McNamara, Kennedy, Johnson—all the guardians of Wilsonian foreign policy—heard the tinkle and rushed to take action. They hardly noticed that none had the blurriest notion of what they were really up to. "I am convinced that it would be disastrous for the United States and the Free World to permit Southeast Asia to be overrun by the Communist North," said Dean Rusk. Why? Had anyone gone to talk to Uncle Ho? Did anyone know if his plans were compatible with US interests? It did not seem to matter to them. Nor did it matter that the actions they were taking were contradictory to even their own stated aims.

"Some others are eager to enlarge the conflict," said President Johnson in 1964. "They call upon us to supply American boys to do the job that Asian boys should do. . . . Such action would offer no solution at all to the real problem of Vietnam. . . . The South Vietnamese have the basic responsibility for the defense of their own freedom."[12]

Thus, did the president repeat what President Kennedy had said before him, and what every American felt in his heart: If the South Vietnamese wanted independence, they could fight for it just as we had. There was a practical consideration behind the sentiment. If the South Vietnamese could not organize or motivate their own people to protect themselves, it would be impossible for foreigners to do the job for them.

No one likes to admit that he is going to war for reasons of vanity or pride. That kind of ambition is, like a bad facelift, not a pretty sight. Ordinary citizens usually turn away from it; they don't like the idea of getting their sons killed and their wallets stolen to support a brassy campaign of self-aggrandizement. So, real ambitions are usually hidden so well that not even the leaders themselves can see their own vanity in them. In 1965, presidential military advisor General Maxwell Taylor explained: "The situation in Vietnam is deteriorating and without new U.S. action defeat appears inevitable . . . the stakes in Vietnam are extremely high. . . . The international prestige of the United States, and a substantial part of our influence are directly at risk in Vietnam. . . . Any negotiated withdrawal would mean surrender on the installment plan."[13]

Not just Johnson, McNamara, and Taylor had their pride on the line but also the whole nation. There may never have been a good reason for fighting in McNamara's war, but Americans began to feel that if they didn't prevail they'd never be able to hold their heads high again.

Still, as late as 1964, Johnson chose not to admit that he would send half a million US boys to do the fighting that Asian boys wouldn't or couldn't do. America was an empire, but still a reluctant one. Maybe he didn't know himself. Besides, it was probably not a good time to mention it. McNamara, in testimony before defense subcommittees of Congress, failed to disclose the level of troop commitments the administration knew would be required. McNamara testified to the Defense Subcommittee of the Senate Appropriations Committee on August 4, 1965, that 175,000 troops would have to be deployed by November, to be followed by another 100,000 the following year. He did *not* bother to say that he already estimated the need for an additional 340,000 men to be added to the tour through the draft and extended tours.

Two years later, McNamara testified before the Senate Armed Services Committee. Asked whether he could provide a monthly breakdown of the costs of Vietnam, he said, "It is almost impossible to do it on a yearly basis, and it is really impossible to do it on a monthly basis. I can tell you how much we are spending in total for defense per month of course, but splitting that into Vietnam and non-Vietnam is honestly almost impossible."[14]

Wilson's platform slogan when he ran for a second term was "He Kept Us out of War." Franklin Roosevelt ran for office saying he would not send troops to fight in Europe's war. And in the election campaign of 1964, Lyndon Johnson maintained that it was still a Vietnamese war, not a US one. The spirit of empire got the better of all of them. Whether you wanted to get into the Vietnam War, or stay out of it, you could find all the reasons and arguments you could want. But the arguments scarcely mattered; temperatures were already rising; war fever was bubbling up all over.

"Aggression and upheaval, in any part of the world," said Lyndon Johnson on the 1964 campaign trail, sounding Wilsonian, "carry the seeds of destruction to our own freedom and perhaps to civilization itself. . . . Friendly cynics and fierce enemies alike often underestimate or ignore the strong thread of moral purpose which runs through the fabric of American history."[15]

By the early 1960s, there was hardly a half-wit in all North America who didn't think that the country was in danger. This time it wasn't the Huns who threatened Western civilization; it was communists. They'd heard it on television. Even the *New York Times* said so.

In a modern democracy, it is relatively easy to stir the masses to absurdity. People are all tuned into the national television stations and read the papers. Just as Americans in 1917 came to believe that their way of life had been put in jeopardy by the Germans, now they came to believe that the communists were a grave and growing threat. If they weren't stopped in Vietnam, said the papers, soon they'd be landing in California. It was preposterous. But that didn't make it unpopular.

In the mid and late-1960s, the war in Vietnam seemed like the biggest, most urgent foreign policy challenge the United States faced. The French were gone; now Vietnam could be added to America's slushy empire. There was little question in Americans' minds that they could succeed where the frogs had failed. Curiously, but not unexpectedly, public support for the war grew as the United States got itself in deeper. The big question—"Why are we involved in this war?"—disappeared, pushed out by a more urgent and practical question: "How are we going to win it?" In the middle of all this, though, the economic aspects (the cost of the war itself) as well as the required level of "boots on the ground" were purposely understated. It was apparent, even within the Johnson administration, that there would be little support for the war if the real costs were known. Head of the Council of Economic Advisors Walter Heller (who resigned in 1966 and was succeeded by Gardner Ackley) said in 1965, "We had no concrete idea how much Vietnam was going to cost. First, I think fundamentally it was being underestimated to begin with. And, second, some of the estimates were somehow or another not getting across the Potomac from the Pentagon to the Executive Office Building, at least not to the Council's part of the Executive Office Building. Anyway, the Council was operating partially in the dark."[16]

After supporting the French, the United States backed the regime of the Diem brothers, a pair of staunchly Catholic conservatives with a talent for corruption and political clumsiness, one of whom was married to a sorceress known as Madame Nhu. As a bulwark against the commies, the Diem regime proved as ineffective as it was quirky. The United States gave the go-ahead to a group of generals to replace the brothers. This decision, like so many others, was not taken after careful consideration of the alternatives by the top policymakers.

McNamara says it was inspired by lower-echelon functionaries who set it in motion while Kennedy, McNamara, and the leading decision-makers were on vacation. Then, it took on a momentum of its own. On November 2, 1963, a group of generals led by General Minh rounded up Ngo Dinh Diem and Madame Nhu. Their hands were bound behind their backs and they were shoved into an armored personnel carrier. When the vehicle arrived at general headquarters, Diem and Nhu had been shot; Nhu had also been knifed several times. The South Vietnamese said it was a suicide. The two were, no doubt, capable of great mischief. But people who have their hands tied behind their backs do not often shoot and knife themselves. The official version of events serves as a eulogy for the entire Vietnam adventure—improbable at the very least, criminal at worst.

Meanwhile, the war ratcheted up another big notch after an incident in the Tonkin Gulf, involving two attacks on US ships. One of the attacks was never confirmed; many think it never happened. The other may have been a mistake. The North Vietnamese now say they never authorized it. Americans said they believed Hanoi was intentionally widening the war. The United States felt it had to retaliate, not for any particular reason, but merely because it felt it had to do something and didn't know what else to do. Before long, the United States had 200,000 of its own troops in Vietnam and was bombing Hanoi "back to the Stone Age."[17]

Finally, after US troop levels in Vietnam reached half a million, and nearly half a trillion dollars (adjusted to year 2000 dollars) had been spent, and noncombatants were being killed or seriously injured at the rate of 1,000 a week (McNamara's estimate), Americans came to their senses. The idealists left the State Department and the Defense Department. Realists, led by Henry Kissinger, came in and figured out how to abandon South Vietnamese allies and sneak out of the war in the least disgraceful way they could.

Vietnam then did fall to the communists and America's erstwhile allies were reeducated. But was the world better or worse? No one knew or cared. After Americans left the place, except for a lengthy discussion of MIA and POWs, Vietnam disappeared from the news. What people had worried about so much had happened. Ho Chi Minh had won. But it seemed to make no difference to anybody. Did the rest of Southeast Asia fall "like dominoes?" Not at all. Cambodia lost its head in a mad frenzy of murder. What that had to do with Vietnam is not entirely clear; the world breathed a sigh of relief when Vietnamese communists invaded the place to restore order.

FACING THE ENEMY

A quarter century later, McNamara and a group of associates confronted a team led by his old adversary, Vo Nguyen Giap, in a series of meetings held in Hanoi, between 1995 and 1998. The exchange was advertised as an attempt to learn something. It is recorded in a book by McNamara, *Argument Without End: In Search of Answers to the Vietnam Tragedy*. Appropriately, there is a photo of that arch-world improver, Woodrow Wilson, at the beginning of the book. We do not know what inspiration Robert McNamara drew from Wilson, but we guess it was the worst sort. Wilson had sent 112,000 Americans to their deaths in World War I in an effort to win a war to end all wars. The result was the opposite of Wilson's stated intention. But instead of reaching the obvious conclusion—that Wilson was a dimwit— McNamara rushed to do something just as foolish.

At the height of the war in April 1969, US troops in Vietnam numbered 543,000, at a cost of $61 billion per year—far, far more than the administration's estimates of $5 billion per year maximum provided back in 1965 (a figure that seemed to emerge time and again amid the vague generalizations McNamara and others offered).

McNamara's book makes amusing reading. It describes a futile effort on the part of the US team to get their Vietnamese counterparts to take a measure of the blame for what they regarded as a "tragedy." The Vietnamese saw no tragedy and accepted no blame. Instead, the way they see it, their country was attacked by foreigners—first the French, then the Japanese, then the French again, with support from America, and then by the Americans. They had undertaken a long, costly war to liberate the country—against a vastly superior military force. It was no tragedy; it was a crime.

On the US side, McNamara and his fellow imperialists were determined to keep morality out of the discussion. They regarded the whole affair as a series of unfortunate errors, miscalculations, misunderstandings, and mistakes. They faced their former enemies not as sinners or criminals, but as incompetents. They seemed practically desperate for the Vietnamese to play along, to admit that they, too, made mistakes that contributed to the misunderstanding that led to the tragedy. But the old Annamites wouldn't cooperate.

Asked, for example, if the North Vietnamese hadn't misread the signal implied in President Johnson's bombing campaign that began March 5, 1965 (called *Rolling Thunder*), the Vietnamese delegates protested. They didn't know it was a signal. They thought the Americans were trying to kill them.

In almost every instance, McNamara and the rest of the US team tried to keep the discussion on strategic issues, diplomatic initiatives, inputs, outputs, throughputs, and other mumbo jumbo. Even three decades after the fact, despite the public weeping, McNamara seems almost not to notice that he sent men to kill who were not always too particular about whom they killed. When a man sticks a knife in his neighbor, it is not easy to disguise what is really happening. The event is right in front of him. But the fog of war, as Clausewitz called it, multiplies by the square of the distance from it. In the Oval Office or the war rooms of the Pentagon, the transactions that took place in Vietnam became "costs" or "losses" or "collateral damage." It was as if they were running an insurance company. The losses were regrettable perhaps, but also excusable and, generally, forgettable.

The Vietnam War, 1961 to 1975, was far bloodier than we are accustomed to think. America lost 58,000 troops. The Vietnamese lost an estimated 3.8 million, according to McNamara. Yet, reading the whiz kid's account of his involvement, it is as if he had never met a single one of them. Every human being in the war was treated as war matériel. They were resources, like bombs and cans of Coke. Treated as assets on the military balance sheet, they are expended as though they were inflated currency.

Robert McNamara saw the war as a bounded, engineering problem. He expected it to be rational, a system that could be modeled and that would yield to practical planning and logical extrapolation. He expected the war could be won simply by increasing the cost to the Vietcong and North Vietnamese. At some point, the cost would become unacceptably high.

In this sense, he was not unlike the geniuses who ran Long-Term Capital Management into the ground in the late 1990s. They thought the financial world could be modeled, too—just as if it were science. They reasoned that the odds of an investment going up or down could be calculated just as you could figure the odds of hitting an iceberg in the North Atlantic. Then you could make your bets calmly, scientifically; after all, it was just advanced mathematics.

The economists in 1998 at Long-Term Capital Management included two winners of the Nobel Prize, but their theories were wrong. Neither investing nor war making is a hard science; they are "human" sciences perhaps, closer to art than science. The difference is obvious. You can heat water to 212 degrees Fahrenheit and it will boil—every time (assuming constant pressure). But put a man under heat or pressure, and the fellow could react in any number of different, unpredictable, irrational, and wholly bizarre ways.

Between 1965 and 1975, the United States stepped up its killing campaign. The Vietnamese suffered hundreds of thousands of casualties as the pressure increased. America was turning up the heat, ready for it to boil over and force the North Vietnamese to the negotiating table. The table was set. But the Americans were astonished when no one showed up. It was as if the North Vietnamese didn't care how hot it got. It was as if they ignored all the resources the United States was bringing to bear and the losses that they were inflicting. It was as if they couldn't count!

It made no sense to McNamara. So, he asked the question of the Vietnamese delegation sitting opposite him in Hanoi, 30 years later. How come all the misery we inflicted on the Vietnamese did not bring them to ask for a settlement? Tran Quang Co replied:

> I would like to answer Mr. McNamara's question. . . . I must say that this question of Mr. McNamara's has allowed us to better understand the issue. During the coffee break, an American colleague asked me if I had learned anything about the U.S. during the discussions of the past few days. And I responded that I have learned quite a lot. However, thanks to this particular question, I believe we have learned still more about the U.S. We understand better now that the U.S. understands very little about Vietnam. Even now—in this conference—the U.S. understand very little about Vietnam.

When the U.S. bombed the North and brought its troops into the South, well, of course, to us there were very negative moves. However, with regard to Vietnam, U.S. aggression did have some positive use. Never before did the people of Vietnam, from top to bottom, unite as they did during the years that the U.S. was bombing us. Never before had Chairman Ho Chi Minh's appeal—that there is nothing more precious than freedom and independence—go straight to the hearts and minds of the Vietnamese people as at the end of 1966.[18]

The Vietnam War was not merely a tragedy, or even a crime. It was a farce. US troops had been sent to kill people they didn't know, in a country they had never been, for reasons none of them could understand, by men as benighted as they were. Ho Chi Minh had expected the United States to come to his aid, not to seek his destruction. Yet, McNamara and President Johnson sent troops to kill people on the basis of an idea so flimsy that, when the war was over, it disappeared without a trace. Gradually, the war was escalated on the basis of a mistake and run as a series of errors, culminating in a disgraceful rout. At every step of the way, US military and civilian officials misunderstood and underestimated their opponents. General William Westmoreland briefed Congress in July 1967: "The situation is not a stalemate. We are winning slowly but steadily, and the pace can accelerate if we reinforce our successes." All we need is more resources!

He could have saved himself the trouble of making it up and taken the communiqué, word for word, sent by French General Raoul Salan, who in October, 20 years before, reported that the Vietminh were on the run. All that were left were isolated bands susceptible to police operations.

"Not once during the war," wrote General Bruce Palmer in his book, *Twenty-five Year War*, "did the Joint Chiefs of Staff advise the commander-in-chief or the secretary of defense that the strategy being pursued most probably would fail and that the U.S. would be unable to achieve its objectives."[19]

Achieve its objectives? No one really knew what America's objectives were. Or if they were attainable. Or, if they really made any difference to anybody in America. The United States had become an empire with scarcely anyone noticing. Its goals were no longer those of its people but of the empire itself. An empire must routinely and habitually contest control of periphery areas. The imperial people had merely come to believe what they had to believe to go along with the program.

The madness began as an oversimplification back in the Eisenhower administration. In 1954, President Eisenhower provided his now famous "domino" speech, by way of explaining that if South Vietnam were lost to communism, all of Indochina would fall. In November 1995, General Vo Nguyen Giap put it to Robert McNamara generously: "Dominoes, dominoes, dominoes—this theory was an illusion. Whatever happened in Vietnam had nothing to do with what happened in Laos, nothing to do with Indonesia. . . . I am amazed that even the brightest people—people like yourself—could have believed it."[20]

Believed it? What was there to believe? That a state—an abstract as well as physical thing—of 35 million people (in 1965) of various cultures, languages, religions, ethnic and racial groups, political preferences, modernization, and sexual preferences, living in a land of 127,000 square miles (about the size of New Mexico), including mountains, swamps, beaches, plains, jungle, hamlets, and cities could be understood as a small, three-dimensional object painted in two colors! The idea was not stupid. It was just absurd. Einstein had said that things should be made as simple as possible, but no simpler. America's empire builders of the 1960s had gone too far. It was as if they had simplified the Old Testament as "Jews kick butts in the Holy Land." They had lost the nuances and details that made it interesting.

Whether Laos or Cambodia would be affected by events in Vietnam, no one could say. But what they could say with complete assurance was that Vietnam was not a domino. If proximity caused nations to change their political systems, why hadn't West Germany become like East Germany? Why did Switzerland keep its federal system when it was surrounded by centralized governments? And who ever heard of dominoes that fell only in one direction? If the presence of a communist South Vietnam might cause Thailand to topple toward communism, mightn't the presence of Thailand on its border cause South Vietnam to topple toward constitutional monarchy?

It was not merely mad to kill people on the basis of the domino theory, it was Wilsonian. But once the madness took hold, there was nothing stopping it. Soon, almost every member of the chattering classes had decided that what was literally and obviously untrue was worth (someone else) dying for.

Thirty years after the fact, McNamara seemed embarrassed to recollect why he and his colleagues once thought the matter was so vitally important. They figured the communists were taking over everywhere. If Vietnam also fell to communists, it would be a disaster. But why? No one seemed to recall.

Yes, there were the dominoes. If Vietnam went communist, so might all of Southeast Asia. We now know that it was nonsense. But what if it had been true? If the people of Southeast Asia wanted to "go communist," who were we to tell them not to? It was only because America presumed to empire that the question even came up. Empires are involved in constant warfare—the struggle to control vassal states on the periphery. Typically, they do so to maintain order throughout the empire, as well as to obtain new sources of tribute. But our answer presumes a logic that isn't there. Empires fight for dominoes—not for any particular, logical reason, but merely because they are empires.

McNamara points out that leading intellectuals, the media, politicians, policymakers, and even street bums viewed the war as a struggle between communism and the Free World.

Could not Vietnam have been independent, but neutral in the Cold War? Why did it matter anyway; Vietnam was still a primitive, mostly agricultural nation. Whichever side gained her allegiance, what did they gain? Nobody ever seemed to ask—either themselves or the other side.

"I am aghast at the shallowness of our thinking on the issue of a neutral solution," writes McNamara. "Why didn't we ask Hanoi for a full explanation of the process they foresaw? If we had asked, and if they had convinced us, for example, that they foresaw reunification taking years, even decades, my god, we would have or should have jumped at it."[21]

In the discussions and confessions 30 years after the end of the war, the Vietnamese said they had been open to suggestion. In retrospect, it looks as though the whole conflict—or at least the bloodiest part—could have been avoided, simply by sitting down and exploring a few issues. But the lunkheads running US foreign policy at the time did not even bother to ask. It was arrogance, no doubt, on the part of McNamara and others, that prevented anyone in the administration from seriously considering *conversation* as an alternative to brute force.

Bad ideas, foolish theories, misconceived campaigns, misunderstood signals—the war in Vietnam began in almost total ignorance and went downhill. Nobody knew anything worth knowing. Nobody understood anything worth understanding. And nobody did anything worth doing.

But we return to the critical question: Americans were dead set against letting Vietnam "go communist." Why? If a group of people in Columbus, Ohio, decided to pool their property and to live collectively, there would be no terrible outcry. (Though eventually, the Feds would probably get them on a weapons or tax charge.) The only plausible reason for being against communism is that the communists were almost invariably world-improvers themselves. They were not content to collectivize their own property, but insisted on collectivizing other people's property, too. Then, when they had made a mess of their own country, they turned their sights on the countries next door.

The feature that made communism barbaric was not that people shared the same toothbrush or denied the profit motive. Instead, it was the common mark of all barbarism—the readiness to use brute force to get what you want. What marks a civilized society, however, is a reluctance to use force, preferring persuasion and cooperation over force and fraud.

There are only two ways to get what you want in life. You can get it honestly, by trade, work, or some other bargain—an economic means of some sort. Or, you can get it dishonestly, by stealing it or taking it away from someone—that is, by political means. There is no other way, save a miracle. This distinction works for "things" such as automobiles and whiskey. It also works for other "wants"—such as sex, ambition, and vanity. We can build our reputations and our own *amour propre* by economic means; say, by working hard we can earn money and feel superior to others. Or we can pick a fight with others to prove we can beat them. Into which category does the effort to "bomb North Vietnam back to the Stone Age" fit? US involvement in Vietnam may have been well-intentioned, but it was missing the point.

188 EMPIRE OF DEBT

Martin Luther King Jr. confronted the contradiction in a famous speech. "My opposition to the war," he said,

> ... grows out of my experience in the ghettoes of the North over the last three years—especially the last three summers. As I have walked among the desperate, rejected and angry young men I have told them that Molotov cocktails and rifles would not solve their problems. I have tried to offer them my deepest compassion while maintaining my conviction that social change comes most meaningfully through nonviolent action. But they asked—and rightly so—what about Vietnam? They asked if our own nation wasn't using massive doses of violence to solve its problems, to bring about the changes it wanted. Their questions hit home, and I knew that I could never again raise my voice against the violence of the oppressed in the ghettos without having first spoken clearly to the greatest purveyor of violence in the world today—my own government. For the sake of those boys, for the sake of this government, for the sake of hundreds of thousands trembling under our violence, I cannot be silent.[22]

If Western democracies have a virtue, it is that they are gradual and consensual—that is to say, that they are civilized. If suddenly the majority of Americans were to decide that every citizen with red hair should be guillotined, it would be an uncivilized thing to do—even if they had voted on it fair and square. It is the means that are the end. The fact that people are willing to get along with one another without resort to violence is what makes a civilized society, not the fact that the particular day-to-day whims of the masses are enacted into law by a group of legislative hacks. Defending Western civilization by bombing North Vietnam was a bit like what Clovis, King of the Francs, proposed to do after he had become a Christian and learned of Christ's crucifixion. Legend has it that Clovis remarked: "If only I had been there with my armies, I would have had revenge against those Jews."

In his private life, Lyndon Johnson understood what the Vietnam War really meant for America:

> I don't think it's worth fighting for and I don't think we can get out. It's just the biggest damned mess I ever saw. . . . And we just got to think about it. I'm looking at this Sergeant of mine this morning and he's got 6 little old kids over there, and he's getting out my things,

and bringing me in my night reading, and all that kind of stuff, and I just thought about ordering all those kids in there. And what in the hell am I ordering them out there for? What in the hell is Vietnam worth to me? What is Laos worth to me? What is it worth to this country? We've got a treaty but hell, everybody else has got a treaty out there, and they're not doing a thing about it.[23]

But America went in anyway. And then the bodies came back in plastic bags.

And even after 30 years, it seems not to have occurred to McNamara that he did anything wrong. Right and wrong seemed to have no place in his analytical brain. Instead, he wondered how he could have done his job better, how he could have fought the war more efficiently, or why he "missed opportunities" to settle it at lower cost. He saw no moral lessons—only practical ones. He looked for no wisdom from the dead, only hints from the living about how to win. If he had only had more information, says McNamara, his world improvements would have turned out better.

Tran Quang Co put him on the spot:

Mr. McNamara admits his mistakes, which we admire, but he unfortunately attributes most mistakes to misjudgments and miscalculations. But we must also ask: What about values and intentions? As I understand it, the right to self-determination—the independence of a nation—belongs to the general values of the world community. What about U.S. support of the French colonialists after World War II, in defiance of its own democratic traditions? What about the direct U.S. military intervention in Vietnam—I mean sending U.S. soldiers to find and kill Southern Vietnamese? And what about the U.S. policy seeking to divide Vietnam for good and to "bomb North Vietnam back to the Stone Age?" We must ask: are these policies consistent with the moral values?[24]

Principles? Morals? There is no room for constitutional restraints, authentic values, or real virtues when you are building an empire. The heart overpowers the brain. Public chatter overpowers private thoughts. Public slogans drown out private acts of decency and courage. Empty words and big theories replace actual thinking. The public itself is charmed and bamboozled, then robbed, killed, or both.

Americans learned nothing from the French experience. De Gaulle warned Kennedy that Vietnam would be a graveyard for US soldiers. It was a "rotten country," he said, unsuitable for Western ways of war. But in the inflationary boom of the first "Guns and Butter" administration, that of Lyndon B. Johnson, Americans thought they could do what the French couldn't. They spent far more money than the French and lost far more men, but Giap beat them, just as he had the French.

While France and America enjoyed their defeats, Vietnam suffered its own dreary independence like a war wound. The whole country oozed a pathetic poverty for the next quarter century, scabbed over with a squalid ideology.

As of 2005, General Giap was still alive. The old man, 91 when he was interviewed by the *Figaro* in 2004, was asked what he thought of America's situation in Iraq: "When you try to impose your will on a foreign nation you will be defeated. Every nation that struggles for independence will win." Woe to empires.

"What we've done," continued the old man, perhaps drifting into senile dementia, forgetting that his comrades set up a police state following his military victory, "was to fight for the right of each man to live and develop as he chooses ... and the right of each people to enjoy national sovereignty."

CHAPTER 8

TRICKY DICK

On August 15, 1971, the administration of Richard Milhous Nixon did something extraordinary. It slammed the "gold window" shut. Henceforth, foreign governments would not be able to redeem their surplus US dollars for gold.

Mention the late president's name, and the average person recalls the crime with which he is so often associated: breaking into and entering the Watergate. But while the public's attention was distracted by Nixon's fumbling sidekicks, another team of Nixon goons was pulling off the biggest heist of all time.

A lumpen investor, a university economist, or a Federal Reserve governor might have read the headlines of the past 30 years without noticing how they tucked together. They might have seen the boom in gold of the 1970s, the bubble in Japan in the 1980s, or the subsequent bubbles throughout the rest of Asia as events as independent of each other as a stolen hubcap in New Orleans and a stolen kiss in Boston.

They might also have looked on the boom and bubble in the United States as unrelated and mistaken the run-up in stock prices as a consequence of the New Era wonder age, the new productivity of information age technology, or the newfound wisdom of the guiding hands at the Federal Reserve. They may even have referred to the productivity miracle as the source of such a wonderful thing. Never, however, would they have imagined that all the great economic and market events of the past three decades found their inspiration in the same place and time: at the hands of Nixon's lackeys in the early 1970s.

What was their crime? Breach of contract? Theft? Fraud? Counterfeiting? It was all those things. They breached the solemn promise of five generations of US Treasury officials and set in motion the worldwide credit bubble of the *pax dollarium* age (see Figure 8.1).

In 1971, the decision to abandon the gold standard was not exactly an improvisation. The decision was part of a series of moves made by the Nixon administration to hold down wages and prices and to check inflation. Consumer prices rose at 4.9% in 1970 and inflation looked as though it was going to get worse. Nixon came to believe that he could control the economy, even though this shift in policy contradicted his own political and economic philosophy as stated in the past.

Arthur Burns, chairman of the Federal Reserve during Nixon's administration, had served as an advisor during Nixon's failed 1960 presidential campaign. At that time, Burns warned Nixon that tight

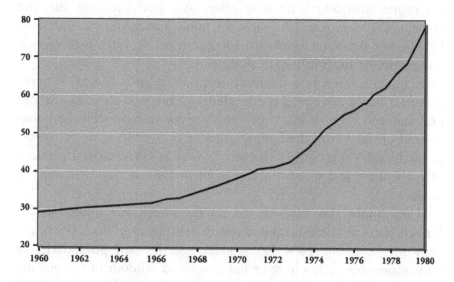

FIGURE 8.1   Consumer Price Index, 1960–1980

Richard Nixon's decision to slam the "gold window" shut has had one demonstrable effect: It set in motion the world-wide credit bubble of the *pax dollarium* age. As a result, the price Americans have to pay for "goods and services" has risen dramatically—and without a pause—ever since.
Source: U.S. Department of Labor, Public Domain.

money policies would worsen the economy, hurting Nixon and ultimately costing him the election. Burns proved to be right: "Now, a decade later, in May 1970, Burns stood up and declared that he had changed his mind about economic policy. The economy was no longer operating as it used to, owing to the now much more powerful position of corporations and labor unions, which together were driving up both wages and prices. The traditional fiscal and monetary policies were now seen as inadequate. His solution: a wage-price review board, composed of distinguished citizens, who would pass judgment on major wage and price increases. Their power, in Burns's new lexicon, would be limited to persuasion, friendly or otherwise."[1]

Nixon agreed with most of it, except the part about limiting controls to friendly persuasion.

Not since the reign of Diocletian had such a powerful empire attempted such an idiotic thing. As part of the big changes in 1971, Nixon created the Cost of Living Council, organized specifically to administer a 90-day freeze on wage and price hikes. Although this temporary measure was removed, inflation returned. In June 1973, controls were reimposed, shortly before Nixon's resignation. Finally, admitting that these policies did not work as hoped, the wage and price control plan was given up in April 1974 during the Ford administration.

PAYING THE PRICE

Financially, the Vietnam War was a mess. The decision-makers had no idea how much the war would cost, or how the bills would be paid. As early as 1965, the McNamara team had an estimate from Army Chief of Staff General Harold K. Johnson that winning the war would require as many as 500,000 troops and five years of fighting. The policymakers were aghast. They were not prepared to commit to anything like that level of involvement—in terms of the numbers of people as well as the costs involved. The chairman of President Johnson's Council of Economic Advisors told the president in 1965, "The current thinking in DOD [Department of Defense], as relayed to me by Bob McNamara on a super-confidential basis, points to a gradual and moderate build-up of expenditures and manpower."[2]

The debate over the real costs of the war continued throughout the entire period from 1964 through 1968. It wasn't until late 1967, however, that LBJ asked Congress for a 10% tax surcharge. That surcharge was approved by mid-1968, but only on condition that Johnson also cut $6 billion from domestic programs—a requirement that hurt him dearly. His beloved Great Society programs, half of the "guns-and-butter" policy defining his presidency, ultimately were curtailed by the escalating costs of the war in Vietnam. But neither the costs of the war nor those of the Great Society were cut enough.

The total spent by the United States on the Vietnam War amounted to more than $500 billion in today's money. That is a lot of money at any time. At first, Johnson assured the nation that the war would not jeopardize his other promises. He had pledged to give away billions of other people's money; the offer was still good, he said. He told Congress in 1966, "I believe that we can continue the Great Society while we fight in Vietnam."[3] As the costs mounted up, government budget officials and his own economic advisors began to worry. The math wasn't working. The president's guns-and-butter policy, a 1960s' version of the Romans' bread and circuses was too expensive. They realized they needed more revenue. Rising deficits and rising inflation levels in the United States worried foreign dollar holders, who began calling away America's gold. Only higher tax revenues could cure the problem (see Figure 8.2).

President Johnson stood his ground. He feared that "all hell will break loose" if he were to request a tax increase. Congress would rather cut the butter than raise taxes or give up the guns. The result would be the end of the Great Society.

Lyndon Johnson had no money of his own to fund the Great Society programs he set in place. He could only give money to one voter by taking it away from another one. Peter had to be robbed if Paul was to be paid.

But theft is not murder, and not only will the majority of citizens in a democracy put up with a little thievery, they will welcome it—especially if it is done on their behalf. The most popular US presidents were those who stole most bountifully. The logic of democratic larceny is that there are always more voters receiving tax money than getting it taken from them. That is the real reason Democrats favor doing something "to help the poor"—there are more of them; you

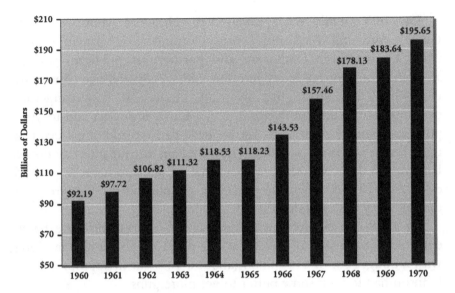

FIGURE 8.2   Federal Outlays, 1960–1970

The total amount spent by the United States on the Vietnam War exceeded $500 billion in today's money. Lyndon Johnson's guns-and-butter policy, a 1960s' version of the Romans' bread and circuses, was too expensive. Rising deficits and inflation in the United States worried foreign dollar holders, who began calling away America's gold.
Source: U.S. Government Publishing Office, Public Domain.

can buy their votes cheaply. Wave a $10 bill in front of a rich man and you will get little attention—in a trailer park, you will draw a crowd. Still, in a fluid society like the United States, there are also a lot of people who hope to get rich some day and want to look forward to holding onto their money if it ever comes their way. So, there is always a certain resistance to higher taxes, and in 1966 and 1967, Lyndon Johnson was loath to run into it.

But there was resistance to bankrupting the country, too. There were still a few geezers in Congress who believed in balanced budgets. So, after the 1966 elections, Johnson's 10% tax surcharge was presented. This, he said, would give the United States "staying power" in its fight with communism. Robert McNamara now claims that he knew the war was hopeless as early as 1964, so staying power was exactly what the United States didn't need. What it needed was the courage to quit. But it is this courage that is most lacking in times of war. People would rather die than admit that they are doing an asinine and pointless thing.

Johnson's tax hike was opposed in the House by Minority Leader Gerald Ford and Ways and Means Committee Chairman Wilbur Mills. The southern Democrats and northern Republicans wanted spending cuts, not tax hikes. Johnson said, "They will live to rue the day when they made that decision, because it is a dangerous decision . . . an unwise decision. . . . I know it doesn't add to your polls and your popularity to say we have to have additional taxes to fight this war abroad and fight the problems in our cities at home. But we can do it with the gross national product we have. We should do it. And I think when the American people and the Congress get the full story they will do it."[4]

By 1968, the empire was going broke. Gold reserves were being depleted. Congress had to act, passing the 10% tax surcharge along with a budget cut of $18 billion (about a 10% cut in appropriations). Johnson had to melt some butter to get more guns.

At the time, Washington still operated on old-fashioned Keynesian economics and a gold standard. Economists believed government could spend more heavily in times of war or times of economic hardship (to "prime the pump"), but it was still widely agreed that what was borrowed must be paid back. Deficits still mattered, partly because they threatened the nation's currency (and its gold backing), and partly because policymakers still thought they would have to make up overspending now by underspending in the future.

Then, as now, taxpayers could be squeezed, but only so hard and only if politically realistic. Otherwise, they would soon start to howl. Redistribution of wealth only works, politically, if someone else's money is being passed around. Taxpayers don't see any advantage in giving up their own money.

Liberal politicians in the 1960s advertised themselves much as George W. Bush does today. They said they were extending freedom at home as well as abroad. "How can anyone say that a nation with an income of more than $800 billion can't afford a $30 billion war?" said Paul Douglas of Illinois.[5]

"Military forces able to defend the cause of freedom in Vietnam and to counter other threats to national security require substantial resources. Yet we cannot permit the defense of freedom abroad to sidetrack the struggle for individual growth and dignity at home," added Johnson.

Vice President Hubert Humphrey joined in, saying that America "can afford to extend freedom at home at the same time that it defends it abroad."[6]

"The United States is not faced—nor could it be faced—with a guns and butter choice. . . . This country has ample resources to prosecute the shooting war and still combat the shortcomings of our own society," continued AFL-CIO president George Meany.[7]

Nor did the people disagree. Americans favored more guns and more butter, over a reduction in spending on either front, by a margin of 48% to 39%, according to a Harris poll.

Until the Vietnam era, after every previous war was over, federal spending dropped. When the Vietnam War ended, however, federal spending continued to go up. The federal budget had been $184 billion in 1969 at the height of the military spending. In 1972, it rose to $231 billion. In 1969, the federal government actually ran a surplus of $3 billion. By 1972, with the war winding down, we expected to see the surpluses continue; but instead the surplus turned into a deficit of $23 billion.

The empire grew, and kept growing. Before launching the attack on the USSR, June 22, 1941, Hitler remarked that the Soviet Union was like a rickety old house. All we have to do, he said, was "kick in the door and the whole thing will fall down." He was 48 years premature. The Soviet Union fell apart in 1989 by itself; America didn't even have to kick in the door. But even after the Cold War was over, the federal budget continued to rise, from $1.14 trillion in 1989 to $1.38 trillion in 1992.

The Great Society was merely the domestic wing of America's new system of imperial finance. Johnson offered more bread and more circuses than any president before him. The five-year cost of administering the Great Society programs was estimated at $305.7 billion (in 2005 inflation-adjusted dollars). This does not include the $250 billion in college loans and grants to 29 million students since 1965 (see Figure 8.3).

The scope of the Great Society was massive, comparable to Franklin Roosevelt's New Deal programs but on a more expensive scale. Even counting only Medicaid and Medicare, the LBJ idea has added trillions to US future obligations: "During [the Johnson] administration, Congress enacted two major civil-rights acts

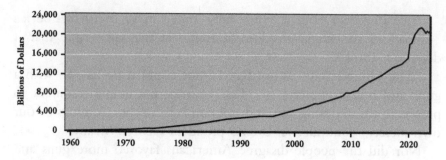

FIGURE 8.3   U.S. Money Supply 1971–2023

The great cost of administering the empire requires an ever-expanding supply of the imperial currency. Since US currency has become untethered to gold, the quantity of paper dollars floating around the globe has ballooned significantly, rendering each dollar a little less valuable than the last.
Source: Federal Reserve, Public Domain.

(1964 and 1965), the Economic Opportunity Act (1964), and two education acts (1965). In addition, legislation was passed that created the Job Corps, Operation Head Start, Volunteers in Service to America (VISTA), Medicaid, and Medicare. Although the Great Society program made significant contributions to the protection of civil rights and the expansion of social programs, critics increasingly complained that the antipoverty programs were ineffective and wasteful."[8]

This expansion had the consequence of creating massive bureaucracies within the federal system. Considering the Medicaid and Medicare costs alone, we have seen exponential growth in current and future obligations, impractical cost-benefit outcomes, widespread waste, and fraud within the medical establishment. The programs were expanded partly to counter growing unrest at home. We should recall that by the end of Johnson's presidency, the country was disturbed. Race riots in the inner cities, massive antiwar protests, and clashes between students and police were commonplace from 1965 onward, and continued into Nixon's reign.

NIXON'S THE ONE

People wanted more bread and circuses. Personal consumption expenditures had expanded significantly since the end of World War II. By 1970, annual expenditures were 4.5 times higher than in 1946. After 1971, when the *pax dollarium* system began, expenditures grew

exponentially. By the year 2000, annual levels were at $6.68 *trillion*—
46 times higher than at the end of the Second World War.

But what followed Nixon immediately was an era of financial turmoil that has rarely been equaled in modern history. The US dollar
plunged precipitously, US unemployment exceeded 10%, oil prices
skyrocketed to $39 a barrel, the Dow Jones Industrial Average fell to
570, gold reached $800 an ounce, and US inflation and interest rates
climbed to double-digit levels.

Imagine investors who bought a 30-year US Treasury bond in
1970. Did they not have a right to expect to receive a dollar back for
every dollar lent? And shouldn't they have been able to expect that
each of those dollars they received—in the year 2000—would be
worth about as much as those they had given up?

We can measure the damage by looking at the price of gold. In
1970, each dollar would buy an investor 1/34 of an ounce of gold.
Thirty-five years later, Mr. Market, sitting as judge and jury, tells us
that a dollar is worth less than 1/425 of an ounce of gold.

Investors, taking the US government at its word, have lost trillions.
The purchasing power of the dollar has fallen precipitously.[9]

Still, so subtle was the theft that the victims have practically
applauded the crime. Over the past century years, they seemed to
think it was making them rich!

PAX DOLLARIUM

Globalized commerce, as practiced by the United States since 1971,
has a fraudulent side. The hegemonic power uses political means;
even when it shops. During the last big boost in the division of labor,
in the 19th century up until 1913, gold backed the money in which
transactions were calibrated. No country—not even an imperial
one—could cheat.

If a country consumed more than it produced, other countries
found themselves with surpluses of the laggard nation's currency.
They then could ask for gold in settlement. Gold was real, ultimate
money. No nation could manufacture it. No national assembly could
undermine its value or pass a law that increased it. When a nation's
gold horde was in danger, it quickly adjusted its policies to correct

the imbalance and protect its gold. The dollar, however, is merely a piece of paper, and since Nixon slammed the gold window shut it is backed by nothing more than the full faith and credit of the United States Treasury. How good a promise is that? No one knows for sure.

The government set up the Federal Reserve in the first place because it wanted a stooge currency. Gold is fine, they said, but it's antisocial. It resists progress and drags its feet on financing new wars and social programs. When we face a war or a great national purpose, we need money that is more patriotic, they said. Gold malingers. Gold hesitates. Gold is reticent. Gold keeps to itself, offering neither advice nor encouragement. Gold has no party affiliation; it doesn't vote. What we need, policymakers said themselves, is a more public-spirited money, a source of public funding, a flexible, expandable national currency, a *political* money that we can work with. We need a dollar that is not linked to gold.

In the many years since the Federal Reserve was set up in 1913, gold has remained as steadfast and immobile as ever. An ounce of it today buys about the same amount of goods and services as an ounce in 1913, and roughly the same amount as it did when Christ was born. But the dollar has gone along with every bit of political gim-crackery that has come along—the war in Europe, the New Deal, World War II, the Cold War, the Vietnam War, the war on poverty, the war on illiteracy, the New Frontier, the Great Society, Social Security, Medicare, Medicaid, the war in Iraq, the war on terror. As a result, guess how much a dollar is worth today in comparison to one in 1913? Five cents.

The Federal Reserve system was set up to provide the nation's empire builders with a convenient, expandable, and compliant money. Whenever they felt they needed more of it, the dollar was right there, ready for duty.

There was a crack in that bell, too. The dollar was ready for service, but its very willingness to serve its masters in Washington made it unreliable to the rest of the world. If the Fed asked the dollar to jump off a cliff, it would do so, no questions asked. This might be a benefit to Washington, but to Tokyo or Peking, it was a risk. At the beginning of 2005, the two nations together held many US Treasury notes that could take a dive at any time.

Since 1971, the United States has added trillions to the world's supply of dollars and credit. During this same time, only about 58,000 metric tons of gold have been brought from the ground. Sooner or later, those extra dollars must be marked to an unforgiving market.

Of course, it hasn't happened yet. Investors are tempted to look out their windows, see the sun shining, and think the dollar will last forever. They have no interest in the financial crimes of the Disco Age.

PART III

EVENING IN AMERICA

The borrower shall be a slave to the lender.

—Proverbs 22:7

CHAPTER 9

AMERICAN MONEY

"It is strange, I mean the way things work out," said a guest at dinner one night. "It seems like a kind of madness wanders around the globe. While, here in Europe, we were trying to batter each other's brains out, you, in America, you were smart. You were sitting back and taking orders. Now you're the ones who have gone mad."

Our guest had described the world of the 19th and 20th centuries—the days when the idea of a US empire was still repugnant and absurd. While wars, revolutions, and pogroms stormed over Europe—and much of the rest of the world—the US kept to itself, reluctant to get involved. Attractive new ideas popped up all over Europe like poisonous mushrooms. But, for the most part, Americans kept their heads. Most went about their business, seeking happiness in their own private ways—trying to get rich. "The business of America is business," Calvin Coolidge explained.

Money isn't everything, we suddenly recalled. Lusting after wealth is not always becoming, not always rewarding, and rarely flattering or dignified. There is something vulgar about the hustle a real business needs ... like sweat stains on a starched shirt or a cold cup of coffee and stubbed-out cigarettes. A person who wants to make a real fortune usually has to grub for it; it's hard to be elegant or refined when you're scratching for cash or market share. But grubbing for money is still better than many other things people do. What follows is a reflection on what the lust for money is better than.

Grubbing for money might be fine for a modest nation working its way up in the world, but is it worthy of a great nation on a roll?

"The trouble with the emphasis in conservatism on the market," William F. Buckley said, "is that it becomes rather boring. You hear it once, you master the idea. The notion of devoting your life to it is horrifying if only because it's so repetitious. It's like sex."[1]

Another old "conservative," Irving Kristol said, "What's the point of being the greatest, most powerful nation in the world, and not having an imperial role?"

"It's too bad," Kristol lamented about money-grubbing, "I think it would be natural for the United States ... to play a far more dominant role in world affairs ... to command and to give orders as to what is to be done. People need that."[2]

"When I think of all the crazy things that went on here in France during the last century," continued our dinner guest, "Or maybe I should say in Europe. You know, we invented most of the awful ideas back then. Deconstructionism, Freudianism, Nazism, Conceptualism, Socialism, Syndicalism, Minimalism, Communism, Functionalism ... come to think of it almost all the worst ideas came from Europe. And even in America, if I'm not mistaken, almost all the new developments in philosophy, art, and architecture came from immigrants ... or maybe refugees ... from Europe. Just about everything. Of course, most of it was harmless. Funny even ... like Dadaism. But politics wasn't so harmless. But now, the world has turned. Now you do what we did. You come up with the new ideas ... and you try to force other people to accept them. You have that ... what do they call it ... neoconservatism."

"We sense that we live in a time set apart," said George W. Bush in his State of the Union 2004 address. What made the time seem so set apart was that the United States had come to resemble a parody of itself; it had come to look like the country leftists had always criticized it for being, but that it had never been: a remarkable combination of self-delusion and self-satisfaction headed for self-destruction. The old conservatives, with their knee-jerk affection for limited government, balanced budgets, and fewer regulations—Republican principles from the Coolidge era—might have saved them, but the old conservatives were gone.

It is a shame about conservatism. Yes, the old sticks-in-the-mud were an impediment to progress. Yes, the old mossbacks were dull and predictable. Yes, their old knees jerked whenever they thought someone might be having fun. Still, we miss those fuddy-duddies. You could count on them to resist the tyranny of the here and now. When something new presented itself, they wouldn't like it. They would resist it, not from any intellectual point of view, but the way a person resists a new pair of shoes or a dog resists a new collar. The new styles might be more fashionable, but that was reason enough to avoid them.

As a creed, conservatism has lost all its adherents, at least in the United States. As a philosophy, it has practically disappeared. As a political movement, with the election of Donald J. Trump, it dropped dead. Everyone likes new things now.

The essential quality of conservatism is not a specific agenda (neither to lower taxes nor to raise the flag), it is merely a way of looking at things—suspiciously—and of reacting to new proposals—dragging one's feet. Conservatives fight against new doctrines like they fought against sushi: they thought it was not only unappetizing; it might be dangerous, too.

But now the geezers have dyed their hair and had their faces lifted. The codgers refinanced their houses, paid with credit cards, and voted for whomever promised them the most of someone else's money. In politics, and in money, the grumps went along with whatever is popular—just like everyone else.

About the only thing you can still count on is vanity—it never seems to go out of style. In the here and now, every generation is the greatest one that ever lived. Every empire is permanent, and everyone who makes trouble for it is an evil subhuman.

In the early part of the 21st century, America's neoconservative heirs to the Wilsons—Woodrow Wilson and Ronald Wilson Reagan—became the earth's most dynamic and ambitious empire builders. Claes G. Ryn in the *American Conservative*, said,

> These Cold Warriors were mostly liberals of a special, ideologically zealous variety. Many of them had come from the extreme Left. They had opposed communism because they had universalistic objectives of their own and did not want any competition. These proponents of a

single model for all societies were able to form an alliance with putative conservatives, who had come to believe during the Cold War that to be conservative was always to be hawkish and assertive in foreign policy. Used to "standing up for America," these nationalistic and saber-rattling conservatives found in the cause of a better world, a new outlet for their desire to exercise American power. Oddly, this coalition to remake the world became known as neoconservatism.[3]

LATE DEGENERATE POPULISM

The neocons preached a rousing sermon of "global democratic revolution," to quote George W. Bush. There is nothing conservative about revolution, but who noticed?

From Hegel, through Marx, Antonio Gramsci, and Cloward-Piven, progressive idealism has sought to maximize the power of the state over the rights of individuals. Politicians and demagogues are preternaturally drawn to power the state affords them.

"During the 1920s and the early 1930s," the economist Thomas Sowell writes, "fascism was not only looked on favorably by the left but recognized as having kindred ideas, agendas and assumptions. Only after Hitler and Mussolini disgraced themselves, mainly by their brutal military aggressions in the 1930s, did the left distance itself from these international pariahs."

Sowell continues providing a warning to our own times:

Fascism, initially recognized as a kindred ideology of the left, has since come down to us defined as being on "the right"—indeed, as representing the farthest right, supposedly further extensions of conservatism.

If by conservatism you mean belief in free markets, limited government, and traditional morality, including religious influences, then these are all things that the fascists opposed just as much as the left does today.

The left may say that they are not racists or anti-semites, like Hitler, but neither was Mussolini or Franco. Hitler, incidentally, got some of his racist ideology from the writings of American "progressives" in the eugenics movement.[4]

In the first administration of the aughts, the neocons had their man in the Oval Office. Secretary of the Treasury Paul O'Neill recalls the leader of the free world had a little trouble following the foreign policy discussions in the White House. But George W. Bush was a shrewd politician who knew a good slogan when someone gave it to him. He saw immediately the advantages of attacking Mesopotamia—it gave him cover to spend more than any president had ever spent, with hardly a peep of protest. Traditional conservatives were struck dumb by this hawkish audacity.

Alas, sometimes it is better to lose a war than to win one. Victory seems to lead to disgrace more often than glory, especially when you are on the road to building an empire. After the West won its Cold War with the Soviet Union, the neocons desperately longed for a new enemy. While they were searching, one of them found the World Trade Towers.

In the opening years of the 21st century, the Huns were America's friends. And the commies its new business partners. Then it was the Muslims of the world who must be defeated! The Muslim mind, according to neoconservative scholars, was locked in the past: it mistreated women, it was anti-democratic, anti-progress, nihilist, and profoundly, irretrievably, stuck in a death struggle with the good guys in the enlightened, free, open-minded, fun-loving, capitalist West. Why this should be so was never clarified. Had not the Muslim mind been around for 1,300 years? Did it not evolve according to its own program, just like the Christian mind, the Confucian mind, or the muddled mind of a Democrat? Were there not many millions of Muslims? Were Muslims less smart than Christians or Jews? And yet, the new conservative thinkers could not imagine that the world would be safe unless Muslims were brought into the empire under their heel.

Twenty years later, a new enemy has been found: Russia. But we'll get to that.

Ronald Reagan had been so successful with his attack on the Soviets' Evil Empire, Republicans hoped for a sequel, never imagining that they might be capable of a little evil themselves. It would be hard, dangerous, and expensive work to transform Islamic civilization, but someone must do it, they said. And only the United States had the military might, the resolve, the courage, the money, and the will to do it. If only the old conservatives' knees still jerked! How they would have harrumphed and gagged.

For here was a new idea—a grand, sweeping new idea—that seemed to call for the most aggressive and activist US foreign policy in US history. Here was a chance for America to entangle itself in foreign military adventures from which it might never get free. Here was an opportunity to vanquish the Muslims, just as Ronald Reagan had beat the Soviets. The United States would make the Islamic world safe for democracy . . . or something like that. Here was a way to improve the world and an almost foolproof way for America to make a public spectacle of itself, go further into debt, and expand its empire!

The old-time conservatives would have been suspicious of such big ideas, especially when they were so flattering. When people flatter you, it is almost certain that they mean to take your business, pick your pocket, or sleep with your spouse. When people flatter themselves, they might just as well put a revolver in their mouth and pull the trigger, for they have lost all touch with reality.

We may be the good guys in the here and now, the old-timers would have said, but if we want to be the good guys in the future, we have to do good things. They would have recalled that people who minded business other than their own almost always came to tears. People are neither good nor bad, the old conservatives would have said, but subject to influence. And by the 21st century, the Lorelei were calling.

Already, many people in the US had begun to wonder: when did we become the "bad guys"? Was it when Teddy Roosevelt conquered Cuba? Or when God spoke to President McKinley in the night, and told him to take the Philippines? Maybe even earlier . . . when Lincoln fought his fellow Americans for four bloody years to keep the South under Union control? Or later, when Woodrow Wilson sent US troops to fight in a war in which they had no business . . . adding two years to the killing, filling up the monuments in France with the names of the fallen . . . and setting the stage for an inconclusive, infelicitous peace?

Traditional US conservatism was not a doctrine of world improvement, but a mood of skepticism. It was undergirded by two important principles. The first principle held that because most innovations are failures, people should view any proposed change to the traditional order with suspicion. That doesn't mean you can't innovate in a society, but the burden of proof should always be on the world improvers to show that their proposed change will make things better—something they can almost never do.

The second principle of old-time conservatism was the political equivalent of Adam Smith's observation about free markets. Smith introduced to the world the concept that "free trade" would benefit individuals and society as a whole. Governments would do better by their citizens if they got out of the way by not following policies that interfere with free trade or markets, domestically and abroad.[5]

The economist and political theorist Friederich Hayek elaborated in *The Use of Knowledge in Society* that information is decentralized—that knowledge is unevenly dispersed among different members of society—and that as a result, decisions are best made by those with local knowledge rather than by a central authority.[6] In short, central planning doesn't work very well, neither in Washington nor in Baghdad. But we add our own little corollary to the knowledge principle—phony knowledge increases the larger the undertaking and the farther you get from it, by the square of the distance and the cube of the elapsed time.

The old conservatives didn't believe in big, elusive ideas either. For example, they didn't really believe in "freedom" per se. "Just don't tell me what to do," they said.

The world can be improved; we don't deny it. Small, private steps tend to take it in the right direction. But on the public stage, the only improvements that make the place better are those that remove the eyesores and prevarications of previous improvers. Ronald Reagan's genius was that he was able to see that the high taxes and the proliferation of federal regulations had not made the world a better place. He realized that he could succeed where they had failed, simply by eliminating them. Milton Friedman's three-part formula for better government—cut taxes, cut taxes, cut taxes—seemed like a decent solution.

Reagan had the right instinct. "Get big guv'mint off our backs" was almost his campaign theme song. When he had the chance, he often did the right thing. Faced with a strike by air-traffic controllers—the only union to back his campaign—he fired 10,000

212 EMPIRE OF DEBT

of them. When he saw some "improvement" created by his predecessors, his instinct was generally to get rid of it.

Reagan's intellectual guidance came largely from George Gilder's
book, *Wealth and Poverty*. Reagan quoted it often. Gilder and Reagan
recognized that a healthy society was not a stable thing, but something that was always coming up with surprising new things:
"Creativity is the foundation of wealth. All progress comes from the
creative minority. Under capitalism, wealth is less a stock of goods
than a flow of ideas, the defining characteristic of which is surprise. If
it were not surprising, we could plan it, and socialism would work."[7]

Gilder was not an academic and certainly not an empty shill for
conservative politicians. Instead, he was a bright observer with a penetrating eye: "Entrepreneurial knowledge has little to do with certified expertise, advanced degrees, or the learning of establishment
schools. The fashionably educated and cultivated spurn the kind of
fanatically focused learning commanded by the innovators. Wealth all
too often comes from doing what other people consider insufferably
boring or unendurably hard."[8]

With George Gilder and Milton Friedman to guide him, later
aided by David Stockman at the Office of Management and Budget,
it looked as though Reagan might actually succeed. He might be able
to stop the growth of government and the elite class it served.

The trouble was that once in Washington, the actor still remembered his lines, but he lost the plot. Almost before he could get his
cowboy boots off, he was making improvements of his own.

This was especially notable in what is known as *foreign policy*.
Republicans had learned their lesson from the Vietnam War. They still
sought to maintain the empire, but by fairly passive means. They
merely hoped to "contain" communism—which they saw as a menace. But Reagan fell under the spell of the proto-neoconservatives in
Washington. Not content to leave things alone, he decided he could
improve the world by actively trying to defeat communism.

This is celebrated as a great and good victory. In her comments on
Reagan's death, Britain's Maggie Thatcher said he would be mourned
by "millions of men and women who live in freedom today because
of the policies he pursued."

Maybe this is true. Maybe it is not. It is impossible to know what
might have happened had Reagan left things alone. Most likely,

communism would have fallen apart anyway, perhaps sooner. When a person's investments go up, they are a genius. Those who failed to invest are seen as fools. By contrast, when investments go down, it is because of events that could not possibly have been foreseen. Likewise, in politics, the link between action and consequence is forged in a way that always flatters the activists. If something turns out reasonably well, it is because some world improver took action and made it that way. If something turns out badly, it is because someone failed to act when they should have. It is always the activists who get the monuments. Abraham Lincoln is credited with having abolished slavery—at a cost of 618,000 US lives, 2% of the entire population. (An equivalent death toll today would wipe out 6 million Americans.) Everywhere else in the world, slavery was abolished—at about the same time—with hardly a single corpse. The Great Emancipator might better be cursed than praised.

Likewise, Woodrow Wilson is given credit for all manner of extravagant improvements. People rarely mention that he almost single-handedly brought about World War II with his meddling in World War I. Instead, when the subject of World War II comes up, Neville Chamberlain's name arises almost immediately. The poor man gets the blame for trying to avoid war—that is, for not taking action when he should have.

Reagan "also helped engineer a huge surge in American patriotism," writes Ross MacKenzie.

The Carter years were a period of American self-doubt about the economy and about American power (with the memory of Vietnam still tormenting most policymakers). Mr. Reagan set about wiping this away. He increased military spending by 25 percent between 1981 and 1985. He talked to the American people, not about malaise (as Mr. Carter had done), but about "morning in America." By the end of his second term, much of the talk about American decline had gone out of fashion: the country regarded itself once again not only as the world's greatest superpower, but also as the world's most dynamic economy.[9]

Soon there was no trace of self-doubt. Instead, there was a bubble in confidence. That alone would be no disgrace, but it came with the most immodest plans for world improvement and the biggest rush of liquidity the water planet has ever seen.

"As we begin, let us take inventory," began Ronald Reagan at his inauguration. His head and heart were in the right place; he sought, at least so he claimed, not to praise the improvements of the past, but to bury them.

> We are a nation that has a government—not the other way around. And this makes us special among the nations of the Earth. Our Government has no power except that granted it by the people. It is time to check and reverse the growth of government which shows signs of having grown beyond the consent of the governed. It is my intention to curb the size and influence of the Federal establishment and to demand recognition of the distinction between the powers granted to the Federal Government and those reserved to the States or to the people. All of us need to be reminded that the Federal Government did not create the States; the States created the Federal Government.
>
> Now, so there will be no misunderstanding, it is not my intention to do away with government. It is, rather, to make it work— work with us, not over us; to stand by our side, not ride on our back. Government can and must provide opportunity, not smother it; foster productivity, not stifle it.
>
> If we look to the answer as to why, for so many years, we achieved so much, prospered as no other people on Earth, it was because here, in this land, we unleashed the energy and individual genius of man to a greater extent than has ever been done before. Freedom and the dignity of the individual have been more available and assured here than in any other place on Earth. The price for this freedom at times has been high, but we have never been unwilling to pay that price.
>
> It is no coincidence that our present troubles parallel and are proportionate to the intervention and intrusion in our lives that result from unnecessary and excessive growth of government. It is time for us to realize that we are too great a nation to limit ourselves to small dreams.[10]

Ronald Reagan called himself a conservative. This part of his inaugural address made us think he really was one. But people come to believe what they must believe in order to play their roles—even conservatives. Reagan's real revolution lay in redefining conservatism as an activist, imperial creed. First, the neocons took over foreign policy. Soon, Americans were stirring up trouble everywhere, from Latin America to Afghanistan. Then, they took over domestic policy. In a few cases, the ghastly remnants of previous improvers—such as 70% top marginal rates—were knocked over. In more cases, new edifices were built up. But the major failure was that the sharp tax cuts of 1981 were not followed by sharp spending cuts. Instead, spending went up. And not just on defense. Reagan had pledged to abolish the Department of Education. Instead, he increased its budget by 50%.

The Reagan Revolution transformed the Republican Party. Rather than continuing to fight a rearguard action against leftist activists, Republicans were emboldened to take the lead, becoming activists themselves. This they did by relying on a monumental fraud.

Murray Rothbard watched Republicans scam themselves:

> In the spring of 1981, conservative Republicans in the House of Representatives cried. They cried because, in the first flush of the Reagan Revolution that was supposed to bring drastic cuts in taxes and government spending, as well as a balanced budget, they were being asked by the White House and their own leadership to vote for an increase in the statutory limit on the federal public debt, which was then scraping the legal ceiling of one trillion dollars.
>
> They cried because all their lives they had voted against an increase in public debt, and now they were being asked, by their own party and their own movement, to violate their lifelong principles. The White House and its leadership assured them that this breach in principle would be their last: that it was necessary for one last increase in the debt limit to give President Reagan a chance to bring about a balanced budget and to begin to reduce the debt. Many of these Republicans tearfully announced that they were taking this fateful step because they deeply trusted their president, who would not let them down.[11]

"Famous last words," wrote Rothbard.

In a sense, the Reagan's handlers were right: there were no more tears, no more complaints, because the principles themselves were quickly forgotten, swept into the dustbin of history. Deficits and the public debt have piled up monstrously since then, and few people care, least of all conservative Republicans. Every few years, the legal limit is raised automatically. By the end of the Reagan reign the federal debt was $2.6 trillion. As of January 2009, it was $11 trillion. In September 2023, it went over $33 trillion. That is merely the current debt. As we will see later, when Treasury Secretary Paul O'Neill totaled up the present value of future obligations minus expected tax revenues, he came to a figure more than four times that large.

Before the Reagan era, conservatives were clear about how they felt about deficits and the public debt: A balanced budget was good; deficits and the public debt were bad. In the famous words of the left-Keynesian apostle of "functional finance," Professor Abba Lerner, there was nothing wrong with the public debt because "we owe it to ourselves." In those days, at least, conservatives were astute enough to realize that it made an enormous amount of difference whether—slicing through the obfuscatory collective nouns—one is a member of the *we* (the burdened taxpayer) or of the *ourselves* (those living off the proceeds of taxation).

Since Reagan, however, intellectual political life has gone topsy-turvy. The idea that "deficits don't matter," came from Michael Kalecki, which was later developed into modern monetary theory. It was popularized and adopted by conservatives after Dick Cheney claimed that Reagan had "proved that deficits don't matter."

Of course, he proved only that you can get away with them ... not that they don't matter. He proved too that the voters don't care about them. And since then, conservatives and allegedly "free-market" economists have twisted themselves inside out trying to find new reasons why deficits don't matter.

Today, if you were to pose the question to the small-town Republican, you might still find a faint residue of the Old Religion. But the poor person has been betrayed by their party, by their representatives, by politics itself, by the lure of empire, and by their own vain and fatal urges. They have come to believe what they must.

There were four key elements to Reaganomics: Restrict the money supply to slow inflation (admirably carried out by Paul Volcker at the Fed). Cut taxes (a 25% across-the-board tax cut was enacted in 1981). Balance the budget by controlling domestic spending. (A complete failure—deficits grew larger than ever.) And reduce government regulation. (Ditto.)

The first two objectives were more or less achieved. They produced more or less what Milton Friedman expected. But neither was an activist measure. Both merely undid some of the worst damage done by previous officeholders. Lyndon Johnson, Richard Nixon, and Jimmy Carter had made a mess of the economy. Ronald Reagan and Paul Volcker helped clean it up. But even the cleanup lacked the necessary suds and elbow grease. Instead, the dirt and clutter were mostly let alone, while new trash was heaped on.

The big cut in taxes gave people more money to spend. Consumers began a buying spree, while government borrowed the money to fund the deficit.

Where did the extra spending power come from? Few people asked. If they had thought about it, they would have realized that, collectively, they were merely going further into debt to upgrade their standards of living. If they had reflected on it deeply, they would have realized that they were running up bills that future generations would have to pay; they were spending money that their children and grandchildren hadn't earned yet. For what was a national debt, but an intergenerational obligation, a burden placed on infants by their parents and grandparents?

Hardly anyone thought about it then—or since.

Reagan's *supply-side economics* was meant to be different from Keynesian economics in that it celebrated the power of the free market to create wealth. If only the restrictions imposed on the economy by previous generations of world improvers could be removed, they said, the economy would boom and people would get rich.

Thus, it came to be that taxes were cut and the economy boomed. But what the new supply-siders had done was nothing more than administer an old-fashioned Keynesian boost. John Maynard Keynes, a British economist of the early 20th century, had given world improvers a tool. He believed that nations could be winched out of recessions by easy credit and government spending. When private spenders eased off, he noted, government could take up the slack—by running deficits. Where would the money come from? He expected governments to run surpluses in good times so they would have money to spend in bad ones. Had government actually done so, the Keynesian system would have at least been honest. But this was the part the politicians never particularly liked, and the part of his plan they never could quite follow. It was all very well to spend money. Only curmudgeonly conservatives complained about that. Otherwise, spending money made everyone happy. But *not* spending money was another matter. Not spending meant less bread and fewer circuses, and fewer clowns on the public payroll. It meant explaining to voters that they wouldn't get the new road or new medical services that had been promised. It meant lower demand and less new money in circulation, the very opposite of the boom everyone loved so much.

Politicians had no trouble giving the economy the boost that Keynes had suggested. But when it came to saving money to have something to give a boost with, the time never seemed quite right. The moment for underspending never seemed to come. Like fat people at a wedding feast, policymakers told themselves they would eat less after the party was over to make up for their gluttony now. But in public finance, there is never a good time for fasting.

When the Reagan team arrived in Washington, the nation had been living with Keynesian deficits for many years. Savers and lenders had grown wary. Consumer price inflation hit 13.5% in 1980. Lenders feared it would go higher still. They demanded protection. In 1980, 30-year mortgages could be had at 15% interest. By the following year, the mortgage rate rose to a peak of 18.9%.

But then, Paul Volcker's anti-inflation policies at the Fed began to pay off. Investors did not yet know it, but the bond market had found its bottom. For the next four decades, bonds would go up. Bond yields—a measure of what people must pay to borrow—went down. Thus, were the two cornerstones of the Reagan era in place—lower taxes and lower real cost of credit. Neither was an improvement to America's system of imperial finance. Both were merely corrections to previous meddling. Taxes had been raised so that the government would have money to spend on its imperial programs: bread and circuses at home, wars at the periphery. High bond yields (a high cost of credit) were the result of Keynesian policies. Neither problem was caused by neglect. Instead, both were the inevitable debris of previous improvements, previous innovations in the field of economics, and previous generations of self-aggrandizing empire builders posing as do-gooders.

After Reagan's tax cuts, US gross domestic product (GDP) grew at an average rate of 3.2% per year throughout the eight years of Reagan's two terms. This was a bit more than the 2.8% average gain in the eight years before and substantially more than the 2.1% of the eight years following. Still the growth was slower than it had been in the 1960s, after Kennedy's 30% tax cut of 1964 produced 5% annual GDP rates. Meanwhile, real median household income rose from $37,868 in 1981 to $42,049 in 1989. This, too, was much better than the rate of growth before or after the Reagan years. But much of it—maybe all of it—came not from real increases in wages, but simply from more people working longer hours, as we illustrated in our previous book *Financial Reckoning Day*.[12]

Real wage increases require three things: First, the society must save money so that it has the capital to invest. Second, it must invest the savings in profitable businesses. Third, these capital investments must result in increased productivity.

Alas, none of these things happened. Instead, these three critical things began trending in the wrong direction. National savings—including public savings—fell from 7.7% in the 1970s to only 3% by 1990. Business investment fell from 18.6% of GDP in the 1970s to 17.4% in the 1980s. And productivity? In the 25 years after World War II, output per employee had risen at an average rate of 2.8% per year. During the 1980s, this rate fell to less than 1%.

There was a bump in productivity after 1995, but this was largely a feature of the Labor Department's new way of calculating it. With falling savings, falling business investment, and (consequently) falling productivity, you could not expect the economy to do very well. It didn't. While the supply side of supply-side economics was a total flop, the demand side was a stunning success. The Reagan team at least figured out how to pay for an empire: borrow.

As a percentage of GDP, federal government receipts fell from 20.2 in 1981 to 18.6 in 1992. But spending rose from 22.9% in 1981 to 23.5% in 1992. Naturally, debts rose.

By the end of 1992, the federal debt was more than $4 trillion. When Reagan took over, it was less than $1 trillion. So far, the numbers were high, but bearable. But the trend was in motion. Deficits didn't matter. So, we got plenty of them. From the year 2000 onward, federal debt grew by more than $1 trillion per year.

No fraud is so lovable as the illusion of getting something for nothing. But something-for-nothing was just what the new conservatives now promised voters—just like the Democrats. The difference was that the Democrats pledged to steal the money from the rich

(Republicans). The Republicans promised to create it in a free economy, like Jesus multiplying the loaves and fishes at Beth Saida. "Voodoo economics," was how George Bush described it.

ORIGINS OF SUPPLY SIDE

When supply-side economics first appeared in the US press, real economists were perplexed. They had never heard of it. There were no university departments specializing in it. There were no peer-reviewed papers. There were no scholarly books describing it. There were scarcely any economists claiming to be supply-siders. It was, apparently, a school of thought without a school. Some wondered if it also lacked a thought.

Traditional economists—mostly empire builders and world improvers, but of the Keynesian variety—had gotten themselves stuck on a teeter-totter. On one end sat inflation. On the other was employment. They could press down on one end, but the other would rise up and hit them on the chin. There seemed to be no way out. No free lunch. It seemed that they would have to pay for every something with something else. If they wanted to reduce inflation, it would cost them jobs. If they wanted to increase employment, consumer prices would rise.

Milton Friedman, among others, warned that Keynesianism was just folderol. As soon as people realized what the government was doing, the jig would be up. They would merely raise prices in anticipation of inflation, without increasing production. *Stagflation*—rising prices in a sluggish economy—would result. Other economists pointed out that any attempt to manipulate the business cycle would fail for the same reason. Once the policy was known, people would adjust their behavior to it, nullifying its effectiveness. They would not mistake inflation for greater demand: They would not increase production; they would not hire more workers; they would not spend more money. The only thing the policymakers could possibly do that would have an effect would be something people did not expect. And that could only be a policy of random manipulations—which would cause further confusion and who-knew-what results. Keynesians, even new Keynesians, never had any real answer to this problem. But that didn't stop them. They decided to ignore it. Meddlers and empire builders can't be bothered with theoretical problems; they are too busy creating a better world!

Stagflation came in the 1970s, just as Milton Friedman had said it would. It was not the better world the Keynesian economists had hoped to create. But it was the world they got. (Like everyone else, world improvers don't get exactly what they expect; they get what they deserve.) Stagflation posed a problem with no easy solution. Prices were rising, but employment was flat. Policymakers wanted to increase employment, but they were loath to add more inflation. They could try to lower inflation, but that would hurt employment even more.

Along came the supply-siders. They had no real solution. But at least they had a way to hide the problem. What both the public and the politicians wanted, they noted, was employment without price increases. They wanted a booming economy and no inflation. Voters wanted money from government; they also wanted to lower taxes.

The trouble with traditional conservative economists was that they were always pointing out the true cost of things. "There's no such thing as a free lunch," was practically tattooed on their foreheads. Conservative economists typically argued against government debt, against deficits, against more spending, and against activism in all its forms; they knew there would be a price to be paid for it, eventually. This attitude made conservative economists deeply unpopular. They were, after all, party poopers. Who would want such a killjoy around? None could ever be elected to high office. The essence of politics was promising things that couldn't be delivered honestly. If a man could get no more from an election than what he actually earned, why would he bother to vote at all?

The supply-siders' proposal seemed to offer something for everyone—at no cost to anyone. Taxes could be cut, said Arthur Laffer; lower taxes would create such a boom that output would go up—eliminating inflation. Government revenues would go up, too—even at lower tax rates. The budget would be balanced. Most important, it offered a way to get conservatives elected—by turning them into big spenders.

REAL BOOMS VERSUS THE PHONY VARIETY

Real booms need real money. Typically, people save money when they are wary and spend it when they are flush. The spending is real. The money is real. The boost in sales is real. The profits are real.

But a boom that people build on phony money is itself phony. Every step of the way takes them in the wrong direction. The demand is an illusion. The spending is a mistake. The money is suspect. And the resulting business profits are not merely temporary, they are nothing more than next year's sales disguised as this year's earnings.

People who borrow money to begin their spending spree contribute nothing to the economy. Every dollar they spend must someday be withdrawn. It must be paid back. Imagine that they borrow $1 million. In a small town, that sum might be enough to set off a boom. They buy a new car. They go out to restaurants. They give money to church and charities. They take a holiday. They order new clothes. They build a new wing on their house. Soon, the money is out of their pocket. But it is not gone. It has found a new home in pockets all over town. And now the butcher, the baker, the builder, the travel agent, and many others are all planning little additions to their own standards of living.

But imagine the disappointment when, the following year, the people who spent so freely no longer come around. They are not seen at the tailor, or at the travel agent, or at the restaurant, or the car dealer. They are not even seen so frequently at their old haunts. Not only do they not spend as freely as they did the year before, they barely spend at all. For now they must cut their regular spending by enough to pay back the $1 million, plus interest. Net spending in the town will actually go down, over a multiyear period, by the amount of interest they pay (assuming that the loan came from outside the community).

(We invite readers to consider the current US situation—with the federal government going deeper into debt at the rate of $2 trillion per year.)

The supply-siders' key insight was that government is essentially a parasite. It lives off its host like a leech. And like any bloodsucker, it has to be careful not to suck too much. Otherwise, it will weaken its host and maybe even kill it. Or, if it sucks too little, it fails to fully exploit the opportunity and invites competition.

The supply-siders' concept was hardly a formula for maximizing individual freedom. On the contrary, it was a formula for financing an empire by increasing government revenues. Arthur Laffer's curve merely illustrates a rational bloodsucker's optimization strategy; they will get the most at a level that is neither too high nor too low. A government that imposes tax rates that are too high weakens the economy and ends up with fewer resources than it might otherwise have. This was a problem with communism—it asked too much of its citizens. The poor schleps were drained dry. The government of the Soviet Union, for example, claimed 100% of each citizen's output, returning just enough "to each, according to his need." Democratic regimes in the West took a lower percentage of their citizens' output. But their hosts thrived, giving the government more money to spend. This was why the West won the Cold War; it had fixed its tax rates lower.

But Reagan's tax cuts were an empty gesture. Without offsetting cuts to federal spending, deficits increased. What really matters to an economy is not the nominal tax rates, but the percentage of the economy's resources taken away by the government. In the Soviet Union, the government's percentage of production, or what might be called its *real tax rate,* while difficult to measure, was very high. That, combined with even more government meddling than in the United States, doomed the Soviet experiment.

Reagan cut nominal tax rates, but government consumed more and more resources. The leech grew. Lower tax rates gave citizens the impression that they had more money to spend. Individually, they did. Collectively, they did not. The program was merely a monumental legerdemain. For every tax-cut dollar that a citizen spent, the federal government had to borrow at least another dollar to keep up with its spending commitments.

Still, citizens thought they had more to spend. They spent it. It was this extra spending—this Keynesian boost of money borrowed by the federal government to replace the forgone tax revenues—that picked up the economy.

And now, pardon us if we go over to this dead horse and lay on the whip again. Reducing taxes is a conservative, anti-activist, anti-world-improving, anti-political, anti-empire gesture. Taxes are imposed by people who pretend that the world will be a better place if your money is taken from you and redirected to others' pockets. Cutting taxes is a way of removing the improvement residues of the past. It is a way of tipping society away from the political means of doing things back toward civilized, consensual, economic life. The lower the taxes—and here, we speak of real tax rates (the amount of resources consumed by the government)—the more modest the world-improvers' ambitions. Lowering tax rates was the right idea. But lowering only nominal tax rates, while simultaneously increasing the government's resources, was a sham.

Because the tax cut was a sham, so was the resulting boom. It was inspired by consumer demand that didn't exist. But the financial world is a complicated, confusing affair with many promiscuous liaisons. Events are engendered by other events. Like a French drama, one door opens, another slams shut as the paramour hastens out the back. They are *path dependent,* as economists say. One event births another. Life was good in the Reagan years. The supply-siders patted each other on the back. "We did it," they congratulated each other. Someone should have asked for a paternity test.

Whereas tax cuts gave consumer spending a temporary boost, bond yields began a long, solid downtrend. The lower cost of credit was a plus for the economy and for the financial markets—at least as important as tax cuts. Falling interest rates made it cheaper to borrow. From experience, people expected prices to go up—which would lower the cost of their loans still further. Rising prices would also undermine the value of their savings. They did the reasonable thing: They borrowed.

Stocks rose. Things were looking up. It was "morning in America." The questions would have to wait until evening.

FUNNY NUMBERS

Since 1913, the cost of do-gooders, empire builders, and world improvers has been adding up. By the 1970s, it had begun to depress productivity rates. Instead of growing at 2.8% per year (the rate since World War II), productivity rose only about 1% from 1973 to 1984. More recently, it has gone flat, or even negative.

But the rates themselves have become fraudulent: In 1995, Department of Labor officials began to crunch the numbers into such odd and awful shapes, even their own mothers would no longer recognize them. The practice known as hedonic price indexing based on "chained dollars" was put into place. Computers came to be valued for their potential to increase productivity rather than their actual cost, dramatically inflating the importance of the tech sector in the economy and overstating GDP so as to make the number useless.

Nearly half the items in America's measure of consumer price inflation are "adjusted"—manipulated—in one way or another.

Between 2000 and the end of 2004, for example, spending on computers rose 9.3%. Since computers became more powerful, however, the number was enhanced to 113.4%. Other numbers in the consumer price inflation calculation were adjusted by the substitution effect. If steak rose in price, the statisticians assumed people switched to mutton, thereby reducing their cost of living.

So did they adjust the price of housing. It cost a lot more to own a house in 2000 than it did in 1980, but the boys went to work on the numbers with pliers and a torch. Soon they had twisted the cost of actually owning a house into the cost of renting the same house; "owners' equivalent rent" they called it. The Consumer Price Index (CPI), of which more than a quarter is the cost of housing, was held down. The credit bubble had a similar effect on used cars. Zero percent financing deals turned heads away from used cars and toward new ones. Used car prices fell—and so did this component of the CPI. Together the two items alone—housing and used cars, along with lower costs from "outsourcing" production to China!—held inflation in check.

We turn back to the Gipper. When Ronald Wilson Reagan was finally carried off in June 2004, the nation said goodbye with a soft heart and a head that had turned to mush. His obsequies were as full of humbug as a national election. The man deserved better. He should have been carried off by six jolly cowboys and bid farewell by honest drunks.

Instead, Reagan was given a send-off worthy of a world-class mountebank. We were told that he was responsible for a huge economic boom in the land of the free. He cut marginal tax rates. He helped get the government off our backs. He defeated communism.

Rod Martin wrote a book praising Ronald Reagan for "saving the world." "Without Reagan," he wrote, "We might all be speaking Russian!" We have nothing against Russian. But we doubt that, in any reasonably imaginable circumstances, Americans could all have learned to speak Russian in a single generation. They are not that good at languages. But it illustrates how the world improvers think: If you want to make a better world, you must make others do just as you do. Martin could not imagine a Russian "victory" without imagining that we had to learn to speak the Russian language. He probably thought we would have to learn to like vodka and dance like Cossacks, too. "[Reagan's] certainty that people everywhere yearned for freedom and that free markets could always outproduce centrally planned slavery drove his strategies where realpolitik could never go. He replaced both containment and détente with his "Reagan Doctrine," proclaiming America would actively roll back its foe by helping freedom fighters behind the Iron Curtain."[13]

What made Reagan so sure that people everywhere yearn for freedom is a mystery; there is no evidence of it. Even Americans, who claim to love freedom as much as anyone, are much more interested in low mortgage rates. They would scrap the entire Bill of Rights in less than 24 hours if it meant guaranteed 10% annual real estate gains. And if free markets could always outproduce centrally planned slavery, why was Reagan so worried about losing out to the Soviets? It was obvious we could beat them—because we could afford far more and better weapons.

Realpolitik was Kissinger's approach to foreign policy. It began by taking people as he found them, whether they wanted Western-style freedom or not, and making the best of the situation. This meant generally trying to avoid conflict without surrendering strategic interests—even imperial ones.

The neo-Wilsonians advising Reagan came up with a more daring doctrine. They wanted to get Kissinger out of the way and remake the world in their own image. Martin does not mention that among the "freedom fighters" that the United States decided to support was, notably, Osama bin Laden. The War on Terror was largely an invention of the neoconservatives. They helped create the enemy and then developed a war against him.

Martin continues: "And free men everywhere, [Reagan] believed, would lay down arms, take up tools and build a new, peaceful, prosperous world for themselves and their posterity, given the chance."[14]

We have never met Rod Martin; we presume he is an honest and decent man. Yet, in this ode to Ronald Reagan and George W. Bush, the man seemed to have taken leave of his senses altogether. Men— free or not—occasionally pick up weapons and begin killing each other. Germany and the Soviet Union battered each other for four years . . . at a cost of 30 million dead. Liberty was not on offer, for neither side.

Yet, Reagan's anti-communism resonated with the voters. He had spent a good part of his career telling the world how bad the communists were. But what was it that was so bad about them? And what business was it of his?

Why was Ronald Reagan so eager to get rid of Bolshevism? As long as you didn't have to live in a communist country, what would it matter to you? Many smart people thought it was a better way. What made the communists a menace was not that they were intent on improving their own world with the benefits of collectivism, but that they were determined to improve our world, too. What made them obnoxious was not their own goofy creed, but their determination to do precisely what Ronald Reagan wanted to do: remake its adversary into something more like itself. Reagan had branded the Soviet Union "an evil empire." But behind the words was a monstrous conceit that, by some special grace of God, he knew how people everywhere were meant to live and how they were meant to govern themselves. It did not matter that 3,000 generations who had come and gone had had other ideas, nor that a third of the world's people alive in 1981 had other ideas. Reagan thought he knew what was best for everyone.

In a strictly economic sense, communism was America's greatest ally. For many decades, it kept millions of people penniless—unable to compete for the world's oil and other resources. While the United States guzzled cheap oil for half a century, communism retarded the economic development of its competitors. Now, every remaining barrel of oil comes on the market with people bidding for it from all over the planet—Americans, Europeans, Russians—and three billion Asians, too!

The Soviets were so discouraged by the Reagan Revolution, we are told, they decided to give up being Soviets; now, they are Russians or Lithuanians or Kazakhs. The Chinese were impressed, too. They became, in many ways, more "capitalist" than the Americans themselves.

And here we see the claptrap wash away, like a receding tide revealing a drowned swimmer. For even though the Russians no longer carried the stain of "communism," by 2022 they were once again America's convenient enemy. The US was laying off its used military equipment (spending billions on new lethal gadgets from its favorite suppliers) and seemed intent on keeping the Russo–Ukraine war going as long as US money and Ukrainian lives were still available. As for China, it had gone capitalist in 1979, after Deng Xiaoping gave it the okay; "to get rich is glorious," he said. You'd think that would have ingratiated the Middle Kingdom to the freedom fighters. But no. Now, they were fighting a new enemy . . . a rival for numero uno status. Communism had nothing to do with it.

MARX'S REVENGE

For the first time in 200 years, the West (including Westernized Japan) faces real competition. The world's largest nations—China, India, and Russia—sat on the sidelines for most of the 19th and 20th centuries. They were too remote and too backward to participate in the great boom that lifted living standards during the reign of the British Empire in the 19th century. GDP per capita rose from barely over $1,000 (in 1990 dollars) in the United States at the beginning of the 19th century to more than $5,000 by its end. China, however, had a GDP per capita of about $600 when the 19th century began. By its end, the figure had fallen to about $525. Indian numbers were about the same, but in the other direction, with a small gain in the 19th century—probably the result of British colonial development. In the 20th century, Russia, China, and India all became victims of self-inflicted wounds; various forms of socialist claptrap took them out of economic competition.

But now they are back, and it is a whole new ball game, as they say. These countries were either on the periphery of US imperial protection or beyond the pale altogether. Either way, they benefited from the order created by the US imperium. Foreign workers seem to be able to make anything we can make—but at much lower cost. Before the COVID struck, India was growing at 8% a year, China at 9%—Russia was booming, too. In addition, they were turning out millions of young people who could make things—graduates in the practical arts and sciences—better and cheaper than we do in the United States or Europe. What's more, the foreigners took the old virtues seriously. They saved their money—the saving rate in China rose as high as 40% of the national income, according to official sources. These savings gave them huge piles of capital with which to build more modern factories and more convenient infrastructure.

The price of labor in the rich countries is high. The average cost of an hour of someone's time in the West—including social charges—is about $20. The average cost of someone's time in China is about the same thing, if you believe the figures. That's why low-cost production is moving to Vietnam, Mexico, and other low-wage countries. Consumers don't particularly care who assembled their gadgets; they only care that they can buy it at the lowest possible price. Labor is the biggest component of the price of most things, so both manufacturers and consumers appreciate lower labor prices. Our old incompetent enemies have learned how to compete. And as long as capital, expertise, and finished products are free to move around, it is likely that global wage rates will grow closer together.

We were told that America became much richer because of Reagan's improvements, but if that is so, why did real wage rates not rise? A person sweats, humps, busses, totes, and schleps today, on average, for about the same real compensation they got before the Reagan revolution fired its first shot. But that is not to say that everything is just the same. Far from it.

By the 21st century, it was clear that the Reagan Revolution had failed. Economists argued over how much of a flop it was. One school of thought, led by Gale Pooley and Marian Tupy, said it had not really failed at all. They reduced product prices to the time it took to earn them. And they determined that people in the 2020s were much better off than those when Reagan was elected. In the same amount of time on the job they could earn enough to buy much more of life's basic commodities: wheat, oil, and so forth.

The trouble was, people do not buy "baskets" of commodities. They buy finished products—autos, houses, food, and clothing. Generally, those things that could be imported—such as a TV screen—were much cheaper. Those that could not be imported—houses, medical care, and an education—were much more expensive. Also, imported goods—or those made domestically but subject to overseas competition—tended to be much higher quality. The same could scarcely said for a university education; by 2023 even the most esteemed colleges were subject to Congressional testimonies over their policies on antisemitic demonstrations and adherence to academic integrity.[15]

We looked at what it actually cost an average worker with an average salary to buy an average house and an average car. We used the Ford F-150, the workhorse of the working class, which was introduced in 1948, for our "average" wheels. As for the house, we simply looked at average sales prices.

The result showed a big loss for the proletariat. The typical wage earner today has to work two to three times longer to be able to afford the major accoutrements of an average life.

But wait. Today's truck is much better. Today's house, too.

Yes, they are better, technologically. But you would expect that the same new technologies—plastics, chips, composite materials, new tools and machines—that make a thing better would also make it cheaper to produce. The quality should have gone up and the cost (in time) should have gone down. Average citizens don't seem better off; they appear to be worse off. Even simply adjusting today's wages with the CPI tells the same tale. The typical working stiff has gained nothing since 1975.

We look on that fact in shock and awe. How could it be that after the biggest explosion of wealth creation in the history of man—with more PhDs on the case, more engineers on the payroll, the internet available to provide the necessary information, central banks at the ready with trillions in cash, and government willing to send out trillions of dollars' worth of "stimmie" checks—the average person was no richer in 2023 than they were in 1975? Indeed, by our reckoning, they were poorer.

We recall the Carter years: The nation was at peace. Despite inflation, Americans were still getting richer. Wages were rising. The country still enjoyed a positive balance of trade, and the rest of the world still owed it more than it owed to foreigners.

Then, along came Ronald Reagan with a message of hope, optimism, and something-for-nothing ... the supply side, the Laffer curve! Suddenly it seemed possible to spend more ... and still have more! Government could cut taxes—and get more revenue, said Laffer. Forget the deficit; it will take care of itself. Somehow. The average person figured they could do the same: borrow more, spend more, and they would get rich.

Pensions were out. Free people could look out for themselves. They could set up their own 401(k) plans and make money in common stocks. All you had to do was buy the companies you liked, said Peter Lynch. The companies themselves could borrow, borrow, borrow ... buy, buy, buy, like Mr. "Winning" himself, GE chairman Jack Welch. The company may get weaker, but the stock would soar.

CEOs no longer had to worry about their employees. Managers could focus on cooking the books to give the impression of maximizing shareholder value. America soon became "shareholder nation"—a whole country of capitalists, all getting rich in the freest, most dynamic economy the world had ever seen.

Now we see that the whole thing was a huge swindle. Supply-side policies may have increased the supply side, marginally. But government never actually lightened up to let people live their own lives in their own ways. Employees never quite got a raise and never got around to putting money into their 401(k) plans; they were too busy trying to keep up with the credit card bills. And managers soon realized that maximizing their own incomes with stock options, bonuses, and rich retirement plans was more rewarding than looking out for shareholders.

As for the capitalists—the millions of lumpen pseudo-investors who owned mutual funds and EFTs—they couldn't tell the difference. They had neither the time or the money nor the training to be real capitalists; they were merely chumps for Wall Street.

And here we are, four decades since Reagan won the White House. In real terms, the average person earns less per hour worked than they did in the Carter years. And the typical household approaches retirement poorer than it would have been in 1980.

America was the world's biggest creditor when Ike was president. By Ronald Reagan's second term, about 15 years into the *pax dollarium* era, the nation slipped to net debtor status. In the following 20 years, it broke all records—becoming the world's biggest debtor. But the borrowing was just beginning. The bubbles were still inflating. The Fed was still pumping up the money supply. And consumers, companies, and the federal government were going deeper and deeper into debt.

And then, 20 years later, the empire creaked and groaned.

Thomas Gale Moore, then a member of President Reagan's Council of Economic Advisors, must have anticipated Ben Bernanke, Janet Yellen, and Jerome Powell when he noticed the United States crossing the creditor/debtor threshold in the mid-1980s. Not to worry, said he, "We can pay off anybody by running a press."

In 1980, people still held parties when they paid off their mortgages. Paul Volcker said that he would bring down inflation rates, and he meant it. You could buy a stock for six times earnings and lend your money to the US government for a 15% yield. Lenders demanded that much because they remembered the inflation of the 1970s. They knew that not every investment story had a happy ending.

Back then, the United States still made things. General Motors was our biggest employer; you could tell what year a car was made by looking at the tail fins. When Eisenhower was in the White House and William McChesney Martin was at the Fed, the United States had most of the world's gold and most of the world's credit. This happy state of affairs persisted until the Ronald Reagan Revolution.

SUNRISE, SUNSET

Under Ronald Reagan, Americans thought they had rediscovered their youth. They couldn't remember ever feeling more confident or more optimistic. Then, 20 years later, in George W. Bush, Republicans thought they saw their hero reincarnate, with another 20 years of prosperity ahead. And it happened again. The same disappointment, followed by new hope. In 2016, they got another chance. Donald Trump said he was a "conservative." On one notable occasion, he clutched the Bible to his heart. And here was a real billionaire ... a guy who knew how to make money ... a tough negotiator who knew what time it was ... a nonpolitician who knew how to shake up America's politics.

Why shouldn't it be morning in America again?

We answer the question directly. It was not morning in America because it was evening. America was not getting more powerful because it was becoming weaker. People were not getting richer because they were getting poorer. It was not 1981 because it was 2016.

Readers who find this an unsatisfying explanation are reminded that it is not your authors who set the planets in motion around the sun and created people—such as they are—out of the dust of the earth. Morning often looks a lot like evening—if you face the wrong way at the right time. But it is the opposite end of the day's cycle.

In 1982, interest rates were high and stock prices were low. In 1982, there were a few people who wanted to buy stocks, and many who didn't. In 1982, America, Inc., looked like a has-been economy. Its currency was widely considered near-trash and its bonds were described as "certificates of guaranteed confiscation."

You could buy nearly the entire Dow for just one ounce of gold. The trend of the time, in 1982, was down. Then smart people considered it eternal. *Business Week* proclaimed that equities were not just in a cyclical downturn, not just sick, but dead.[16]

As the moon looked down in summer 1982, it shone on a wall of worry so high that only a knuckleheaded contrarian would think of climbing it. Every headline seemed to give another reason the bear market would last forever. Every poll showed that consumers expected it. Every price seemed to confirm the everlasting trend; the sun had set forever; the black of night was permanent.

And yet, at that very moment, had investors turned around, they would have noticed a brightening in the eastern sky. Over the next four decades, the sun rose higher and higher, until investors were so encouraged by the favorable growing conditions that they scattered their seed like confetti at a victory parade. Did anyone doubt that it would take root in the hard concrete of lower Manhattan's financial hothouse or the thin soils of the technology sector?

Every day comes to a close ... and every trend reaches its end. By 2020, everything that had been in 1980 had become its opposite.

In 1980, few people wanted to buy stocks. In the first quarter of the 21st century, there were few people who didn't want to buy them. Interest rates were high in 1980 (following roughly 32 years of rising yields). By the end of the trend, in 2020, you needed a microscope to see them. The yield on the two-year Treasury bill, for example, was 11% in 1980. Forty years later, it was only 0.11%, down by 99%. Stocks, too, saw a similar rise (bond prices go up as yields go down). From less than 1,000 on the Dow in 1980, they rose to over 36,000 in 2021.

But how do you account for it? How come the financial world should change so dramatically while the economy—based on average earnings—stays the same?

A WORLD OF DEBT

"Estimates vary," Pete Peterson points out in *Running on Empty,* his vast inquiry into the impending bankruptcy of the US government, "depending on methodology, but the numbers are all vast."[17] Peterson pointed to studies done on the future obligations of the Social Security and Medicare trust fund alone. That was in 2004. The year before, the American Enterprise Institute projected a $45 trillion shortfall; $47 trillion countered the International Monetary Fund in 2004; the National Center for Policy Analysis and the Brookings Institution came up with $50 trillion and $60 trillion, respectively, in their own research reports published in 2003.

Those are were already incomprehensibly large numbers. But they turned out to be chicken feed. From 1999 to 2023, for example, federal debt leaped by $27 trillion. In just two years of the Republican Donald Trump's administration, deficits totaled nearly $6 trillion. Taking household, corporate, and federal debt and then adding the unfunded liabilities—Social Security, Medicare, veterans' benefits, and the like—brought the total to over $200 trillion. It was debt "out the wazoo."

As an empire matures, the imperial citizens believe more and more extravagant things. By the opening of the 21st century, Americans were spending more than they earned. Each day brought more new debt than real new wealth. Yet, almost every quarter showed growth in GDP. Americans mistook this growth for progress. They knew they had the world's best economy, its best system of government, and its finest culture. They could not imagine that they were growing poorer. But here we turn again to the living and the dead for elucidation. Supply-sider Jude Wanniski admitted that real growth had come almost to a halt: "In the United States, my own work shows that between 1945 and 1971, when the dollar was fixed to gold at $35 oz under the 1944 Bretton Woods arrangement, the real economy in the US grew by 4 percent per year. From 1971 when the dollar was floated to 2004, real growth of the US economy has only a pitiful 0.3 percent per year."[18]

The growth, such as it was, in the US economy, came about by virtue of increased emphasis on the present tense. Americans came to despise the past and neglect the future. The lessons of the dead and the desires of the unborn were both ignored. Instead, all that seemed to matter was consumption in the here and now.

A dead man, F. A. Hayek, explained the consequences: "The economy in its entirety must continue to decline so long as more is being consumed than produced, and some part of consumption therefore takes place at the expense of the existing capital stock."[19]

Without a theory, Hayek might have said, the facts are mute. But by the year 2023, facts and theories had become blabbermouths. They said whatever came into their noggins. Trouble was, the facts had been corrupted so they no longer told the truth. And the old theories that might have been used to interpret the facts had been abandoned in favor of new, more convenient delusions. Americans could now run up as much debt as they wanted, said the new theorists.

The US economy may or may not have been "growing" in post-Reagan years. But if traditional, time-tested theories about how wealth and poverty are correct, thank God it was not growing more. Every step it took moved it deeper into debt and closer to bankruptcy.

CHAPTER 10

THE EMPIRE OF DEBT

Let us take a moment to stand back and gaze at America's great Empire of Debt. It is the largest edifice of debt ever put up. It sustains the most magnificent world economy ever assembled. It supports more people in better style than any system ever before devised.

Not only is it incomparably effective, it is also immeasurably entertaining. For it has its burnished helmets and flying banners; its intellectuals and its gladiators; its Caesars, Antonys, Neros, and Caligulas. It has its temples, its forum, its Capitol, its senators; its praetorian guards; its via Appia; its proconsuls, centurions, and legions all over the world as well as its bread and its circuses in the homeland; and its costly wars in periphery areas.

The Roman Empire rested on a classical model of imperial finance. Beneath a complex and nuanced pyramid of relationships was a foundation of tribute formed with the hard rock of brute force. America's Empire of Debt, on the other hand, stands not as a solid pyramid of trust, authority, and power relationships but as a rickety slum of delusion, fraud, and misapprehension.

In 2005, real estate was "where it's at." In June 2005, more than a third of the houses sold in the previous 12 months were not primary residences, but second homes or investments. The trend continued apace until the financial panic of 2008.

Down at the bottom of the pyramid were petty agents spreading deceit and misinformation. You would think a new buyer could trust a certified tax advisor to give sound counsel. Instead, buyers were urged to speculate on the most bubbly property market in US history. Naturally, the lumpen went for it, aided no doubt by a whole industry of professional dissemblers. Press reports told us that appraisers routinely stretched valuations to help close a deal. Mortgage lenders knew perfectly well the appraisals were lies, but they winked at them with one eye while winking at the borrower's phony income declaration with the other. Again, according to the press reports, lenders no longer verified income claims. They had gone blind!

In California, house prices raced so far ahead of incomes that barely 1 in 10 buyers could afford the median house. Yet thanks to "creative finance," more houses were being sold than ever before.

Thus the foundation of the debt pyramid was laid down in a bed of mutual deceit and cupidity, and covered with another level of fabrications. Lenders did not stick around to see how the loans worked out. Instead, they pretended the credits were good, and packaged the mortgages into convenient units so that investors could buy them. The financiers knew damned well that many buyers couldn't really afford to pay for the houses they bought, but they saw no point in mentioning it. Nor did the investors want to know. They were in on the scam, too. The smartest of them even figured out how it worked. The Fed held down short-term rates below the inflation rate so that investors in long-term mortgage financing and buyers of US Treasury obligations could make an easy profit.

Further up the steps of imperial debt were whole legions of analysts, economists, and full-time obfuscators whose role was to make us all believe six impossible things before breakfast and a dozen more before dinner. Economists at the Bureau of Labor Statistics did to numbers what guards at Guantanamo did to prisoners. They roughed them up so badly, they were ready to say anything. In June 2005, it was reported that productivity was increasing at a 2.9% rate—the fastest pace in nine months. Productivity was supposed to measure output per unit of time. But the yardstick was bent by the government's statistical brownshirts, who said that if a computer this year can process information 10 times as fast as one produced last year, the worker who assembled it has multiplied their output 1,000%.

This abuse of statistics is part of what allowed Americans to deceive themselves about their own economy. It was healthy, they said. It was growing. It was stable.

Economists, commentators, and policymakers took up these distortions and added their own twists. It was obvious to anyone who bothered to think about it that an economy that spends more than it earns is in decline. But try to find an economist willing to say so! They'd all become like rich notables in the time of Trajan, doing the emperor's work whether they are on his payroll or not. They would tell you the economy is expanding, but it was an expansion similar to what happens when compulsive eaters escape from a fat farm; the longer they are on the loose, the worse off they become. It was an expansion of consumption, not wealth-producing, job-creating investment.

On the issue of the trade deficit, they said what the senators and consuls wanted to hear, as Levey and Brown did in *Foreign Affairs* magazine: "The United States' current account deficit and foreign debt are not dire threats to its global position, as would-be Cassandras warn. U.S. power is firmly grounded on economic superiority and financial stability that will not end soon."[1] In fact, the story of international trade, circa 2005, was the most preposterous tale economists ever told. One nation bought things that it couldn't afford and didn't need with money it didn't have. Another sold on credit to people who already couldn't pay ... and then built more factories to increase output.

Every level colluded with every other level to keep the flimflam going. On the banks of the Potomac, people of all classes, rank, and station were pleased to believe that all was well. And there, at the Federal Reserve headquarters, was another caste of loyal liars. Alan Greenspan and his fellow connivers not only urged citizens to mortgage their houses, buy SUVs, and commit other acts of wanton recklessness, but also they controlled the nation's money and made sure that it played along with the fraud.

From the center to the furthest garrisons on the periphery, from the lowest rank to the highest—everyone, everywhere willingly, happily, and proudly participated in one of the greatest deceits of all time. At the bottom of the empire were wage slaves squandering borrowed money on imported doodads. The plebes gambled on adjustable rate mortgages. The patricians gambled on hedge funds that speculated on huge swaths of mortgage debt. Near the top were Fed economists urging them to do it! And at the very pinnacle was a chief executive, modeled after whom—Augustus or Commodus?—who cut taxes while increasing spending on bread, circuses, and peripheral wars.

The spectacle was breathtaking. And endlessly entertaining. We were humbled by the majesty of it. Everywhere we looked, we saw an exquisite but precarious balance between things that were equally and oppositely absurd.

On the one side of the globe—in the Anglo-Saxon countries in general, but the United States in particular—were the consumers. On the other side—principally in Asia, notably China—were the producers. One side took, the other made. One borrowed, the other saved. One consumed, the other produced.

This is not the way it was meant to be. When America first stooped to become an empire, she was a rising, robust, energetic, innovative young economy. And for the first six decades of her imperium—roughly from 1913 until 1977—she profited from her competitive position. Every country to which she was able to extend her *pax dollarium* became a customer. Her businesses made a profit.

But gradually, her commercial advantage faded and her industries aged. The very process of spreading the soft warmth of her protection over the earth seemed to make it more fertile. Tough, weedy competitors sprouted all over the periphery of the empire—first in Europe, then in Japan, and later, throughout Asia, even areas she had never been able to dominate. By 2023, China had leapfrogged other periphery competitors to become not just an economic competitor to the United States but also, increasingly, a political and military one.

By the early 21st century, the costs of maintaining her role as the world's only superpower, and its only imperial power, had risen in excess of 5% of her GDP, or $558 billion per year. Not only had she never figured out a good way to charge for providing the world with order but also order was working against her. The periphery economies grew faster. They had newer and better industries. They had higher savings levels and much lower labor rates, lower taxes. They had few of the costs of bread or circuses and none of the costs of policing the empire. They were freer, lighter, faster. Every day, the competitors took more of America's business, assets, and money. If the empire were an operating business, accountants would say it was losing money.

The empire no longer pays because the entire Western world—including Japan—has lost its competitive edge. Globalization of the *pax dollarium* era served the United States well after World War II. America was the world's leading exporter. But Europe also thrived in the 30 years after the war—*les trente glorieuses*, as the French call them. Then, in the 1980s, the Japanese took over as the leading economy of the advanced world.

And now, the pax wrought by the American empire works against America. Asian factories are newer and more modern. Asian workers are younger and cheaper. Now, every business day that passes, the Asians grab a little more of the US market. And every business day puts Americans $2 billion further beholden to its mostly Asian creditors.

"GM plans to cut 25,000 jobs in the U.S." The headline appeared on the front page of the *International Herald Tribune* in mid-June 2005. Elsewhere in the paper was a status report explaining that China's Chery Automobiles planned to begin exporting the first of 250,000 Chery Crossovers to the United States in 2007. For every job lost by America's preeminent industrial company, China was planning to export 10 new cars. Scarcely a year later, at the end of 2008 during the panic and bailout period, China was actively considering buying all three of America's automakers.[2]

It was not just manufacturing that was moving to periphery states. The advent of high-speed, inexpensive communications, along with cheap computing power, enabled Asians to compete in service sectors as well. Anything that can be digitized can be globalized—architecture, law, accounting, administration, data processing of all sorts, call centers, record keeping, marketing, publishing, finance, and so forth.

What was left for the developed economies? What could they do? Here is where European and Anglo-Saxon economies parted company. The Europeans emphasized high value–added products such as luxury goods and precision tools. They clung rigidly to the wisdom of the old economists, refusing to expand consumer credit and refusing to use massive doses of fiscal stimuli to increase overall demand. House prices rose sharply in Paris, Madrid, and Rome. But there were few signs of speculation. Houses were not refinanced readily. They were not "flipped." There was little creative finance. Nor was there a big run-up in consumer debt, or a big run-down in savings rates. Credit cards were still comparatively rare. Unemployment was high, for Europe's policy managers tolerated neither marginal jobs nor marginal credits. Europe was rigid and dull, economically, but relatively solid, with a positive balance of trade.

The Anglo-Saxon countries took a different route. During a time when the Bank of England has regularly moved interest rates up and down to deal with changes in economic conditions, the European Central Bank sat on its hands.

The general consensus was that Europe would be better off if it acted a bit more like the Anglo-Saxons: manipulating interest rates to encourage consumer debt. American economists imagined themselves carefully analyzing the data and coming to a logical conclusion. What they did not realize was that their numbers, conclusions, and views of the world had become nothing more than stones in the immense pyramid of *consuetude fraudium* of the advanced empire.

The numbers were frauds. If you were to look at the percentages fairly, the European economy actually looked no worse than its Anglo-Saxon competitor—with a similar rate of growth, higher unemployment, but better productivity and less debt.

As the Anglo-Saxon economies lost their competitive edge in manufacturing, they tried to make up for it by encouraging consumption. This was the biggest fraud of all. At first, higher consumption feels good. It is like burning the furniture to keep warm; it feels good for a moment. But the sense of well-being is extremely short-lived. When people borrow and spend, they feel as though they are getting richer—especially when their houses are rising in price. The increased consumption even shows up, indirectly, in the GDP figures as growth. But you don't really become wealthier by consuming. You become wealthier by making things you can sell to others—at a profit. The point is obvious but, at this stage of imperial finance, it was inconvenient.

The homeland's losses—measured by a negative balance of trade—began in the mid-1970s. Less than 30 years later, government and consumers were running up debts at an alarming rate. What else could they do? The only way Americans could continue their imperial role—which meant more to them than ever because it was now the only source of national pride left to them—was to borrow (see Figures 10.1 and 10.2).

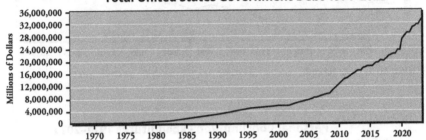
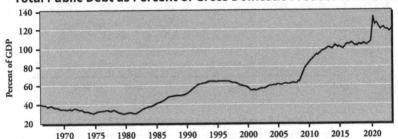
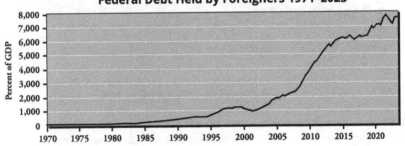

FIGURE 10.1 New Borrowing by Federal Government

"Reagan proved deficits don't matter." Beginning with President Reagan in 1980, total government debt rose, debt as a percentage of GDP followed suit and an increasing amount of that debt was marketed overseas. Local governments sold their own debt to a larger market as well.

Source: https://fred.stlouisfed.org/series/GFDEBTN
Source: https://fred.stlouisfed.org/series/GFDEGDQ188S
Source: https://fred.stlouisfed.org/series/FDHBFIN
Source: https://fred.stlouisfed.org/series/SLGSDODNS

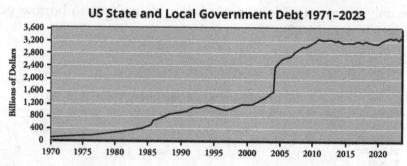

FIGURE 10.1 (Continued)

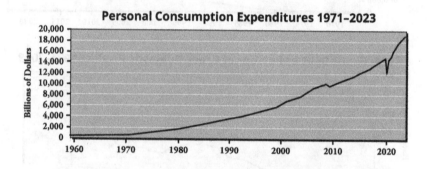

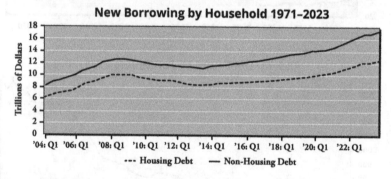

FIGURE 10.2 New Borrowing by Private Households

Personal consumption and the accumulation of household debt in the US followed the same trends established by local, state and federal governments. Credit cards, home mortgages and car loans all hit historic rates of increase in the 21st Century. Personal savings fell.

Source: https://fred.stlouisfed.org/series/PCE
Source: https://www.newyorkfed.org/microeconomics/hhdc
Source: https://fred.stlouisfed.org/graph/?g=VtLo
Source: https://fred.stlouisfed.org/series/DTCTLVENANM (New Car Loans); https://fred.stlouisfed.org/series/DTCTLVEUANQ (Used Car Loan)
Source: https://educationdata.org/student-loan-debt-statistics

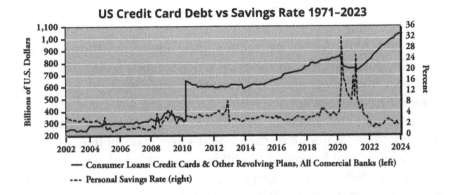

US Credit Card Debt vs Savings Rate 1971–2023

— Consumer Loans: Credit Cards & Other Revolving Plans, All Comercial Banks (left)
--- Personal Savings Rate (right)

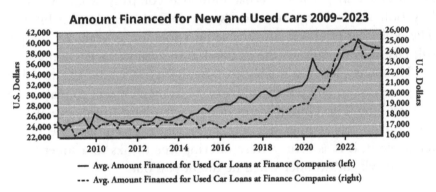

Amount Financed for New and Used Cars 2009–2023

— Avg. Amount Financed for Used Car Loans at Finance Companies (left)
--- Avg. Amount Financed for Used Car Loans at Finance Companies (right)

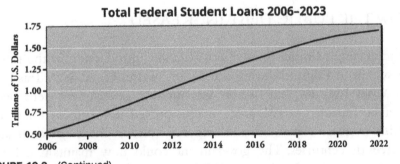

Total Federal Student Loans 2006–2023

FIGURE 10.2 (Continued)

The global economic system in the *pax dollarium* era was perfectly balanced. For every credit in Asia, there was an equal and opposite debit in the United States. And for every dollar's worth of demand from the United States, there was a dollar's worth of supply already waiting in a container in Hong Kong.

But while the imperial finance system was flawless, its perfections were devastating.

In mid-2005, Americans saluted their imperial standards. They gratefully pasted the flag to their car windows, their jackets, their hats, their beer mugs, their shirts, and even their underwear (never once in Europe have we seen anyone with a national flag anywhere except at a parade or a public building). Americans are proud of their empire—and should be. Without it, they could never have gotten so far in debt. What central banker would fill his vault with Argentine pesos or Zimbabwe dollars? What drug dealer or arms seller would want Polish zlotys in payment? What insurance company would want to buy Bolivian or Kyrgyzstan bonds to cover its long-dated liabilities? The dollar has not been convertible into gold for 37 years. Yet, people still take it as though it were as good as the yellow metal—only better. Ultimately, lending money to a foreign government is a bet that the government will put the squeeze on its own citizens to make sure you get paid. The United States doesn't even have to squeeze. When one foreign loan comes due, other foreigners practically line up to refinance it; it is as if they were offering free drinks to a street bum, just to gawk and wonder when he might pass out.

HOW THE PUBLIC DEBT INCREASED

"Since Prime Minister Sir Robert Walpole's introduction of the funding system in England during the 1720s," writes H.-A. Scott Trask for the Mises Institute, "the secret was out that government debt need never be repaid. . . . Walpole's system proved its worth in financing British overseas expansion and imperial wars in the eighteenth and nineteenth centuries. The government could now maintain a huge peacetime naval and military establishment, readily fund new wars, and need not retrench afterward. The British Empire was built on more than the blood of its soldiers and sailors; it was built on debt."[3]

The new system was slow to catch on in America. Jefferson was against it. In 1789, in a letter to James Madison, he wondered whether "one generation of men has a right to bind another." His answer was "no." "The earth belongs in usufruct to the living," he concluded. "No generation can contract debts greater than may be paid during the course of its own existence."[4]

An intergenerational debt is an odd thing. Say a man buys a house. He may leave the house to his children, with a mortgage owing. The children were not party to the mortgage contract, but they take the bequest in good grace.

The house may have a mortgage or it may need a new roof. A gift is a gift, encumbered or not. If it is too heavily burdened with debt, they could simply turn it down; they never made a deal with the mortgage company and are under no obligation to pay it.

Suppose it is credit card debt. Say the man used the money to take a trip around the world. But the trip wore him out; no sooner does he return home than he collapses of a heart attack. Are the children under any obligation to pay the credit card bills? Not at all.

It instead becomes "public" debt. What kind of strange beast is this? One generation consumes. It then hands the next generation the bill. The younger generation never agreed to the terms of the indebtedness. They are party to a contract—and on the wrong end of it, we might add—that they never made. Indentured servants only had to work seven years to pay off their indenture. This new generation, however, will have to work their entire lives.

Such arrangements are often excused as part of the "social contract." But what kind of contract allows one person to take the benefits while sticking the costs to someone else?

But dead people don't talk, and the unborn don't vote. Politicians in the US—just as those in Britain, Italy, and Germany—gradually came to see that they could get the benefits of spending money in the present, while passing on the debts to the next administration and the next generation. Then, as now, war provided cover for excess spending. First, there were the debts from the American Revolution, which were paid down quickly. Then came the War of 1812, Mexican War, and the War Between the States. Each time, spending was increased, debts were taken on, and then, after the war, the debt was paid down, or paid off completely.

World War I saw federal debt explode from $3 billion to $26 billion. Presidents Harding and Hoover paid it down to $16 billion. But then came the Great Depression, Roosevelt, and World War II. By 1945, federal debt had reached $260 billion. Then came something new. The war did not end. It continued as the Cold War, and instead of the debt being paid down, it was increased.

Under Ronald Reagan, America's debt seemed on course for Mars. Less than $1 trillion in 1980, it soared to $2.7 trillion before

Reagan left office. One might have expected some relief after the Cold War was over. But the habit of debt is hard to break. By the time George W. Bush took office, the debt had risen to $5.7 trillion.

Mr. Bush, a conservative, might have seized the opportunity to pay down the debt. The nation was at peace and expected huge budget surpluses. He promised as much when he stood before a joint session of Congress in 2001 and announced his budget.

"That night," Paul O'Neill tells us in the book by Ron Suskind, *The Price of Loyalty,* "Bush stood before the nation and said something that knowledgeable people in the U.S. government knew to be false."[5]

Generations of Republicans had promised balanced budgets. Only war had permitted them to continue running up debt. With no war, the Republicans squirmed. But since 1917, wars had always seemed to come along just when they were needed, and now they included a remarkable event: 9/11. All of a sudden, another strange war was announced against an enemy no one could find on a map—a *War on Terror.* Now, the war, the spending, and the debts could go on forever.

In the following 24 months, the Bush administration added more debt faster than at any time in the first 200 years of the nation's existence. It was shocking then. But Obama, Trump, and Biden merely continued the spendthrift trends. And after a decade of zero interest policy and quantitative easing, the Treasury and Federal Reserve colluded to save the financial markets, and feed the Empire all the credit it needed. Consumers refinanced their homes repeatedly. The government justified its spending on wars and social programs by keeping its own interest rates low.

MAESTRO'S PERFORMANCE

In February 2005, Alan Greenspan gave a speech in honor of the first modern economist—Adam Smith. The Fed chairman journeyed to Fife College, in Kirkcaldy, Fife, Scotland, where Smith was born in 1723. There, he commented on Smith's work: "Most of Smith's free market paradigm remains applicable to this day," said he.[6]

In particular, the world seems to have discovered that independent buyers and sellers are better at delivering the goods than government planners.

This would have come as a shock to George Orwell. Writing at the beginning of World War II, Orwell expressed the belief of millions: "I began this book to the tune of German bombs. . . . What this war has demonstrated is that private capitalism—that is, an economic system in which land, factories, mines and transports are owned privately and operated solely for profit—does not work. It cannot deliver the goods."[7] See Figure 10.3.

Orwell was wrong. Capitalism delivered the goods better than socialism, a fact that even nearsighted journalists and central bankers were eventually able to see. But even after the fall of the Berlin Wall, continued America's most celebrated central banker, there was "no eulogy for central planning."

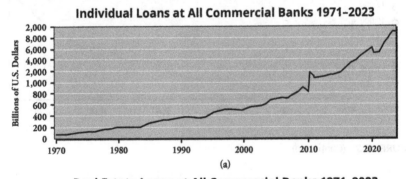

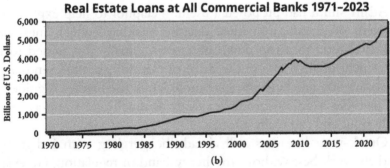

FIGURE 10.3 (a) Individual Loans at All Commercial Banks 1971–2023, (b) Real Estate Loans at All Commercial Banks 1971–2023, (c) NYSE Margin Debt 1997–2023, and (d) United States Corporate Debt 1971–2023.

Corporate debt, commercial and non-commercial real estate loans and stock trading on margin all became acceptable means of conducting business. "Markets make opinions." The empire of debt encouraged indebtedness at all levels of US society.

Source: https://fred.stlouisfed.org/series/CONSUMER
Source: https://fred.stlouisfed.org/series/REALLN
Source: https://www.advisorperspectives.com/dshort/updates/2024/01/16/margin-debt-up-6-0-in-december
Source: https://fred.stlouisfed.org/series/BCNSDODNS

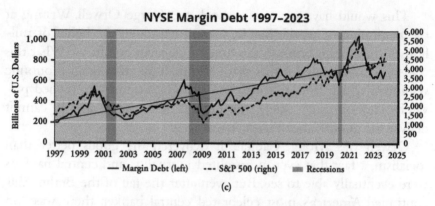

NYSE Margin Debt 1997–2023

— Margin Debt (left)   --- S&P 500 (right)   ▬ Recessions

(c)

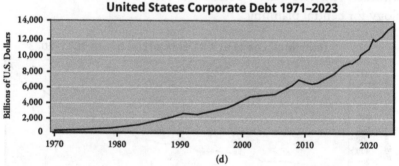

United States Corporate Debt 1971–2023

(d)

FIGURE 10.3 (Continued)

Adam Smith had proposed a useful metaphor to help explain how a system of private, individual decision-making—which must have looked chaotic to a top-down observer—actually functioned to the betterment of all. A rise in the price of pigs, for example, sends a signal to the hog raisers to produce more. Thus, the market is guided by an "invisible hand" to produce exactly as much of a thing as people really want and can really afford.

Quick-witted readers will already be gurgling with indignation. Markets work best without the heavy hand of regulation, Greenspan acknowledged. But he seemed to exempt, conveniently, the credit markets. The maestro's speech hit a false note; rather like President Bush's approach to evangelical democracy, it seemed to miss the point. Instead of letting lenders of credit and demanders of it be guided by an "invisible hand," for years the Fed chief's boney paws have drawn them together. Mr. Greenspan's "Open Market Committee," not the open market, has largely determined the rate at which lenders will lend, short term, and at which borrowers will borrow.

Why is it that what is good for the goose of lumber markets, stock markets, grain markets, laptop computer markets, and almost every other market under heaven is not good enough for the gander of the credit market? The answer is not one of logic, but of convenience. Most of the time, political leaders prefer easier credit terms than buyers and sellers would determine on their own. In setting its key rate, the Open Market Committee is likely to set a rate that is to the politicians' liking.

New Yorker columnist James Surowiecki's book, *The Wisdom of Crowds*,[8] makes the point that two heads are better than one. Groups of people can be smarter than individuals. A market, theoretically, can do a better job of finding the right price for a thing. A market is supposed to aggregate the private opinions and independent judgments of thousands of individuals. Generally it succeeds. But on occasion, the market slips into crowd-like behavior—whipped to excess by the financial media or the financial industry.

And sometimes, the whole market is deceived by its own central planners. Rather than allow lenders and borrowers to decide for themselves what rates they would accept, the central planners at the US Federal Reserve decided for them. How they can know exactly what lending rate such a large and infinitely complex economy needs has never been explained. But, historically, from the Fed's lowest rate to its highest, there are about 1,200 basis points. On those odds alone, they have almost certainly chosen the wrong one. There are times—indeed most of the time—when political leaders prefer easier credit terms than buyers and sellers determine on their own. In setting its key rate, the Open Market Committee tends to set a rate much more to the politicians' liking than the one offered by Mr. Market. A lower rate, that is. But as Schumpeter points out, any stimulus in excess of actual savings is a fraud.

This artificially low rate gives the illusion that there is more money available than there really is. Hardly anyone ever complains. Consumers feel they have more money to spend than they really have. Producers sense a demand that really isn't there. Undeserving politicians get reelected. And conniving central bankers are reappointed.

The "information content" of the Fed's low rate misleads everyone. They proceed happily on the long, slow process of ruining themselves, unaware that they are responding to an imposter. Only much later does the deception become a problem.

Friedrich Hayek explains: "The continuous injection of additional amounts of money at points of the economic system where it creates a temporary demand, which must cease when the increase of money stops or slows down, together with the expectation of a continuing rise in prices, draws labor and other resources into employments which can last only so long as the increase of the quantity of money continues at the same rate—or perhaps even only so long as it continues to accelerate at a given rate ... would rapidly lead to a disorganization of all economic activity."[9]

The way it works is simple: An economy is geared to produce for real demand. Or it is misled by artificially low interest rates to produce for a level of demand that doesn't exist. The deceit can go on for a long time. But, eventually, some form of adjustment must take place—usually, a recession restores order by reducing production and consumption. Generally, the correction is equal to the deception that preceded it.

But the Bank of Alan Greenspan thought it could avoid these periodic bouts of sanity. Fed Governor Ben Bernanke proposed "global cooperation" in a November 21, 2002, speech. Then, in May 2003, he went to Japan urging concerted action. The Fed was prepared to sacrifice the solvency of American consumers, he told the Japanese. Tax cuts and low interest rates could still induce them to buy things they didn't need with money they didn't have. But Japan had to help hold down US interest rates—by buying up dollars and dollar-denominated assets, notably US Treasury bonds.

This is what happened next, according to Richard Duncan:

> In 2003, and the first quarter of 2004, Japan carried out a remarkable experiment in monetary policy—remarkable in the impact it had on the global economy and equally remarkable in that it went almost entirely unnoticed in the financial press. Over those 15 months, monetary authorities in Japan created ¥35 trillion. To put that into perspective, ¥35 trillion is approximately 1 percent of the world's annual economic output. It is roughly the size of Japan's

annual tax revenue base or nearly as large as the loan book of UFJ, one of Japan's four largest banks. ¥35 trillion amounts to the equivalent of $2,500 for every person in Japan and, in fact, would amount to $50 per person if distributed equally among the entire population of the planet. In short, it was money creation on a scale never before attempted during peacetime.[10]

Why did the Japanese create so much money? Because they needed to buy from their citizens the dollars they had accumulated by selling things to Americans. Had they not done so, their currency would have gone up—making their products less competitive on the US market. Had they not done so, the dollar would have fallen much further against other currencies. Had they not done so, the Japanese would not have had the dollars to buy US Treasury bonds. And had they not bought so many of them, US interest rates would have risen, consumers would have had less money to spend, and probably the whole world would have had an economic crisis. Duncan continues:

> Intentionally or otherwise, by creating and lending the equivalent of $320 billion to the United States, the Bank of Japan and the Japanese Ministry of Finance counteracted a private sector run on the dollar and, at the same time, financed the U.S. tax cuts that reflated the global economy, all this while holding U.S. long bond yields down near historically low levels.
>
> In 2004, the global economy grew at the fastest rate in 30 years. Money creation by the Bank of Japan on an unprecedented scale was perhaps the most important factor responsible for that growth. In fact, ¥35 trillion could have made the difference between global reflation and global deflation. How odd that it went unnoticed.[11]

FLIGHT TO HAZARD

As the empire matured, Americans developed new ideas and attitudes to go with it. We have already shown how they took on the beliefs of an imperial race, ready to mind everyone's business but their own. Financially, their beliefs changed, too; people switched their attention from assets to cash flow, from balance sheets to monthly operating statements, from long-term wealth building to paycheck-to-paycheck financing, from saving to spending, and from "just in case" to "just in time."

It was a flight to hazard that became more hazardous with every takeoff and landing.

It was as if a strange new trade wind had been stirred up in the Pacific and blew across the country. Year after year, it blew stronger, until practically every tree and street sign, all across the country, leaned toward empire. Gradually, all of America's institutions and attitudes were bent by the new wind.

The federal government ran a fairly tight ship until the Johnson and Reagan years, and then the wind caught it. Soon, it was under full sail, flying toward record deficits and unheard-of debts.

The Federal Reserve braced itself under the iron hand of Paul Volcker (1981–1987). Then, it was Alan Greenspan's turn at the helm. Soon, the Fed was not only bent over along with everyone else but also actually flapping away itself—increasing the blow.

Consumers had a hard time keeping their feet on the ground. Every time they ventured outdoors, the strong wind pushed them toward more and more dangerous debt. When once they considered a heavy mortgage a risky thing, they came to see it as no risk at all. The gush of air picked up their houses and lightened the load. As interest rates dropped, they couldn't wait to refinance and then refinance again, each time "taking out" a little more equity.

The wind bent consumers' attitudes toward debt and twisted the lending industry into such comely new forms: How could they resist?

In spring 2006, *Grant's Interest Rate Observer* paused to observe something unusual: Rarer even than a banker with a heart, it had discovered one with a brain.

The late Vernon W. Hill was a banker from a small town that must be in a gully; the winds of modern debt financing didn't seem to reach it.

"We feel the U.S. is in trouble, with major weaknesses and unpleasantness ahead," he said. "Whether inflation or deflation lies ahead, or some kind of both, we believe many borrowers will be unable to repay their loans as scheduled."[12]

None of the reasons Mr. Hill mentioned were original: little savings, little investment in productive industry (much of what was invested went into short-lived software), and the illusion of wealth that accompanies rising house prices. With little real investment in new factories or new methods of production, few good-paying new jobs were created. In such an economy, a banker without a brain walked lightly and lent heavily. For the president of Monroe County Bank, however, you got the impression that every step toward a new loan was uphill. He lent almost reluctantly, wondering how borrowers would be able to repay.

While other bankers were moving more and more of their money into real estate loans, Mr. Hill was warily reducing his bank's exposure—especially to residential property. Home mortgages were less than a third of commercial bank loans in 1980. Now they were nearly two-thirds. Other bankers lent to anyone who could sign their name, provided they were buying a house. Mr. Hill wanted to know how the borrower would be able to pay back the loan if—heaven forfend—the borrower's house didn't go up in price by 20% per year.

These were not the sort of practices that would make Mr. Hill's establishment the "Bank of the Year" or get his photo on the cover of *BusinessWeek*. Not in 2005. His was not the bank of the present. It may have been the bank of the past. That it might also be the bank of the future was in nobody's mind.

Not only was the Monroe County Bank out of step with most other lending institutions, it seemed to be marching in the opposite direction—back to the future. We had never met the man or visited his office in Forsyth, Georgia. But had we to enter the bank, we would have expected to find a man behind an old-fashioned ledger at an oak desk . . . and a spittoon in the corner. Were we to ask for a loan, we would have expected a disapproving look, followed by a polite, but severe inquiry into our personal finances. No, these were not the methods of the typical banker in the 18th year of Alan Greenspan's reign at the Federal Reserve System.

Nor was Mr. Hill's approach to the credit industry particularly profitable. He admitted he would have earned more money by doing what other bankers did. Most bankers borrow short and lend long. As long as long rates are higher than short rates—and they do the math right—they will make money. Mr. Hill's approach, borrowing long and lending short, was a curiosity in the banking industry. It forwent current profits in favor of a more solid balance sheet. And when long rates rose, which they will do, sooner or later—both Mr. Hill and your authors were sure of it—Mr. Hill would have the last laugh. Compared with most bankers, it would be far easier for him to collect his credits and pay his liabilities.

Stocks are buoyed up or thrown down as the market's view of the firm's value changes. Profit-making enterprises' value depends on how much profit they make, a figure subject to change and speculation. But the value of a house changes little over time. Year after year, it is the same roof, the same walls, the same cozy warmth and convenience. The value that an owner-occupied house gives cannot be amended, jiggled, bent, written down, cooked up, or restated. No clever CFO can smooth its earnings. No fast-talking promoter can hype up next year's sales. It is what it appears to be and nothing more: home sweet home.

But with the complicity of the entire credit industry, except for one bank in Forsyth, Georgia, Americans came to believe that the very same dull and lifeless bricks they knew so well—along with the fading paint, the stained carpets, the leaking taps, and cracking driveways—had a near-magical quality; they could make them rich. They believed that the house was an "investment," different from stocks only in that it was safer and more profitable. They knew from their own, direct experience that the house is not a profit center but a cost center. Each month, the place must be maintained. Money must be spent on it. They also knew that—other than the aforementioned service the house renders to its occupants—there is no output. There is nothing that comes out the back door that can be sold. As a business, it is a losing proposition, and they knew it. It produces nothing; no revenues are realized. No profits are earned.

And yet, homeowners also believed that they could go to friendly lenders from time to time and "take out" cash—as if the place had been accumulating earnings. What they were taking out, they believed, was merely surplus equity. They figured that if last year they had, say, $200,000 worth of house, this year they must have $250,000 worth of house. They could "take out" the $50,000 extra and spend it—just as if the house had earned $50,000 in profit—and still have their $200,000 worth of house.

They did not ask themselves where that $50,000 came from. They did not find it at all extraordinary that an item they knew to be a cost center could also produce more in "profits" each year than they earn in income! Nor did they wonder how there could be so much untapped value locked up in their house, when they knew full well that they and their family used every room.

Mr. Vernon W. Hill considered this wealth an illusion, as we did. He believed it would lead to big problems among borrowers and lenders. To avoid the big problems personally, Mr. Hill, like Warren Buffett, lived in the same house he bought nearly 40 years ago.

Mr. Hill required prospective borrowers to show him their finances without considering the house they lived in. Whatever value there is in the lived-in house, he said, is "inactive." It doesn't really earn any money for you; if you were to sell it, you would just have to buy another one. And you can't ship it to China to pay for your flat-screen TVs or to Japan to pay for your SUV.

It was not that Mr. Hill was necessarily opposed to the great empire; he just didn't seem to care. But a view more typical of the average lender, and average economist, was expressed by a pair of economists, mentioned briefly previously, writing in the *International Herald Tribune*. Mr. David H. Levey was formerly managing director of Moody's Sovereign Ratings Service. Stuart S. Brown is a professor of economics and international relations at Syracuse University. The two argued that "U.S. Hegemony Has a Strong Foundation." The two were talking big. They were talking macroeconomics, with no trace of Mr. Hill's modest insights, or his private knowledge, or his 37 years of experience lending money, or the keen and immediate attention of having his own money at stake.

What Levey and Brown were trying to tell us is that we had nothing to worry about. Yes, it was true that we Americans spent 6% more every day than we earned. Yes, $11.5 trillion worth of US assets were in foreign hands and our net international investment position had gone negative at more than $3 trillion. And yes, it was true that we saved nearly nothing. But we could still feel good about ourselves, they said.

The numbers obscure "the United States' institutional, technological and demographic advantages," they said. What were those advantages? The two never quite said. But what could they say? Other countries have different institutions. Others have different demographics. Others use different technologies. Who knows which are an advantage and which are a hindrance? You only know—and then, only by inference—after the fact. At the height of its bubble in 1989, it was widely presumed that Japan had all the advantages. Hardly a single issue of the business press failed to mention them. Now, 15 years and a major slump later, Japan seemed to have all the disadvantages, while the advantages somehow crossed the Bering Strait into North America.

The mainstream press told us how dynamic, flexible, and open the US economy was. At the end of their article, Messrs. Levey and Brown told us that the only real threat was that "protectionism and isolationism at home will put an end to the dynamism, openness and flexibility that power the U.S."[13]

We can't help but remember French military policy after the Franco-Prussian War. Led by Colonel Grandmaison, the French allowed words to replace tactics and strategy. *Élan* was the word. It meant "spirit" or "force of will." When World War I began, the French attacked on horseback, swords glittering. What élan! What style! What blockheads. The German machine guns opened up and soon the ground was covered by handsome young soldiers. Élan proved great for poets but bad for France's military.

One hundred years later, Americans put on their own gaudy tunics—so proud of their "dynamism," their "flexibility," their "openness." Who cared that they spent more than they could afford? Who worried that we had no savings and now depended on the kindness of strangers to maintain our standards of living? Who realized that the Chinese or Japanese could bring the US economy to its knees with a single word?

But so what if the Chinese and Japanese sold our bonds, we still had our houses!

The two economists noted that "when you include capital gains, 401(k) retirement plans, and home values, U.S. domestic saving is around 20 percent of GDP, the same as in most other developed nations."[14]

They should have talked to Mr. Hill. They didn't seem to realize that home values are "inactive." We have yet to hear of a factory built with increases in house prices. We have yet to see a debt paid from a rising house price—without an equal debt arising somewhere else.

"Much of our meager savings and massive borrowing has gone into housing," said the Monroe County banker. "How convenient it would be now if mansions and subdivisions could be exported, to improve our foreign trade balance. Since they cannot be exported, perhaps the foreigners who own our massive debts can be repaid by coming to live in our McMansions, with homeowners serving as houseboys and house maids to the visiting Japanese and Chinese owners of our debt."[15]

"The United States economy is growing," said Paul Volcker, "on the savings of poor people."[16] Or, as Marshall Auerback put it, we had become a "Blanche Dubois" economy—we had delusions of grandeur, and yet, we were completely dependent on the kindness of strangers just to keep going.[17] Poor people made things, and then financed the consumption of them by rich people.

Americans deceived themselves with the fanciful notion that people who live in hovels, eat disgusting animals, and earn less than 1/20 as much per hour would be willing to finance our new houses and new wars forever. Why? Our economy is so "dynamic" ... so "flexible" ... so "open"—the poor peasants can't resist!

FRUGAL TO A FAULT

As the gusts of credit, debt, borrowing, and spending blew across the nation, very few of the old attitudes and institutions were left standing. Apart from Vernon Hill and a few others, lenders stopped worrying about the quality of their borrowers. Savings and loan businesses might as well have dropped the word *savings* from their names. And calling lenders *thrifts* was practically a lie; the whole industry bent to a new task—to load up consumers with as much debt as possible.

There was a time when thrift was a virtue. "A penny saved is a penny earned," dead people whisper. Accountants with sharp pencils even noticed that a penny saved was more than a penny earned, 40% to 50% more; it was not subject to state, local, and federal income taxes.

But in America, thrift came to be regarded no longer as a virtue but as a mental disorder.

Evidence came from a magazine spotted on Long Island, again through the ever-observant *Grant's Interest Rate Observer*. The publication, entitled *Real Simple*, told the story of a poor woman named Morning Naughton, 34 years old in the flesh, hundreds of years old in spirit.

If the phone didn't ring at an expensive jewelry store, it was Ms. Naughton who wasn't calling. If no one was admiring the new SUVs in a North Carolina showroom, it was Ms. Naughton who stayed at home. If you were to check the credit card records for sales of expensive vacations, fancy hotel rooms, extravagant fur coats, or top restaurants, you would not find Ms. Naughton's name.

Alas, said *Real Simple,* the woman had a real problem; she was "frugal to a fault."[18]

"She has never had credit card debt, she pays all her bills on time and she typically saves $500 each month—on a salary of about $30,000," we are told. "Her husband, Jason Michaels . . . worries about her inability to indulge herself . . . or him." The plot thickens. "And he wonders if her scrimping sends the wrong message to their child." "I realize she can't help herself," says Jason. "But her obsession with saving can drive me nuts."

But never was there a problem under the bright sun of America that didn't have some sort of fraud creeping in the shadows behind it. Reading about Ms. Naughton, economists saw a threat; if other consumers were to do the same, the whole shebang would be in trouble. Psychologists, however, saw an opportunity; some would prepare 12-step programs to help overcome it. Others would offer drugs and counseling.

Both economists and psychologists could relax. If frugality is a disorder, it was too rare to worry about. The odds of coming down with it were as remote as integrity in public office. Besides, thrift—even if it were a disorder—is one that comes and goes. If people are saving too much, or too little, just wait; it will go away.

Ms. Naughton—through no fault of her own—tumbled into an unusual situation. One generation creates; the next dissipates. One generation earns; the next burns. One generation composes, the next disposes. Morning Naughton was merely born at the wrong time.

"In the 1970s," began a recent letter from a reader of our daily e-mail, the "Daily Reckoning," "I recall seeing many people, children of the Depression, ravaged by inflation. They remembered the 'bad times' and were loath to take on debt—even if it would have been prudent to borrow and pay back in cheaper dollars. In the face of rising prices, they would slam their wallets shut or buy used, rather than new—'I'd never pay that much for a new car!' They held their dollars, steadfastly refusing inflation hedges, and watched, even increased their dollar position, as the inflation storm ravaged their holdings."

"When Morning was 9," continues the *Real Simple* analysis, "her parents divorced, and she moved with her father to Cape Cod. Her dad did some construction work to make money, but he was an artist at heart. . . . She worked at a multitude of odd jobs, including baby-sitting, to make money. At age 10, she opened her first savings account. At 13, she started paying all the bills by filling out the information and having her dad sign the checks. . . . 'My childhood left me with this extreme anxiety about parting with money. I always need a safety net.'"

She may have been the only American on two legs who still worried about falling. But she could always try therapy. "Were it not for her husband and child, Morning . . . might not be motivated to change," *Real Simple* explained.

"After more than 20 years of belt-tightening, Morning knows she needs to relax. 'I don't want [my son] Spencer to grow up with the same money anxieties I have,' she says. 'Being so frugal has become a burden, and I want to change. But it's hard after a lifetime of being this way.'"

We wished her luck. But we offered advice: Don't change too much. Old habits might turn out to be useful. Who knows? Frugality could make a comeback.

THE OWNERSHIP SOCIETY

A great empire can be viewed as a vast public spectacle. It begins with a bold crime, develops into a farce, with petty acts of tomfoolery and fraud along the way, and ends in shame, regret, and disaster.

The Medicare Drug Benefit program, enacted during Bush's first term, was meant to cost $400 billion during its first 10 years. Turns out, the official estimates included 2004 and 2005, that is, two years before the program existed. The real 10-year cost of the program floated through the news months later at $720 billion. Americans voted for their representatives in Congress and the White House; the politicians voted for the free drugs. Thus, was the divine right of the majority—the brute power of the more to tell the few what to do—

purified by the ballot box. The polite forms of the old republic were respected. But the essential act was a sin and a crime. Why should some Americans get drugs at other Americans' expense? Is it not larceny on the part of one and complicity on the part of the other? And how will those "others" pay for it; were they not already on the hook for $44 trillion in unfunded federal obligations?

But now the scam is the law of the land.

George W. Bush wanted to create an "ownership society." But it was a strange form of ownership. Much of what Americans believed they had title to actually belonged to someone else. Their retirements and health benefits, for example, must be stolen from other people before they could be handed out. Even things they thought they paid for were actually on the balance sheet of other people. More and more houses were really owned by mortgage finance companies. Cars were owned by GMAC and other auto financers. People expected to retire on the equity locked up in their houses. But they owned less of their own houses than ever before. And Social Security? A forensic accountant could pore over the books for a thousand years and never find a trace of the cash supposedly stashed away for Americans' retirement. It doesn't exist.

Mr. Bush said he wanted to change that. He wanted Americans to own their own retirement funds—with private accounts invested in stocks. The young had wised up to Social Security. There was no way they could get a decent return on investment in Social Security; they wanted out. The old were alarmed, too; they were afraid that the something for nothing they'd grown to expect would turn out to be more nothing than something. And the Bush administration wanted votes from both groups. So, it did what you would expect: It deceived and dissembled.

Fast-forward 13 years, members of Klaus Schwab's World Economic Forum would be treated to a video entitled *You'll Own Nothing and Be Happy* purportedly regaling the exact opposite of George W. Bush's vision.[19] The phrase took the internet by storm, and remains a meme to today.

Alas, it doesn't matter what we think about it. Empires—like history—have thoughts of their own, and a will toward their own end.

CHAPTER 11

MODERN IMPERIAL FINANCE

A new piece of research from Princeton's Center for the study of the brain was reported in the press in the early aughts.[1] Poking around, the scientists thought they found something new that would explain Americans' reluctance to save money.

Decisions are made in two parts of the brain, the researchers told us. The first part is the lateral prefrontal cortex. This is where advanced, logical thinking is supposed to happen, such as when a person decides which investment to make or which automobile offers the most value for the money. Deeper down in the gray matter is another decision center, the more primitive limbic system, where people actually decide which car to buy—usually the one that best suits their own prejudice. If buyers think they are a manly man, they buy a big US-made truck, or maybe a Hummer. If they prefer to think of themselves as an intellectual, they go for a foreign make, maybe an Audi or a Volkswagen. Behind the wheel of a German car, they feel at one with Hegel and Schopenhauer. Or, if they are a hip environmentalist, they will want to advertise that, too; in a sleek hybrid or an EV, maybe a Tesla, they will feel as smug as a teetotaler in a beer hall. Forget the logic of whether there will be charging stations nearby when advancing beyond the perimeter of its battery life.

Researchers believe that the limbic system decides our likes and dislikes, and tells us how to react to immediate stimuli. When a dump truck cuts you off in traffic, the limbic system almost automatically wants to cock your right arm and middle finger in the traditional salute, before your lateral prefrontal cortex can warn you against the gesture. Your first option is, rightly, to apply the brake or swerve.

In the upper part of the brain, Americans realized that they needed to save for their retirement. But the limbic system insisted on buying a new wide-screen TV instead. Though the researchers' report was circulated in the media as though it meant something, it left us only more puzzled than before. When did Americans acquire this limbic system, we wondered? Up until 1980, US savings rates were about 10% of incomes. Did some kind of evolutionary mutation occur in the early years of the Reagan administration?

And how come the Chinese didn't seem to have the same problem? As previously mentioned, they saved 25% of their incomes, while Americans saved less than 1%. Someone ought to pry open a Chinese skull and take a peek to verify this, but our guess is that the Chinese have limbic systems, too. Similarly human ones.

At least the scientists were wise enough to realize that not every thought that passes through the human brain makes any logical sense. The most powerful thoughts—strong enough to put the average American's retirement financing, and even their life, in jeopardy—are not logical at all, but instinctive, atavistic, and primordial. Driven by passion.

GLOBALIZATION AND ITS DISCONTENTS

Two thousand years ago, St. Peter urged a crowd to "turn away from this lost generation." W. H. Auden spoke of the "low, dishonest decade" before the Great War. Could our own generation be low, dishonest, and lost? We had come to believe that things will last forever that couldn't possibly be true for even a minute. Early in his tenure, Fed governor Ben Bernanke told Americans that they were doing the world a great favor by borrowing its surplus savings. The globe suffers from a "glut" of savings, said he. Americans counted on overseas savers to lend them money. The overseas savers, said Bernanke, counted even more on US spendthrifts to borrow it. With the empire of debt firmly established, the logic somehow worked.

And yet, the trouble with this analysis is not that it is flawed, but that it didn't go quite far enough. The transaction Bernanke described is only half complete. It is like a man who gets dressed in the morning by putting on his shirt, but forgets his pants. He goes out on the street and looks ridiculous. Anyone who looks at Bernanke's half-dressed explanation wants to point and giggle. He has forgotten the essential part—how and when the lenders get repaid. Borrowers only do lenders a favor when they are capable of repaying it on the agreed terms. If they cannot, the transaction becomes a big disappointment for the lender. Incomes in the United States are stagnant, or actually falling. That was true in the early editions of this book. It's still true in 2023.

We face more and better-organized competition than at any time since the beginning of the industrial revolution. Tech companies grab a lot of the headlines. We're currently in the throes of an artificial intelligence bubble on Wall Street. So the illusion continues. Yet, globally the pool of people willing to work hard for $3,000 a year is enormous, and growing. Given such competition, why would US wages go up? And without higher wages, how will Americans ever pay back what they have borrowed?

But the world's financial plumbing had become so curiously put together that the oddest things had been mistaken for commonplace. A decade of zero interest rates, globally, led by the Federal Reserve, seemed to new entrants into the market as if that was the norm. Pensions and hedge funds then began to plan, or bet, accordingly.

When we turned on the stove the champagne fizzed out. We opened the faucet and it ran with Kentucky bourbon; the whole thing was strange, but it didn't take long to learn to like it. The US economy had been so strong for so long, people all over the world had come to accept its currency as though it were real money; they took it and asked nothing in return. In exchange for a shipment of TV sets, the Japanese took a wad of $100 bills and called it even. And here is another remarkable thing: The bills tended to stay overseas—where they were used to buy another form of US paper, Treasury bonds. The United States could print as many $100 bills as it wanted. So could it issue as many bonds and notes as it pleased. As long as people didn't try to exchange them for other forms of wealth—all was well.

Rev. Al Sharpton is clean. He is not an economist. He was against outsourcing. That those qualifications did not cinch the 2004 Democratic presidential nomination for the man disappointed many people. That he had not been outsourced himself disappointed many others. For surely a clever fakir could be found in India who would be ready to make a public spectacle of himself at half the price. For that matter, all of Washington could be outsourced to the banks of the Ganges at a fraction of the price, but no one has yet suggested it.

Joined by Dennis Kucinich and Ralph Nader, Sharpton believed the United States should disavow free trade altogether. As long as we are members of the World Trade Organization, explained Kucinich in a debate, we cannot "protect the jobs . . . this is the reason why we have outsourcing going on right now. We can't tax it. We can't put tariffs on it."[2] Kucinich turned out to be appropriately correct 10 years later when Donald Trump flamed the passions of populism to millions of Americans, mostly in the "flyover" states who starting asking the question, "What went wrong with America?"

To be nonpartisan about it, all the candidates' positions on outsourcing were preposterous or scurrilous. There were those who wanted to stop it. And those who saw no problem with it. Every opinion was fraudulent, delusional, or dumb. It was widely believed that the Chinese were stealing US jobs. Their factories hummed and belched smoke while US factories went silent and sent up weeds in the parking lot. And then began to get serious about cutting carbon emissions when the rest of the world only appeared to show up at summits and conferences to talk about it. Globalization, exportation of US industry, to most readers concerned with the issue and are reading this book, turned out to be a double-edged sword. Sure, corporate America could save on labor, resources, and manufacturing costs. Yes, Americans could reap the benefits of cheap stuff—toys, sporting attire, electronics, tools—shopping at Walmart, Best Buy, or Home Depot. But where did the "good" jobs and communities go?

The world has been globalized for a long time. English people in 1910 could sit in their parlor off St. James Park at the center of what was then the world's greatest empire and drink tea that came all the way from Ceylon in cups that came all the way from China. Then, putting down their drink, they could pick up a Cuban cigar, put it to their lips . . . and perhaps sprinkle a few ashes on the carpet that they had bought in Egypt or the leather boots they had ordered from a shop down the street that sold Italian goods. They could buy stocks in New York as easily as they could pick up oranges from Spain or the latest French novels to make their way across the channel.

But globalization is not without its discontents. In 1910, England had been the world's number-one superpower and the world's greatest economy for two centuries. But global competition had recently edged the British out of the top spot. US gross domestic product (GDP) surpassed it at the turn of the century. Germany marched by a few years later. Relatively, England, that "weary Titan," was in decline, and the globalized economy that the British Empire helped create worked against it.

Still, why would the English complain? They lived well—perhaps better than anyone else. Even if they didn't, they thought they did. The rest of the world was content. People liked buying and selling. People in Europe liked globalization, because it brought them oranges in the wintertime. People in the warm latitudes liked it because now they had someone to buy their oranges. Even then, people spoke of the "annihilation of distance" and assumed that more miles would be destroyed in the years to come.

Globalization is nothing more than the extension of the division of labor across international boundaries. One of your authors passes much of his time in France. In his little village are the vestiges of a self-contained community. As recently as the end of World War II, almost everything people needed was produced right there. The farms grew wheat. Farmers raised vegetables, cows, pigs, and chickens. There was a machine shop, a forge, and a woodworking atelier. There still remain the *Versailles boxes,* in which lemon trees were planted. The boxes allowed the trees to be moved into heated space in the winter. Otherwise, they would freeze and die.

But as distance was annihilated, commerce in lemons was born. There was no longer any need to plant lemon trees in transportable wooden boxes when lemons could be shipped, quickly and cheaply, by the millions. One country can produce lemons. Another can produce machine gun cartridges. Individuals, towns, enterprises, regions can divide up the labor, work more efficiently, and produce more things at lower cost. Everyone involved gets a little richer.

You'll recall our distinction, dear reader: There are only two ways to get what you want in life. You can do so honestly or dishonestly. You can get it by working for it or by stealing it. You can get it by trade and commerce or by force and fraud. You can get it by civilized methods or by barbaric ones. You can get rich by "economic means" or by "political means," as the great German sociologist Franz Oppenheimer put it. Globalization is merely an elaboration of the economic means of getting things. It requires civilized relationships for trade to work; people must get along with each other. They must rely on others—even other people in strange, faraway places—for important, maybe even essential, items. They must also be able to count on the medium of exchange for trading goods and services. If they can't trust the imperial money, they will switch to something else.

The end of history has been announced several times. But it never seems to arrive. People always tend to think that what is will remain, that present trends will continue at least indefinitely, and perhaps forever. When the going is good, they tell themselves that the odds of anything going wrong are like the extreme edges of a bell curve—vanishingly small. But people badly "underestimate the persistence of history's traditional side, the rise and fall of empires, the rivalry of regimes, the disastrous of beneficent exploits of great men," wrote French historian Raymond Aron.[3] That is to say, they tend to ignore the political means that shake things up and the rare "fat tail" events that make history interesting. Fat tails are those uncommon things that bunch up way out on the extremities of bell curves. They are things that shouldn't happen very often, but that tend to happen more often than people expect. That is why the tail ends of bell curves have little bulges in them—or *fat tails*.

Such a fat tail happened in 1914. A European war came after nearly 100 years of peace and progress. People thought the war could not happen. And if it did happen, they said, it would be short and sweet. As we have seen, they were wrong on both points. Again, in the 1930s, came another "fat tail" event—a great depression. And once again, globalization entered a shrinking phase. Fast-forward to 2001 a bubble in tech stocks that had forecast the end of history also busted, followed by a real estate and derivative panic in 2008 and another "unpredictable" event in 2020 when the world's populations submitted to a lockdown of the entire economy owing to a global pandemic that no one, allegedly, foresaw.

Some experts think globalization can flourish only under the protection of an imperial armada, such as that of Great Britain in the 19th century and the United States in the 20th. They are plainly wrong. Sometimes trade arrangements are elaborated. Sometimes they are trimmed back. The presence or absence of a sheltering empire is a factor, but certainly not an essential one. Switzerland has always enjoyed healthy trade with its neighbors, despite never being part of an imperial system. And even within an empire (such as within the Soviet Union), trade might be more difficult than trade between independent states.

Still, in the free world until 1989, and now almost everywhere, a *pax dollarium* greatly aided the cause of globalization throughout the second half of the 20th century. When the British pound was the currency of trade during the Victorian Age it was backed by gold. The US dollar post–Bretton Woods and the cessation of World War II enjoyed that same stability, until 1971. Since then, the world's reserve currency has been backed only by the "full faith and credit" of the imperial government.

America—and much of the rest of world—enjoyed a great boom after World War II. They were years of high growth, low inflation, and high employment. Tom Wolfe called it a "magic economy." Real incomes doubled from the late 1940s to the early 1970s. So did household income and consumption per capita. People were twice as rich because they produced twice as much as they had a quarter century before. Productivity, or output per worker, rose 100%.

But in 1973—two years after Richard Nixon took the nation off the gold standard—the economy lost its magic. No one knows exactly why. But that didn't stop people from having opinions about it. Conservatives thought economic policy had been too socialist; there were too many rules, too many taxes, and too many government expenses. Liberals thought there needed to be more controls; economists needed to manage the economy better, like the Japanese did. They also blamed free trade, which they saw as a threat to America's developed industries.

It took many years to achieve, but year after year, all the world's leading industrialized nations added laws, regulations, and taxes designed to make things better. And all these Wilsonian improvements cost money, reduced investment, or merely slowed down the economic machinery.

Taxes took resources out of the productive economy and moved them into government spending—which was essentially current consumption, with little future payoff. Taxes also discouraged investment by reducing real rates of return. This was especially important as inflation rates rose because taxes applied to the entire nominal gain, not the actual, real profit. An investment might double in nominal value. But if the value of the currency fell in half during the same period, investors had not made a dime. Still, the Internal Revenue Service would tax their nominal profit as if it were real. Also, as the government began supplying more and more "bread" to those who needed it—welfare, social security, health benefits, job protections, entitlements—people saw less need to stock their own cupboards.

When Ronald Reagan first entered the White House, the rate was over 8%. "Gross national savings" (calculated by deducting capital imports from total domestic savings) were nearly 20% of GDP in 1980. They fell to 15.6% in 1989 and then to less than 14% in 2007. Following the pandemic in 2023 the national savings rate dropped to just 3.4%.[4]

Net national savings are even worse. You get the net figure by subtracting depreciation of the capital stock. As the economy became more and more reliant on communications technology, the rate of depreciation increased. New computer systems and communications software just don't last as long as a new auto plant. Net national saving had been 8% of GDP in the 1970s. It averaged only 3.4% in the 1980s. By the 1990s, it was down to 3%. And in 2004, the number sank to 1.6%.

By the end of the financial crisis in 2008, the net national savings rate had dropped negative for the first time since the Federal Reserve started tracking the number in 1947. In 2009 it registered −2.9%. The national rate returned to positive (barely) for the next decade, but by the time inflation began to take its toll in 2023, the rate again dropped below zero—the only time it has done so without a declared crisis or emergency of some political acknowledgment.[5]

With no savings of their own, the country has relied on foreigners to do the savings for them. But not only did the foreigners have to save, they had to be willing to buy US financial assets—mainly Treasury bonds—denominated in US dollars. If they grew tired of it, or wary of it, the dollar could collapse. Fears of such a collapse caused investors in US treasuries to endure their "worst year ever" in 2022 before a respite in 2023.[6]

The odd thing about the spurt of globalization in the opening decades of the 21st century was that it was so lopsided. The United States took, but it didn't give. It borrowed, but it didn't pay back. It bought, but it didn't sell. It imported, but it didn't export. The only reason foreigners put up with it is that they assumed their dollars would be as valuable in the future as they are now. They assumed that the trends of the previous 50 years would continue unchanged. They assumed that no terrorists would knock off an archduke, that they would never want for bread, and no fat tail would plop itself down in the currency markets.

Americans and their politicians preferred to see neither a glass half empty nor a glass half full, but one that was full to the brim. All they really wanted to do was get their sip.

Of so little interest and importance was the trade deficit that, at the nation's two political conventions, it was hardly mentioned. Theories emerged that it was and is because the trade deficit exists and grows the dollar maintains its value globally. Too bad if you happen to use the same currency to buy eggs, bread, and gas. Everything for policy-makers was almost perfect for decades, said the Republicans—and getting better and better every day. Everything was almost perfect, said the Democrats—but the Republicans were making a mess of it. "Outsourcing" was a problem, all agreed. The trade deficit, however, didn't matter. When was the last time you heard anyone talk seriously about the trade deficit? Savings invested in production, exportation of goods returning value to the homeland? Soundbite politics don't express or handle these archaic economic values very well.

Back when Paul Volcker was at the Fed, the central bank's role was to, as his predecessor William McChesney Martin had articulated, "take the punch bowl away" before the party got out of hand. Volcker did it at the end of the 1970s—sending Treasury yields above 15%. The party animals were so mad, they burnt an effigy of Volcker on the Capitol steps. Still the Fed brought inflation under control and prepared the way for the boom of the 1980s and 1990s. But by 2005, the party had gotten so wild that people were dancing on tables and putting lampshades on their heads. And Ben Bernanke and Alan Greenspan were creeping over to the punch bowl with grins on their faces and bottles of gin in their hands. Janet Yellen couldn't find a party she didn't want to attend. Jerome Powell showed up to the party late and found himself studying Paul Volcker's words and actions to a far greater degree than anyone imagined.

TAKE IT AWAY, MAESTRO

As the early days of the new century unfolded, the US economy had been in "recovery" for more than 37 months. It was an odd recovery. No one was quite sure what it was recovering from. There had been a recession in 2001 and 2002. But it was a curious recession. GDP growth went negative. Yet, consumer spending and credit continued to expand. Ironically, we'd see the same pattern two decades later when the economy was doing great following the economic turmoil of the pandemic period.

If recessions are meant to correct the mistakes of the previous expansion, the mid-2000s one was a failure. Consumers should have spent less and increased savings. Then, after the recession was over, they should have had money to spend in the following expansion and a pent-up desire to buy what they had not bought during the recession.

The expansion was doomed from the beginning. Consumers had never stopped spending. So, when the economy turned around, they had saved no money. The only way they could continue spending was by borrowing more. The Fed helpfully dumped more alcohol in the bowl—lowering rates to make it easy for them. But by this time, the whole economy had become so woozy that the extra consumer spending had much less positive effect on the real economy than had been hoped. Americans borrowed and spent. But, in the new globalized economy, much of what they bought came from Asia—particularly China—which could turn out consumer goods at a lower cost than the United States.

What America really needed was not a consumer binge, but a capital spending boom. It needed to invest in new factories, new plants, and new jobs. The jobs would have given consumers real new income, with which to buy more goods and services and sustain the expansion. But gross investment—which had averaged 18.8% in the pre-Reagan years—had begun dropping the year Reagan entered the White House.

By 2004, it had fallen to 1.6%—even dipping below zero periodically. People were spending, but on consumption, not future production. The gewgaws and gadgets bought from China merely put Americans further into debt. Neither jobs nor incomes improved. Typically, at this stage of a recovery (June 2005), 10 million more new jobs should have been created. Likewise, incomes went up $300 billion less than they should have, based on the pattern of previous recoveries. These numbers will seem quaint to current readers, but not the trends.

Many economists—including Alan Greenspan—maintained that the lack of jobs was a sign of something good happening. "Productivity," they said, "accounts for most job losses, not outsourcing." In our current economy the focus on job openings and the unemployment rate obscures the fact that many Americans are starting to sniff the ill winds and are wondering what will become of their retirement savings. And asking whether their day-to-day, week-by-week expenses are sustainable.

"Over the long sweep of American generations and waves of economic change," explained the maestro Dr. Greenspan, "we simply have not experienced a net drain of jobs to advancing technology or to other nations."[7] Could something be different this time? Could this be a kind of "new era" in US economic history? The answer we give is "yes" ... but we will give it later. Here, our burden is more modest, and our proof comes more readily to hand. For here, we argue only that America's leading economic and political policymakers are either rascals or numbskulls. Or both.

Major tops in the credit cycle seem to correspond with major bottoms in economic thinking. From high offices all over the nation came the explanations, excuses, rationales, and obiter dicta; we don't know whether they were corrupt or merely stupid. But when the guardians of the public financial mores began urging people to acts of recklessness, the country was in trouble. Buy more, said one Fed governor. Borrow more, said another. Don't worry about debt, interest rates, or the loss of jobs, said the captain of them all. It was as though the National Council of Bishops had come out with a public statement urging wife swapping. The experience might not be unpleasant, but it is unseemly of them to say so. Whatever their words were at the time, they took hold. The trends have remained and have only grown on the abacus of the national ledger.

"Go out and buy an SUV," urged Fed governor Robert McTeer.[8] Seventeen million people heeded his call each year, from 2001 to 2005. Now the call to arms is to finance EVs and get on board with net-zero 2030!

On February 23, 2004, the Fed chief urged Americans to switch from fixed rate mortgages to ARMs—mortgages with adjustable rates, which left them much more exposed to interest rate increases, at the very moment when the Fed was increasing them. Many of the folks who refinanced their mortgages to lock in lower than 3% mortgages 2016–2020 are reeling with confusion now that rates have returned a somewhat historical norm of 6.8% to low 7%.

If anyone could be held directly and immediately responsible for the record level of America's foreign and domestic debts, it was Alan Greenspan. He had brought about a binge of borrowing by lowering interest rates down to Eisenhower-era levels. But spiking the punch was not enough; he was urging consumers to have another drink. His disciples followed suit for nearly two decades.

The erstwhile Fed chairman had an uncanny way of arriving at ideas at a time when they would be of most benefit to his own career and of most danger to everyone else. To Greenspan, the conservative economist, the stock market looked "irrationally exuberant" in the mid-1990s, until a member of Congress pointed out to him that he would be better off keeping his mouth shut. A goldbug in the 1970s, Greenspan became the biggest purveyor of paper money the world has ever seen. Similarly, large federal deficits seemed at odds with his creed until it suited him to think otherwise. The new US empire needed easy money and almost unlimited credit: for 19 years Alan Greenspan made sure it got them.

Markets make opinions, say old-time investors. Mr. Greenspan's opinions neatly corresponded with the market for his services. As the debts and deficits mounted up, Greenspan underwent an intellectual metamorphosis. An article in the New York Times explained:

Many mainstream economists are worried about these trends, but Alan Greenspan, arguably the most powerful and influential economist in the land, is not as concerned:

In speeches and testimony, Mr. Greenspan, chairman of the Federal Reserve Board, is piecing together a theory about debt that departs from traditional views and even from fears he has himself expressed in the past.

In the 1990s, Mr. Greenspan implored President Bill Clinton to lower the budget deficit and tacitly condoned tax increases in doing so. Today, with the deficit heading toward a record of $500 billion, he warns more emphatically about the risks of raising taxes than about shortfalls over the next few years.

Mr. Greenspan's thesis, which is not accepted by all traditional economists, is that increases in personal wealth and the growing sophistication of financial markets have allowed Americans—individually and as a nation—to borrow much more today than might have seemed manageable 20 years ago.

And here the article strikes gold:

This view is good news for President Bush's re-election prospects. It increases the likelihood that the Federal Reserve will keep short-term interest rates low. And it could defuse Democratic criticism that the White House has added greatly to the nation's record indebtedness.[9]

Out of convenience, rather than ideology, Mr. Greenspan came to see goodness in all manner of credit. Since he became head of the Federal Reserve system, debt levels rose from $28,892 for the average family in 1987 to $101,386 in 2005. Mortgage foreclosure rates, personal bankruptcies, and credit card delinquencies rose steadily. Mortgage debt rose $6.2 trillion during his tenure at the Fed. By January 2005, it had reached $8.5 trillion, or approximately $80,849 per household.[10]

But none of this seemed to bother the chief of America's central bank nor its chief politicians. The era of Greenspan spawned an entire generation of consumers, bankers, and policymakers who came to believe cheap and easy credit was not only the norm but to be expected when financial stress arrived unannounced.

WHAT DID ALAN DO?

For years, we have been working on Greenspan's obituary. As far as we know, the man is still in excellent health. We do not look forward to the event; we just don't want to be caught off guard. Maybe we could even rush out a quickie biography, explaining to the masses the meaning of Mr. Greenspan's life and work.

We see something in Alan Greenspan's career—his comportment, his betrayal of his old ideas, his pact with the devil in Washington, and his attempt to hold off nature's revenge at least until he left the Fed—that is entertaining and educational. It smacks of Greek tragedy without the boring monologues or bloody intrigues. Even the language used is Greek to most people. Though the Fed chairman speaks English, his words often needed translation and historical annotation. Rarely did the maestro make a statement that was comprehensible to the ordinary mortal. So much the better, we guess. If the average person really knew what was being said, they would be alarmed. And we have no illusions. Whoever attempts to explain it will get no thanks and might as well tell their teenager what is in their hot dog.

Alan Greenspan was the most famous bureaucrat since Pontius Pilate. Like Pilate, he hesitated, but ultimately gave the mob what it wanted. Not blood, but bubbles. Greenspan's role in the empire was more than that of a Consul or a Proconsul. He was the Prefect. He was the quartermaster who made sure the empire had the financial resources it needed to ruin itself.

We don't know how heaven will judge him. According to the central bankers' code, Greenspan has committed neither sin nor crime. He is seen as a paragon of virtue, not vice. Yet, as Talleyrand once remarked to Napoleon, "Sire, worse than a crime, you have committed an error."[11]

When the winds of imperial debt finance blew, Mr. Volcker planted his feet and stuck out his jaw. His successor, Mr. Greenspan, tumbled over. The Fed chairman's error was to offer more credit on easier terms to people who already had too much. During Greenspan's reign at the Fed, more new money and credit was created than under all the rest of the Fed chiefs combined. Consumer debt rose to its highest level in history, the ratio of debt to income also rose higher than it has ever been. The effect was to inspire bubbles all over the world and to transform the United States from the world's largest creditor to its biggest debtor.

What the Greenspan Fed had accomplished was to put off a natural, cyclical correction and transmogrify an entire economy into a monstrous *economic* bubble. A bubble in stock prices may do little real economic damage. Eventually, the bubble pops and the phony money people thought they had disappears like a puff of marijuana smoke. There are winners and losers. But in the end, the economy is about where it began—unharmed and unhelped. The households are still there and still spending money as they did before. Only those who leveraged themselves too highly in the bubble years are in any trouble.

But in Greenspan's bubble economy, something awful happened. Householders were lured to take out the equity in their homes. They believed that the bubble in real estate prices created wealth that they could spend. Many did not hesitate. Mortgage debt ballooned in the early years of the 21st century—from about $6 trillion in 1999 to $12 trillion at the end of 2008—increasing the average household's debt by $60,000. Americans still lived in more or less the same houses. But they owed far more on them.

We had given up all hope of ever getting an honest word out of the Fed chairman on this subject when, in early February 2005, the maestro slipped up. He gave the aforementioned speech in Scotland entitled "Current Account." Jet-lagged, his defenses down, the poor man seems to have committed to the truth. If it seems like we're unduly focused on the events between 2001 and 2008, it's true. Even a couple decades later, we're fascinated by the willingness the proletariat went along with the charade. Following the events of 2008 and 2009 the narrative just got more surreal and odd. Free money led to excessive financial decisions. Excess finance led to social changes of a magnitude we wouldn't have imagined but probably could have forecast. Then, if we weren't producing goods and exporting them anymore, citizens turned to real estate. Financiers turned the paper—home mortgages, home equity loans, car and student loans—into securitized investments for sovereign wealth funds; federal, state and local pension funds; 401(k)s; and industrial-strength IRAs—into "investment-grade" products to set their sales teams on. In hindsight, it wasn't such a great trend to invest in.

"The growth of home mortgage debt has been the major contributor to the decline in the personal saving rate in the United States from almost 6 percent in 1993 to its current level of 1 percent," Alan Greenspan admitted at the time. Thus, did he bring up the subject. Then, he began a confession: The rapid growth in home mortgage debt over the past five years has been "driven largely by equity

278 EMPIRE OF DEBT

extraction,"[12] said the man most responsible for it. By this time, listeners were beginning to take notes. And pretty soon, even the dullest economist in the room was adding two plus two. Mr. Greenspan lowered lending rates far below where a free market in credit would have put them. With little to be gained by putting money in savings accounts and a lot to be gained by borrowing, households did what you would expect; they ceased saving and began borrowing. What did they borrow against? The rising value of their homes—"extracting equity," to use Mr. Greenspan's jargon. The Fed chairman had misled them into believing that the increases in house prices were the same as new, disposable wealth.

But the world's most famous and most revered economist didn't stop there. He must have had the audience on the edge of its chairs. He confessed not only to having done the thing but also to having his wits about him when he did it. This was no accident. No negligence. This was intentional.

"Approximately half of equity extraction shows up in additional household expenditures, reducing savings commensurately and thereby presumably contributing to the current account deficit. . . . The fall in U.S. interest rates since the early 1980s has supported home price increases," continued America's answer to Adam Smith.[13]

"Lacking in job creation and real wage growth," explained Stephen Roach,

> private sector real wage and salary disbursements have increased a mere 4 percent over the first 37 months of this recovery—fully ten percentage points short of the average gains of more than 14 percent that occurred over the five preceding cyclical upturns. Yet consumers didn't flinch in the face of what in the past would have been a major impediment to spending. Spurred on by home equity extraction and Bush administration tax cuts, income-short households pushed the consumption share of U.S. GDP up to a record 71.1 percent in early 2003—an unprecedented breakout from the 67 percent norm that had prevailed over the 1975 to 2000 period. . . .[14]

Since the fall of the Berlin Wall, nearly everyone seems to agree that central planning is bad for an economy. The central planners, as any Economics 101 student can tell you, do a poorer job of delivering the goods than the "invisible hand" of the market.

Joseph Schumpeter sharpened the point: "Our analysis leads us to believe that recovery is only sound if it does come from itself. For any revival which is merely due to artificial stimulus leaves part of the work of depression undone and adds, to an undigested remnant of maladjustments, new maladjustments of its own."[15]

The US economy faced a major recession in 2001 and had a minor one. The newborn slump was strangled in its crib by the most careless central planners who ever lived. Alan Greenspan cut lending rates. George W. Bush boosted spending. The resultant shock of renewed, ersatz demand not only postponed the recession, it pushed consumers, investors, and businesspeople to make even more egregious errors. Investors bought stock with low earnings yields. Consumers went further into debt. Government liabilities rose. The trade deficit grew larger. On the other side of the globe, foreign businesspeople worked overtime to meet the phony new demand; over the two decades of these policies, China has enjoyed a capital spending boom as excessive as any the world has ever seen.

At the time of Greenspan's later tenure we couldn't help but ask our own Fed chairman, guardian of the nation's money, custodian of its economy, night watchman of its wealth: "How could you do such a thing?" He turned a financial bubble into a worldwide economic bubble. Not only were the prices of financial assets ballooned to excess, so were the prices of houses and the debts of the average household. And the economy itself was transformed.

The housing bubble that began as a consequence of interest rate policy decisions in response to the collapse of the tech bubble in the late century was no longer an investment phenomenon but an economic one affecting almost everybody. In some areas, half of all new jobs were related to housing. People built houses, people financed houses, people remodeled houses, people sold houses to each other, and people put in so many granite countertops that whole mountains had been flattened to quarry the stuff.

CHAPTER 12

SOMETHING WICKED THIS WAY COMES

The force of a correction is equal and opposite to the deception that preceded it. Alan Greenspan, George W. Bush, Janet Yellen, Joe Biden, and all the great nabobs of positivism assure us that there was nothing to fear. Whatever challenges lie ahead, America is more than ready for them.

We always try to get our day off on the right foot by reading Friedman's column before breakfast. There is something so gloriously naive and clumsy in the man's *pensée* that it never fails to brighten our mornings. It refreshes our faith in our fellow people; they are not evil, just mindless. We have never met the man, but we imagine Friedman as a high school teacher, warping young minds with drippy thoughts. But to say his ideas are sophomoric or juvenile merely libels young people, most of whom have far more cleverly nuanced opinions than the columnist. You might criticize the man by saying his work is without merit, but that would be flattery. His work has negative merit. Every column subtracts from the sum of human knowledge in the way a broken pipe drains the town's water tower.

Not that Mr. Friedman's ideas are uniquely bad. Many people have similarly puerile, insipid notions in their heads. But Friedman expresses his hollow thoughts with such heavy-handed earnestness, it often makes us laugh. He seems completely unaware that he is a simpleton. That, of course, is a charm; he is so dense you can laugh at him without hurting his feelings.

Friedman writes regularly and voluminously. But thinking must be painful to him; he shows no evidence of it. Instead, he just writes down whatever humbug appeals to him at the moment, as unquestioningly as a mule goes for water.

One of the things Friedman worried about, early in the 21st century, was that the world would "go dark." As near as we can tell, he meant that the many changes wrought after 9/11 were changing the character of the nation, so that "our DNA as a nation . . . has become badly deformed or mutated." In classic Friedman style, he proposed something that any 12-year-old would recognize as preposterous: another national commission! "America urgently needs a national commission to look at all the little changes that were made in response to 9/11," he wrote.[1] If a nation had DNA, and if it could be mutated, we still are left with the enormous wonder: What difference would a national commission make? Wouldn't the members have the same DNA? Or should we pack the commission with people from other countries to get an objective opinion—a UN panel and a few illiterate tribespeople for cultural diversity?

Friedman's oeuvre is a long series of "we should do this" and "they should do that." Never for a moment does he stop to wonder why people actually do what they do. Nor has the thought crossed his mind that other people might have their own ideas about what they should do and no particular reason to think Mr. Friedman's ideas are any better. There is no trace of modesty in his writing—no skepticism, no cynicism, no irony, no suspicion lurking in the corner of his brain that he might be a jackass. Of course, there is nothing false about him either; he is not capable of either false modesty or falsetto principles. With Friedman, it is all alarmingly real. Nor is there any hesitation or bewilderment in his opinions; that would require circumspection, a quality he completely lacks.

Friedman feared that he might not approve of all the post-9/11 changes. But so what? Why would the entire world "go dark" just because US stooped to create an empire? The idea was nothing more than another silly imperial conceit. America is not the light of the world. Friedman can stop worrying. The sun shone before the United States existed. It will shine long after she exists no more. But, without realizing it, imperial conceits were all Mr. Friedman had to offer, one after another. He knew what was best for everyone, all the time.

But even at his specialty, Friedman is second-rate. It is not that his proposals are much dumber than anyone else's, but he offers them in a dumber way. He sets them up like a TV newscaster, unaware that they mean anything, not knowing whether to smile or weep. He does not seem to notice that his own DNA has mutated along with the nation's institutions, and that he does nothing more than amplify the vanities and prejudices that pass for the evening's news. Is there trouble in Palestine? Well, the Palestinians should have done what we told them. Have peace and democracy come to Iraq? If so, it is thanks to the brave efforts of our own troops. Is the price of oil going up? Well, of course it is; the United States has not yet taken up the comprehensive energy policy he proposed for it. And why did they vote Donald Trump into office; they must not have paid attention to Friedman. The *New York Times* columnist's world is so neat. So simple. There must be nothing but right angles. And no problem that doesn't have a commission waiting to solve it.

It must be unfathomable to such a man that the world could work in ways that surpass his understanding. In our experience, any man who understands even his own thoughts must have few of them. And those he has must be dumb.

But we enjoy Friedman's commentaries. The man is too clumsy to hide or disguise the awkward imbecility of his own line of thinking. The silliness of it is right out in the open, where we can laugh at it. Arabs ought to shape up and start acting more like New Yorkers, he believes. If they don't want to do it on their own, we can give them some help. He says we can send "caring" and "nurturing" troops to "build democracies" in these places, "protect the rights of women" and lower carbon footprints, too. But he doesn't understand how armies, empires, politics, or markets really work. US troops can give help, but it is the kind of help that Scipio gave Carthage or Sherman gave Atlanta. Armies are a blunt instrument, not a precision tool.

In 2003, Friedman was urging the Bush administration to attack Iraq. But wait, he wondered "how do we get the Sunni Arab village to delegitimize [whoa … a big word hiding a whole dictionary of lies, fibs, prevarications, *malentendus*, misapprehensions, miscalculations, guesswork, hallucination, conceit, and mendacity] suicide bombers?"

Wait. Delegitimize suicide bombers? We didn't know they had ever gone legit. Besides, isn't it a problem that solves itself? There can't be many repeat offenders.

But Friedman has another solution. Propaganda! "The Bush team needs to be forcefully demanding that Saudi Arabia and other key Arab allies use their news media, government, and religious systems to denounce and delegitimize the despicable murder of Muslims by Muslims in Iraq."[2]

That ought to do it. What was wrong with the Bush team? Why didn't they think of that? "Forcefully demand" that the Arab states do more propaganda. Yes, problem solved.

By the way, your authors have no position on foreign policy. We only notice that the people who do have them are idiots.

Still we are not going to criticize Friedman. There is no sport in it. The poor fellow is evidently handicapped. He only sees things in two dimensions, like a drawing by a five-year-old with only one eye. He seems to have a one-eyed proposal each week: a "Reform Revolution" (whatever oxymoronic thing that is), "nation building," "a Manhattan project to develop a hydrogen-based energy economy," a "National Commission for Doing Things Right," a "Patriot Tax" of 50 cents a gallon on gasoline, a "Reform India" proposal, and many others too numerous and absurd to mention.

Friedman provided much rich entertainment for years, inadvertently, as people laughed at his silly columns. If only he'd used a question mark from time to time!

(We will send Friedman a whole box of question marks, suggesting that he sprinkle them through his columns.)

In 2003, the US government tossed the question marks aside and invaded Iraq (which had nothing to do with suicide bombings or terrorism). And now with the passage of time—and with the corpses, from two decades of empire building, now stacked to the rafters—our laughter is less jolly.

Ten years after the Iraq invasion, Charlie Rose on NPR asked Friedman if he still supported the war. Here is his reply:

What they [Islamic extremists] needed to see was American boys and girls going house to house—from Basra to Baghdad—and basically saying: Which part of this sentence don't you understand? You don't think we care about our open society? You think this [terrorism] fantasy [you have]—we're just gonna let it grow? Well, suck. on. this. That, Charlie, was what this war was about. We coulda hit Saudi Arabia. . . . We coulda hit Pakistan. We hit Iraq because we could.[3]

How's that for deep thinking? We hit Iraq because we could. And now we can hit Russia . . .without even poking our heads up out of the trenches! Why do we hit Russia? Because we can!

By this time, George W. Bush was gone. Barack Obama was in power. But no matter which party held the White House, US foreign policy was in the grips of a group of pompous, self-congratulatory, empire-building nitwits, who described themselves oxymoronically as "progressive conservatives"—David Frum, David Brooks, Bill Kristol, and the king and queen of neoconservatives, Robert Kagan and Victoria Nuland. They were neither progressive—because they aimed to restore a very ancient authoritarian system, not because they were "conservative." They were the exact opposite: activists. They were all determined to counter the "corrosive cynicism about public action" (the sort of thing you are reading now).

They urged "action." They wanted "leadership." They wanted an empire that the whole world would admire. Or, if not admire, at least fear. And they got it!

David Brooks described it as "national greatness conservatism." It was more muscular, more focused, with a greater sense of purpose than real conservatism. "Wishing to be left alone isn't a governing doctrine," he and coauthor Bill Kristol pointed out in the *Wall Street Journal*.[4]

Being left alone was okay for real conservatives and for a modest constitutional republic, but it wouldn't do for an empire. And it fell to Tom Friedman to take out the big words and sell it to the masses.

But by 2016, the message needed an update. America's roly-poly empire of faux capitalism, *pax dollarium*, firepower, and debt has helped establish order throughout most of the world. That order was immensely helpful to Americans in the first 60 years of the US imperium. We made things that we could sell throughout the world—at a profit.

But then, although the US-imposed imperial order might or might not still have benefitted Americans in the 21st century, it was the foreigners who were clear winners. Real wages rose in Asia. In the United States, they were stagnant.

By then, the logic of human jealousy—and imperial finance—had shifted. The United States was becoming less willing to provide a public good—order—for no other return than the opportunity to compete on a level playing field. Industries in the United States were old. Its leadership was old. Its population of baby boomers was old; it was no longer as competitive. Average incomes were up. But the money was more and more skewed toward the better zip codes. Half of the gains went to the top 10%. Take that out of the "average" calculation, and real incomes for most real people, were down significantly. And they were beginning to resent it. They didn't necessarily understand what was going on—what politician or mainstream columnist would tell them—certainly not Tom Friedman. But they knew something was wrong. America had slipped. They wanted someone who could tilt the playing field further in their direction.

And so, they elected a man who otherwise seemed unelectable: Donald J. Trump. He made a promise that no mainstream politician—Republican or Democrat—could match. He would "Make America Great Again." Hilary Rodham Clinton could only stare in amazement. "America already is great," she replied.

What both she and Friedman had not noticed was that America had squandered her lead. It's huge advantage was fading. If the United States had been using real money, and investing it in real factories, real jobs, and real new wealth-building innovations, it would still be competitive on the world market. Instead, it invaded Iraq, Afghanistan, Libya; ginned up an additional war between the Ukraine and Russia; spent an estimated $1.5 trillion per year (as of 2022) on its imperial program; and squandered time and treasure.

The entire program was based on fraud. The money wasn't real money. Interest rates were phony. Even the wars were phony wars, launched under false pretenses for no real purpose other than to make the warmongers richer and more powerful.

And now, the US had a "reformer," a disrupter, in the White House. And a perfect one he was; here was a bull in the china shop who didn't break so much as a teacup. The disappointment of the Trump years was not that he didn't make America great again; that was probably far beyond his means. But he didn't have to make it so much worse.

The empire is financed on credit. Debt builds up. Unless it is brought under control, eventually, the debt tail will wag the dog. But instead of reducing US debt (Mr. Trump actually promised to eliminate it), the Trump team exploded US debt in a manner never before seen.

Looked at in constant 2021 dollars, Trump increased federal spending by $366 billion per year. That is four times as much as Barack Obama. It is six times as much as Ronald Reagan. And 10 times as much as Bill Clinton.

This, of course, led to deficits. Trump's deficits, averaged over his four years, came to 9% of GDP. Even during the Kennedy-Johnson years, the increase was less than 1% per year. Under Obama, the deficits came to nearly 5%. But no other president even came close to Trump's levels.

The deficits needed to be filled with borrowed money. During Trump's term, the extra debt mounted up at the rate of $2 trillion per year. That is twice the rate of the Obama team, and by eyeball averaging, about six times the level under Ronald Reagan.

The Trump promise was to "drain the swamp," cut spending, reduce regulation, and thereby restore America to what it had been and should be again. The idea was simple enough. It didn't require much deep thought. But you had to actually do it, not just bluff and bluster about it. What Trump did was to fill the swamp with more slimy spending than any president ever had before him. Federal spending as a percentage of GDP rose from about 19% when George W. Bush took office, to 22% when Donald Trump won the White House. Thereafter, in 2020, it reached to almost 32%. When Trump's possessions left Washington for Mar Lago, the swamp was deeper than ever.

You'd think, with so many political disappointments, futile wars, and rampant chicanery in public policies, an observant reporter for the *New York Times* would have learned something. For there he was, still drawing a salary from the newspaper, Tom Friedman. And after so many of his suggestions and ideas have proven either idiotic or disastrous, he still offers more of them. The *Times* devoted a full page and a half, in its September, 16, 2023, international edition, to his views on the Russo-Ukrainian war

The man is still a bad writer. But he is no ordinary bad writer. He is one with a real talent for taking complicated, nuanced subjects and not making them seem simple, but just simple-minded.

And still, he is desperately in need of question marks. There's always more to the story. Problems do not respond to commissions and good intentions. And people do not always get what they want; sometimes they get what they deserve.

Twenty years later, after the Iraq debacle, America was hitting another nation: Russia. The warmongers and empire builders were still at it: drumming up support for more glorious intervention. Here's Bill Kristol, raising money for a group called "Republicans for Ukraine": "When America arms Ukraine, we get a lot for a little. Putin is an enemy of America. We've used 5% of our defense budget to arm Ukraine, and with it, they've destroyed 50% of Putin's Army. We've done all this by sending weapons from storage, not our troops. The more Ukraine weakens Russia, the more it also weakens Russia's closest ally, China. America needs to stand strong against our enemies; that's why Republicans in Congress must continue to support Ukraine."[5]

This was not an original idea. By the 23rd year of the 21st century, the rot had already gone deep, and expressed itself as peculiar form of stupidity. Mitch McConnell explained why aid to the Ukraine really had little to do with any concerns for democracy or justice: "American support for Ukraine is not charity. It's in our own direct interests—not least because degrading Russia helps to deter China."[6]

How Russia became an enemy of the US was never clarified. Nor did we need to know what we were deterring China from doing, or why. By then, there was no need. Everyone now knew how the game was played. Also in September 2023, Joe Biden gave a remarkable speech to the UN. He told the assembled notables such a series of whoppers we half expected his pants to erupt in flame. He made it known that America was in full support of "sovereignty," "territorial integrity," and "a world governed by basic rules that apply equally to all nations."[7] He went on to characterize the Russo-Ukrainian war as Russia's "war of conquest."

How the delegates must have chuckled to themselves. They knew full well that of all the UN's 193 members none violated those basic rules more often or more flagrantly as the US. In the 21st century alone, its soldiers had intervened—often with remotely launched drones—in Afghanistan, Iraq, Yemen, Somalia, Libya, and Syria. It also sponsored dozens of "regime change" efforts—including one in 2023, in which the elected and popular president of Pakistan, Imran Khan, was replaced in a coup d'etat. His sin? He was too "aggressively neutral" on the Russo-Ukrainian war.

Probably the most remarkable evidence of hypocrisy was the US-led attack on Serbia in 1998. It did so, it said, to support the Kosovans' struggle for independence. What had happened to its high regard for "independence" when Russia sought to aid the Donbas separatists, in the Russian-speaking area of Eastern Ukraine, 25 years later?

In his weekend word mulch, Friedman explained that he visited Kyiv for three days (not mentioning that in his un-jetlagged moments he was shown only what the powers-that-were there wanted him to see, and only speaking to "experts" who agreed with his opinion). Now an expert himself, his doubts are gone. The scales lifted from his eyes; where he once saw through the glass darkly now he sees clearly, face to face. Like the catastrophic campaign in Iraq, he saw no need for nuance. No point in looking at it from the "other side." No reason to find a peaceful way out, and no curiosity about how it started or how it might end. It is a fight between good and evil, as all wars are, according to Friedman; he is on the side of the angels, of course.

There is no need to talk to any of the 2 million refugees who fled—to Russia!—to escape the fighting. Nor is there any cause to speculate about Putin's security concerns, either. Nor about the encroachment of NATO, nor about the coup d'etat orchestrated by the CIA and the US State Department in 2014, nor even about whether a boundary dispute on the Eurasian steppe was really worth the risk of a nuclear war.

He follows this up with this gem: "One need only look into the eyes of Ukrainian soldiers back from the front, or talk to parents in the streets of Kyiv, to be stripped of any illusions about the moral balance of this war. I was in the country for just three days . . .

"This is as obvious a case of right versus wrong, good versus evil, as you find in international relations since World War II."[8]

How could the journalist have an opinion on the "moral balance" without taking a glance at the other side of the scale? Did he attend a conference in Moscow? Did he talk to Russian veterans? To any of the victims of the Ukraine's firepower? No? We didn't think so.

Thank Tom Friedman, the sultan of sap, for removing all the hesitations, balancing, and second thoughts that might have saved a sensible person. Friedman merely clarified that what Putin was doing "is evil." There was really no reason to say more. You can't compromise with "evil." You can't try to "see it from his perspective." There's no middle ground.

Friedman, though, had another full page to fill. So he launched into one of the lamest geostrategic justifications for war since the Wehrmacht invaded Poland.

"Without the Ukraine, Russia ceases to be an empire. . . ." This left us stunned. Where were the question marks? Really? Why? There are plenty of other foundling countries Mother Russia could take in. And why would we care whether Russia were an empire, or not?

Russia has made no claim on the Ukraine. It has only taken over the Eastern provinces. It says it has done so partly because that is where the people live whom it wants to protect. The Kyiv government banished the Russian language; Russian speakers, who are dominant in the region, apparently welcomed the "regime change."

The other reason Russia has provided for its invasion is that it is afraid that NATO—egged on by people like David Brooks and Tom Friedman—might pose a threat. An attack from "the West"? Seems unlikely to us. But Russia's been down that road; it doesn't want to go there again.

Justified or not, those are the things Putin really seems to care about. But the mainstream media barely mentions them. It describes the war in terms that leave no space for exploring "the other side." So often are the adjectives *brutal* and/or *unprovoked* used to describe it, there is probably a whole generation of young people who think they are permanently attached, like *high dudgeon* (we've never heard of someone stomping out of a room in *low dudgeon*) . . . or *high tea* (whoever has *low tea*?).

But the attack was clearly not unprovoked. Instead, it appears to be just what America's empire architects wanted to see. NATO Secretary-General Jens Stoltenberg accidentally brushed up against truth when he told the EU how the war actually got started: "The background was that President Putin declared in the autumn of 2021, and actually sent a draft treaty that they wanted NATO to sign, to promise no more NATO enlargement. That was what he sent us. And was a pre-condition for not invading Ukraine."[9]

That was, after all, the deal made between Russia and the West—including leaders of Germany, France, the UK and the US—that allowed the reunification of Germany in 1990. Russia would agree to reunification. But the West had to respect Russia's security interests and not allow NATO to creep to the East.

US Ambassador to Moscow, William Burns, who later became head of the CIA, reminded the Bush administration of this promise in 2008. His memo—"Nyet Means Nyet"—famously recalled that bringing NATO up to Russia's border was a "red line" that shouldn't be crossed.

Unless, of course, you really wanted to provoke a war.

Even Zelensky's own team admitted that the real cause of the war wasn't Putin's desire for conquest; it was NATO enlargement. Oleksiy Arestovych, former advisor to the Office of the President of Ukraine under Zelensky, declared that "with a 99.9% probability, our price for joining NATO is a big war with Russia."[10]

Russia tried to avoid war, asking the West to honor the terms of the Minsk II Agreement, allowing for autonomy for the ethnically and culturally Russian areas along the Russian border.

Finally, at the end of 2021, Putin made another effort to avert war, proposing a US-NATO Security Agreement. That is the agreement that Mr. Stoltenberg mentioned. The US rejected it and offered no counterproposal.

Nor was the attack especially brutal. The war began in February 2022. By September, 2023, 18 months later, the *New York Times* said about 500,000 people had died. The last time Kyiv was a battleground, in 1941, German and Soviet forces lost that many men in just 10 days of fighting.

But none of this—no *arrière-pensées*, no extenuating circumstances, no alternative narratives—was of interest to Mr. Friedman. Instead he put forward childish quips like this one: "Putin lately has stopped even bothering to justify the war—maybe because even he is too embarrassed to utter aloud the nihilism that his actions scream: *If I can't have Ukraine, I'll make sure Ukrainians can't have it, either.*"[11] Again, the question marks appear. Putin was now fighting a defensive war; the Russians were dug in, more or less at the Dnieper, the frontier between Russian-favoring Eastern Ukraine and the Ukrainian-oriented region to the West. There was no evidence, none, that he was trying to destroy the whole country. And there was ample evidence that if he went on a war of conquest, he would find little success. Putin had just showed the world he didn't have the firepower.

And here's another Friedmanian geopolitical thought vacuum: "Most Americans don't know a lot about Ukraine, but I say this without any hyperbole: Ukraine is a game-changing country for the West, for better or for worse depending on the war's outcome. Its integration into the European Union and NATO someday would constitute a power shift that could rival the fall of the Berlin Wall and German unification."[12]

A power shift from what to what? What power does NATO lack now that it would acquire by enrolling the Ukraine? And why would that be a good thing?

Not waiting for questions, much less for answers, Friedman goes ahead, like a blind man in a sorority shower room, hoping to get lucky: "It is very hard to stop a leader who has no shame or conscience. On Tuesday Putin told an economic conference in Russia that the 91 felony counts filed against Donald Trump in four different U.S. jurisdictions represent the 'persecution of one's political rival for political motives' and show 'the rottenness of the American political system, which cannot pretend to teach democracy to others.'"[13]

We're not sure what Putin was trying to say. Is US democracy rotten because Donald Trump allegedly committed 91 felonies? Or because his enemies are using the judiciary system to persecute him? Either way, he has a point. But what is Friedman's point?

He doesn't say. Instead, he goes on and on and on: "'Human morality must win this war,'" Zelensky said. "'Everyone in the world who values freedom, who values human life, who believes that people must win. And our success, the specific success of Ukraine, depends not only on us, on Ukrainians, but also on the extent to which the entire vast moral space of the world wants to preserve itself.'"[14]

Good luck on that one. When did "human morality" win a war? Wars are won by tanks, guns, bombs—none of which could give a damn about "morality." The "morality" angle is brought out later. Winners put the losers on trial, who are clearly "immoral," making the winners, necessarily, the ones with the halos. If Japan had won WWII, albeit a rather fantastic alternative history, Harry Truman would have been hung for dropping the atomic bomb on two civilian targets: Hiroshima and Nagasaki. Who would have the "moral space" then?

In addition to the absence of question marks is the absence of irony, or a sense of non sequitur. After telling us that the Ukraine is fighting the good fight, we discover from Friedman that it is having a good time doing so: "Despite the ongoing war, Ukrainian start-ups brought in more than $6 billion in revenue in 2022—$542 million more than in 2021—and have tripled in valuation since 2020. . . . In a normal year, Ukraine was graduating 130,000 engineers—more than Germany and France. . . ."

"Besides military and cyber start-ups," Friedman quotes an employee of one of the startups "the street I live on has three or four new restaurants that are very European in feeling. It is a cultural revolution."

And then, we find out what a great success the EU has been:

> [T]he E.U. is a quiet, boring miracle. Adding Ukraine to it would make it only stronger.
>
> By pure accident, I was reminded of just how important this could be on my trip home. As I sat at Warsaw's Chopin Airport, I watched German Lufthansa planes land on Polish tarmacs. I saw three Hasidic Jews saunter by in their distinctive black coats and hats, the fringes of their prayer shawls dangling from their white shirts. With Poland now in the E.U., I could overhear chatter in several languages, some of which I couldn't identify, in the 360 degrees around me.
>
> In 1939, the arrival of a German plane in Warsaw meant death and mayhem would soon follow, especially for my ancestors. Now, it's just a fast way to Frankfurt.[15]

Huh? Pure Friedman. Makes no sense. So what if, after passing through Warsaw airport, he believes the EU is a success? What does he know? If it is such a great success, why did the English vote to leave it? We don't know, but surely he could use some of those question marks we're sending his way.

And because we're heavily into question marks, Hitler unified Europe, the first person to do since Napoleon. Now, the EU has done it again. Who's to say that some new madness mightn't take hold? Would the EU stop it? Or amplify it? And how does this have anything to do with the Russo-Ukraine war?

We don't know. Neither does Tom Friedman.

Every empire begins with a humbug. Later it develops into mass illusion, self-congratulation, hallucination, farce, and finally disaster. You rarely know quite where you are. Because every tunnel has a light at the end of it, and every imbecility has dozens of politicians, such as Joe Biden and Donald Trump, and plenty of "journalists," such as Tom Friedman, who are ready to promote it as truth.

Only when the empire reaches its disaster phase that the question marks finally appear.

Only as of spring 2024 have they begun to appear.

PART IV

FIN DE BUBBLE

There's something funny going on over there at the bank.

—Jimmy Stewart, *It's a Wonderful Life*

CHAPTER 13

WELCOME TO SQUANDERVILLE

The citizens of Squanderville, as Warren Buffett called the United States, were a happy bunch. They believed happy things; it didn't bother them that the things they believed were impossible. We animated the story in our documentary following the first edition of this book.

After 20 years of mostly falling interest rates, mostly falling inflation rates, and mostly rising asset prices (stocks and real estate), people had come to believe that this is the way the world works: Interest rates mostly go down, and house prices mostly go up; it goes on forever.

Even the professionals in Squanderville had never been more certain. We remember a prevailing view in 2005 was investing for the long run was prudent because stock prices always go up. And real estate? Who believed house prices would fall? Almost no one. Although it is all very well to think happy thoughts and spend happy money, it is savings and investments that produce real jobs and real earnings. An era, a generation's worth of time, of low interest rates and policymakers who didn't really understand the economics of it led to the idea it could last ad infinitum.

As the years go by, Squandervillians make less and less that they can sell abroad, and consume more and more from overseas. So, when they spend money, much of it goes to buy products from Thriftville.

(Buffett's term, perhaps he had Asia in mind.) The industrious people of Thriftville used the money to hire more workers, build more factories, import more technology, and improve their products. Thus, did the authorities in Squanderville find themselves in a remarkable position: They could still use monetary and fiscal policy to create a boom, but the boom happened in Thriftville!

The happy residents of Squanderville hardly knew or cared. The latest job numbers were celebrated; who bothered to notice that the new jobs were not quite as nice as the old ones? While companies laid off relatively highly paid people in the manufacturing sector, other companies hired relatively more cheap employees in the service sector. General Motors declined; Walmart grew.

What would happen if real estate prices actually started to go down? What if the "Magnificent 7" stocks—Apple Inc., Amazon.com Inc., Alphabet Inc. Meta Platforms Inc., Microsoft Corp., Nvidia Corp., and Tesla Inc.—didn't continue to bolster the stock market? Soon, the homeowners of Squanderville and their lenders might be faced with a brief interval of horrible sanity. They might be unhappy. So far that hasn't happened for a select few.

THE WAY WE LIVE NOW

As the 21st century opened and began to evolve, the corpus of the world financial system became even more grotesque than it had been in decades before. Connecting the thigh bone of bond yields to the hip bone of Asian purchases of US bonds to the vertebra of credit expansion, we stood back in awe and wondered: What kind of monster was this? It looked like a creation of Frankenstein. When we began the writing of this book, the trends seemed to lead in a direction that would not end well. In 2023, as we update, many of the threads of the sweater are held by who control wealth in Asia, the Middle East, and in sovereigns the US empire can only pretend to have its historic influence.

Whatever it was in the early 2000s, it was no ordinary economy—it had a hunchback and two club feet. Jobs that ought to exist didn't. Income that should be helping consumers to spend wasn't there. Savings that were vitally important to economic growth had disappeared. After the pandemic, the jobs numbers didn't make sense to Jerome Powell or a host of financial journalists who were trying to read the tea leaves. Would rapid rate hikes in the overnight rate cause a recession in the economy? The fact that no one really knows is telling.

The best way to understand America's economic predicament is to look at it as a system of imperial finance. The United States is an odd and reluctant empire. Its body parts fit together, but only in an absurd and comic way; it's the imperial backbone that gives it shape.

Only an empire can run such a trade deficit for many years. Only an empire can maintain so many expensive outposts all over the world. Only an empire's money will be accepted by so many people in so many different places. The US empire, circa 2005, still set the trends in fashion, arts, style, and manners—but it neglected engineering, science, and homeland-bound industries. It depended on the periphery states for its savings and its consumer goods. As an empire matures, its center weakens and its backbone bends under the weight. Eventually it either passes off its imperial burden to a friendly power to which it becomes beholden—as England did to America between 1917 and 1950—or its back breaks.

LA BUBBLE EPOQUE

After investors have lost a lot of money in one bubble, they practically can't wait until the next one comes along. In the 1960s boom, anything with *-onics* in the title sold for far more than it was worth. If you added *-onics* to your company name, you were almost sure to be a rich man the next day.

In the boom of the 1990s, the magic syllables were *dot-com*. Remember Dr.Koop.com? Furniture.com? Webvan? So many examples come to mind. It is like trying to select the dumbest member of Congress; we don't know where to start. The dot-coms were so popular with investors—and mining companies so unpopular—that at least one firm that supposedly had been mining gold switched to supposedly becoming a dot-com to take advantage of it.

Near the end of the tech bubble, an e-trading firm ran an arresting advertisement. It showed a doctor peering down at a trader on the operating table; the doctor says, "Why ... he's got money coming out the wazoo!"

Five years later, you could replace the e-trader with a house flipper. Whether they were trading houses or stocks, Americans enjoyed the new empire of debt. Coast to coast, money was coming out of wazoos all over the place.

"If you can fog a mirror, you can get a home loan," said a mortgage analyst to the *Los Angeles Times*.[1] In the past, being able to fog a mirror was a necessary requirement for credit. Only now had it become sufficient. If the present trend continued, soon lenders would not even bother to hold up the mirror.

There was no particular reason why the dead should be denied mortgage credit; they would probably be at least as good risks as many of the living who were getting it. Maybe better. At least they don't skip town or wear out the carpet.

Between 2001 and 2005, the property bubble raised house prices in California by $1.7 trillion. That was equivalent to 35% of personal income. The whole economy not only enjoyed a rising real estate market but also it depended on it. Coast to coast, people bought big houses they couldn't afford. They expected to sell them to someone else for more than they paid for them. What they did not expect was to pay for them themselves. How could they? What would they pay for them with?

No one seemed interested in actually owning real estate. Houses had become like futures contracts. People traded on margin and never took delivery. Houses were financial assets to be actively managed, just as though they were stocks or a sailboat. When interest rates dipped, new credit was unfurled; the house was refinanced at a lower rate with the borrower often taking out a little cash to spend. If rates seemed to be going down, more sailcloth was hoisted at an adjustable rate to catch the favorable wind.

What if rates rose? What if the weather turned bad?

The average Americans lived in a suburban house thought to be worth $188,800. Since stocks began to decline in January 2000, their net worth had not necessarily declined, but it had become less abstract; they now had to live in it. Even in Philadelphia.

A housing bubble in Philadelphia? It seemed almost impossible. Who would want to buy a house in Philadelphia, much less at a premium? But house prices rose in Philadelphia, and even in Baltimore.

Parents and grandparents had been loath to spend more than 25% of their incomes on rent or a mortgage. Now, people were spending more than 50%. The ratio of household debt to disposable personal income rose from 77% in 1990 to 127% by the end of 2007.[2]

There was disappointment built into this delightful show. It is all very well that the world financial system matches up borrowers with lenders, but the matchmaking works only if it produces satisfying results. If you match a princess with a frog, when the poor girl bends down to give the amphibian a kiss, something remarkable better happen or there will be regrets. Reproaches. Maybe lawsuits.

Just as travelers are never really sure they've had a good trip until he gets home, you never know if a loan is a good one or a bad one until the money makes its way back to the lender. That is where the disappointment is likely to come. Are lenders too lenient? We would know when the money got ready for the return portion of the trip. Our guess was that not as much would make it home as people expected.

"The boom in interest-only loans—nearly half the state's home buyers used them last year, up from virtually none in 2001—is the engine behind California's surging home prices," said the *LA Times*.[3]

California house sales hit a new record in February 2005. And again in March. And again in April. Housing starts nationwide were at a 21-year high. All over the 50 states, people were buying, flipping, refinancing.

"It is as if you were paid to live in California," said a skeptic to the *LA Times*.[4] Prices rose 22% in 2004. It meant that an average homeowner, with an average $400,000 house, added $88,000 to his net worth. He did this without lifting a finger.

In the Bay Area, houses were selling for half again as much as people asked for them. The *LA Times* mentioned a house offered for $980,000 that sold almost immediately for $1.5 million. The *Times* told of a young woman who bought her first house with no money down and "interest only" payments. In 2001, fewer than 5% of new houses were purchased with "interest only" mortgages. By mid-2005, the total was nearly 50%. From the newspaper report, the woman appeared to be headed toward a financial crisis. Homeownership, she believed, would bail her out. She told the paper that she intended to use her equity to pay down her credit card debt! More of the *Times* article: "I have $40,000 in student loans from my master's degree," she said. "I have high credit card debt. I'm a typical American. And yet they wanted to give me more debt to buy a house."

"If you're like me, you're so incredulous that anyone would give you any money whatsoever, you just close your eyes and sign the papers. . . . I would have signed anything."[5]

On the East Coast, the situation was not much different: "An expert was interviewed by the New York Times. He remarked that in the past real estate investors expected annual rental returns of 8 percent to 10 percent of the purchase price. But such a 'historical perspective' was wrong, he said. It caused investors to pass up good opportunities. What they needed was a 'fresh prospective': 'They're not being foolish; they're looking at it differently than people who have been in the market for a long time.'"[6]

Forget the wisdom of the dead, in other words. This was a new era.

People bought property as they had bought tech stocks five years before—without any regard for earnings. It was all a greater fool's game—betting that someone would come along who was an even bigger numbskull than you were. The game continued such a long time that people came to see it as eternal. And the more confidence people had in it, the more reasons they invented for it to go on. Most experts cited "demographic factors" as guaranteeing higher residential property prices. There were supposed to be many more people who would need a roof over their heads in the years ahead. According to the theory, there were so many new immigrants and baby boomer children that the homebuilders couldn't keep up with them. Prices would rise. Why the homebuilders would build enough houses to keep up with the demand was a matter of debate. How the new buyers would be able to pay higher prices—when incomes were falling—was not clear either.

A major reason given for why stock prices had to continue rising in 1999 was that so many people were putting so much money into stocks for their retirements. The logic was supposedly irrefutable: The baby boomers must save money. They had no choice but to put it into stocks. Stocks had to go up.

The reasoning was perfect—as long as stocks went up. But then something happened: Stocks went down. Baby boomers felt little desire to buy stocks. But the "demographic factors" argument was still perfectly serviceable for the housing market. It would work fine, too—until houses went down in price. Then, miraculously, the multitudes in need of housing just vanished.

On April 10, 2005, an article entitled "The Hunt, Becoming a Mogul Slowly" appeared in the *New York Times*. It told the story of a 25-year-old New Yorker who had been making real estate deals ever since 2002. Drawing on this deep well of experience, the young Trump offered advice. "An apartment is more attractive to me when other people want it. While the price might seem expensive now, it might not be expensive six months to a year from now. We overbid to capture the opportunity." By some instinct, he had captured the gist of the efficient market hypothesis—and applied it to real estate. Whatever price he paid was okay—because it was the price others were willing to pay.

The *Times* article told us that "his success has inspired six of his young, former-renter friends, to follow in his experienced footsteps," because "I made it seem like a very cool thing to do." Meanwhile the real Donald Trump said he was getting a million dollars a pop just to tell young mogul-hopefuls his secrets.[7]

In mid-2005, you only had to get in a cab to realize that the real estate boom had become a bubble. Cabdrivers would point out how much houses had gone up. While once they gave tips on tech stocks, now they told you which neighborhoods were likely to experience the greatest price inflation. Listen carefully, and you were likely to overhear drivers on their cell phones talking to real estate agents about their new condos.

The trick was to find a "fixer-upper," do a little cosmetic work on it, and put it right back on the market. So many people were looking for fixer-uppers that canny sellers were considering deliberately making a wreck of their houses—so prospective buyers could hallucinate about how much money they would make after fixing them up.

In spring 2005, the Federal Deposit Insurance Corporation (FDIC) identified 55 areas in the nation that it said were undergoing a boom in residential real estate. These were areas where prices rose 30 percent or more over the preceding three years. Not in 30 years had so many parts of the country experienced such a boom, said the FDIC. Even in the last boom of the 1980s, only half as many areas met the test.

THE SAGE OF THE PLAINS

"A lot of the psychological well-being of the American public comes from how well they've done with their house over the years . . . ," said the Sage of the Plains, Warren Buffett, in April 2005. "Certainly at the high end of the real estate market in some areas, you've seen extraordinary movement. . . . People go crazy in economics periodically, in all kinds of ways. Residential housing has different behavioral characteristics, simply because people live there. But when you get prices increasing faster than the underlying costs, sometimes there can be pretty serious consequences."

"You have a real asset-price bubble in places like parts of California and the suburbs of Washington, DC," added Charlie Munger.

Buffett: "I recently sold a house in Laguna for $3.5 million. It was on about 2,000 square feet of land, maybe a twentieth of an acre, and the house might cost about $500,000 if you wanted to replace it. So the land sold for something like $60 million an acre."

Munger: "I know someone who lives next door to what you would actually call a fairly modest house that just sold for $17 million. There are some very extreme housing price bubbles going on."[8]

"Flipping real estate . . . without getting burned," is a headline from the weekend *Seattle Times*.[9]

There's something about a bull market that weakens brains and permits senseless metaphors. The *Times* could have said, "Flipping houses without having them fall on your head" or "How not to get burned in a red-hot real estate market." But the hacks in Seattle didn't bother to think about it; who did? Everybody knew property was hot, and everyone knew you could get rich—fast. By April 2005, the press was beginning to report on people who had quit their jobs to get in on the house bubble before it went sour, we mean, before it popped.

The *Times* article referred to "30-something investors" who had left gainful employment to invest in real estate. What they were doing had little in common with real investment, but neither they nor the reporter seemed to realize it. The houses they bought rarely yielded any real, net income. What they were really doing was gambling on rising property prices.

It was much like the end of the 1990s when young investors were quitting their jobs to day-trade stocks. As long as stocks were rising, these traders were geniuses. When the stocks went down, they were idiots.

"I lost a ton of my portfolio in 2001," the *Times* quoted a rising property mogul. The man fired his financial planner and put his money in a self-directed IRA that he could use for speculating in houses, practically day-trading them. "By the end of the year we'll be doing two or three a month," said he.[10]

DELUSIONS OF MEDIOCRITY

Another similarity between the bubble in tech stocks at the end of the 1990s and the housing bubble in 2005 was the rise of "clubs" designed to help members speculate in the company of others. At the end of the 1990s, people joined investment clubs so they could yak about stocks with other people who didn't know anything either. In 2005, they joined real estate clubs. There were at least 177 of them by mid-year. Members got together to talk about "techniques" and "strategies." Four of these "strategies" were recorded for the benefit of future Donald Trumps, and perhaps history, in the *Times* article: (1) Buy a house, hold it, and sell it later, (2) buy a house, fix it up, and sell it, (3) flip the damn house before you actually have to pay for it, and (4) rent the house for more than it is worth, giving the tenant the right to buy it in the future.[11]

We were tempted to add exclamation marks after each strategy. But the items scream such imbecility that amplification seems unnecessary. They reminded us of our own dictum about stock market speculators of the late 1990s: There is smart money; there is dumb money; and there is money so moronic it practically cries out for court-ordered sterilization.

They say on Wall Street that no one rings a bell at the top of the market, but so many bells were ringing in spring 2005 we thought we would go deaf—or mad. Playmate of the Month Jamie Westenhiser was abandoning a promising career as a model to take up real estate investing.

What would make a nice girl like her end up in place like that? Maybe it was the 12.5% gain in real estate nationwide in the previous 12 months? Or maybe it was the 50% increase in housing prices in five years? In hot markets—such as California, Florida, and Washington, DC—prices had gone up 60% in two years.

It was a "real estate gold rush," said the cover of *Fortune* magazine. But Americans were suffering from delusions of mediocrity. They took for normal what was actually extraordinary.

Prices of US residential real estate, in real terms, rose 66% between 1890 and 2004. But all the increase happened in just two brief periods: right after World War I, and after 1998. Other than those two periods, the real price of housing was either flat or falling. The big difference between the period following World War II and the 1998–2006 era was that after the war the US economy was growing and healthy. America not only had a positive trade balance but also had the most positive one in the world. Wages were going up so people could afford more expensive houses. Families were expanding faster than the economy so they needed more houses.

But by the end of the century, incomes were stable or shrinking. The nation spent more than it earned; it desperately counted on rising house prices—and the savings of poor people in foreign countries—just so it could continue living beyond its means. And Playmates of the Month were giving up strutting their stuff to invest in real estate. This was not a normal situation.

Other news stories told of friends who were teaming up to buy houses—they had become too expensive for a single couple to afford on its own. The main cause of foreclosure was divorce, because neither spouse could afford to keep the marital home. Imagine two couples. You might think the risk would double. In fact, it probably quadrupled—or more. Either couple might break up. Even more likely, the two couples might decide they can't stand each other. A lender would have to be brain-dead to agree to such a deal. But in 2005, many did.

This is the great comedy of the financial markets. They put fools together with their money just so the market can get a good laugh by taking it away from they. These "investors" thought they were geniuses. They thought their techniques and strategies were making them rich. Of course, tech stock speculators also thought they were getting rich. Then, they lost "a ton" of their portfolios. It is amazing that they had a ton left. But that would go soon.

As prices rose early in 2005, Congress wanted to know if the Fed might raise rates faster than anticipated. It looked as though the bubble in real estate was getting out of hand. Don't worry about it, said the world's most famous economist; inflation was no problem.

"The economy seems to have entered 2005 expanding at a reasonably good pace, with inflation and inflation expectations well anchored," Alan Greenspan told the nodding heads on the Senate Banking Committee. "The evidence broadly supports the view that economic fundamentals have steadied."[12]

He must not have looked out the window that day. For the very same day, as headlines made clear, inflation and inflation expectations—notably in the housing market—were under full sail in hurricane-force winds.

The cost of housing, in many areas of the country, was not just inflating—it was blowing up like a front-seat air bag. In Alan Greenspan's hometown, Washington, DC, prices were rising six times faster than GDP growth. Buyers were not looking for a place to live; they were speculating—betting that their neighbor, the Fed chairman, would continue giving away enough money to make them rich. Even unsuspecting new home buyers became speculators. The market dictated it.

Meanwhile, the house flippers were driving around in new Mercedes, making big money by buying and selling each other's houses. One genius bought a condo before it was built. He flipped it to another investor, who held it until it was completed, making a bundle when he sold it to a professional couple who intended to stay for two years and then sell (at a huge profit) to other buyers. All of them were making the smart moves—buying with little money down and making minimum monthly payments on adjustable rate mortgages. And all of them were getting richer—or so they believed—as long as prices continued to rise. They talked about it at cocktail parties. They looked at their balance sheets with pride and pleasure, and if they needed cash, they "took out a little equity" as easily as calling for a pizza.

Pity the poor renters. They were the sort of people you wouldn't want your offspring to date, let alone marry. They were the poor losers who forgot to buy tech stocks in the late 1990s and now were missing the real estate bubble. They were the quiet, lonely dorks who never got invited to parties and had nothing to say—except an "I told you so" that they had been holding onto for years, waiting for the right moment.

AMERICANS GET POORER

"This is the greatest crisis facing the country that people can do something about," wrote the once-comedian Ben Stein in *Forbes*. Stein was talking about people who failed to save enough for retirement.

"With less than 20 percent of U.S. workers now in employer pension plans (many of those plans are on shaky financial footing) and with Social Security typically replacing less than 40 percent of pre-retirement income, personal saving has never been more important," continued Stein. And yet, few people save any money.

"Savings rates have never been lower," Stein explained. "In 1999, the national savings rate dipped below 3 percent for the first time since 1959, according to the U.S. Commerce Department. It has been declining further since then, and in 2004 it was at a mere 1 percent. The low savings rate, coupled with large deficit financing by Asian banks, is dangerous for the U.S. But it's more dangerous for individuals." Following the pandemic era, savings also plummeted to record lows while consumer debt increased at a dramatic pace.

People are forever crying alarm about this or that. There is a crisis in health ... a crisis in moral values ... a crisis in the Middle East ... or in the newspaper trade. For all the whining, there is usually little that can be done about the emergency, and if it is left alone, it generally takes care of itself in its own way.

"Nearly 28 million U.S. households—37 percent of the total—do not own a retirement savings account of any kind," continued the *Forbes* article, "Among the households who owned a retirement savings account of any kind as of 2001, according to a 2004 report by the Congressional Research Service (CRS), the average value of all such accounts was $95,943. That number was distorted by the relatively few large accounts, and the median value of all accounts was just $27,000.

"The median value of the retirement accounts held by households headed by a worker between the ages of 55 and 64 was $55,000 in 2001," the CRS says. To that, Stein added that "just 11 percent of all Americans have retirement savings of $250,000 or more."[13]

You can jabber to people about saving money until your jaw falls off; they're not going to put an extra dime in a savings account—not when property prices or the stock market are going up at 10% per year and the Fed is still giving away money. Eventually, however, the things that must happen do happen. Of course, that's when people wish they had saved money. That's when they really need it. That's when the whining really begins.

Saving—like manufacturing—is one of those early-empire virtues that was once an important part of the US economy but seems to have gotten exported. The Chinese now make our products and do our saving for us. As mentioned, they save more than 25% of their income. For decades, they had so much of savings, they were thankful to the US for taking it off their hands.

But what goes around comes around. When the US real estate bubble popped, some of that old virtue began to make its way back home. Americans started to save again. Whereas they put aside only a penny on the dollar in 2005, soon they are likely to set aside 10 cents or more. The savings crisis will be over. A new crisis can then begin: a depression.

In traditional economic theory, people save. Their savings are borrowed by entrepreneurs and businesspeople to build new enterprises, new factories, and new consumer items. This new output is then sold at a profit, which creates new jobs—and higher incomes—that give people more purchasing power, more savings, and so forth.

But in America's fabulous 21st century bubble economy, things happened so much differently that we wondered, is the theory mistaken, or are Americans? Hardly a dime was saved. But Americans spent more than ever.

Something was and is wrong. The picture was and still is grotesque, unnatural.

The problem with not saving money is that you won't have any. If you want to do anything beyond what you're already doing, you have nothing saved up to do it with. Even current levels of consumption cannot be maintained. Factories wear out and need to be rebuilt.

Competitors race ahead. There is no standing still. You are either going forward or falling behind. "Day by day, all the earth ages, drooping unto death," goes an old Anglo-Saxon saying. You need a reserve of "energy"—savings—to give it life again.

THE COMING CORRECTION

Tout passe, tout casse, say the French. Everything goes away. Everything breaks down. Nothing is born that does not die. Nothing begins that does not end. There is no morning without an evening, and no silver lining without a cloud. Empires come. Empires go.

In the financial markets, the "going" phase is called a *correction*. It is intended to correct the excesses and mistakes of the expansion phase. In a bull market, there are corrections that bring extraordinary gains down to more modest ones. In a bear market, corrections—which soften extraordinary losses into more ordinary ones—are known as *rallies*.

Generally, the force of a correction is equal and opposite to the deception that precedes it. And the pain it causes is directly proportional to the pleasant deception that went before it. The period from 2019 to 2023 requires one.

America's empire of debt rests on many huge deceptions that we have described in this book:

- That one generation can consume—and stick the next with the bill
- That you can get something for nothing
- That the rest of the world will take US IOUs forever—no questions asked
- That house prices will forever go up . . . even now
- That US labor is inherently more valuable than foreign labor
- That the US capitalist system is freer, more dynamic, and more productive than other systems
- That other countries want to be more like America, even if it is forced on them
- That the virtues that made America rich and powerful are no longer required to keep it rich and powerful

- That domestic savings and capital investment are no longer necessary
- That the United States no longer needs to make things for export

It's extraordinary that these deceptions are more pronounced as the first quarter of the 21st century nears its end. In particular, deception that sent credit expansion soaring between 2001 and 2005 came eagerly from America's own central bank. In the ensuing decades bankers, investors, and politicians got used to it. By setting the key lending rate below the current inflation rate, the Fed misled almost everyone. Even themselves, it turns out.

Throughout the boom years of 2002 to 2005, the great deceiver, Alan Greenspan, appeared before the US Senate and dissembled. Not only did inflation present no clear and present danger but also neither did Americans' debt loads, nor did the negative numbers in the current account. Mr. Greenspan, who surely must have known better, found nothing to dislike and nothing to worry about.

So, we stop, draw breath, and wonder.

The deception was so large, we wondered how it could ever be fully corrected. We speak not merely of Mr. Greenspan's perjury before Congress, but of the larger deception, in which Mr. Greenspan played a leading role.[14]

The promise of US capitalism is that it makes people richer, freer, and more independent. But since the introduction of the Fed and the rise of the empire, the currency in which Americans keep score has so addled the figures, we scarcely know if we are winning or losing. The dollar we knew as a child—in the 1950s—is only worth a tenth as much today. The average household today has far more of them than we did. In 1950, US household debt to disposable income, which is basically after-tax income, was 34% (if disposable income was $10,000, households had $3,400 in outstanding debt).

Almost every American believes they are richer. Certainly, compared with the Old World, Americans have no doubt that the rise of their empire improved every subject's life. Is it true?

We pause to deliver a shocking update.

People love myth, fraud, and claptrap—especially when it flatters them. Maybe their food, life expectancy, crime rates, transportation, liquor, and architecture are nothing to brag about, say Americans to each other, but when they grub for money, they grub good. "Old Europe," they say, making a comparison, "is too rigid, fossilized, hide-bound . . . a museum."

And yet, even this is a fraud. Despite Laffer's curve, Reagan's revo-lution, Greenspan's bubbles, and the ensuing Bernanke and Yellen effort to make money free, the US economy has done no better than Europe.

Early in the century, the trend was already apparent. The *Economist* examined the evidence in 2005:[15] Everybody believed that America grew a lot faster than Europe over the previous 10 years. But the fig-ures, in terms of GDP/person were very close—2.1% per year for America against 1.8% for Europe. Take out Germany—which strug-gled with absorbing its formerly communist cousins from the East—and the two regions were exactly the same.

And productivity? A study by Kevin Daly, an economist at Goldman Sachs, found that, after adjusting for differences in their economic cycles, trend productivity growth in the euro area had been slightly faster than that in America over the 10-year period.[16]

What about jobs? America is the greatest jobs machine on the planet, right? Again, excluding Germany, jobs in the rest of Europe grew at the same pace as in America.

It's true that Americans earned more and spent more than Europeans . . . but they worked a lot more hours.

Europeans simply enjoyed more leisure.

But what about the post-2001 "recovery"? Wasn't it much more vigorous in America than in Europe?

Well, only on the surface. Spiked up by the biggest dose of fiscal and monetary juice in history, America's economy slightly outpaced Europe's. But the figures are hard to compare. Europe calculated GDP growth more conservatively than America, and understated the truth, rather than overstated it, as they did at the Labor Department. More important, America's jolt of growth came at great cost. Although Europe got no net stimulus, America got enough to give it the shakes.

Said the *Economist*,

Super-lax policies of the past few years have left behind large eco-nomic and financial imbalances that cast doubt on the sustainability of

America's growth. From a position of surplus before 2000, the structural budget deficit (including state and local governments) now stands at almost 5 percent of GDP, three times as big as that in the euro area. America has a current-account deficit of 5 percent of GDP, while the euro area has a small surplus. American households now save less than 2 percent of their disposable income; the savings rate in the euro area stands at a comfortable 12 percent. Total household debt in America mounts to 84 percent of GDP, compared with only 50 percent in the euro zone.[17]

Barely had the 21st century begun and America found itself in a remarkable position. It had what it believed was the world's most powerful economy and the world's most powerful military force. Like the defunct Soviet Union, it had a sickle in one hand and a hammer in the other. The sickle, alas, had an awkward bend in it.

Since 1990, income for the average US household rose only 11%[18] while average household spending jumped 30%.[19]

How could people spend so much more money without earning more? The connection between earning and spending has been deracinated. Outstanding household debt doubled to more than $10 trillion between 1992 and 2004, even adjusted for inflation. By 2023, that figure had skyrocketed to over $17 trillion.[20] Interest on average consumer debt in the US passed $1 trillion dollars in early November of the same year.[21]

Americans have been determined to live large and live better than they can afford. In the early 2000s, they did this by what economists called *smoothing* income. Anticipating higher incomes in the future, young families spent the money right away (e.g., buying bigger houses than they could afford). Nationwide, house sizes grew 30% since 1980, said Cornell economist Robert Frank.[22] Even people in their 50s and 60s looked forward to higher incomes or miracles.

Some economists referred to the whole phenomenon as the "democratization of credit." "Innovation and deregulation have vastly expanded credit availability to virtually all income classes," said the Fed chief.[23] He did not mention his own role in this democratic revolution. He was too modest. He was a Danton and Robespierre put together. The Fed chairman accomplished more than all the nation's innovators and deregulators put together. Dropping the price of credit below the inflation rate, he offered the entire world something for nothing. Thanks to him, every person could get themselves into financial trouble, not just kings, speculators, and financiers. He made it possible for lending institutions to extend such a long rope of credit to the common person that millions were sure to hang themselves.

We turned to the dead for an opinion. But it was hopeless; the corpses knew even less than we did. They couldn't even imagine what was happening. Borrow against your house when you don't have to? Buy a house as an "investment"? Take out "equity"? Depend on foreigners to balance your "budget"? Live beyond your means and expect Third World wage earners to make up the difference? The ideas that Americans once took for absurd, they now took for granted.

The baby born when the empire began in 1913 came into the world with nothing but owed nothing. Now, a baby comes into the world owing their share of a huge public debt—one that is growing by more than $1.8 trillion per year. What would the dead say?

WHAT WILL HAPPEN TO AMERICANS' DEBTS?

"He that dies pays all debts," said Shakespeare.[24] Who pays these debts? And how?

When people cannot pay their debts, they do not pay them. But the debts do not cease to exist. They are merely "paid" by someone else—the creditor. In the case of America's debts to foreign nations, this can be achieved in three ways: The currency in which the debt is denominated can be devalued against other currencies, the currency can be made less valuable through inflation, or the debt can be repudiated. One of these things—or all of them—is likely to happen. And, in fact, it is happening.

Repudiation has a long and squalid history. If a person can get away without paying their debts, they will generally figure out why they shouldn't have to pay them. In public life, the reasons are often very good ones. When a new political regime takes over, why should it be stuck with the bills of the old one? When the Bolsheviks took over Russia in 1917, they made Tsarist bonds worthless. Why should they pay bills that they never agreed to? Why should they honor commitments of one capitalist to another? They didn't pay. And why, after 1919, should the new German republic have to pay the Kaiser's bills? France, Britain, and the United States had defeated the Kaiser; let them pay his debts!

The idea of public debt is an attractive nuisance. A parent would not have dinner in a fine restaurant and send the bill to their child. Nor would the parent say to the restaurateur: Hold the bill for my unborn grandchild. But such is the state of faith in democracy that a relatively small group is not only willing to stick its heirs or enemies with costs to which they would never consent but also is happy to do so. Politics is a pernicious and barbarous occupation.

Generally, the public has only the dimmest, most remote idea of the kind of obligations that are being contracted on its behalf. If asked about them directly, many—if not most—would surely object. But who asks? Besides, the unborn don't vote. And neither do foreigners. Or even out-of-staters.

In America, several states—Michigan, Mississippi, Arkansas, Louisiana, and Florida—totally and permanently repudiated their debts in the panics of the 1840s. In the 1880s, many Southern states repudiated the debts that had been run up by illegitimate carpetbagger governments. But the United States doesn't have to repudiate. Its debts are denominated in its own currency—the value of which it can control. Having the world's reserve currency means you can stiff your creditors without ever having to say you're sorry.

AMID THE BUBBLE DETRITUS

Among the many remarkable stories that appeared in the press in the bubble years, the story of Mr. Asakawa stood out.

The United States economy has been so strong for so long, people all over the world have come to accept the imperial currency. By 2005, no one had more of it than poor Mr. Asakawa in Tokyo. The man controlled the biggest stash of US paper in the world. His life had come to imitate a popular joke. "A man who owes his banker $100,000 can't sleep at night," the joke begins. "But when a man owes his banker $1 million, it's the banker who can't sleep." Mr. Asakawa is the central bank's banker. At the end of 2004, he held an estimated $700 billion worth of US dollar–denominated paper assets in his vault at the Finance Ministry. Beside his bed was a blue plastic monitoring device that would go off like an alarm clock when the dollar fell out of a given trading channel. We suspect Mr. Asakawa, did not often sleep soundly.

A relatively modest drop in the dollar's value would mean huge losses to Japan's central bank and other dollar holders. But what could Mr. Asakawa do? His infernal alarm alerted him to drops in the dollar/yen exchange rate. But he merely aggravated himself and his wife. He could do nothing about it. The Asians owned so many US dollar assets that any attempt to sell would cause the very thing they most worried about—a drop in the value of their single biggest asset.

We understood why Mr. Asakawa would be alarmed. What bothered us was why no one else seemed to be. With as much as $100 trillion of the world's wealth denominated in dollars, how did the world watch so complacently as the value of its main asset was marked down? In 2002, the dollar went down against the euro by 10%. Then 20%. And then 30%. When Warren Buffett began putting his money in euros, he could buy one for just 86 cents. By early 2005, the euro cost nearly $1.36. In Europe, the dollar had lost about 40% of its purchasing power.

We look back on these stories and marvel how little has changed. Except, perhaps, the excess.

CHAPTER 14

KINGDOMS ARE OF CLAY

The merde began hitting the fan in summer 2007. Why do we care about it now? Other than the lessons history teaches, the policy response to the financial crisis set the stage for a decade of cheap credit and mounting debt. It's easy to say in hindsight, but remember, the first edition of this book was written before the crisis unfolded. Let's return.

"We are seeing things that were 25-standard deviation events, several days in a row," said David Viniar, CFO of the smartest financial firm in the world, Goldman Sachs.[1] According to Goldman's mathematical models, August, Year of Our Lord 2007, was a very special month. Things happened in that month that were only supposed to happen about once in a blue moon.

Either that, or Goldman's models were wrong. Hmm.

We recall looking out our window. Outside, we saw a summer day much like any other. And inside, what we saw in the news was also rather typical—a credit crunch. No, credit crunches don't come along every day, nor do 100,000 years separate one from another. In recent history there was the crash of the dot-coms, the crash of Long Term Capital in 1998, and the crash of 1987; looking forward, there was 2008, 2015, and 2020. Who expected the inflation of 2021–2023? Not the federal government

Outside of the United States, there have been a number of credit crunches, in Japan, Russia, Mexico, and various Asian countries. China, now.

When you make loans to people who can't pay the money back, trouble is only a couple of standard deviations away. During the first eight months of 2007, some 1.7 million houses were caught up in foreclosure proceedings in the United States. That was just the beginning. At that stage, the amounts of money weren't very large, not by Wall Street standards. But when the money didn't show up, it had an alarming effect. Citigroup said it was $13 billion short. Morgan Stanley was said to be facing $8 billion in losses. Merrill Lynch set records with estimated losses of $18 billion. The cat still had Goldman Sachs's tongue. Nearly two decades later, little has changed.

Already, back then, heads had begun to roll. First, Warren Spector of Bear Stearns got axed. Then, it was Peter Wuffli at UBS. He was followed by Stan O'Neal of Merrill Lynch. O'Neal made the headlines when he was pushed out of the corporate jet with a "golden parachute" valued at $160 million. After O'Neal hit the ground, Charles Prince of Citigroup, America's largest bank, was chucked out.

What went wrong? The business model seemed so pure and simple. You simply bought up subprime loans from the knaves who made them, and then you cut them up, slicing and dicing them into a kind of mortgage spam. You got the rating agencies to bless them, and then you sold them off to naive investors. The idea was to earn huge fees up front, while laying the risk onto the fools who bought the stuff.

When the going was good, it looked as though no business could be better. You were providing a valuable public service, helping people buy houses they couldn't afford by redistributing the risk from the people who incurred it to people who had no idea it was there. And in the process, you earned such large fees you would get your picture in the paper, build a huge mansion in Greenwich, Connecticut, and acquire some abominable, but very expensive, paintings to put on the walls. What could go wrong?

Everything. The *Financial Times* provided more detail on what happened at Citigroup: "The bank reported that, at the end of September, it had around $2.7 billion of unsold collateralized debt obligations—pools of debt securities that are repackaged and distributed to other investors.

"But it also had $4.2 billion of subprime loans it had bought in the past six months, and about $4.8 billion of loans to customers which were secured by subprime collateral. In addition, the bank had $43 billion of exposure to the most highly rated tranches of CDOs based on subprime mortgage assets."[2]

It turned out Citi was a fool and knave at the same time. It sold dubious subprime debt to its customers. But it bought it, too, and took it as collateral.

Gary Crittenden, Citi's chief financial officer, claimed that the firm was simply a victim of unforeseen events. The losses were "driven by some events that have happened during the month of October," he said, referring to downgrades by rating agencies. No mention was made of the previous five years, when Citi was busily consolidating mortgage debt from people who weren't going to repay—pronouncing it "investment grade," mongering it to its clients and stuffing it into its own portfolio—while paying itself billions in fees and bonuses. No, according to the masters of the universe, downgrades by Moody's and Fitch's were completely unexpected, like the eruption of Vesuvius; even the gods were caught off guard. Apparently, as of September 30, Citigroup's subprime portfolio was worth every penny of the $55 billion Citi's models said it was worth. Then, the moon turned blue.

Looking back we continue to wonder why these details don't matter anymore.

CARTOON CAPITALISM

Meanwhile, America's largest mortgage finance companies, Fannie and Freddie, had so much water in their lungs it was announced that it would take at least $25 billion of the public's money to save them. Possibly $300 billion. Were it up to us, we would have left them on the beach.

Instead, the US Senate bent down and pressed its blubbery lips onto those gaping traps of the mortgage twins, gurgling into them a corrupt breath of life. Because the two held one out of every two mortgages in the nation, in effect, Congress was nationalizing the US housing stock itself. Henceforth, citizens would pay not only their taxes to the government but their mortgage payments too.

At a speech at our annual conference in Vancouver, James Kunstler seemed positively delighted. Finally, gasoline over $4 a gallon was doing what generations of artistic scorn could not: destroy Fannie and Freddie's collateral. Kunstler's critique of US suburban vernacular architecture is that its products are not real houses at all, but "cartoon houses." They have porches that look like real porches from a distance, but they are too narrow to sit on. They have shutters, too, nailed to the wall, making them completely useless. The streets are all names after things they replaced and no longer exist; orchards, fields, farms, forests. The houses may have "picture" windows—looking out on nothing—or no windows at all. And they wouldn't exist at all were it not for cheap credit and cheap gasoline.[3]

Of course, the same may be said of America's—and Britain's— entire economies during the previous 20 years. The loose credit that built cartoon houses also constructed cartoon economies; they looked like real economies, but they were essentially perverse, consuming wealth rather than creating it. How it has sustained for most of the 21st century, as we know it, remains an inquiry in our sight.

For proof in the early years, you had only to look at Fannie and Freddie. Here were two companies that appeared to be helping Americans own houses. But since they were created, homeowners' equity—that portion of the house actually owned and paid for by the homeowner—fell from 70% to below 50% to a record low in the fourth quarter of 2008 of just 44%. By mid-2008, nearly 9 million Americans had zero or negative equity—and house prices were still falling.

How came this to be? The answer was simple. The looney-tune approach to finance radiated to all points of the economy. People pretended that they earned more—spending more and more money to buy more and more goods and services, while wages did not really increase. Then, they bought houses—believing the roofs over their heads were investments, rather than consumer items. With no down payment, no proof of income, and zero interest loans, for most of the new buyers, home ownership began as a dangerous conceit. And now that the roofs were caving in, it was a staggering burden.

The "consumer economy" has always been a mockery. No serious economist ever suggested that you could get richer by consuming wealth. But that didn't make consumerism unpopular. The more people consumed, the more GDP went up. GDP measured output, not wealth creation; but who could tell the difference? Besides, spending made people feel as though they were getting richer.

Then, whenever consumers threatened to come to their senses, the Fed rushed to "stimulate" them—by giving them more of what they least needed: more credit. More spending kept the cartoon economy running—enabling the consumer, the businessperson, and the speculator to add to their burden of debt. In 1971, when the United States went off the gold wagon, household debt was less than 50% of GDP. By 2008, it was almost 100%.[4] Today, in the third quarter of 2023, it has mounted, post-pandemic. US households owe a grand total of $17 trillion.

Even the rentiers were bamboozled by their own cartoon claptrap. Stocks rose from 1982 to 2000, fell heavily to 2002, and bounced back. But for the previous 10 years, shareholders had gotten little for their effort. In July 1998, the London index, the FTSE, hit a high of 5,458. In July 2008, it fell to 5,625. And in America, if stock prices were quoted in gallons of gasoline, the Dow would take the driver no further in 2008 than it did 40 years before.

The cartoon capitalists did it all backwards; they were supposed to exploit the workers, not be exploited by them. But while investors were going nowhere, corporate managers and Wall Street hustlers were getting rich. The two bozos running Fannie and Freddie, for example, pocketed about $32 million between them in 2007—a year in which the companies lost almost $5.2 billion—not to mention the losses to shareholders. And on Wall Street, managers paid out $250 billion in bonuses in the four years leading up to the credit crunch. The firms declared a profit and paid bonuses when the bets were made; they didn't wait to see how they turned out. Thus did the big banks and big brokers become capitalists without capital, dependent on the gullibility of investors to keep them in business. And when investors began to wise up, they turned to the public for capital support.

What kind of scam was this? It may look like capitalism from a distance. But this was not real capitalism; this was cartoon capitalism—run by clowns, who sold freak investments to chump investors, and encouraged the lumpen householder to ruin himself.

THE DUMBEST PEOPLE IN AMERICA

Where did he go wrong? The question probably crossed his mind, perhaps even when he mounted the scaffold on January 21, 1793. The Bourbons had been the most successful family in Europe. They had ruled Europe's biggest and richest country since Henry IV. And now they were on thrones all over Europe. But in the language of the City, Louis 16th blew himself up. He was supposed to be an absolute monarch. Ah . . . there was the dynamite! He believed it. He had surrounded the Parliament with troops and turned the country against himself. And now, he had absolutely no control over anything. Not even the power to save his own skin.

Poor Louis! He already had the bag over his head. And the blade at his neck. He must have felt like the dumbest person in France.

Dick Fuld must have felt pretty dumb, too. His firm had survived the Civil War, the Railroad Bankruptcies of the late 19th century, the Bankers' Panic of 1907, the Crash of 1929, the Great Depression, World War II, the Cold War; Lehman Bros. had outlasted spats, prohibition, and disco music. But it couldn't keep its head through the biggest financial boom in history.

John Edwards claimed the title of the "dumbest man in America" when the press got wind that he was two-timing his wife and running for president at the same time. But in 2007–2008, Edwards had more competition every day. In January 2007, the financial industry put a value on Lehman Bros.—a company it knew well—of $48 billion. On September 15, 2008, the bid went to zero. Then came more disquieting news: The world's largest insurance company, AIG, was failing. Martin Sullivan had run it into the ground, said the analysts. It needed an $85 billion bailout.

There was no one there to bail out Louis when he needed it. France was not too big to fail; it was too big to bail out. And everything had been going so well! When Jacques Turgot was controller-general, he was getting rid of the internal customs barriers, lifting price controls, and abolishing the trade guilds and the corvee (the system of forced labor used to build roads). The political system was being reformed, too, evolving toward a parliamentary democracy.

But along came those plucky Americans to stir up trouble. They sucked France into war with Britain. France supplied money, matériel, and troops—landing 5,000 soldiers in Rhode Island and ultimately winning the war by blockading Lord Cornwallis at Yorktown.

"The first shot will drive the state to bankruptcy," Turgot warned the king. He was almost right. By 1786, the French were in desperate straits, with half the population of Paris unemployed and a national debt equal to 80% of the GDP. The French were counting on the Americans to begin repaying their $7 million in loans, but the United States was broke, too. And soon, French credit was so bad, the king could no longer borrow from the moneylenders in Amsterdam nor even from his own creditors in Paris. Having borrowed too much, Louis no longer had any room to maneuver. All he could do was to march up the scaffold steps like a real monarch.

Nearly 200 years later, the heads rolled on Wall Street. But who was the dumbest? Surely Dan Mudd and Dick Syron at Fannie and Freddie were still in the running. Even with the deck stacked in their favor (they borrowed money more cheaply than their competitors because everyone knew the government wouldn't let them go under), they couldn't stay in the game. Finally, as expected, the Fed had to step in and bail them out.

The previous 15 years had been too kind to finance. Wall Street was essentially a debt monger; and in the boom, nobody didn't want to borrow. Financial profits soared. Since 1980 the profits of the US financial sector as a portion of GDP went up 200%. Industry owners and managers could have taken their money off the table and retired to Greenwich. But on the back of this outsized success grew a monstrous hump of self-delusion; the masters of the universe began to believe their own grotesque guff. The financial markets were perfect, said the academics. All-knowing and all-seeing, they wouldn't make a mistake! The chiefs at the big financial firms must have thought they supped with the gods themselves; they had the paychecks to prove it.

Of course, some Wall Street bosses were more cunning than others. In selling itself to Bank of America, for example, Merrill Lynch dodged the scaffold; but it becomes a ward of the state, almost like Fannie and Freddie before they were taken over completely.

The old regime on Wall Street was dominated by just five large investment companies. In just a few weeks, in fall 2008, their debt bombs blew up, and the entire, independent investment banking industry disappeared.

NOBEL PRIZE LOSERS

The financial industry has been widely criticized. But then, it was just doing what it always does—separating fools from their money. What was extraordinary about the bubble years was that there were so many of them. There is always smart money in a market-place . . . and dumb money. But in 2007 there were trillions with no brains at all. What other kind of money would pay Alan Fishman $19 million for three weeks' work helping Washington Mutual go bust? With the Federal Reserve's help, those free money years continued until 2020.

Behind the dumb money were some of the smartest people in the world—with bogus statistics, the claptrap theories, and the swindle science.

"Six Nobel prizes were handed out to people whose work was nothing but BS," says Nassim Taleb, author of *The Black Swan*. "They convinced the financial world that it had nothing to fear."[5]

The theorists convinced themselves of two things that everyone knew were untrue. First, that "economic man"—the person they were supposed to know so well—had a brain but not a heart. They were supposed to always act logically and never emotionally. But there was the rub, right there; they had the wrong person. The second was that you could predict the future simply by looking at the recent past. If the geniuses had looked back to the fall of Rome, they would have seen property prices in decline for the next 1,000 years. If they had looked back 700 or even 100 years, they would have seen wars, plagues, famines, bankruptcies, hyperinflation, crashes, and depressions galore. Instead, they looked back only a few years and found nothing not to like.

If they had just looked back 10 years, says Taleb, they would have seen that their "value at risk" models didn't work. The math was put to the test in the Long Term Capital Management (LTCM) crisis, and failed. Their models went sour faster than milk. Things they said wouldn't happen in a trillion years actually happened while Bill Clinton was still in the White House.

In the real world, Taleb explains, things are stable for a long time. Then, they blow up. Then, all the theories and regulators prove worthless. These blowups are inevitable, but unpredictable . . . and too rare to be modeled or predicted statistically. "And they are almost always much worse than you expect," says Taleb.[6]

THE BRIGHT SIDE OF THE BREAKDOWN, SORT OF

But who could honestly say they weren't enjoying the financial crisis? It unhorsed cavalier fund managers; it turned the masters of the universe into servile waiters; it made Nobel Prize winners look like morons. The rich, the proud, the pompous, the vain, the incompetent—surely there was a God, an "invisible hand," giving them all a whack on the head!

And there were the regulators, too! Under their very noses the biggest scams in history went unnoticed. America's Securities and Exchange Commission (SEC) alone—to say nothing of the countless other cops on the financial beat—had 3,371 employees playing the piano in 2006. If you can believe it, not a single one of them noticed what was going on in the back room. Even after rummaging through Bernard Madoff's back office twice in three years, they still didn't know. They must have been like pets watching an orgy, with no idea what to make of it, but wagging their tails and vaguely wanting to get in on the action.

In two days just before Christmas 2008, Bernie Madoff's managed accounts were thrown into a "spiral of horror," said one fund manager. Tipped off by his own sons, the feds went to Madoff's apartment. They graciously asked if there was perhaps a misunderstanding. No, replied Madoff, "there was no innocent explanation."[7]

Soon, the press, investors, regulators were all howling for Bernie Madoff's head. But he was a hero to us. He did the world a great favor, giving us all a remarkable and vivid lesson in investing, in pyramid schemes, in the markets, and Wall Street. As a result of such eye-opening instruction, Bernie Madoff will save more investors more money than the SEC ever will. They'll think twice before giving money to friends to invest for them. They'll raise their eyebrows and their doubts when someone promises them consistent, high rates of returns.

The feds charged Madoff with running a $50 billion Ponzi scheme. Charles Ponzi took money from investors and then used their money to pay out profits to earlier investors. As long as the new money kept coming into the system, it worked like a charm. So what's the difference between Madoff's Ponzi scheme and the scheme run by Wall Street—in which all the investment houses, the rating agencies, the mortgage companies, Fannie Mae, Freddie Mac and the regulators themselves were all complicit? As long as new money was coming into the system, who complained?

Reports said Madoff promised investors steady 10% returns. How could he do that? Of course, he couldn't. Stocks had gone nowhere for the previous 10 years. The average rate of return? Zero. Promising 10% was clearly an exaggeration. Delivering it was surely a crime. But investors must have guessed that he was swindling his retail trading customers in order to deliver steady, above-market returns to his investment accounts. They may not have understood how it worked, but they didn't want it to end.

Nobody is as easy to scam as a scammer, and Madoff scammed them all.

Of course, he should have gotten the gallows; we don't dispute it. But, often, there's not a lot of distance between the hanged man and mob that is lynching him. John Law in early 1700s France would set the tone for the modern financial era.

The people who most wanted to see Bernie swing were the people who invested money with him. Most were very sophisticated investors. They knew perfectly well that there is no magic way to transform a zero-return market into a 10% return market. If they were to get 10%, they knew they had to take a big risk. They just didn't know what the risk was. It turned out to be the risk that Bernie Madoff was lying.

And what about the bubble economy itself? Wasn't it also a giant pyramid scheme with a huge, huge risk attached? It promised speculators enormous profits, but how could it deliver? It paid out money from new participants to the old participants. Without new money coming in, it would implode. Over the next decade, the Fed delivered.

As former Citigroup CEO Chuck Prince put it, "As long as the music was playing, they had to dance. But didn't they know the music would stop, leaving them in an awkward and embarrassing position? Wasn't it as obvious to them as it was to us?"[8]

Apparently not.

And what about the investors? Weren't they trying to get something for nothing out of the bubble economy? And the rating agencies? They must have known that subprime debt was dangerous. Even we knew it. The math didn't add up. Why did they give it Triple A ratings? And what about the SEC? It has thousands of smart analysts, accountants, and investigators. How could they all be so stupid as to miss the biggest investment bubble in all history, right under their noses? And what about Alan Greenspan, who actually encouraged households to take out subprime mortgage loans? Weren't they all in on the scam? Weren't they all complicit? A decade and more later we realize the it not only caused mayhem in the financial market but to the government itself. We still want to ask, "when is it the government's job to bail out speculators on specious financial products?"

Madoff's charm was that he outfoxed the foxes and outscammed the scammers. He out-Ponzied Charles Ponzi. He out-Princed Chuck Prince. He could have taught the Egyptians how to build pyramids. In the history of high-stakes grifting, he outdid them all. A Robin Hood with Alzheimer's; he stole from the rich. If he'd only remembered to give to the poor, he'd be a hero to everyone!

Besides, how hard was it to give away new houses to people who didn't have any money, or get people who didn't speak English to sign toxic mortgage documents? Child's play, really. And the executives with their millions in bonuses, and humbuggers like Richard Fuld, their marks were mostly ordinary stock market investors; low-hanging fruit compared to the coconuts Madoff plucked. Rather than go after the widows and orphans, he swindled the smartest money in the world: money managed by family offices, the old Jewish money from New York and south Florida, London's Man Group, Switzerland's Union Bancaire Privee. He even flimflammed the hedge funds, and took billions from his oldest and dearest friends. A real democrat, he took money from his own tribe, his own clan, and his own golf club buddies. Billions of it. Even more impressive, he did it not with hyperbole, but with relative modesty. He promised only 10% per year, which didn't seem like much during the bubble epoque.

And now, historians look back and wonder: How could people have been so stupid? The answer is simple: In a bubble, it pays to be stupid. You buy something at a lame-brained price, and it goes up. Not only did stupidity pay, it paid well. Running a suicidal bank paid better than robbing one. Hedge fund managers got paid more than contract killers or stick-up men.

But "when the tide goes out, you see who's been swimming naked," says Warren Buffett.[9] By the end of 2008, investors hadn't seen the tide so low in many years; the view was nauseating, hideous. More than $30 trillion had been lost—so much that it threatened to turn the lights out on the entire world economy.

THE FIX IS IN

"They are in trouble in New York," said J. P. Morgan to Bishop Lawrence.[10]

In October, 1907, J. P. Morgan was 70 years old, and attending a church meeting in Richmond when the importance of the sacred was disturbed by the urgency of the profane. Telegraphs kept arriving from New York; they warned of a disaster. According to Dun's Review, 8,090 companies had failed in the first nine months of 1907. Then, a failed takeover of the United Copper Company caused a panic.

"A correction is equal and opposite to the deception that preceded it," Morgan would have said, if he'd thought of it. Since he didn't, it falls to us.

Morgan had been around the block when it came to money. He had taken over his father's banking business decades earlier. He'd seen panics, crashes, bankruptcies. And, now, it must have seemed that his whole life had been spent training for this one test. He returned to New York; crowds of investors looked to him to save the day. And he did. He put his own money on the line to help shore up troubled companies. He rallied friends, colleagues, and competitors to do likewise. A trust was in trouble, then the New York Stock Exchange itself, then the City of New York—one after another, Morgan brought in the financiers, came up with the money, bullied and cajoled, until the storm had passed and they could all enjoy a good drink.

And when it was over, Senator Nelson W. Aldrich, realizing what Morgan had done said: "Something has got to be done. We may not always have Pierpont Morgan with us to meet a banking crisis."[11]

As it turned out, Pierpont Morgan was a ghost four years later. But in that same year, 1913, the US Federal Reserve was set up to fill his big shoes. In 2009, it's the Fed that is being tested.

Armageddon seemed to arrive in Manhattan on Monday, September 29, 2008, not just in New York, but in Moscow, Hong Kong, London, and Frankfurt, too. Germany hastened to succor bank account holders. In Reykjavik the pandemonium was so hot it seemed to melt the ice. Then, on Tuesday, plagues and locusts were loosed on the world: The US stock market fell hard again. Japan was sinking into the sea. Brazil's market was down 51%, year to date. Central banks were cutting rates like pulpwood. Even so, unemployment was still on the rise. Consumer spending was falling. House prices were going down.

Of course, the world improvers couldn't sit idly when there was so much in need of improvement. They soon began intervening, in the usual clownish ways. Short selling was blamed for more accidents than alcohol. And everywhere, the authorities were getting ready for show trials, perp walks, and public hangings. Was it fair, Congressman Henry Waxman wanted to know, that Richard Fuld should be paid $480 million for his role in bankrupting the 158-year old Lehman Bros.?[12] Congressman Waxman seemed to think that something needed fixing. But that just goes to show how little he appreciated the free market. Investors handed Fuld that money of their own free will; they got exactly what they deserved. The system was fixing itself.

When investors had the wind at their backs, they were ready to believe the most outrageous things: that the financial sector could get rich by lending money to people who couldn't pay it back, and that a whole economy could flourish by luring consumers to spend more than they could afford. These hallucinations created an immense worldwide bubble of debt and dollars. But now, the wind had swung around. A huge anti-bubble was forming—equal and opposite, in true Newtonian form—a financial whirlpool marked by exaggerated thrift, debt destruction, and sweaty-palmed investors.

And where was Morgan when we needed him? Where was the Fed? Ten years before, the giant hedge fund—LTCM—had overdone it. As in 1907, according to Roger Lowenstein's account, "Rushing for the exits ... [traders] posed a danger not only to themselves, but to the entire world financial system."[13] So, the Federal Reserve Bank of New York called in the big financial houses to help with the rescue. It worked. The crisis was averted. LTCM's positions were liquidated in an orderly way, just the way Morgan would have wanted.

But this time, the fixers were at work, but the fix didn't seem to stay fixed. Bad positions couldn't be unwound in an orderly manner; there were too many of them. And it was not just a handful of speculators who were getting whacked—it was half the population of the United States of America and Great Britain. Trillions of new cash and credit were being pumped in. The Fed was buying trillions worth of "assets" you would throw out of your refrigerator. Her majesty's government became proprietor of 50 billion pounds worth of banking shares; the government of George W. Bush was preparing to enter the banking business, too. But as trillions went in, trillions more leaked out. Stock prices were still going down. Property prices were going down. Jobs were being lost. Ships were idling in port. It was not just a few investment decisions that were being corrected; in other words, it was the delusions of an empire.

"These prices make no logical sense," said a Wall Street trader, referring to mortgage-backed derivatives at Walmart-style discounts, and missing the point. Markets are not scientific. They are poetic. After the liquidity comes the liquidation. After the outsized recklessness comes the appropriate regret. After the empire come the barbarians.

HELP IS ON THE WAY

"The private market has screwed itself up," explained Representative Barney Frank, "and they need the government to come help them unscrew it."[14] (He left out the extenuating circumstance that the US money supply, the shortest term lending rates, Fannie Mae, Freddie Mac, the Fed, the Federal Housing Agency, the SEC, and a whole plethora of commissions and meddlers—as well as one of out of every four dollars spent—were all under government control all along!)

On September 19, 2008, the US Congress put its back to saving the empire's financial system.

"We're not going to Christmas tree this bill," was how Senator Chris Dodd supposedly described how Congress would deal with Treasury Secretary Henry Paulson's proposed bailout plan. We had never heard *Christmas tree* used as a verb. But leave it to a Washington hack to turn Christendom's sentimental icon into a lobbyists' grab-fest. As soon as the bill arrived, the boys on the hill began decorating it, hanging baubles on every limb. They agreed on the major issues; but they were still going to take a few days to get the thing all trimmed out before it became law. The Dow shot up as investors waited for the lighting ceremony.

The plan was simple enough, but the chutzpah of it was breath-taking. He was proposing a $700 billion program, in which the government would buy up Wall Street's mistakes—otherwise known as "cash for trash." Henry Paulson said he had no choice: "We did this to protect the taxpayer," said the former Goldman chief.[15]

Everyone was getting in the act, condemning the markets and offering advice. Politicians, investors, comics . . . even the clergy. Yes, the archbishop of Canterbury said that men had put too much faith in the market, and that this faith had become a sort of "idolatry." He thought the government should be held in higher esteem, while the decisions and plans of free men should be curbed. More regulation is needed, said he, praising Britain's ban on selling financial firms short.[16]

The poor Church of England had a fool as its top man. But you could hardly blame a man of the cloth for believing that markets had failed; the idea was as widespread as an STD; he probably got it the same way, that is, simply by hanging around with the wrong crowd.

Typical was this from Garrison Keillor: "[T]hat's why we need government regulators. Gimlet-eyed men with steel-rim glasses and crepe-soled shoes who check the numbers and have the power to say, 'This is a scam and a hustle and you either cease and desist or you spend a few years in a minimum-security federal facility playing backgammon.'"[17]

Out on the prairie, one could imagine all sorts of things. But it's not as if there were no bureaucrats on the job between 2000 and 2007. How did one imagine that these same regulators, who missed the biggest bamboozle in market history, were now going to be able to clean it up? How would bureaucrats—charged with protecting the public's money—recognize a scam more readily than investors whose own money was on the line? What information do the bureaucrats have that is not available to the public? What theory do they follow that is unknown to investors? What meat do they eat, what wine do they drink, that prevent them from falling prey to the delusions and temptations to which all flesh is heir?

This is what Hayek termed the *fatal conceit*, that public officials—armed with the power to force people do to what they say—will do a better job of running things than people can do for themselves voluntarily. The markets had failed, or so everyone said. But what had not failed?

Neither the masters of the universe on Wall Street, nor the geniuses at the rating agencies, nor the saints at the SEC—and certainly not the poor lumpen investor—understood what was going on. None had gimlet eyes. Instead, all their eyes bulged with admiration at the financial engineers' handiwork, and with greed at how much money they could make.

And yet the new plan put $700 billion in the hand of GS14s, clerks, hacks, and appointees. What are they supposed to do with it? Buy "assets" that Wall Street wanted to dump. How were they supposed to know what the assets were worth? If they paid too much, the government would take a big loss. If they paid too little, at least according to the dim light coming from the Christmas treers, it wouldn't bail out Wall Street enough and the economy might sink into a deep recession. So what were these derivative contracts really worth? No one knew. Values had become like the face of God, or the meaning of *is*. They floated in the ether; they played cards with Jimmy Hoffa. But, oh happy day for the public sector, that great untapped reserve of investment wisdom. Here was an opportunity to buy up those pearls that the swine on Wall Street didn't want.

And not only had they to do something, they had to do it fast.

"Our entire economy is in danger," said the chief executive.[18]

"The time has come to save capitalism from the capitalists," wrote Luigi Zingales of the University of Chicago.[19]

Could any scriptwriter have come up with such a preposterous story? Could any director have found such a clownish cast of characters?

It was only a few months earlier that all the leading men and women of this drama claimed to believe in free enterprise so fervently they were willing to spend hundreds of billions of dollars forcing it on others. It was free enterprise that separated us from the barbarians and made the country rich, they said. But now, they were turning many of these free enterprises over to the bureaucrats to run, and desperately trying to make sure that the others didn't go broke. It was a strange kind of laissez-faire—capitalism without the creative destruction. Capitalism without bankruptcy. It was like taking the alcohol out of Guinness; what was left was bitter and pointless. But an epochal shift had begun—from capitalism to state-sponsored socialism, from white collar grifters to stick-up men, from subtle swindle to naked larceny.

And then, on September 19, 2008, Ben Bernanke and Hank Paulson appeared before Congress and warned that if Congress didn't put up $700 billion of taxpayers' money pronto, the whole world economy could melt down.

"If we don't take action to rescue the economy," said Mr. Bernanke, "we may not have an economy on Monday."[20]

Of course, this alarm turned out to be as silly as their previous assurances. Monday came. Tuesday. Wednesday. The economy did not stop functioning. It wasn't exactly business as usual . . . except in the US Congress, where the Christmas tree decorating party continued. To the bailout bill were attached these and other baubles:

Sec. 101	Extension of alternative minimum tax relief for nonrefundable personal credits
Sec. 102	Extension of increased alternative minimum tax exemption amount
Sec. 201	Deduction for state and local sales taxes
Sec. 202	Deduction of qualified tuition and related expenses
Sec. 203	Deduction for certain expenses of elementary and secondary school teachers
Sec. 204	Additional standard deduction for real property taxes for nonitemizers
Sec. 205	Tax-free distributions from individual retirement plans for charitable purposes
Sec. 304	Extension of look-thru rule for related controlled foreign corporations
Sec. 305	Extension of 15-year straight-line cost recovery for qualified leasehold improvements and qualified restaurant improvements; 15-year straight-line cost recovery for certain improvements to retail space

Sec. 307   Basis adjustment to stock of S corporations making charitable contributions of property

Sec. 308   Increase in limit on cover-over of rum excise tax to Puerto Rico and the Virgin Islands

Sec. 309   Extension of economic development credit for American Samoa

Sec. 310   Extension of mine rescue team training credit

Sec. 311   Extension of election to expense advanced mine safety equipment

Sec. 312   Deduction allowable with respect to income attributable to domestic production activities in Puerto Rico

Sec. 314   Indian employment credit

Sec. 315   Accelerated depreciation for business property on Indian reservations

Sec. 316   Railroad track maintenance

Sec. 317   Seven-year cost recovery period for motorsports racing track facility

Sec. 318   Expensing of environmental remediation costs

Sec. 319   Extension of work opportunity tax credit for Hurricane Katrina employees

Sec. 320   Extension of increased rehabilitation credit for structures in the Gulf Opportunity Zone

Sec. 321   Enhanced deduction for qualified computer contributions

Sec. 322   Tax incentives for investment in the District of Columbia

Sec. 323   Enhanced charitable deductions for contributions of food inventory

Sec. 324   Extension of enhanced charitable deduction for contributions of book inventory

Sec. 325   Extension and modification of duty suspension on wool products; wool research fund; wool duty refunds

Sec. 401   Permanent authority for undercover operations (as related to tax provisions)

Sec. 402   Permanent authority for disclosure of information relating to terrorist activities (as related to tax provisions)

Sec. 501 $8,500 income threshold used to calculate refundable portion of child tax credit

Sec. 502   Provisions related to film and television productions

Sec. 503   Exemption from excise tax for certain wooden arrows designed for use by children

Sec. 504   Income averaging for amounts received in connection with the Exxon Valdez litigation

Sec. 505   Certain farming business machinery and equipment treated as five-year property

Sec. 506   Modification of penalty on understatement of taxpayer's liability by tax return preparer

Subtitle B—Paul Wellstone and Pete Domenici Mental Health Parity and Addiction
Equity Act of 2008

Sec. 601	Secure rural schools and community self-determination program
Sec. 602	Transfer to abandoned mine reclamation fund
Sec. 702	Temporary tax relief for areas damaged by 2008 Midwestern severe storms, tornados, and flooding
Sec. 704	Temporary tax-exempt bond financing and low-income housing tax relief for areas
Sec. 709	Waiver of certain mortgage revenue bond requirements following federally declared disasters
Sec. 710	Special depreciation allowance for qualified disaster property
Sec. 711	Increased expensing for qualified disaster assistance property[21]

TOO BIG TO BAIL

How heartwarming it was to see the meddlers and world improvers get a second wind. It was like driving around in a 1933 Chevy, or throwing rocks at the gendarmes. The old, gray commies felt young again! Impetuous! Brainless!

And every capitalist was behind the bailout program, too. All over the world, markets were out; state-sponsored meddling was in. Free market principles are fine—until prices start going down!

Even Russia got into the act. New to counterfeit capitalism, it was getting the hang of it fast, pledging $20 billion in the fight to keep stock prices from falling to what they are really worth.

Then, not to be left behind in the hysterical absurdity, SEC honcho Christopher Cox announced a list of 799 financial stocks on which shorting was to be banned. In Britain, the Financial Conduct Authority's ban on shorting financial shares lasted into 2009. But Pakistan got the King Canute Memorial Prize: By law in that benighted land, stocks couldn't go below their August 27, 2008, close.

But all the whiners and world improvers were missing the elegant mischief of capitalism. The markets were working fine. Capitalism, in 2007–2008, was doing just what it should do: It was separating fools from their money.

In the space of six months, it scratched 10,000 Porsches, destroyed more monuments than Cromwell, and squeezed the rich harder than

Mitterrand. It would have taken an army of dreary Bolsheviks decades to redistribute so much wealth; and it wouldn't have been half
as much fun.

SAID THE JOKER TO THE THIEF

What a bunch of numbskulls: Greenspan, Paulson, and Bernanke!
Every word they said was financial poison. This was the same Alan
Greenspan, who had lobbied to allow the banks to enter the securities business 20 years before. From the *New York Times*, November 19,
1987: "Mr. Greenspan said opening new business to banks would
improve their profitability and long-term prospects, provided that
safeguards assured that their deposits were not used to finance securities operations. He also said the proposal would draw more needed
investment into the banking industry.

'Repeal of Glass-Steagall,' Mr. Greenspan said, 'would respond
effectively to the marked changes that have taken place in the financial marketplace here and abroad.'"

By 2003, evidence was beginning to surface suggesting that the
deregulation of the markets was not without risk. In particular, the
derivatives market was going wild. But Mr. Greenspan seemed not to
notice the danger: "'What we have found over the years in the marketplace is that derivatives have been an extraordinarily useful vehicle
to transfer risk from those who shouldn't be taking it to those who are
willing to and are capable of doing so,' he told the Senate Banking
Committee."[22]

Then, in 2005: "Greenspan relaxed about house prices . . . ,"
reported the *Financial Times*.[23] "Most negatives in housing are probably behind us . . . ," said the same sage in October 2006.[24]

"We believe the effect of the troubles in the subprime
sector . . . will be likely us . . . ," said his successor, Ben Bernanke, in
March 2007.[25]

Then, as more signs appeared that America's system of imperial
finance was breaking down, the more its leaders went blind.

"I don't think we're headed to a recession," said George W. Bush.[26]
"I don't think I've seen any scenario where the US taxpayer needs to

be stepping in with more taxpayer dollars," added Henry Paulson.[27] Then, on March 11, the Treasury secretary went on to explain that the fallout from subprime mortgages was "largely contained"[28]

The very next day, Bear Stearns CEO Alan Schwartz told the world that his firm faced no liquidity crisis. In an exclusive interview with CNBC, he said the rumors were unfounded: "We finished the year, and we reported that we had $17 billion of cash sitting at the bank's parent company as a liquidity cushion," he said. "As the year has gone on, that liquidity cushion has been virtually unchanged."[29] That same week, SEC chairman Christopher Cox added that his agency was comfortable with the "capital cushions" at the nation's five largest investment banks.[30]

Four days later, the cushions seem to have miraculously disappeared. Bear Stearns faced bankruptcy brought on by collapsing subprime prices. In a desperate measure, the firm sold itself to J. P. Morgan the next day for $2 a share—a 98% discount from its high of $171.

But by July, several things were clear: The subprime problem was not contained, the banks did not have enough cash, and every official—public or private—who opened his mouth was either a joker or a thief. On July 16, Fed Chairman Bernanke told Congress that troubled mortgage giants Fannie Mae and Freddie Mac were "in no danger of failing."[31]

On September 6, the US government nationalized both Freddie Mac and Fannie Mac, wiping out the shareholders.

"I believe companies that make bad decisions should be allowed to go out of business," opined George Bush.[32]

But by the middle of September, the financial authorities—who neither saw no evil nor heard any—were on the case. On September 19, US Treasury Secretary Paulson took aim at the problem he never saw, calling on Congress to ante up the aforementioned $700 billion. Whence cometh the $700 billion figure? "It's not based on any particular data point, we just wanted to choose a really large number," said a Treasury Department spokeswoman.[33]

"I got to tell you," said Paulson on November 13, "I think our major institutions have been stabilized. I believe that very strongly."[34] Two weeks later, America's largest bank and its largest automaker, desperate, stood on a ledge, preparing to jump.

O! BAMA! THE WHOLE WORLD TURNS ITS WEARY EYES TO YOU . . .

And so it was that the presidential campaign of 2008 was held against the backdrop of crashing imperial finances. Under pressure from the knuckleheads in his own party, Obama picked up a babbling hack as his running mate—and ran right into his own fraud. Joe Biden was to Obama what Monica Lewinsky's blue dress was to Bill Clinton— the dumb thing that revealed the spoken lie.

Biden demolished his own presidential campaign in 1987 by pretending to be British Labor politician Neil Kinnock. Not only did he recite Kinnock's lines about being the first in his family to go to university, he also stole his identity, claiming that his father had worked in the coal mines. His own father was actually a polo-playing car salesman from Baltimore. But if the media hadn't stopped him, he would probably be collecting Kinnock's pension by now.

Apparently, the better you know Biden, the less you like him. In his home state, 97% of voters refused to back him in the presidential primary. But that was Biden in the 1980s. In the 2000s, Biden was, supposedly, on the ticket because he knew who Saakashvili was. In truth, he was there because the old nags in the Democratic Party wanted someone they could trust on the ticket—a real go-along, get-along backslapper. They turned to Biden, in other words, not for change, but to avoid it. Americans don't mind a liar in high office, but they were suspicious of one who can't keep his lies straight. For a few weeks, Obama's support softened.

But then, it was McCain's turn to stumble over his own scam. The candidate who was so concerned about national security chose a baroque woman from Alaska as his number two. Voters imagined her hands on the nuclear button and shuddered.

And so the electorate spoke. And it said, "Give us Obama."

And it came to pass that the man called Obama was given unto them. Mr. Obama became the president-elect of all the Americans. Nobody's coffee tasted better on Wednesday morning than it did on Tuesday. But all over the world, people felt better about themselves, as if the human race had achieved something important.

Commentators drew all the wrong conclusions and made fools of themselves. Some thought it meant America's redemption from the sin of slave trade. Others saw a historic transformation that they couldn't put in words and shouldn't have tried.

"A new World Dawns," proclaimed Britain's *Daily Mirror*.[35]

"They did it. They really did it," wrote the *Guardian*. "The American people yesterday stood in the eye of history and made an emphatic choice for change. . . ."[36]

It's the "End of the National Nightmare," said *TIME* magazine.[37]

People looked at Obama and they thought they saw a young Kennedy; they thought they might be able to rerun the tape from an earlier period in US history and do a little editing. They longed for the new frontier without the Vietnam War, a Camelot without Lee Harvey Oswald.

Amid the effervescence came the French. Obama's victory "arouses a wild yet reasonable hope," claimed Bernard-Henri Levi in the *Financial Times*. Mr. Obama's election will affect us in "at least three concrete ways," he continued, it will be "a decisive turning point in dealing with the 'racial question' in the U.S. . . . hope for an America that began doubting its 'famous missions' . . . and with Obama representing the USA, anti-Americanism . . . will have a harder time surviving and it will be forced to revisit its sales pitch."[38]

They shouldn't let French philosophers comment on US politics; they take the whole thing far too seriously. Besides, you never know what they are talking about anyway. Nobody knows what America's "famous mission" is—certainly not the Americans themselves. And if those are his "concrete" ways, we're glad Mr. Levi is not building bridges. There was nothing concrete about the hopes Mr. Obama's victory aroused. Just the contrary: They were all gas. But *Le Monde* saw it clearer. Not only was the paper happy to see the United States finally rinse the stain of racism out of the Stars and Stripes, it was glad to see Americans give free market capitalism the flush, too.

Obama will be "reviving the role of regulation in the U.S.; [devising] tax policies to smooth out increasingly wide socio-economic divides; planning a health-care system appropriate to the country's wealth," said the paper.[39] In other words, he will be putting in a system of state-directed capitalism, just like they have in France.

None of the commentators really understood Obama's triumph. They saw in it a yearning for truth and a stretch for progress. It was nothing of the sort. The last thing voters want is the truth; they will reject it if it is put in front of them. Instead, what they want is diversion from the real world. What they hope to get from their leaders is something for nothing. If they could only get from politics what was rightfully theirs from their own labors, what would be the point of voting? No, voters always hope for something more: a fantasy. Something to cheer them up when they are down. Or something to give them a fright when they are up.

The last period of great national trial, 1914–1945, with its wars, epidemics, Dust Bowls, hyperinflation, Great Depression, mass murders, bankruptcy, and revolutions, was the era in which Americans elected Franklin Roosevelt. He told them they had "nothing to fear but fear itself." It was all in their heads! It was a whopper, but it was the whopper they wanted to hear.

In the United States of America, in the late imperial period, the Bush administration worked hard to make people fearful—with its torture chambers and preposterous "threat levels." But the terrorists wouldn't cooperate, they failed to blow up even a trash truck. Then, in fall 2008, the mob began to sweat for real. People were afraid of losing their houses, their jobs, and their retirements. That's why Obama won; it had nothing to do with national redemption or Sarah Palin. When the world was safe and plush, the mob wanted to feel the frisson of danger. What the public wanted in November 2008 was safety: a movie with a happy ending, not a horror flick. Obama appeared the calmer, more intelligent, candidate. Voters could imagine him as the "black Roosevelt" giving soothing fireside chats and telling the lies they most wanted to hear.

And so, in the national narrative, one cockamamie bamboozle took the place of the one that went before. Americans were supposed to have been racists; now they were supposed to be color-blind. They were supposed to have been fearful; now they were supposed to be confident. They were supposed to defend free market capitalism to their last breath; now they turned to the state and begged it to protect their last dime.

THESE FIREFIGHTERS ARE PYROMANIACS!

In the preceding 100 years there were only two fires similar to the inferno that began in fall 2008. The first conflagration was in 1929, centered in New York. The second was in 1990, when Tokyo went up in flames. In both instances, rescuers took extraordinary measures. And in both cases, they not only failed to save the economy, they scorched it even more. Obviously, few economists share this analysis with us. The few who do are probably either insolvent or insane, or perhaps both. So, the burden of proof is on us.

We begin by calling a ghost as an expert witness: "Liquidate labor, liquidate stocks, liquidate the farmers, liquidate real estate. . . . It will purge the rottenness out of the system . . . values will be adjusted, and enterprising people will pick up the wrecks from less competent people. . . ."[40]

That was the advice from US Treasury Secretary Andrew Mellon. In October 2008, scores of commentators went to the cemetery. Not one channeled Mellon. Instead, they summoned the shadow of Franklin Roosevelt. He "understood that his first job was to restore confidence," wrote David Brooks in the *New York Times*.[41] Over in the *Financial Times*, Martin Wolf even quoted Roosevelt's puerile remark that "the only thing we have to fear is fear itself."[42] What about 25% unemployment, one might have asked?

"[W]e might have done nothing. That would have been utter ruin. Instead we met the situation with proposals . . . of the most gigantic program of economic defense and counterattack ever evolved in the history of the Republic. . . . Some of the reactionary economists urged that we should allow the liquidation to take its course until we have found bottom. . . . We determined that we would not follow the advice of the bitter-end liquidationists. . . ."[43]

That quotation comes neither from Paulson nor Bernanke, but from another ghost. Herbert Hoover has gotten the reputation for being a "do-nothing" president. Would it were so! When Herbert Hoover passed the baton to Roosevelt, his can-do meddling had already helped turn a financial crisis into a Great Depression. You see, ghosts are often morons, too.

Poor Andrew Mellon was shouldered aside in the early 1930s. Then, Hoover got to work. His first improvement is known to us by two blunder buddies who turned it into law: Misters Smoot and Hawley. The idea was to protect US business by imposing higher tariffs on foreign trade. A group of 1,000 economists, bankers, and other notables realized that blocking trade at the onset of an economic slump would be suicide. They urged him to veto the bill. But Hoover believed in tariffs as he believed in almost all other forms of government interference. He signed the bill with approval. He called on the Fed to provide "an ample supply of credit at low rates of interest,"[44] and initiated a program of public works, including the Hoover Dam, a massive lump of concrete that blocks the Colorado River. He threatened federal regulation of the New York Stock Exchange and attacked short selling.

Hoover's chief concern seemed to be to hold up the price of labor. He cut off immigration, in an effort to keep out wage competition. Then, he got the business community to pledge that it would not reduce wages. Because the cost of labor was then too high for the closely shaved profit margins, businesses could not hire. Unemployment rose.

Roosevelt was a better politician, which is to say, he was more shameless. He attacked Hoover for spending too much money, won the presidency, and then spent more. He began so many agencies and projects—from the Agriculture Adjustment Act to the Civilian Conservation Corps to the Social Security Act—that he practically ran out of alphabet. He also imposed wage and price controls, as well as limits to executive salaries.

In his classic book on the subject, *America's Great Depression*, Murray Rothbard, once professor at the University of Las Vegas, now among the forgotten dead, explains that a properly functioning economy is balanced. One industry enjoys an expansion, another suffers a contraction. But sometimes there is a "cluster of errors" that causes a major boom. Whence cometh these errors? Who is responsible for them? Rothbard identifies the culprit: "monetary intervention in the market, specifically bank credit expansion to business."[45] If Rothbard were still among the quick, he'd probably be pointing his finger at Alan Greenspan, the arsonist who lowered the key US lending rate to an "emergency" level of 1% and held it there long after the emergency was over. Then, he'd probably point at Ben Bernanke, who continues to add kindling, and to Hank Paulson, who led Goldman Sachs while it created trillions of dollars' worth of asset-backed explosives and sold it to financial institutions all over the world.

"The boom . . . is the time when errors are made . . . ," Rothbard continues. "The 'depression' is actually the process by which the economy adjusts to the wastes and errors of the boom. . . . Far from being an evil scourge, [the depression] is the necessary and beneficial return of the economy to normal. . . . Evidently, the longer the boom goes on the more wasteful the errors committed, and the longer and more severe will be the necessary depression readjustment."[46]

But here come the firefighters with yet more dry wood! After stoking the flames with easy credit, they bring more. Professor Rothbard, reviewing the record of the post-1929 rescue team came to this conclusion: The authorities "met the challenge of the Great Depression by acting quickly and decisively . . . [using] every tool, every device of progressive and 'enlightened' economics, every facet of government planning to combat the depression."[47]

Yet, the conflagration didn't go out. It intensified. An expected recovery in 1931 went up in smoke, says Rothbard, thanks to government interference. Instead of a panic and quick recovery—a la 1921—the US economy went into a long, hard on-again, off-again depression that put a quarter of the workforce out of a job. It might have lasted until the 1950s had it not been for the biggest public works program of all time: World War II.

"The guilt for the Great Depression," Rothbard writes, "must, at long last, be lifted from the shoulders of the free-market economy and placed where it properly belongs: at the doors of politicians, bureaucrats and the mass of 'enlightened' economists. And in any other depression, past or future, the story will be the same."[48]

Six decades and half a world away, the Japanese proved him right. In January, 1990, a spark touched off the Nikkei Dow. Soon, Japan's miracle economy was in trouble. Bankruptcies rose. Profits fell. Banks teetered. But the Japanese had their economists, too. And soon, they were doing what Hoover and Roosevelt had done before them. As to monetary stimulus, the Bank of Japan's key lending rate was cut from 5% down to "effectively zero." And there were plenty of fiscal stimuli too. Japan's government did just what Keynes recommended—it spent money.

Keynes's idea was already 2,000 years old when he thought of it. It came right out of the Bible story of the seven fat years and the seven lean years. Pharaoh knew people wouldn't be smart enough to save grain for themselves. They'd make a mistake—they'd eat it all. So he stocked up grain in the fat years, then released it to the people when the lean years came. Keynes said the government should do the same: run surpluses in the good years and deficits in the bad ones. Since then, of course, governments have proven very able at running deficits, even in the fat years. It's the surpluses they have trouble with. So, instead of giving out stored-up grain, they give out grain that hasn't even been planted yet.

The Japanese government went on a spree of what Alan Booth calls "state sponsored vandalism" in the 1990s, taking the budget deficit to a remarkable 5% of GDP in 2002.[49] Roads to nowhere, concrete shorelines, bridges and dams. Japan, per square mile of available territory, covered 30 times as much surface in concrete as in America. The Japanese were spending beaucoup money; in 1996, the Shumizu Corporation even announced plans to build a hotel on the moon using specially developed techniques for making cement on the lunar surface.

Once again, these heroic efforts produced nothing more than farcical consequences. The Japanese economy is still barely on speaking terms with prosperity. And the Nikkei Dow closed 2008 at 9,043—30,000 points below the high it set 20 years earlier.

GONO COMETH

"It was horrible! Horrible! Like lightning had struck. No one was prepared. You cannot imagine the rapidity with which the whole thing happened. The shelves in the grocery store were empty. There was nothing you could buy with your paper money."[50]

In 1993, Friedrich Kessler, law professor at Harvard, described an event from his past: the Weimar Republic's hyperinflation. He might have been describing the future, too.

By the beginning of 2009, all over the world, the inflation pumps were running hot. In Australia, the government announced a stimulus program. Checks of $1,000 per child will be sent to deserving parents. Senior citizens will get $1,400.

The Japanese had a 5 trillion yen rescue program . . . and then, two weeks before Christmas, they threw in 4 trillion more. Europeans were in for $1.8 trillion. But in the United States, the pumps were practically burning up. The Americans put up

$8.5 trillion, including $120 billion to bail out a group of foreign countries, as well as the homeland. And that was before adding in Obama's bailouts.

"I am confident that the Fed would take whatever means necessary to prevent significant deflation in the United States," Ben Bernanke assured Congress, adding that "a determined government can always generate higher spending and hence positive inflation."[51]

So determined was the US Fed since 1970 that the dollar lost more than three-quarters of its purchasing power. But now, all over the world, prices were falling. Inflation was no longer a sure thing. For the first time since the 1930s much of the world ran the risk that inflation rates will turn negative.

Ben Bernanke was wrong about many things; but as to the Fed's ability and determination to destroy the dollar, he will almost certainly be proven right. Having inflated so many bubbles—including the monster in private debt that had just blown up—the Fed chief was confident that he would have little trouble inflating another one in public debt. And then, when that blows up, it will wipe out two problems at once. Americans will be eager to spend their money again, rather than save it, and their debts will go up in smoke.

The Federal Reserve was bailing out the bankers, the insurers, the mortgage lenders, the automakers, and half of Wall Street. But who would bail out the Fed? What would happen when the Fed's credit got marked down? As we write, at the debut of 2009, that story will have to wait for a later book. Still, we will take a guess: In the firestorm that is coming, even the devil will sweat.

For the 15 years leading up to 2009, the US money supply has grown about twice as fast as GDP. Federal government liabilities, meanwhile, grew three times as fast. In 1929, America's debt was equal to about one and a half times its gross domestic output. During the 1930s, output fell and the debt peaked out at 2.5 times US GDP. By 2008, total debt had risen to a record 3.5 times GDP. Meanwhile, the money supply grew at a 15% annual rate between 2007 and 2008—almost four times the growth in GDP. And by the end of the year, 2008, US money supply was growing at a 10% annual rate, while output was actually shrinking.

Although the empire is already effectively broke, nevertheless, the debit sides of its ledgers grow heavier and heavier. The deficit for fiscal year 2008 added half a trillion in new debt. And estimates of the bailout costs are growing rapidly.

Where will the government get that kind of money? There were only two possibilities—one honest and depressing, the other corrupt and alarming. We recall that there are only two ways to get what you want: by civilized means or by barbaric ones. The US Treasury is confronting that choice as we write. It can borrow honestly. Or it can print money. If it borrows, the world enjoys no net increase in financial resources. Borrowing for bailouts merely takes resources from projects that might have been worthwhile and diverts them to the losers. Interest rates rise, as a consequence of the extra borrowing; higher rates generally worsen the economic picture. If, however, the US government prints the money—or if it created it "out of thin air," to use Lord Keynes's handy phrase—the results will be even worse. Inflating the money supply with new currency, a la Argentina or Zimbabwe, wipes out debts. But it destroys faith in the dollar and brings down the US-dollar based imperial money system. Why would they do such a thing? Because they have no choice. The empire's debts are too great. They can't be paid . . . they must be liquidated.

If this were an earlier phase of the imperial cycle—such as in 1920—Americans would have taken their losses, liquidated their mistakes, and bounced back stronger than ever.

If it had been in the 1930s America—or even in Japan 60 years later—the losers would have taken their losses with good grace, occasionally jumping out of a skyscraper or stepping in front of a bullet train to obliterate the disgrace. The government would have contented itself with honest trickery and the usual harmful bumbles: lowering interest rates to zero and borrowing massive amounts of money to spend on wasteful public works projects.

But this is 2009 . . . not 1920 . . . nor 1929 . . . nor 1989. And it is America, not Japan. The Fed's key lending rate is already at zero and the empire totters on spindly old legs. It has grown tired and has been burdened with so many fixes, rules, privileges, and safety nets that it cannot compete in many key industries. It is already the world's biggest debtor with total debt of $33 trillion—a burden that is expected to increase by about $7 billion every working day.

At this stage, Americans do not boldly face the future—they want protection from it. Capitalism is separating the fools from their money, but fools vote. And in the late stage of an empire, they vote for bread, circuses, and bailouts. There are more debtors than creditors in the United States of America; and so, the feds flex every flabby muscle trying to protect them. How? By destroying their currency.

In fall 2008, it was as if the laws of nature had been suspended.

Exhibit A: a corporate bond from International Paper Company that, in November of 2008, had a yield of nearly 10%. Compare that to the yield on US Treasury paper. A 91-day T-bill yielded practically nothing. Even yields on the 10-year Treasury notes were sinking to levels never before seen—approaching 2%, about half the official rate of consumer price inflation. The "spreads" between corporate bonds and US government bonds were wider than at any time since America's Great Depression. Why?

The cost of the world's bailout efforts was soaring. Yet, the more bonds the US government sold to finance the rescue efforts, the more the demand for them grew. The more determined the Fed become to prop up losing bets, in other words, the more people lined up to lend them money. Never before were US bond yields so low nor confidence in America's credit so high. It violated common sense, as well as the law of supply and demand. Remarkably, the further in debt government went, the more the debt was worth. If the Fed can get away with this, gravity will be the next to go.

But nothing is more remarkable than the credulity and gullibility of the world's patsies. Bernie Madoff's oldest friends would come up to him and practically beg him to take their trust funds. People joined his Palm Beach country club just to get close enough so they could stuff large wads of cash in his pockets. And now, investors practically trip over one another in their eagerness to lend money to world's biggest debtor.

Once a bubble in one sector has burst, you can't reinflate it. All you can do is to inflate other bubbles. After the bubble in the tech sector popped in 2000, for example, the Fed manned the pumps. But they couldn't get the tech stocks reinflated. The Nasdaq never recovered. Instead, the Fed pumped up a huge bubble in private debt—with gassy bulges in housing, finance, commodities, emerging markets, and many other sectors. Now that bubble has burst and the Fed, once again, is working up a sweat trying to reflate it. This time,

348 EMPIRE OF DEBT

it's blowing up the biggest bubble in *public* debt the world has ever seen.

Even *Le Monde* noticed:

> The governments of the entire world are beginning to create moun-
> tains of debts in order to finance their bailout plans, their stimulus
> programs and their budget deficits caused by the recession. Even
> so, the rate at which the U.S. and European countries borrow on
> the financial markets is near the lowest in history. It is only barely
> above 2% for 10-year loans to America and slipped under 3% for
> the German equivalent at the end of 2008. . . . Some economists
> ask themselves if a bubble in government debt isn't in the process
> of forming . . . and they ask themselves what will happen when it
> eventually explodes. . . .[52]

We think we know what happens. The whole system of imperial finance gets flattened.

In a broad sense, the social welfare economies of all the advanced Western nations are nothing more than Ponzi schemes. Typical is the Social Security system of the United States of America. It survives only as long as there are enough new contributors to cover the promises made to the old ones. As in any Ponzi scheme, the first ones into the system do very well. The very first beneficiaries put in little and got a lot out, depending on how long they lived. But as time goes by, the deal goes bad. Middle-aged people today would be better off with a private pension system, and the young are unlikely to see any benefits at all.

John Law never lived to see America's system of public finance at work. Nor did Charles Ponzi. But even without a paternity test, each would have recognized it as his own.

Bernie Madoff is still alive as of this writing. He is the world's reigning champion, title holder in the Ponzi league. Yet, compared to America's system of public finance, his scheme was penny ante . . . chickenfeed. The nature of the scheme is most easily under-stood by looking forward rather than backward. President Obama announced two weeks before he was sworn in that Americans faced "trillion dollar deficits for years to come." Already, the estimate of the deficit for 2009 was $1.18 trillion. Some experts predicted a deficit over $2 trillion. At least one guessed that it would come in over $3 trillion, if not in 2009 then the following year.

These huge deficits did not seem to disturb the sleep of the homeland bound citizens. A trillion-dollar annual deficit, over five years, would add about $50,000 to each family's burden of debt. But some intuition assured Americans that they will never have to pay it. By instinct alone, they knew it was a Ponzi scheme.

Of course, every Ponzi scheme must end. The day is long past when Americans could say "we owe it to ourselves." A large part of US borrowing is taken up by foreigners. At least a quarter of America's public debt is in the hands of non-US citizens. China alone has bought a trillion dollars' worth of it. And if the foreigners don't continue to pony up the dough, the United States will run out of money. Why do the foreigners buy US debt? They do so in the hope of getting the money back, with interest. But how can the United States pay back the money it borrows? It has no earnings. It has no surpluses. Instead, it must borrow more to service past borrowings. It must depend on bad money to come in so the good money can go back out. It is a scheme John Law would love, Ponzi would be proud of, and Bernie Madoff can envy, for its organizers never go to jail.

As we write, foreign lenders have still not wised up. But they've got less new money to lose. Americans are not buying the way they used to; world trade is contracting fast.

Trenton no longer takes. So Tianjin no longer makes. And Tianjin's entrepreneurs no longer turn up at the central bank with piles of dollars to exchange for yuan. Which leaves China's central bank with fewer dollars to buy up US Treasury debt.

The whole system is breaking down. Most likely, it cannot be repaired. The empire of debt is collapsing.

Central bankers, as everyone now knows, are rascals and scalawags. Gideon Gono is no exception. But there is something heroically imbecilic about the man. While most economists hedge and weasel, Mr. Gono goes boldly, recklessly forward—where no central banker has dared to go, at least not since the worst days of the Weimar Republic. Mr. Gono stands tall . . . a colossus of error . . . an Olympus of bunglement.

It is easy to criticize the chief of Zimbabwe's national bank. In fact, it is hard not to criticize him. Keynes warned that "there is a lot of ruin" in a nation. Mr. Gono's contribution to economics is to show how much ruin there is.

What Gono wrought—as reported by the press in autumn 2008—sounded like hell: The trash piled up in Harare and the water system no longer worked. Vendors sold bottles of water for $25 US. Cholera broke out, and anthrax, too. Shops were empty. People were hungry. Nothing worked. Even the forces of law and order went on the rampage, breaking windows and looting what little remained in the shops. The soldiers and police had not been paid, at least, not with real money.

Between August 2007 and June 2008, the Zimbabwean money supply increased 20 million times. Naturally, this led to the kind of spectacular increases in consumer prices that modern economists had only seen on newsreels. Consumer price inflation was clocked at 2,000,000% in mid-2008. By the end of the year, it was said to have sped up to 230,000,000%.

Of course, Mr. Gono rolled out all the usual inflation fighting measures—all, that is, except for the one that works. Prices were controlled. Mr. Gono personally went around, found shop owners who had illegally raised prices, and had them arrested. Bank withdrawals were limited to 500,000 Zimbabwe dollars per day. If you wanted to buy 2 kg of sugar, for example, you'd have to stand in line for four days at an automated teller. But at the rate of consumer price inflation in November 2008, you could stand in line at the automatic tellers every day for eternity and never get enough money to buy a drink of water.

Still we salute Gideon Gono. He may be a moron, but at least he's a useful one. Better than another bad theory, he has provided a bad example. In an age when central bankers all over the world desperately try to avoid a decline in the cost of living, Mr. Gono has proven that there are worse things.

But despite the news from Zimbabwe, Gonoism is gaining admirers in the rest of the world. Because the old "hair of the dog that bit him" technique isn't working. The world has had too much credit; the Fed want to give it even more. With $10 trillion in "stimulus" efforts all over the planet, they are not giving only a hair of the dog, they are throwing in the whole damned kennel. But you can't help an obese person by giving them another helping of dessert. And you can't cure an alcoholic by offering them free drinks. In short, you can't help someone who is deeply in debt by lending them more money.

So, central banks are trying new techniques. Ben Bernanke is not yet dropping hundred dollar bills out of helicopters, as he once promised, but that cannot be far off.

Surely, Gideon Gono must feel his chest swelling with pride. He must be in line for a Nobel Prize . . . or a hanging. We quote his approving words: "Banks, including those in USA and Britain are not now just talking of, but actually implement flexible and pragmatic central bank programs where these are deemed necessary in their national interests.

"That is precisely the path that we began only four years ago in pursuit of our national interest and have not wavered from that critical path despite the untold misunderstandings, vilification and demonization we have endured from across the political divide."[53]

Most deserving of Gono's praise is the Fed's new policy of "quantitative easing" or "credit easing," as Bernanke called it. These are code words for printing money. Rather than recapitalize the bankers, the central banks buy debt directly from the government. This permits the government to finance its stimulus plans without putting pressure on the debt market. It also acts like a gush of wind on a stack of dollar bills.

When central banks buy their own government's debt, they create money out of thin air for the purchase. The money supply increases. If they do enough of this money creation, the quantity of money overwhelms the quantity of goods and services that it can buy. Result: inflation, sometimes modified by the prefix *hyper-*.

That is the Fed's goal. If they can cause the value of the dollar to drop against consumer goods and investment assets, they will spur people to get rid of dollars quickly. This will, according to the theory, not only reduce the burden of debt for individuals and the government but also increase economic activity. As of this writing, they have only begun this process, and it has not been very successful. But we have faith; in the end, they'll get the hang of it.

THE LINT AGE

When Ben Bernanke gave his speech to the London School of Economics on January 13, 2009, a friend was on scene. Terry Easton put a tough question to America's central banker: Aren't your interventions just making the situation worse, he wanted to know.

Amid the blah ... blah ... blah ... of Bernanke's response was this: "The tendency of financial systems to boom and bust ... is a very long-standing problem ... but I think it's very important for us to try to put out the fire ... then you think about the fire code."[54]

In his 1988 book, *The Collapse of Complex Societies*, Joseph Tainter argued that all societies, like all organisms, are doomed. Tainter studied ancient Rome as well as the Mayan civilization. He noticed that problems always blaze up. Each one—whether climatic, political, or economic—rings the firehall bell. And each solution—and readers may substitute the word *bailout* for solution—brings more challenges and takes more resources. Finally, the available resources are worn out.[55]

Tainter observes that when the costs become high enough, people seem to give up. By the end of the Roman era, for example, the burdens of empire were so heavy that people sold themselves into slavery to get free of them. So many people did so at one point that the authorities had to come up with another solution: They outlawed the practice. Henceforth, Roman citizens were required by law to remain free![56]

An earlier philosopher, Giambattista Vico, writing in the 18th century, put the beginning of the decline of Rome roughly at the time of the Great Fire during Nero's reign. Nero, partly to pay for his postfire reforms and reconstruction, began taking the gold and silver out of the coins. All civilizations go through three stages, Vico said: divine, heroic, and human. The divine period is ruled by the gods. The heroic period is marked by victories and statues. Then comes the human era. (Here, we permit ourselves to add a footnote to Vico's oeuvre: The coin of the realm in early periods is the gods' money: gold. Later, people switch to money of their own invention: the kind of money you make from trees.) This last stage, says Vico, is when popular democracy arises, along with rational thinking and what Vico delightfully calls the *"barbarie della reflessione"* [the barbarism of reflection]. In earlier eras, people do what their gods and leaders ask of them. In the final era, they ask, "what's in it for me?"[57]

Even as late as the early 1960s, John F. Kennedy could still appeal to heroic urge without drawing a laugh. "Ask not what your country can do for you," he said in his inaugural address, "ask what you can do for your country."

But 11 years later, Richard Nixon, like Nero before him, began the process of debasing the money. That was a solution, too; the United States had spent too much. Nixon would worry about the fire code later. First he opened up with the firehose: He defaulted on America's promise to exchange dollars for gold at the statutory rate.

Barack Obama tried a Kennedyesque appeal to civic high-mindedness in early 2009. We need to "insist that the first question each of us ask isn't 'what's good for me?' but 'what's good for the country my children will inherit?'" said the president-elect.[58] But now, like Doric columns in a trailer park, the words are ornamental, not structural. They are the homage that one age pays to a better one.

We are in the 21st century now. Barbarous reflections rise up like swamp gas. The whole place stinks of them. Bernanke and Obama offer solutions. But their plans to save the world from a correction are little more than a swindle of the next generation. They offer to bail out the mistakes of one generation with debt laid onto the next.

"Regarding the current financial meltdown," writes Rony Teitelbaum,

> it is very clear that two main factors underlie the political reactions to the crisis, the first being pressure originating from ties between the financial and the political elect, manifested by taxpayer bailouts of large institutions that continue to deliver bonuses to the executives and donate to political campaigns. For those of us who are not blind, these are clear signs of political corruption which would have made the worst Roman emperor blush. The second factor is political pressure originating from the mass public. The kind of solutions offered so far, and I may add which were received with very warm enthusiasm, were tax rebates and gasoline tax holidays. These are actions aimed at a public who "impatiently expected quick and obvious results," to quote Cary's description of Roman society in AD 300. [*A History of Rome*].[59]

Circa 2009, there is hardly a soul in the entire world who has not been corrupted by the *barbarie della reflessione* of the late imperial period. Both patricians and plebes are for bailouts. Both business and labor back stimulus programs. The taxpayers and the politicians who rule them are of one mind. Liberal, conservative, rich, poor, Republican, Democrat all speak with a single voice: "Screw the next generation!"

The Golden Age of US capitalism is over, in other words. In the space of half a century it passed from gold, to silver, to paper . . . and is now somewhere between plastic and navel lint.

THE TRIUMPH OF OSAMA BIN LADEN

Finally, we turn back to the dead. "Been there, done that," the shades whisper again. "You think you're so smart . . . ," they continue, and then the spooks laugh so hard they can't finish the sentence.

There are a number of theories of history. Hegel, Vico, Spengler; destiny, dialectic, the clash of civilizations. They are a penny a dozen, and still overpriced.

"The history of the world is but the biography of great men,"[60] was Thomas Carlyle's small-change addition to the genre. He thought individual people had a decisive effect. But not only do people come to think what they must think when they need to think it, they also do what they must do. Then, they imagine that it is they who control history, and not the other way around.

"Encourage your enemy to expend his energy in futile quests while you conserve your strength. When he is exhausted and confused, you attack with energy and purpose."[61]

This is from an ancient Chinese text known as the *Thirty-Six Stratagems* or *36 Strategies* first published in the western world by Harro von Senger. Osama bin Laden must have read the book. In a report that appeared in the *Guardian* in November of 2004, the Al Qaida leader outlined his strategy: "'Bleeding America to the point of bankruptcy' was what he was up to, he said in a videotape. He even did the math. 'Every dollar spent by al-Qaida in attacking the U.S. has cost Washington $1 million (£545,000) in economic fallout and military spending,'" said the report.

"'We, alongside the mujahideen, bled Russia for 10 years, [in Afghanistan] until it went bankrupt and was forced to withdraw in defeat. . . . So we are continuing this policy in bleeding America to the point of bankruptcy.'"[62]

How many people can boast of bin Laden's triumph? He brought down not just one empire, but two. His band of terrorists leeched the Soviets so well, they fainted. His campaign, with CIA support, put nearly a half-million Soviet soldiers out of service, mostly because of illness, and destroyed billions' worth of irreplaceable military matériel.

It was no coincidence that the Soviets lost Afghanistan in the same year their empire disintegrated. Then, Osama turned on the world's only surviving empire. The story of Osama's attack on the United States of America will be more familiar to readers than it is to us. It succeeded beyond Osama's wildest imagination. With a band of just 19 suicidal fanatics, he was not only able to bring down two of America's iconic buildings but also panic the empire into slitting its own wrists.

In 2003, America's war in Iraq and other expenses created a deficit of $377 billion. At the time, the total US debt was $7.4 trillion. Now, the cost of the war in Iraq in itself is estimated to mount up to $2 trillion. Bin Laden—the son of a billionaire—had found the weakest section of the empire's walls: its finances. The terrorist strikes could have been turned over to the usual gumshoes—the FBI and local gendarmes. The actual perpetrators were in cinders; still, good police work and the cooperation of foreign law enforcement agencies might have brought more perps to justice, at negligible additional cost.

But the empire had George W. Bush in charge of its military and Alan Greenspan in charge of its money; these two exterminating angels were ready for the job ahead of them. Besides, it had been slapped in the face! America didn't have $2 trillion to spend on a pointless war. But bin Laden had delivered a challenge to the empire's amour proper. In effect, he suckered the fattest man on earth into having another éclair.

Two trillion was just the beginning. The attack on the World Trade center induced a hysteria. It followed the collapse of the Nasdaq and coincided with a cyclical downturn in the US economy. In the general panic, the Bush administration believed that the US economy needed to be goosed up, at all costs. Thus it was that the greatest stimulus package of all time was unleashed, as described in this book—a massive turnaround in public spending, from positive to negative—along with the most aggressive cuts in interest rates in many years. The bubble in the Nasdaq was soon replaced by much bigger bubbles: in housing, finance, derivative debt, art, private equity, student loans, and other forms of private debt. The explosion of those bubbles has now blown up the whole system of imperial finance.

Now, for the first time in 25 years, global trade is shrinking. The US trade deficit is declining, along with China's exports. Economies naturally expand and naturally contract. In an expansion, world trade increases. In a contraction, it diminishes. Typically, big increases in global trade correspond with the rise of imperial powers—armed forces large enough to protect trade routes guarantee the safety of merchants and enforce a uniform, reliable commercial code. Trade expanded greatly during the Roman Empire and then contracted sharply when it fell. The Mongol Empire, too, created a huge free trade area in Eurasia. Then, the British and other European powers expanded their sphere trade along the shipping lanes, throughout most of the world, until they were rolled back from much of Eurasia by the advance of other hostile empires—the Soviet Union and China.

The last major boom in world trade came with the Reagan administration. The free-marketers in the 1980s—both in England and America—lowered taxes and reduced barriers to commerce. Then, a remarkable thing happened: The Soviet Union collapsed, leaving its member states and client countries free to enter into trade with the West. China also realized that its rice bowl would be fuller if it, too, began selling to the West, rather than threatening it.

That Golden Age of ebullient world trade is now over, too, because the empire that nurtured has peaked out. And now, Mr. bin Laden, holed up in his grim refuge, can cherish his own conceits: that he is the hero who slayed two empires, rather than just another lunkhead doing history's dirty work.

"Kingdoms are of clay," said Marc Antony, before killing himself.

CHAPTER 15

TURNING ARGENTINE

We [Bill Bonner and wife] visit our ranch in northwestern Argentina once a year, just to make sure things are running smoothly. It is a remote place, five hours from Salta city on a dirt road. Because it is so far from civilization, we always imagined that it would make a good refuge if things got really tough. A serious war, maybe a global computer or internet breakdown, fuel shortages, riots. . . .

Our only worry was that, when a crisis came, we wouldn't be able to get here. Planes would stop flying. Borders would close. Credit cards would be useless. But we were lucky.

In the COVID crisis of 2020, we had a unique opportunity. We got to see if we could really get to our getaway when we needed to get there. We also got to see what a real financial crisis looks like, trapped as we were in Argentina. And as a bonus, with the luxury of broadband, we got to watch as another great nation—the US—headed in the same direction.

We landed in Salta, Argentina, in mid–March 2020. International flights stopped two days later. We promptly drove to the ranch and were told not to leave.

Which was just fine by us. We had nowhere to go, anyway.

"What a place to enjoy the end of the world," said Elizabeth.

Talk about social distance! We were in a dry, sparsely populated area. And we were on the far side of a river, with only the footbridge that most people are afraid to cross. Nobody is going to "drop over" for a visit. No postal carrier delivered the mail. And we had no reason to leave. Here was where we fattened our calves. We grew onions, lettuce, potatoes, and beets. We had a spring for water. And we'd brought down a stock of our own wine, enough for a couple of months.

No conferences. No coffees. No drinks. No PowerPoint or meetings. No cocktails. No tête-à-têtes. Nowhere to go. Nothing to do. What a charming interlude! Most of our life is spent getting and spending. Now, we could do neither. A period of enforced idleness; a pause in the rush of life. Like moments spent in a quiet graveyard, or on the edge of a cliff, were only a step away from eternity.

In *The Decameron*, 14th-century author Giovanni Boccaccio sets his tale in an abandoned countryside villa, to which 10 young people have fled to escape the Black Death. They pass the time with tales, some of them so racy they were scrubbed clean by translators.

And now, here we were in San Martín, waiting, and wondering how it will all turn out.

A week later . . .

- Italy had blocked internal travel.
- Three out of four US small businesses said sales were down.
- James Bullard, president of the Federal Reserve of St. Louis, said US GDP could be cut in half, worse than the Great Depression.
- The bond market staggered as issuers, including the federal government, desperately tried to raise money.
- And the "rescue" package in Congress had grown to $2 trillion.

It was starting to look like Revelation's pale horse. In fact, with a total of just 470 people dead, the US was in such a tizzy, you'd think a whole cavalry of riders, white as chalk, had appeared on the White House lawn, led by the devil himself. "Emergency war powers" were being invoked to fight a "war" on a molecule.

But a pale horse appeared back in 1918 as well. In a few months, the Spanish flu killed some 675,000 Americans, equivalent to about 1.2 million today. Cities and local communities coped as best they could. But there was no panic. No state of emergency was proclaimed. No "shelter in place" orders were given. No face masks were distributed. No testing programs put in place. No stores closed. Nobody (unless they were actually sick) failed to show up for work.

The only major public health initiative, undertaken in some cities but not others, was that schools closed early for the summer. And what the authorities didn't do for citizens' health, they also didn't do for their money. No "stimulus" was given, deficit run, interest rates cut. There was no emergency spending or helicopter money. Stores remained open. Steel furnaces ran hot. Restaurants served meals.

Unemployment grew, mostly because of the soldiers coming back from the war in Europe. But, by the end of 1919, when it was all said and done, it had risen to only 4%. Otherwise, things continued as usual. US debt went down. And the stock market went up!

Back in 1918, America still had a more-or-less free economy. Its price signals were still reliable. The Federal Reserve had been set up, but not yet flexed its muscles. The dollar was still backed by gold, limiting the Fed's power to print. The idea of bailing out a private business would have seemed outrageous. And the idea of sending people checks willy-nilly, preposterous, and impossible.

But, come 2020, hardly anyone questioned it. The government had so fouled the economy that you could barely take a step without needing to clean your boots. And the approach of a virus gave it the green light to bring out the seven princes of hell to do their diabolical mischief.

Underway was the biggest money-printing scheme ever seen in North America. Businesses, weakened by Fed policies, would be bailed out. Bad managers, who used the Fed's low interest rates to shovel billions to their shareholders and themselves, would be rescued by taxpayers, their jobs saved, their fortunes revived. Even ordinary families, whose votes were needed in the next elections, would be given bribes.

Yes, we were launched on the wildest experiment ever undertaken north of the Rio Grande. We were going to find out how far we could go—with bailouts, fake money, stock purchases, government price controls, and negative real interest rates—before the whole thing blew up.

And we were watching it from a country that had had so many blowups already, maybe we could learning something. So, while keeping an eye on events in North America, we paid attention to those in South America, too; coming into focus, little by little, was the future.

EVERYONE GOES CRAZY

"Can you believe what's going on?" said a farm manager. "It's like everyone has gone crazy. We have no cases here in the valley, but I had to go through six roadblocks just to get here. We're not even allowed to go into Molinos to buy fuel."

"Crazy?" replied a neighbor, rolling his head backward. "I've been living with craziness all my life. One disaster after another. You're lucky," he continued, pointing at us. "Here in Argentina, we're so used to craziness that we couldn't live without it. It's the craziness that keeps us sane. You don't have that problem in America. . . ."

"I remember," he went on, recalling the inflation of the 1980s, "you'd go out for a beer and a cigarette and, while you were sitting at the bar, the price of the beer would double." He roared again.

The inflation rate then, in Argentina, was about 50% per year. You could change a dollar for 300 pesos, on the black market, of course. That is something you learn quickly—to use the "informal" economy to get what you need.

"But you know something else," our neighbor was helping us to understand financial life in what Donald Trump called a "sh★thole country." "It's never quite as crazy as you think. There's always someone with his hand in the cookie jar."

In the US, at that very moment, so many hands reached for the cookies, it took 800 pages in the CARE Act to list them all. Congress was giving away the equivalent of 10% of GDP. Who didn't want a hand in that?

Perhaps the most appalling thing of all was that Congress passed this monstrous bill on a voice vote. Only one member of Congress objected, and he was widely ridiculed, as though he was stopping an ambulance from getting to the scene of an accident.

LEARNING TO TANGO

Argentina was once the world's second-richest country, at least by some tallies. The expression "as rich as an Argentine" led prominent European families to hope a gaucho would scoop up their daughters.

Some did. And for almost a century—1850–1950—Argentines enjoyed wealth and status that was the envy of the world.

Today, Argentina still has many rich people. But it has a lot more poor people. And, generally, its people are getting poorer, not richer. What happened? Nothing out of the usual. Juan Perón, a young military officer, visited Italy in the 1930s. He saw how Mussolini rose to power and how he could harness the aspirations of the masses in a democratic system. He returned to Argentina and put his lessons into practice.

Argentina is a big country, but most of its people live near the capital, Buenos Aires. Appealing to these "urban mobs"—many of whom had already been infected by one of the many imported -*isms*: syndicalism, communism, socialism, anarchism—Perón was elected president in 1946.

Reducing the program to its bare bones, the idea was to promise the voters "something for nothing." Then, the government delivered what it could, with much of the bounty ending up in corrupt pockets and secret bank accounts. Inevitably, the government spent too much money, and lenders balked at lending more. Then, it simply printed up the money it needed.

There is nothing very original or imaginative in the formula. It is tried and true. And it soon becomes a habit that is hard to break.

We first visited Argentina in the late 1990s. We were invited to the Casa Roja to meet then-president, Carlos Menem. At the time, Argentina was enjoying a boom. After going through a disastrous spell of hyperinflation, bankruptcy, defaults, military coup d'etat, mass murder, and near civil war, Menem had instituted a new currency (not the first!), which was pegged to the dollar. The peg guaranteed that lenders would get back their money in good order. It stabilized the financial system and returned the economy to prosperity.

But old habits are hard to break. And by the end of the 1990s, Argentina once again appeared to have borrowed too much money. How long would it be able to maintain the peg, people wondered?

In our meeting with Menem, we put the question directly: "Are you going to be able to stick with the program, with the dollar and the peso linked together, one-to-one," we asked?

"Of course, we will," came the answer.

Menem explained that Argentina's prosperity—its growth, its financial stability, and the integrity of its economy—depended on a solid peso, which in turn depended on the peg to the dollar.

All that was true.

"So, there is no way we'd do away with the peg," he concluded.

Which was false.

About three weeks later, the Argentine treasury announced that it could not pay its bills. The banks were closed. The peg was removed. Bonds collapsed. The economy was shattered. Foreign bondholders spent years in court, trying to get their money back. A US hedge fund, Elliot Capital Management, even managed to seize an Argentine naval vessel when it docked in Ghana, for nonpayment of debt.

More than two decades has passed between the time President Carlos Menem vowed to preserve the peso at a one-to-one exchange rate with the dollar. This was enough time for another complete boom-to-bust cycle. Spend too much, print too much, go broke, and then, do it all over again.

The federales north of the Rio Grande were picking up the tricks, but not learning the lesson. Hardly had Donald Trump passed out the pens—souvenirs of one the most reckless, foolhardy, and asinine pieces of legislation of all time, a $2.2 trillion boondoggle designed to get Democrats and Republicans re-elected—than the numbskulls came out with yet another $2 trillion scheme. It was the next installment of Congressional efforts to help the country weather the destructive blows inflicted by the coronavirus. Donald Trump explained: "With interest rates for the United States being at ZERO, this is the time to do our long awaited Infrastructure Bill. It should be VERY BIG & BOLD, Two Trillion Dollars, and be focused solely on jobs and rebuilding the once great infrastructure of our Country!"[1]

Yes, Democrats and Republicans got together, Trump and Pelosi, fools and the knaves, for sure, though it was hard to tell which was which, and agreed to put an end to the way America did business. No more give and take, no more win-win, no more getting and spending. No more free markets or honest prices.

Now, the feds were in charge. The government would soon be spending over half of GDP. Yes, it was an old-fashioned, stark-naked, banana republic, money-printing lollapalooza.

Dow 50,000! A cup of coffee $25!

THIEVES IN THE NIGHT

You can get away with a lot in the fog of war. And, like so many of America's wars in the last 100 years, the war on the coronavirus was a smokescreen for insiders to shift power and wealth to themselves.

Whether WWI, Vietnam, or the Ukraine, here's how it works. First, both the press and the government hype up the threat. The mob becomes hysterical. It hears lurid tales of how evil the enemy is. In WWI, Americans read about Germans bayonetting babies and mass-raping nuns. Come Vietnam, we were told the reds would reach Detroit if not stopped in Da Nang. The wars spilled over to the home front, too; in 1975, we were warned marijuana would make us a nation of heroin addicts. In 2003, we heard Iraq had "weapons of mass destruction."

Next, as the hysteria grows, more and more of the nation's output and energy is shunted toward the war effort. In WWI, automobile factories were commandeered to build tanks. Since 2001, the War on Terror chewed up some $5 trillion. During the 50-year War on Poverty the feds spent $22 trillion, according to a Heritage Foundation estimate.[2] The totals in foreign aid to Ukraine and Israel have barely begun to be tabulated.

And, finally, new "emergency" legislation gives the feds more power to keep people from challenging the "war" narrative. In 1918, under the presiding eye of Wilson, the Sabotage and Sedition Acts allowed the feds to punish anyone who deigned to "willfully utter, print, write, or publish any disloyal, profane, scurrilous, or abusive language about the form of the Government of the United States."[3] In 2001, amid the heat of the war fever, the Patriot Act was passed, giving the government broad powers to eavesdrop, seize property, and invade privacy. It was an "emergency" measure, but its worst features are still the law of the land.

Again in 2020, the new stimulus measures were accompanied by broad efforts, many of them clandestine, to prevent dissent. Did the COVID virus come from a lab? Did it really pose a threat to most people? Were "shutdowns" effective? How about masks? Alternative opinions, even from certified academic experts, were suppressed.

War is the health of the state, said Randolph Bourne.[4] And here she was, fat and sassy, a little fleshy from overfeeding: the state has rarely been healthier. Why? Because she's at war, a perfect war, with a virus that couldn't really do her any harm.

With no serious questions allowed, no debate permitted, and no proof required, most national and local governments adopted the now-familiar measures: social distancing, face masks, and so forth. These led to a drastic cutback in wages, sales, profits, tax revenues, and GDP. Those losses were and mostly permanent.

If a person misses work one day, that day's production is gone forever. They might try to make it up on the morrow, but then lose whatever they had planned for that day. A month of idleness equals about 8% of annual GDP—that's a recession. Two months is a depression. That's what the feds had wrought.

Of course, the threat posed by the virus turned out to be much overhyped, like the threat of the Vietcong in the 1960s, drugs in the 1970s, and terrorists back in 2003. Nonetheless, the feds declared war. The politicos loved it. It put the nation's resources at their disposal, giving them more power and money.

And it gave them a chance to prove our dictum: There's no natural calamity they can't make worse. How? In the time-tested way of Roman emperors and Argentine politicians: a diet of inflation, spiced up with a war. We were all gauchos now.

The "conservatives" were technically the ones in charge, but there was nothing conservative about their policies. In April, for example, the president proposed paying the medical expenses of uninsured COVID victims. But what about people with cancer, lung disease, or hemorrhoids? The Secretary of the Treasury proposed a 71% increase in funds to small business. Normally, businesses earn the money to cover their costs. That's how a real economy works. A baker makes money by baking, not by getting a check from the government. That didn't seem to matter.

In 1803, French economist Jean-Baptiste Say noticed that it wasn't money that made people rich: it was output, the ability to produce goods and services. In other words, money has no value of its own. It is only given value by the number of goods and services that are available to buy with it. Give a million dollars to a castaway, and it's worthless. Give it to an Argentinian, and they can live like a monarch.

But now, before our very eyes, we were watching Say's insight put to the test. In this wondrous new age, where Anything Was Possible No Matter How Ridiculous It Was, the feds yelled loud and clear: FREE LUNCHES. Sure! Didn't sell any cars last month? We'll make up the money. Couldn't go to work? We have a check with your name on it. Your restaurant served no meals, your cruise ship didn't leave the harbor, nobody bought your planes? Problem solved: We'll pass out some Franklins, Jacksons, and Grants.

Can fake money replace real output? We were going to find out. But those who pay the piper call the tune. In a healthy economy, the producers call it, because they're the ones with the money. But in an unhealthy, fake war, fake money, fake lending rates, fake profits economy, the feds became disk jockeys.

Yes, it was time to tango.

Nuttier and nuttier.

I don't think we should ever shake hands ever again.

—Dr. Anthony Fauci

That did it for us. We were convinced. America's war on Covid was being run by morons. People have been shaking hands for 3,000 years. It is a sign of good intentions, whether in friendship or sealing a deal. It is just one of the many customs and manners that mark civilized life. But Dr. Fauci seemed to think that the only thing that matters in life is not getting sick.

If staying alive were the only aim, we would all stay home, all the time. Like business magnate Howard Hughes, we would shuffle around our houses with tissue boxes for shoes and use the tissues to pick things up for fear they might have germs on them.

But did that mania prolong Hughes's life? When he died in 1976, he was just 70 years old. Though still one of the richest men in the world, he looked as if he had starved. He was 6'4" tall, but weighed just 90 pounds. He was so unwashed, unkempt, and unfed that the FBI had to check his fingerprints to identify him.

What kind of a damned fool would want to live like that?

Our heroes were once people who stood up to authority. Now, the heroes—Trump or Fauci, take your pick—locked up seniors in their nursing rooms and imposed on the nation a kind of martial law, with curfews, bans, interdictions, and millions under house arrest.

In Michigan you could go to the supermarket, but you can only buy the "essentials." And what was essential? Lottery tickets! In Baltimore, thank the lord, liquor was considered essential.

People were collared for conducting church services or surfing. Gone was the right to peaceably assemble. And forget about a speedy trial or due process of law. The courts were closed!

And almost everyone went along. If they thought it might extend their lives by only a few days, they would gladly sit in solitary confinement, wash their vegetables in bleach, surrender their right to surf or to worship, and give the old Bill of Rights the heave-ho.

And many gladly denounced their neighbors for taking more than one walk per day.

"The whole aim of politics is to keep the populace alarmed (and hence clamorous to be led to safety) by an endless series of hobgoblins, most of them imaginary," said Baltimore's own H. L. Mencken.[5] Was the COIVD-19 pandemic "mostly imaginary"? It didn't matter. The feds were not going to let a good crisis go to waste. In a bold move, initiated in the United States by Donald Trump, the US government quarantined the healthy for the first time in human history.

By mid-April, the whole world economy was collapsing. Demand for oil was so weak that the black goo was selling for less than $20 a barrel. There was so much of it sitting around that oil tankers were being used for storage, with rental rates as high as $300,000 per day (about 20 times the normal rate).

The Trump team promised small businesses a kind of eureka loan, one that didn't have to be repaid. The Payroll Protection Plan, they called it. Naturally borrowers lined up, and the Small Business Administration was processing faster than Frank Perdue processed chickens. The press reported that they had been carefully examining 6,547 applications each hour for the last three weeks. That was 109 every minute; one every half a second. They checked out the facts, verified the value of collateral, and assured themselves that everything was on the level. After all, they were giving out as much as $2 million each time!

Who got the money? We don't know. But, like subprime mortgages in 2007, all you needed was a pulse. The *New York Times* later reported the total of fraudulent loans at $76 billion.[6] NBC News called it "the biggest fraud in a generation."[7] Prison inmates got PPP loans. Rappers. NFL stars. Hedge funds got the money, too.

For some, that wasn't even enough. Also on the scene was a White House wannabe, billionaire Mark Cuban, who claimed to be a "fiscal conservative," with yet another plan to spend other people's money.

"It's time to face the fact that PPP didn't work," Cuban told CNBC. "Great plan, difficult execution. No one's fault. The only thing that will save businesses is consumer demand. No amount of loans to businesses will save them or jobs if their customers aren't buying," parroting the Keynesian idea that consumption—and not production—drives the economy. He then proposed: "We need to consider an interim spending stimulus program. All 128m households could get a $1k check every 2 weeks for the next 2 months that MUST BE SPENT WITHIN 10 DAYS OF RECEIPT OR IT EXPIRES."[8]

NOT JUST FINANCIAL LOSSES

On the other side of the globe, the elder of your two authors' wives, Elizabeth, rode to see her neighbor. Ramón had turned up on horseback after lunch the day before, reporting that his wife was in tears. So Elizabeth went over to see what was wrong.

"Marta's okay," she reported. "She's been isolated for a month and it's getting to her. Ramón is always out with the cattle or machinery. He's happy. But she stays inside and watches too much TV. She's not afraid of the virus. She just misses her children and grandchildren and is afraid that this lockdown is ruining their lives. She thinks it's unfair that their lives are put on hold to protect her."

In a prosperous country, the war on COVID-19 cost many young people their earnings and their jobs. And many of those jobs will never come back. Their careers were stifled. Their family plans were delayed; some never happened at all.

But in a country like Argentina, the consequences could be much worse.

Another neighbor is an old man, Manuel, bent by age and infirmity. He has an open wound in his abdomen. His intestines were exposed. We were never clear on what was wrong with him. But he needed medical attention. And in the "lockdown," there was none available. Doctors did not come to the local clinic. Buses did not run up and down the valley to take him there. No medicines were available. And no nurses either.

Fortunately, our farm manager came from the city each week. He brought supplies. We were able to get clean dressings and some basic antibiotics. Still, he should have been in a hospital.

Almost miraculously, he pulled through. Many others—who delayed doctors' visits, ran low on medicines, or needed more care—probably didn't.

Exchanging freedom for security; getting neither.

The *federales* alarm the public with invented hobgoblins and use the crisis to extend their own power. The masses have a complementary flaw: they *want* to be scared. And once they are, they beseech authority, vote for bullies and windbags, and support jackass protection rackets.

The mob is always timorous and always ready to give up its dignity and independence in exchange for "security." We let airport goons frisk us, even though we've never once planned to blow up a plane. We don't smoke, even in a sidewalk café, for fear the cops will arrest us. We are careful in the words we use, often afraid to say what we really think.

And now Americans cowered in their homes, so afraid. Lunatic regulations were issued, as if to mock common sense. You were allowed on wet sand but not dry sand. You were allowed to drive in a car with your family but not to get into a boat. You could be put in jail for violating the lockdown, but criminals were let out, because staying in prison might be a risk to their health.

Capitalism on the way up; cronyism on the way down.

Capitalism built the United States. People worked hard, took risks, made money, lost money. Investors, managers, and day laborers all grew richer together. By 1999, the tree of the US economy was magnificent, spreading its limbs from sea to shining sea. But the leaves were already turning yellow and beginning to slide off the branches. The bugs and worms of lifelong bureaucrats, swamp critters and Deep State parasites had made their nests in it.

And then, after 2000, three things fell upon it like a woodsman's ax. First, the George "Dubya" Bush administration ginned up wars against terror and Iraq. Next, the Obama administration, faced with the crisis of 2008–2009, added $10 trillion of debt to the government ledger to bail out the good, the bad, and the ugly. Had old-fashioned capitalism been left to do its magic, the fund manager up on the 25th floor might have toted his losses, reviewed his options, and exited by the window that capitalism left open for him. Instead, cronies sent him a check.

Then the third, the cruelest cut of them all: Donald Trump vowed to Make America Great Again. And then, the wind picked up. Under cover of COVID, the remaining leaves were blown away. Now, the naked branches, corrupt and bent by special pleading, were exposed for all to see.

Locked down, but not alone.

We'd met our new friends clandestinely at the only hotel in the area. They were French, a psychiatrist and her neurologist husband. They arrived just as the country was shutting down and locking up.

"The whole thing is unbelievable," said the shrink. "At first we were quarantined in our room for two weeks. Then the hotel closed and everybody left. The manager, the maids—everybody. But we had nowhere to go, so they just left us here. Fortunately, they gave us the keys to the wine cellar and the kitchen. As for the bidet, we realized how important that was soon enough when we ran out of toilet paper."

What have we learned from the shutdown? The importance of a wine cellar and a bidet.

"Fortunately, or unfortunately, we have the internet," her husband continued. "I follow the news. I can't understand what's going on. *Mon Dieu*. It's just a virus. There are about a million people in this province the size of Texas. And only three cases of the virus, all of them people who had just come from Spain, and none very serious. Yet they stop you from going to work or to restaurants or driving down the road. It's crazy. A lot of these people need to work to eat.

"Speaking for ourselves, we're okay. I'm enjoying a rest. And my wife's been able to keep working. She gets together with her patients via video conferencing. And her business is doing well. Her patients are trapped in their houses and apartments. They're getting crazier and crazier. . . ."

It sounded like the same thing was happening in Washington. The US deficit was already heading to $4 trillion for the year, yet here came another budget-buster to "top up" the aid package. And just to make sure nobody got in the way of their spending, the swamp denizens were out to eliminate the only member of Congress who hasn't toed the line. Kentucky's Thomas Massie dared to make the totally uncrazy suggestion that, if the people's representatives were going to spend the equivalent of 10% of GDP, they should at least go on the record.

"Gotta get rid of him," said Republican fixers. The last thing you want in a nuthouse is a sane person. He makes the inmates feel crazy.

Argentina, a case study. What would happen when you suppressed supply and pumped up demand. Inflation?

Economists like to study Argentina. It's the only country in the world to go from one of the world's richest to sh*thole status, thanks entirely to government policy.

In 1982, the military dictatorship went to war with Britain, paying its expenses with printing press money. By the following year, it had to issue a "new peso," worth 10,000 old pesos, and, when that failed to stop inflation, another currency, the austral, was substituted at the rate of one per 1,000 pesos.

"I remember the late 1980s," said our administrator in Salta. "I was a student in Buenos Aires. My parents had to send me money every day so I could eat. I'd rush to the supermarket. They had staff who spent all day changing prices, trying to keep up with the inflation."

While the Argentine currency collapsed, the US dollar was king. It had already become fake money, but fake money is fine as long as it acts like the real thing, with interest rates falling and prices looking stable. People are happy to take it in payment for goods and services. They are happy, too, to leave it in bank accounts or under mattresses. And when there is a crisis, they want more of it. But that gives it power, and power corrupts.

Americans, with only faint memories of mild inflation in the 1970s, expect a return to "normal" soon. But the Argentines knew better. They knew that it was not the 1970s that was the aberration, it was Paul Volcker's remarkable victory over inflation, the Chinese entry into the world economy, and a 40-year stretch of money-printing without consumer price inflation. They knew, too, that, when Americans caught on to the money-printing scam, they wouldn't be able to resist it. Printing money is a hard habit to break.

In 1881, President Julio A. Roca brought out the Argentino de Oro, a gold coin with 0.2334 ounces of gold. They say there are still some in the vaults of the Argentine Central Bank, but the country had been buried under repeated blizzards of paper money. Zeroes had been added and stripped away. Yet the Argentino de Oro, the gold coin minted more than 100 years previously, never lost a dime of value. A friend explained: "This Argentino de Oro, whose original price in 1881 was 5 pesos, would be valued today at 452.3 quadrillion (that is 15 zeros) pesos, a 9.4 quintillion percent "return" on the investment, measured in the original currency."

The important thing, though, is not that the gold coin was a good investment. It wasn't. It was exactly the same coin in 1990 that it had been in 1881. It had produced nothing. And yet, if you had held the gold coin, rather than the paper peso, it would have prevented the loss of 99.999% of the wealth represented by the original peso.

Changing the currency does nothing to halt inflation. As long as the government funded itself with newly printed money, the people didn't care whose picture was on it. By 1989, the inflation rate hit 12,000%, and riots broke out in the streets.

The austral replaced the peso, and then that too was tossed on the monetary trash heap. Finally, a new "convertible" peso was introduced: one new peso was equal to 10,000 australes. Convertibility was the key; this was the new currency introduced by Carlos Menem (mentioned previously) and linked to dollars. You know the story. It worked, for a time. Inflation almost disappeared. The economy began a rebound.

But by the early 2000s, the peg had been broken. When we arrived in March 2020, a dollar would get you 90 pesos on the black market, of course. By late April, it was more than 100. And now, October 2023, the official rate is one to 350. Unofficially, out on the street, black market traders will give you 900 pesos for a dollar.

THE ROUGH RIDER

It was now autumn on the pampas. We had been taking pot shots at the Trump team for mishandling the COVID crisis for only

372 EMPIRE OF DEBT

two months. Some readers didn't like it. One recommended we read Roosevelt's "The Man in the Arena" speech. The essential part we reprint here: "It is not the critic who counts; not the man who points out how the strong man stumbles, or where the doer of deeds could have done them better. The credit belongs to the man who is actually in the arena, whose face is marred by dust and sweat and blood. . . ."[9]

But Roosevelt is one of the saddest figures in US empire history. Born rich, he never had an honest job in his life and never added a penny to the world's wealth. In this speech, given at the Sorbonne in Paris, he lauds the risk-taker, the doer, the striver and achiever, yet his own big achievements were amateurish, lethal, and mostly came at someone else's expense.

In his hand-tailored uniforms, with his private army of dreamers, schemers, and vainglorious world improvers, he was the picture of the warmongering martinet. It was he who was largely responsible for getting the US into two pointless wars, the Spanish American War and WWI, at a cost of 120,000 dead Americans along with millions of dead Spaniards, Cubans, Filipinos, Germans, and French. Of course, the old Blunderbuss didn't like critics. They didn't just point out how "the strong man stumbles." They told him what a clownish jackass he was.

Running out of metaphors.

We were only two months into the experiment, and we were already running out of metaphors.

The old standards—printing money "out the wazoo" "to beat the band" "like nobody's business"—no longer seemed up to the challenge. We'd seen fake money before, but this was something else.

America's paper money system began on August 15, 1971, and the whole scam probably would have blown up by the 1980s but for the Fed Chair Paul Volcker. In a rare display of courage and fortitude (for a public official), he forced the dollar to act as though it were real money. While inflation and interest rates rose to double-digit levels in 1980, he put the Fed's key lending rate up to 20%. It caused a recession. But it saved the fake dollar system.

This gave the dollar a longer life span than expected and led people to think that it was a reliable currency, long term. If ever there were another crisis, they said to themselves, there would surely be another stiff-necked public servant like Volcker to set it straight.

But then, in 2020, we were 49 years into the fake money system. The printing presses were running hot. And we seemed to have passed the point of no return, without a Volcker in sight. Necessity is the mother of invention, but it is also the deadbeat parent of catastrophic mischief. Their backs to the wall, people were ready to do almost anything, no matter how idiotic or preposterous.

Sooner or later, a "necessity" arrives, a threat—usually a "war" or threat of insurrection. Rudolf von Havenstein, in charge of money printing in the Weimar Republic, said he had to print trillions of marks in order to head off the Bolsheviks. Instead, he brought on the Nazis.

THE MIRACLE OF TABACAL

Stuck in Argentina, we were learning as much as we could from a failed economy. But that's not to say that everything has failed. What follows is a brief history of one of the most successful investments of all time. It was daring, bold, difficult, but ultimately very profitable, creating one of South America's largest fortunes and nourishing the political career of the man who might have kept Argentina from going broke.

We're talking about Tabacal, an enormous sugar cane operation in northwest Argentina. We bring it up because it tells us something about the world as it was in the early 20th century . . . and the world as it is 100 years later.

The story begins in 1916. It was then that Robustiano Patrón Costas got off the train in Orán, Argentina, and became convinced that the area was suitable for a modern sugar mill. It seemed very unlikely at the time. The surrounding countryside was a wilderness, with very few people and none of the support infrastructure that a large plant would need: no towns, no skilled laborers, no roads, no electricity. Nevertheless, he got together a group of investors and began a breathtaking project that today seems almost impossible.

They had to clear thousands of acres, with much of the work done with shovels and pickaxes. An extensive irrigation system had to be built, with a river diverted into canals, gates, dikes, and hundreds of miles of ditches. The land had to be plowed and planted. Pests and plant diseases had to be identified and defeated. A railroad, with 16 engines and 1,500 freight wagons, had to be built to transport the cane to the mill.

And that was just the beginning. In cutting season, 8,000 laborers were needed. Where would they live? What would they eat? And what about the thousands of permanent employees? Where would their children go to school? Where would they pray? And what if they were sick?

So Patrón Costas and his associates built a whole town, too. Houses—clean, neat, modern, laid out on tree-lined streets—churches, schools for 1,200 students, bakeries, sawmills, two barber shops, wood shops, metal shops, a theater, tennis courts, polo fields, and a hospital that provided not only nursing but X-rays and surgery, too.

A dairy provided milk. A farm provided fruit and vegetables. The bakery processed 12,000 pounds of flour each day. And the sugar mill itself was similarly immense, powered by its own electric plant. In 1945, it produced 51 million kilos of sugar and 4 million liters of alcohol. By the 1980s, it was the largest sugar mill in the world.

The investors and workers prospered together. The mill brought in thousands of local people with no skills and no money, many from the indigenous tribes of the area, and turned them into carpenters, cooks, machinists, bakers, drivers, and even chemical engineers.

Patrón Costas gained such a reputation that he ran for president of Argentina in the 1940s. Alas, the appeal of risk-taking, hard work, and real growth was already waning. People like capitalism on the way up; they prefer socialism on the way down. Patrón Costas lost to the socialist Juan Perón. The country has been sliding ever since.

The remarkable thing is that, even with 100 years of technological advance, and an abundance of capital, it would be nearly impossible to build Tabacal today. It took 17 years of struggle for the project to prove itself. Who would risk their money for such a long-term payout now? Instead, the ambitious young person becomes a fund manager or develops a new app and plans to go public within 36 months.

Someone with an idea as big as Tabacal would be doomed to failure. The "Indigenous people" would stop them. The "environmentalists" would stop them. The tax department, labor unions, banks and lobbyists, the politicians and bureaucrats, the whole "community"—all would stop them from putting a stake in the ground.

And if, by some miracle, they did overcome such powerful opponents, they would be regulated and controlled, their margins would evaporate in the heat of inflation, and their profits would be taxed away. They would realize that, in order to survive, they'd have to become a crony. They'd say they were combating climate change with "green" technology, that they were putting women and minorities on their board, that they were creating a safe place for their employees.

And then, instead of making money selling sugar at a competitive price in a free market, they'd ask the government for low-cost loans, tariff protection, and emergency subsidies.

Sic transit gloria capitalista. June came to the valley, and things in America got worse. While the media and mobs focused on the struggle between red and blue, liberal and conservative, Republican and Democrat, the battle that really mattered was not even noticed.

It was the battle between the Deep State elite, with all their beefed-up military hardware, unlimited funding, and self-serving crackpot ideas, and "the people" of America.

And the people were losing. The balance between freedom and government was tipping dangerously toward the feds.

Was there any limit? The "social contract" is a myth. There is no such contract. We never saw it. We never agreed to it. And what kind of "contract" can be forced on people, then changed by one of the parties but not the other?

Still, the "social contract," vague as it is, summed up the basic bargain: the feds treat us fairly and we let them take our money and boss us around. But the bargain has shifted over time, little by little, in the feds' favor.

During the Great Depression, the Roosevelt administration never ran a deficit over 7% of GDP. The Trump administration was headed for 20%. Even in the middle of World War II, the US government spent only 40% of GDP. In the second quarter of 2020, the US 61%.

Senator George Frisbie Hoar saw it coming in 1898. Thanks to its foreign wars, he predicted, the US would be "transformed from a Republic founded on the Declaration of Independence, guided by the counsels of Washington, the hope of the poor, the refuge of the oppressed, into a vulgar, commonplace empire founded on physical force, controlling subject races and vassal states, in which one class must forever rule and the other classes must forever obey."[10]

One of the lessons of history is that an army used to trampling on the helpless abroad will one day be used to trample on the helpless at home. And there is never a lack of crises that need to be trampled.

COVID, said the feds, needed to be stamped out immediately, and neither the First Amendment (guaranteeing the right to assembly), nor the Sixth (guaranteeing a fair and speedy trial before punishment), nor the Ninth (guaranteeing your rights that are not specifically in the Constitution), were seen to have the slightest bearing on the matter.

After the US took over the Philippines in 1899, Mark Twain put it thus: "We have pacified some thousands of the islanders and buried them; destroyed their fields; burned their villages, and turned their widows and orphans out-of-doors; furnished heartbreak by exile to some dozen disagreeable patriots; subjugated the remaining millions by Benevolent Assimilation, which is the pious new name of the musket. And so, by these Providences of God—and the phrase is the government's, not mine—we are a World Power."[11]

Being a great nation seems to chafe against being a good one.

By midsummer, the presidential elections in the US were hogging media attention. The two candidates—Trump and Biden—went after each other like gauchos in a barroom fight, knives in hand, they wanted to draw blood, but not too much.

POLITICS ON THE PAMPAS

Here in Argentina, the election strategy that works is simple: Destroy the economy, make people dependent on government, and print money for giveaways to the urban masses.

Former Argentine president Juan Perón proved that it worked in the 1950s, and hardly anyone since has won Argentina's Pink House without following the formula. The only remaining competition was between conservative Perónists and liberal Perónists.

And now, in both Trump's and Biden's proposals, we saw the ghost of Perón. Both aimed to seduce the common marginal voter with an illusion: that the *federales* can make people better off by rigging the economy as they please and passing out printing press money. The *Washington Post* described Mr. Biden's program thus: "The Biden plan includes '$400 billion for products and materials our country needs to modernize infrastructure, to replenish our critical stockpiles, and to enhance our national security.' The plan also promises to fight unfair trading practices; fund green energy; support a caregiving and education workforce; add more money for education; and secure the Affordable Care Act."[12]

But Biden and Trump weren't the only candidates. Kanye West also threw his hat into the ring. His promise? He would hand out more money. "The maximum increase would be everybody who has a baby gets a million dollars or something in that range," said West. West also said that marijuana "should be free."[13]

Why not? When you can print all the money you want, why not spend it any crazy way you choose? Like lottery winners and mental defectives, fake money lovers indulge their fantasies.

NO POT WITHOUT A CHICKEN

No pocket left unpicked. No cliché left behind!

The charm of Argentina is that people are used to crises. They know they can't trust their government or its money. They expect corruption, inflation, devaluations, protests, and defaults. In April, a key witness against the vice president in a bribery case was murdered the day before he was supposed to testify.

By contrast, most Americans enjoy a sudsy inebriation of naivety, delusion, and printing press money. Protected by two vast oceans, they have never been seriously invaded, bombed, or occupied (we put aside the flukey War of 1812). Nor have they ever had to live under communism or fascism or a dictatorship, nor ever experienced hyperinflation. They live in a bubble: "It can't happen here."

At the time of the founding of the US Republic, however, people had seen what paper money had done to England and France, and what their own "continentals" had done during the Revolution. The continental was paper money created to fund the Revolution. By 1780, it "expired without a groan," having lost 99.9% of its value.

So when the founders wrote the Constitution, they included a clause designed to protect us from the printing presses, requiring that nothing "but gold or silver" be used as money. Now the feds issue a dollar without a speck of gold or silver in it. As such, this "money" from the government is untethered and counterfeit.

Because real money is part of the real world. It is limited, like time. You can't create more time just because it would be nice to have an extra hour's sleep. That's why gold is so useful as money. Each ounce of gold has to be discovered, dug out of the ground, processed, and stored. It takes time, investment, skill, and resources to produce gold, just like any other kind of wealth.

Gold connects "money" to the real world of time, sweat, toil, and risk. And, in that real world, any decision must be considered in light of trade-offs. How much time will it take? How much resources will it use? What does it take away from the other things we need?

Usually, these questions are reduced to a single one: how much does it cost? But did anyone bother to ask that critical question as the COVID programs were rolled out? Even when the programs are quoted in dollars—a $3 trillion bailout, say—these are just numbers. They no longer represent real costs, real sacrifices, or real trade-offs. It was assumed that no one will ever pay them.

A $3 trillion bailout should come with a $30,000 tax surcharge for every federal taxpayer. The year's federal budget deficit was $4 trillion. But what taxpayers saw an extra $40,000 charge on their tax bill?

Today, there is no price too high, no program too lunatic. Because everyone knows the money is phony, the economy is counterfeit, the programs are fake, the stock market is fraudulent, and a bad moon is rising.

SLIPS AND SLIDES

So what happened to Argentina? One of our friends in Buenos Aires, an American who has lived in the country almost all his life, wondered: "I've thought about this for years. Same sort of people. (Europeans). Similar physical country, with same resources. Even the same basic institutions and constitutions.

"Argentina just seemed to go sour in the 1950s. . . . I'm talking about the way people thought . . . and the way they acted. America was different, people were more independent . . . and more willing to support basic ideas of justice and fairness.

"But I have to say . . . what I see happening in the US now reminds me of what happened here a few decades ago."

As recently as the 1960s, Argentina had about the same GDP per capita as Japan. And the country has no social or cultural reasons that might explain its collapse. Why did it fall so far behind the rest of the Europeanized world?

The first problem was democracy itself. In 1905, a new law gave all men the vote. This meant the proletariat, concentrated in Buenos Aires, was able to outvote the richer, land-owning elite and more traditionally minded farmers. Pernicious ideas began pouring into the capital along with the new immigrants, including ideas from the "reform" movements popular in Europe, such as those championed by Britain's *Beveridge Report*.

But Juan Perón was not of the Beveridge mold. He took Mussolini and Hitler as his models. The Germans and Italians were lucky: their "reformers" were defeated in World War II. The Perónists were not.

As mentioned, Juan Perón was elected president in 1946. He set about the typical European reforms: pensions, medical care, minimum wages, a "13th month" salary bonus, and so on. For this, he needed money. Argentina's most lucrative sector was agriculture, so Perón took control of exports, using farm revenue to fund his schemes.

Thanks to its exports, Argentina had always run a trade surplus. But by the third year of Perón's presidency, the surplus had turned into a deficit. Inflation increased to 33% by 1949. Strikes were common. In a remarkably short time, the economy was a wreck. This brought a wave of dissent. So Perón called the protestors *traitors* and had them arrested and tortured.

Such corruption soaked through the entire society and still saturates it today. From the largest corporation to the humblest taxi driver, nothing in Argentina is completely straight. Dishonesty, double-dealing, inflation, defaults: they are all part of public life. And there's no sign of that changing any time soon.

"If you tried to follow all the laws," explains our friend, an attorney, "you'd go out of business.

DELUSIONS AND FANTASIES

In 2020, politics muscled into our private lives, like Antifa crashing a kumbaya singalong. At the Democratic Convention, Joe Biden said, "[I won't] put up with foreign interference in our most sacred democratic exercise: voting."[14]

It took a remarkable suspension of disbelief to think foreigners would want to diddle with US elections. We had a worn-out husk, ready to go along with everything, on one side. On the other was a delusional grifter, who might do anything. Why would any foreign nation bother to meddle? As Napoleon put it, "Never interrupt your enemy when he's making a mistake."[15]

But the mistake lay deeper than the candidates. Americans from both political parties now favor more government spending, more bailouts, more giveaways, and more meddling with trade, industry, and commerce.

Surely, the dollar would suffer. The feds would print money to cover their excess spending. Then, eventually, prices would rise. It happened to Diocletian. It would surely happen to Joe Biden.

WEEP FOR THE NATION

"It's madness. Weep for the nation."

A neighbor stopped by. He was talking about Argentina. The Argentines were running out of money. Real money. Which for them is US dollars. Compared to their pesos, the dollar was golden. But, according to Bloomberg, they only had $6 billion left. Not much when you have $323 billion in foreign debt.

Of course, the gauchos had been down this road so many times, they could drive it drunk, with their eyes closed. In 2001, they set a record, defaulting on $95 billion in loans. In May 2020, they defaulted on $65 billion. And by September they were lifting the seat cushions, looking for loose change. What to do? Raise taxes.

Going forward, Argentines seeking to purchase dollars for savings would need to pay a new 35% tax on top of the previous 30% so-called solidarity tax, and they'd still be limited to exchanging no more than $200 a month. The extra levy would also affect credit card purchases in dollars.

But Argentines can spot thieves, even with their masks on. Within seconds of the tax hike, there were lines in front of the black market currency dealers. People were eager to trade wads of pesos for a few US dollars. Overnight, the exchange rate rose from 130 pesos to the dollar to 150.

SOCIETIES EVOLVE

Politically, in Argentina and America, the conservatives, and the restraint they used to bring, are gone. Socially, the middle ground was disappearing: You were either red or blue, with us or agin' us. Economically, an explosive crescendo seemed to be approaching.

Societies are always evolving: taking up new things, leaving old ones behind. A half century ago, they left behind the gold-backed dollar. At the time, to many, it seemed like an improvement. But soon it became a hustle. It was a way to fund deficits and wars. Businesses, households, and the government all realized that borrowing money was easier than earning (or taxing) it. Now it's a full-blown racket.

It took a hundred years for the Fed to run up its first $3 trillion in holdings. It added another $3 trillion from March through May 2020. It was then promising to add nearly $5 trillion more.

Even the Argentines didn't go this far; their credit was never that good. In the COVID panic, they made the same mistake: locking down the productive economy in order to protect the unproductive part. And, yes, they too tried to replace real output with fake money, printing pesos and giving them to unemployed people. But at least they left the helicopters on the ground. No $1,200 "stimmie" checks dropped from the sky.

The difference was that everyone in Argentina knew the government was broke. Give them money? They would head straight for their nearest currency trader. By comparison, Americans are monetary naïfs. Inflation is a distant memory. The feds could hand out trillions, but no one wondered where it came from. No one imagined that the well might go dry.

TURNING BACK TO GOLD

Traditionally, gold was the best defense: a "last resort" money for at least 3,000 years. A cache of gold coins and objects, buried in England in the 8th century, was discovered a few years ago. Since its burial, England suffered wars, Viking invasions, the Norman Conquest, plagues, bankruptcy, bombing, and the decline of its once mighty empire. But not only were the coins still valuable when they emerged from the dirt, they were more valuable than when they went in.

Our guess is that gold will continue to do its work, especially in the first phase of the coming crisis. People will become more and more concerned about the dollar, the economy, and the stability of the country. They will buy gold as protection, even as they are unsure what they are protecting themselves against.

Not that gold will be a panacea. Desperate governments will call those who try to escape the currency crisis "parasites," "profiteers," or "class enemies." Gold may be banned, taxed, or even confiscated. In 1933, by executive order, Roosevelt made private ownership of gold illegal, subject to a $10,000 fine (a lot of money back then) and 10 years in jail. Contracts stipulating payment in gold were nullified. The ban was enforced for the next 40 years.

Today, people have another option: cryptocurrencies. Theoretically, bitcoin is superior to gold. It's easier to exchange and hide, there's no need to lug bags of gold coins around or to pay someone to store them for you and, unlike farmland, it doesn't need to be managed. It may be harder to tax, too.

But gold is a work of nature; Bitcoin is a work of people. And, so far, people's works have proven transitory. Bitcoin was a clever innovation, but there are millions of clever people. Who knows which of them will find a better bitcoin?

A friend wrote to caution us. "It is way too soon to write an obituary for the US dollar," he wrote. And he's right, of course. We are headed into a period of depression, political and social instability, and claptrap financial policies on a scale never attempted. The blowout inflation will come, but not right away. In the short run, the dollar might strengthen, not weaken.

But, no pure paper money has ever lasted for an entire credit cycle. The dollar will not be the first to rest among the shades. And its inevitable decline and fall will bring down the whole US capital structure: stocks, bonds, debt, credit, pensions, insurance payouts, Social Security, Medicare, the empire—the whole shebang.

For the first 189 years of the Republic, the economy grew strongly, with not even a hint of monetary stimulus (setting aside the War Between the States, when both sides did print money and fell into recession). As recently as the late 20th century, growth remained healthy, with scarcely any money printing. It wasn't until 1999, more than 200 years after the dollar was introduced, that the Fed began administering large doses of fake money. Between 2007 and 2021, it added $8 trillion to its balance sheet as growth rates fell.

Fake money is the poison that will eventually put the dollar in its grave. But there's no need to call the undertaker just yet. It will take years for the toxin to do its work. Just remember, you don't want to be holding your wealth in dollars when the organ music starts and the smell of lilies fills the funeral parlor.

TRUMPED

In 2016, Mr. Trump set forth a set of goals and promises, somewhat incoherent, which could broadly be summarized as follows:

- Build a wall (widely interpreted as a metaphor for tighter border controls, less immigration, and more protection for native-born Americanos).
- Pull out of the unwinnable wars in the Middle East.
- Cut the trade deficit (favoring domestic manufacturers).
- "Drain the swamp" (i.e., cut the "permanent government" of lobbyists, cronies, hacks, and has-beens).
- Put China in her place.
- Repeal and replace Obamacare.
- And balance the budget and pay off the federal debt.

Making no judgment as to whether they were worth doing, as near as we can tell, all were failures. There is no wall. The forever wars continue. The trade deficit is higher than ever; the swamp deeper; China stronger. Obamacare is still the law of the land. The budget is far out of balance. Federal debt is greater than ever.

During the four years of Trump's leadership, America's public debt grew faster as a percentage of GDP than under any US administration in the last four decades. When Obama left office, government debt was 100% of GDP. After just four years of Trump, it had risen to 135%, the biggest one-term increase in history.

A LONG BATTLE … LOST

Nearly 50 years ago, I, Bill Bonner, then a callow youth, naive and foolish, played a small role in trying to force some restraint onto federal finances: I pushed for a balanced budget amendment. I thought that requiring the feds to operate on a pay-as-you-go basis would keep the devil on a diet.

But the drive for such an amendment ran right into the swamp, where it sank without a trace. Restraint was the last thing the insiders wanted. And that was in the mid-1970s, when the deficit was running between $50 and $70 billion per year and total US debt, from the beginning of the Republic until the beginning of the Reagan administration, had still not reached $1 trillion.

Nearly 50 years later, we're no longer callow, the US owes $33 trillion, runs annual deficits of more than $1 trillion, and seems determined to stick with this kind of banana republic financing until the jungle swallows it up, like some ancient civilization.

But what can you do? The days are long past when we thought we could amend the Constitution, or even keep our hair from falling out. We're no longer so innocent. Fake money doomed the republic. And now it dooms the empire, too.

Marta works for us at our house at the ranch. She comes down from her mountain *puesto* (outpost) on foot, a hike of about six hours. She and her family are about as unsophisticated about money as anyone in Christendom, living in a mud house with a dirt floor. Their hands are as hard as boot leather. They get no newspapers. Watch no TV.

But even Marta is hip to the dangers of inflation.

"Could you change pesos for dollars?" she asked on the Saturday before we left.

You know you are near the popping of a stock market bubble when taxi drivers begin giving you stock tips. But where are you when subsistence farmers, high in the Andes, begin hedging currencies?

JAVIER VERSUS THE WORLD

"Today, I'm here to tell you the West is in danger," the newly elected president of Argentina, Javier Milei, began his address to the anointed gathered in Davos, Switzerland, for the World Economic Forum (WEF) on January 18, 2024.[16] The WEF is an annual event attended by gads of political leaders, their minions, tech billionaires, Hollywood A-listers, nongovernmental aid workers, climate change activists, and any other globalist world improvers who can get an invitation, afford it, and secure accommodations. Climate activists blocked a private airport leading up to the meeting in 2024 because so many private jets were used by the world's elite to get there. Milei flew to Davos in coach.

"In recent decades," Milei set the tone for his address, "the main leaders of the Western world have abandoned the model of freedom for different versions of what we call collectivism. Some have been motivated by well-meaning individuals who are willing to help others, and others have been motivated by the wish to belong to a privileged caste."

Regarding the history of his own country Milei warned the audience: "Thirty-five years after we adopted the model of freedom, back in 1860, we became a leading world power. And when we embraced collectivism over the course of the last 100 years, we saw how our citizens started to become systematically impoverished, and we dropped to spot number 140 globally."

And yet:

If we look at the history of economic progress, we can see how between the year zero and the year 1800 approximately, world per capita GDP practically remained constant throughout the whole reference period.

If you look at a graph of the evolution of economic growth throughout the history of humanity, you would see a hockey stick graph, an exponential function that remained constant for 90% of the time and which was exponentially triggered starting in the 19th century. . . . Now, it's not just that capitalism brought about an explosion in wealth from the moment it was adopted as an economic system, but also, if you look at the data, what you will see is that growth continues to accelerate throughout the whole period.

And throughout the whole period between the year zero and the year 1800, the per capita GDP growth rate remains stable at around 0.02% annually. So almost no growth. Starting in the 19th century with the Industrial Revolution, the compound annual growth rate was 0.66%. And at that rate, in order to double per capita GDP, you would need some 107 years.

Now, if you look at the period between the year 1900 and the year 1950, the growth rate accelerated to 1.66% a year. So you no longer need 107 years to double per capita GDP—but 66. And if you take the period between 1950 and the year 2000, you will see that the growth rate was 2.1%, which would mean that in only 33 years we could double the world's per capita GDP.

This trend, far from stopping, remains well alive today.[17]

The immense progress and prosperity accrued in countries governed by democratic capitalist systems, Melei believes, is under direct attack, even by many of the members of the WEF assembled to listen to him. Not that the "outsider" who campaigned for president carrying a chain saw to his campaign events was new to controversy. The prop was intended to convey what he intended to do to Argentina's administrative state should he be elected.

"Today," Melei observed for WEF elites,

states don't need to directly control the means of production to control every aspect of the lives of individuals. With tools such as printing money, debt, subsidies, controlling the interest rate, price controls, and regulations to correct so-called market failures, they can control the lives and fates of millions of individuals.

This is how we come to the point where, by using different names or guises, a good deal of the generally accepted ideologies in most Western countries are collectivist variants, whether they proclaim to be openly communist, fascist, socialist, social democrats, national socialists, Christian democrats, neo-Keynesians, progressives, populists, nationalists or globalists.

Ultimately, there are no major differences. They all say that the state should steer all aspects of the lives of individuals. They all defend a model contrary to the one that led humanity to the most spectacular progress in its history."[18]

Melei's full address is worth a read.

"Many Americans are in a tough spot right now," Connor O'Keefe wrote commenting on Melei's speech for the Mises Institute. In a hopeful essay entitled "The United States Needs Its Own Javier Melei," O'Keefe argues,

Eighty years of inflationist monetary policy has made life more expensive. And the heavy government involvement in many of the most important sectors—including healthcare, housing, education, and energy—has made it harder for younger Americans to afford the same lifestyles [13] as previous generations.

Further, the Federal Reserve's manipulation of interest rates has left the American people heavily in debt, low on savings, and forced to weather the recurring nightmare of the boom-bust cycle. Meanwhile, as Washington's decades of foreign intervention pre-dictably blow up [14] in its face, politicians are calling on the American people to fork over an ever-increasing amount of money in the futile effort to sustain an unchecked global empire. All while, at home, the government remains unable or unwilling to protect the lives [15] and property [16] of millions of Americans.

We may not yet have a poverty rate over 40 percent or infla-tion north of 140 percent like Argentina, but we're on a trajec-tory [17] that leads straight to that kind of economic ruin. It doesn't have to be this way. We know the way out.[19]

We applaud O'Keefe's optimism. But having witnessed the trajec-tory of the empire in the early decades of the 21st century, we won-der. Even if we do know the way out, it will take twin epic political and financial and crises before the populists come to their senses and the adults come back into the room. As they finally seemed to have done in Argentina.

"Crucially," O'Keefe suggests a course to set post-crises, "we need to put an end to Washington's drive for a globe-spanning empire. The American people have been forced to fund coups, bombing campaigns, and full-on wars that have killed millions and made the world less stable. History is full of empires overextending themselves and collapsing. Let's opt out of our own downfall."[20]

CHAPTER 16

GRAY SWANS

Among the jitter and jive from the World Economic Forum event Melei addressed in Davos was this gem. The elites are beginning to worry about a revolt of the masses. CNBC reports: "A growing detachment between political leaders and populations presents the biggest risk in a busy election year, according to Allianz CEO Oliver Bäte.

"The Allianz Risk Barometer published this month noted that political risk was already at a five-year high in 2023, with some 100 countries considered at high or extreme risk of civil unrest.

"Asked on the sidelines of the World Economic Forum in Davos, Switzerland, on Tuesday what he considers the main global risk at present, Bäte pointed to a lack of trust from populations in their governments across major democracies . . ."[1]

Why might the people lose faith in their deciders?

What went wrong in the 21st century is becoming a popular subject for historians. Here's Ed Snowden, now "on the lam" in Moscow: "If I had to explain how the American Century collapsed in just 3 points, I might say:

- Impoverishing the worker via union-busting & off-shoring
- Unleashing the state by abandoning the gold standard
- Continuously erasing essential liberties post-9/11."[2]

"EXORBITANT PRIVILEGE"

Snowden gets two out of three, which is not bad. The end of the gold standard allowed government spending, debt, and cockamamie projects to increase enormously. And, he's right that the feds took advantage of a fearful population, post-9/11, to grab more power in the Patriot Act. Union busting and off-shoring, too, may have contributed to lower compensation for the working classes, but the real source of the trouble was the funny money itself. Rather than make things and trade with other producers, Americans could buy on credit.

That is the benefit of what Giscard d'Estaing called the "exorbitant privilege" of having the world's reserve currency. After 1971, other countries took America's green paper and treated it as real money.

But there was a big downside. The situation was a little like that of Spain after the conquistadores had seized the gold of Mexico and Peru. Ships ladened with gold arrived in Spanish ports. The Spaniards were rich. The easy money from the new territories undermined honest industry. In the bubble economy of the early 16th century, Spain developed a trade deficit similar to that of the United States today. People took their money and bought goods from abroad. By the time the New World mined petered out, the Spanish were bankrupt. The Spanish government defaulted on its loans in 1557, 1575, 1607, 1627, and 1647.

REVOLT OF THE MASSES

An honest economy functions as people exchange goods and services for money and use the money to buy goods and services from others. They all become better off, together. Distort the money and you distort the whole transaction and sour the relationship between buyers and sellers. Some people no longer have to give to get; they just have to get their hands on this cheap "money."

The new money, created by the Fed passed through Wall Street. Much of it stuck to greedy hands.

No surprise then, that in the period 2009 to 2023, the fellow with a hedge fund, an IPO, a SPAC, venture capital, or just an investment portfolio watched his stocks rise by 87% after inflation. The poor working stiff, however, put his savings into a bank account, collected almost no interest, and its real value fell by 45%.

But now, America's paper money is petering out, too. The feds can still print it, but the inflation cat is out of the bag. More printing leads to higher prices and higher interest rates.

And now, the workers of the world are losing faith in their leaders. Why? Because the decisions made by the deciders were almost unbelievably bad. Iraq, Afghanistan, Patriot Act, Wall Street bailout, zero interest rates policy for 10 years, stimmies, lockdowns, Inflation Reduction Act—in every instance doing nothing would have been far preferable.

And thanks to this deranged activism, by 2024, the feds had added $29 trillion to the US national debt.

Are the elites stupid? Why did they make so many bad decisions?

CORRUPTING POWER

We've hammered on this nail many times, but we'll give it another whack. The future is unpredictable. But things follow patterns. Power corrupts, as Lord Acton reminds us. There is always an elite that takes control of a society. Over time these smart "deciders" find ways to make their own lives richer, more secure, or more illustrious.

Wars are losers for the people. But they are much beloved by the firepower industry; trillions of dollars come their way. Giveaways and boondoggles do little to help the common person, but they are great for the parasites, the grifters, and the insiders. Wall Street—and the whole investor class—made an estimated $30 trillion in "excess wealth," thanks to the Fed's low rates.

But what about the people themselves? Why do they go along? How come they now cling to two proven failures—Trump and Biden? Where are the lynch mobs? Where is the rope? Where is the candidate promising real reform?

Everyone plays their role in the glorious theater of history. The people, in a late, degenerate empire, have their bit parts, too. They give a "triumph" to their incompetent generals. They re-elect their jackass politicians. They cheer their own destruction and kiss the boots that kick them.

Thirty years ago, we looked into the future and set a goal for readers: "Two hours or so away from major cities, you are living in a sparkling clean, secure community. Your assets are intact, and in fact they are worth more than ever. You don't need to live in a big town. Computer and two-way interactive video connect you with like-minded people all over the world. You not only work but even shop, take courses, and visit your doctor through the communications network."[3]

That was our forecast in 1993. Only two years after Al Gore invented the internet. Word for word. Only two years after Al Gore "invented" the internet.[4] It is now a reality

A half century ago, Bill Bonner led a group called the National Taxpayers Union (NTU). We've been sounding the alarm about deficits ever since—first, in our public interest group, later, in our investment research company. (For nearly 30 years, Addison Wiggin ran a sizeable portion of the research company also dedicated to the same aims.)

From its inauspicious beginnings, NTU grew to become one of the most powerful citizens' organizations in the United States. The group helped the overhaul of the federal tax code under President Reagan in 1986 and championed the cause for a "Taxpayer Bill of Rights" in the late 1980s and 1990s.[5]

But we became aware as early as the 1980s and Reagan's strategy in the Cold War to spend the Soviet Union out of existed that the NTU had no hope of stopping the federal government's reckless spending. It was like arguing with a drug addict. Members of Congress would tell you what you wanted to hear. But they really just wanted more, more money to hand out to their favorite lobbyists.

In the mid-1980s, we moved on. Instead of trying to save the country, we'd at least try to save ourselves and our readers. Our investment publishing firm grew to have subsidiaries in 10 foreign countries, with more than a billion dollars in annual sales worldwide.

Most important, we gained contacts, leads, and insights.

My early business partner, James Davidson, went to Oxford. He met a fellow student, Bill Clinton, who later provided valuable context. Between us, we learned the benefit of getting in touch with the people who really knew what was coming down the pike—the deciders themselves—such as Margaret Thatcher, Milton Friedman, and Alan Greenspan. And we teamed up with others to learn more. Lord William Rees-Mogg, for example, was a former editor-in-chief of *The Times* of London, vice chairman of the BBC, and confidant of powerful British figures like Margaret Thatcher and Lord Rothschild. He was also a director of London's Private Bank and financial advisor to some of the world's wealthiest families.

Lord Rees-Mogg joined us as chairman of our London-based research arm, Fleet Street Publishing. He also coauthored a number of important books with Davidson, including *The Great Reckoning*, *Blood in the Streets*, and the *Sovereign Individual*. More important still, Davidson and Rees-Mogg pioneered a new way of understanding powerful financial trends, which I'll tell you about in a minute.

We wrote several books, including the early editions of the book you hold in your hands.

Though we write books, most of all, we read them. We study history. True, we're economists and investment advisors, and we have very useful connections in politics, finance, and the intelligence community. But our hobby, what we love best, is studying the past and using it to forecast the future. We'd do this even if it didn't pay a cent.

Sometimes the cycles of history are quite precise and mathematical. Other times we have to read hundreds of books and apply seasoned judgment just to get a glimpse of where the trends are headed.

History may not repeat itself, exactly. But there are templates, patterns, and cycles that help us to understand what comes next.

AVOIDING THE "BIG LOSS"

Our main goal in researching and writing about these trends, cycles is to avoid the Big Loss.

The idea of the Big Loss comes from the great investment writer Richard Russell. He pointed out that most people make most of their money incrementally, over a long period of time. They earn; they save; they invest. If they're lucky they end up with a nice little pile of money, but only after they are well into middle age.

The danger is not that they will miss the next great investment opportunity—AMZN, Google, Netflix, and so on. Those opportunities are few and unpredictable. Thousands of new companies emerge. Few survive.

The real danger for most people, over the age of 55, is not missing out on some unknown new innovation. Instead, it's getting whacked by something well-known that turns out to be untrue.

In the late 1990s, the threat of the Big Loss came from the faith that people placed in new technology—specifically, in the internet and its spin-off dot-coms. Heavily investing in the sector would be okay for a young person. They usually don't have much to lose, and the most important thing for them is to learn. The popping of the dot-com bubble provided a lesson they wouldn't soon forget.

The next Big Loss came in the real estate market. It looked like a sure winner. In 2002, the median house sold for $145,000. By 2007, it was $215,000. In other words, it gained about $15,000 per year. Assuming the buyer put down a 20% deposit, that was a return on cash of nearly 50% per year for five years. Smart investors figured out how to leverage it—"flipping" houses themselves or investing in housing-related industries.

There was a lesson to learn there, too. Over the next five years, the median house lost $45,000 in value. Buyers in 2007 would have seen their entire 20% deposit wiped out. As homeowners, they could hold on for another five years and they would have been okay. Prices came back. But the speculator, flipping multiple houses or buying shares in a go-go mortgage lender, was doomed. In June 2009, in an article cleverly titled "Angelo's Ashes,"[*] the New Yorker looked back at one of the great mortgage finance businesses and its founder, Angelo Mozilo: ". . . Countrywide Financial Corporation was regarded with awe in the business world. Fortune published a story in September, 2003, called 'Meet the 23,000% Stock,' which said that Countrywide had 'the best stock market performance of any financial services company in the Fortune 500, measured from the start of the Great Bull Market over two decades ago.' Shareholders who had invested a thousand dollars in 1982 would in 2003 have more than two hundred and thirty thousand dollars."[6]

On January 11, 2008, Bank of America announced it would buy Countrywide for four billion dollars in stock—a sixth the amount of its market value before the crisis began.

That was a loss of 83%.

BONDS GO BUST

The next big opportunity for a Big Loss came in cryptos. A few people got rich—especially those who got out early. Most cryptos were dreamy scams. Pity the poor investors who put their whole wad into them.

And then came a Big Loss in an area that should have offered no loss at all—bonds. An oft-stated allocation rule is that you should subtract your age from 100; the remainder is how much of your money you should have in stocks. Obviously, as you get older the allocation to equities (considered risky) goes down.

The rest, typically, is invested in the safety of bonds. But bonds are less safe, now that the feds have shown themselves willing to "print" their way out of any emergency. That's why we have no bonds in our own portfolio. Since 2020, the US Aggregate Bond Index is down 17%. After inflation, investors have lost about a third of their value.

US Treasury bonds should be about the safest credit in the whole world. But they've been going down for the last 39 months, the longest drawdown in history, so odds are that they will recover in the months ahead. But they are far from safe.

The Big Loss always comes as a surprise. You think you can depend on real estate, bonds, stocks? Where will the next Big Loss come from?

THE INFORMATION REVOLUTION

"Information" is not the same as "energy." Take away the energy and billions of people die. But take away the Information Revolution and what happens? That would only send us only back into the 1980s. We're old enough to recall the "world before the internet" and what we remember about it was this: It wasn't bad. Maybe even better.

The things that matter—the things we could feel, see, hear, and taste—have always mattered. Following the Information Revolution they were very similar to those we have today. We lived with central heating and air conditioning. We ate food that came from all over the world. We laughed at ourselves and others. We watched TV for amusement and read the newspapers for information. All in all, it was a satisfactory time.

After 1990 things generally went downhill. Growth rates went down. Debt went up. Wages went nowhere. Our politics became disagreeable and dysfunctional. And we couldn't laugh the way we used to—so many ideas, topics, and memes become off-limits.

And somehow, with all that information at our fingertips we lost track of things we had known by men who have been dead for hundreds of years: You can't spend your way to prosperity. You can't bomb your way to security. The Bush, Obama, Trump, and Biden administrations tried to do both.

The major difference between before and after the Information Revolution was that post-1990, we had many more ways to fritter away our time and our money. In 1990 approximately zero time or money was spent in thrall to electronic devices, because there weren't any. Today, the average American spends eight hours and five minutes per day on digital devices.[7] In other words, most of our waking hours are spent looking at a video screen.

And the typical family today is likely to spend as much on phone, streaming services, and electronic hardware as it spent on rent in the 1980s.

NOT THE FIRST TIME

We make no judgment as to whether this is a good thing, we only note that it didn't really seem to increase Americans' wealth, health, or the quality of their lives.

But let's turn back to the specific question: Are the makers of these electronica—the Magnificent 7 stocks—setting up investors for the Big Loss?

The answer: yes, probably.

Every once in a while, investors come to believe that a stock or a group of stocks will be their ticket to wealth. They buy the favored asset. Its price increases, suggesting to other investors that they should "get in," too. The price goes up further, proving that they were right and drawing in even more investors at even more unrealistic prices.

The Nifty Fifty, dot-coms, houses and mortgage finance, pot stocks, cryptos, NFTs fractional ownership—this won't be the first time.

Psychologically, you tell yourself you'll just get out if the go-go favorites begin to go down. But when they slip, you're not ready to give them up. "They'll go back up," you say to yourself. Then, when they slip further you don't want to take the loss. "It's just a dip," you say, "I'll wait for the bounce; then I'll sell out." Then, after a further drop in price, you say: "Geez, I can't sell now; I've lost too much money." You wait. The price bounces. You still don't sell; now you think you were right all along. Then, the stock goes down again. And finally, you give up, you sell at the bottom. You have just taken the Big Loss.

Most of our subscribers are over the age of 50. They make money slowly and carefully, from their businesses, their professions, and their investments. They build their wealth over an entire career; the worst thing that can happen is that they lose it, because they don't have time to make it back.

PEACE OF MIND

Taking the big tech as a whole, the sector has a price to earnings ratio (P/E) of 36.[8] So, if you were to buy the whole bunch, lock, stock, and silicon chip, and collect all the earnings, you'd have to wait a long time to earn back your money. After taxes, assuming earnings remained constant, it would take you until about 2080.

Of course, most of us will be dead by then. And the world will be much different—especially the world of new technology. In half a century, the companies themselves will probably be worth very little.

Nobody is going to buy the whole companies. Instead, they are going to buy tiny pieces of them, aka, stocks. And stock prices go up and down. When we compare the Dow 30 industrial stocks to gold, for example, we see that we could have bought the entire Dow, back in 1929, for 18 ounces of gold. Today, how much will the leading Dow stocks cost? You guessed it, about 18 ounces of gold.

So, you can't really expect capital appreciation from your stock investments. In real money terms—gold—you'll get nowhere.

What you can expect is a share of the earnings. That's why owning a business of your own is usually better than owning a stock in someone else's business. When you own it yourself, you get 100% of the profits to do with as you please. When you own stock in a public company, you only get what the directors give you—usually a dividend of less than 5% of your investment. But here, too, the Magnificent 7 stocks are likely to be a big disappointment. The current dividend yield on the group is only 0.18%. So, if you invest $100,000 you can expect a dividend check of $180—about enough for a bus ticket to the annual shareholders' meeting, maybe.

In short, in dividends as well as capital gains, the reward is likely to be small. The risk, however, is that you'll take the Big Loss, something we'd prefer to avoid.

THE DEBT, THE DOLLAR, AND THE POINT OF NO RETURN

A bubble in tech stocks are one thing. What about a bubble in the currency itself?

Figure 16.1 shows total Federal debt as a percentage of gross domestic product (GDP) going back to the pivotal "disco age" event in 1971. Debt-to-GDP is a measure of what a country owes with what it produces on a very large scale. The ratio is one metric used to reliably indicate a country's ability to pay back its debts.

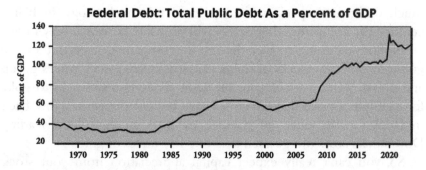

FIGURE 16.1   Debt-to-GDP Ratio Hits 128%.
A study published by Hirschmann capital revealed: "Since 1800, 51 out of 52 countries with gross government debt greater than 130% of GDP have defaulted, either through restructuring, devaluation, high inflation, or outright default." In 2020, the US debt-to-gdp ratio hit 128%. The upward trend line remains intact.
Source: US Federal Reserve St. Louis. https://fred.stlouisfed.org/series/GFDEGDQ188S

For seven decades, long before the pandemic, the peak in the ratio was 146% in 1946. The United States ran up a hefty bill while financing its own troops in World War II as well as with the aid it rendered to the Allies. Once the war ended, so did the deficit spending and borrowing.

The Korean "Police Action," for example, was mostly paid for with tax revenues. Under the Eisenhower administration year-over-year deficit spending approached zero. Ike set the tone. And despite the "butter and guns" campaigns of Johnson and the inflationary mayhem of the Nixon and Carter eras, the debt-to-GDP remained fairly constant.

By 1981, before Reagan took over policy, the debt to GDP-to-ratio had reached a post-war low of 31%. And now?

Following a huge spike in federal spending during the COVID lockdowns, the ratio hit 128% in 2020. The spike is easily explained. The economy, which had come to a virtual standstill because of government enforced lockdowns, shrank. As the economy began to open back up, GDP began to recover; government spending did not.

The current ratio is 123%. Why does that matter?

"When a government debt-to-GDP ratio goes over 130%," writes Dan Denning of Bonner Private Research, "it almost always marks a point of no return for a monetary regime."[9]

Denning cites research published by Hirschmann Capital. In a report published in 2020 Hirschman showed that, "Since 1800, 51 out of 52 countries with gross government debt greater than 130% have defaulted, either through restructuring, devaluation, high inflation, or outright default."[10]

"The U.S. is at an historical tipping point," Denning explains. "We've been at war with 'terror' for over twenty years and at war with crime, drugs, and poverty for a lot longer). History shows that any time a government lives this far beyond its means, some sort of default is inevitable. It's our view that 'high inflation' will be the form of default this time around—*a 'soft default.'*"[11]

Among the nondiscretionary spending items the US government has to "print money" for is interest on debt already incurred. Interest on the national debt alone is forecast to cross the headline-grabbing sum of $1 trillion in 2024.

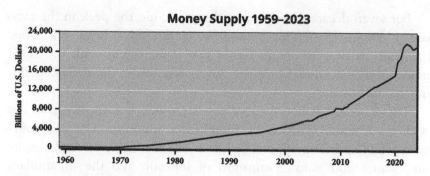

FIGURE 16.2 Money Supply Soars: The Root Cause of Today's Inflation.
Money supply in the US had been trending steadily upward since the dot.com bust in 2001. The pandemic era economic disruption and resulting policies really kicked "cash" into high gear resulting in a 40-year historic rate of inflation.
Source: US Federal Reserve, St. Louis. https://fred.stlouisfed.org/series/M2SL

"Once you have to print money hand over fist just to keep up with your spending each year," Denning observes, "you're on your way to monetary ruin. The United States is well on its way."[12]

Which helps to explain why the Federal Reserve has also been grabbing headlines in a blow-by-blow cage match with 40-year inflation highs since 2021.

Figure 16.2 captures the nature of the Fed's challenge. The money supply has grown by 36% since March 2020 and grown by over 160% since the zero interest rate policy and quantitative easing era began in response to the global financial crisis of 2008—2009.

"Inflation is not a price problem," Denning gets to the crux of the matter. "It's a money problem, a *too much* money problem. Yes, supply chains are a factor in today's prices. And yes, food and energy prices are higher because of the war in Ukraine—where the world gets a lot of its food, fertilizer, and energy. But today's CPI [Consumer Price Index] number is the harvest of years of too much money printed by our central bank policy makers."[13]

"There is no need for a country with a printing press and the world's reserve currency," Denning asserts, "to ever formally default on debt."[14]

And there's the rub and what makes the BRICS+ countries— Brazil, Russia, India, China, South Africa—attempt to develop a viable alternative currency to the US dollar, a primary target for a what economists call a "gray swan" event.

COMETH THE GRAY SWAN

A "gray swan" is a term used by economists to describe "a potentially very significant event whose possible occurrence may be predicted beforehand but whose probability is considered small."[15]

In other words, a grey swan event can be reasonably forecast given a current trend. But given human beings being abnormally hobbled by the "normalcy bias" most people don't expect the events will actually ever happen. And yet these events do happen. "Because there is a slight chance the event will occur it should be anticipated, particularly as it could shake up the world economy and stock market," *Investopedia* blandly advises.[16]

We've been tracking gray swans all our lives. In the late 1980s, we were concerned about a coming crash in Japan. The crash did come in 1989. Japanese stocks have still not recovered. In our daily investment e-mail, the *Daily Reckoning*, we warned about a crash in the US stock market in 1999. The dot-coms crashed the following year.

The original edition of this book was written in 2005–2007, and as you're aware, we told readers to get out of speculative real estate. The subsequent mortgage finance collapse caused 4 million people to lose their homes.

For years, after 2010, we warned that the Fed's ultra-low rates and the Treasury's money printing would lead to consumer price inflation. By 2022, inflation ran as high as 9%. Astute readers have made a fortune following some of our advice; more important, many have avoided the Big Loss.

We've been fortunate. We are interested in, explore, and write about alternative ideas. We've been at it for a long time. As you have likely gathered, we're often at odds with the politicians and the legacy press. The mainstream—media and politicians—cannot admit that there are problems. They are often the cause. Sometimes right. Sometimes wrong. But always on the case.

Now, we believe, the world is on the cusp of more important changes than any we've described before. More important, even, than any of the crises mentioned here. In the next 18 months, more money will be made—and lost—than ever before in world history.

Among the candidates for disruption: the US will lose the "exorbitant privilege" of printing the world's reserve currency.[17]

THE WORLD'S RESERVE CURRENCY

You'll recall (from Chapter 8) in 1971 the US abandoned the Bretton Woods Exchange Rate system, which allowed foreign governments to exchange their holdings of US dollars with US gold held in reserve. After seeing the US rack up enormous debts on a failed war in Vietnam, social Johnson's Great Society, and the War on Poverty, foreign governments cried foul and wanted to take shipment of their gold. Nixon realized he had to end the era of gold-backed dollars or risk depleting the nation's gold reserves.

Closing the "gold window"[18] presented its own set of global economic challenges. The US dollar had enjoyed reserve currency status for 27 years. The dollar was the currency of choice for most nations of the world during the rapid economic expansion following World War II.

With a stroke of panic-inspired statesmanship, President Nixon and then Secretary of State Henry Kissinger convinced King Faisal of Saudi Arabia to accept only US dollars as payment for oil. In exchange, they pledged to protect the Saudi monarchy, and all its oil fields, from anyone who might choose to seize them, enemies domestic and foreign alike.

King Faisal agreed. And, by 1975, he had persuaded the member nations of OPEC to agree, too. Kissinger christened the pricing mechanism the "petrodollar." Rather than being backed by gold, the dollar would be backed by the global oil market. The agreement was so successful it prolonged the dollar's status as the world's "reserve currency" for another 50 years—sans gold.[19] It also pitted the empire irreparably against the Soviet Union, Libya and Iran.[20]

Likewise, the monetary innovation known as "petrodollar recycling" was born.[21] The phenomenon that gave birth to our unprecedented 50-year secular bull market in US bonds.[22] Warren Buffett is quoted to have dubbed it as one of the most "extraordinary" bubbles in financial history.[23]

Buffet's "extraordinary bubble" allowed the empire's citizens its delusions—to live beyond their means, to print unlimited amounts of money at virtually *no* cost, to spend more than earned, consume more than produce, import more than export. Ultimately, the economic bubble allowed the US government to borrow *excessive* amounts of money at *obscenely* low rates and build up *enormous* trade and budget deficits with few adverse effects.

The security agreement behind the petrodollar emboldened the US military to establish its presence globally. Beyond the Middle East, it maintains troops on every continent. "As of September 2022," reads a report by Hope O'Dell, "there were 171,736 active-duty military troops across 178 countries, with the most in Japan (53,973), Germany (35,781), and South Korea (25,372). These three countries also have the most U.S. military bases—120, 119, and 73, respectively. There are around 750 U.S. military bases in at least 80 countries, though Al Jazeera says the number 'may be even higher as not all data is published by the Pentagon.'"[23]

Alas, not every nation is so amenable to continue to grant the US its exorbitancy. In 2006, a report titled *Iran Next U.S. Target* sighted the launch of an Iranian oil exchange as Americas number 1 threat, hailing it to be the real "economic weapon of mass destruction."[24] The report was voted by alternative media outlet Project Censored as one of the top 10 censored stories of that year.[25] By 2008, despite all US efforts to crush it, Iran managed to successfully and silently get a version of this exchange up and running.[26] The early exchange was a beta test to establish its validity on global commodity markets priced outside the dollar.

In late August 2023 the so-called BRICS nations—Brazil, Russia, India, China, and South Africa—gathered in Johannesburg, South Africa, for their annual meeting. The moniker "BRICS" was originally an acronym coined in 2001 by former Goldman Sachs economist Jim O'Neill who used it in a paper to "highlight the economic potential of Brazil, Russia, India and China for future investors."[27]

Despite statements from the host country South Africa that an alternative currency to the dollar was not on the agenda for the meeting, Brazilian president Luiz Inacio Lula da Silva broke ranks and made the proposal a talking point all the same.[28] During the meeting, the member nations also voted to accept Argentina, Egypt, Ethiopia, and the United Arab Emirates to join as full members from January 1, 2024.

Notably, Saudi Arabia, and Iran—the principle benefactor and detractor, respectively—of the petrodollar, were also invited.[29]

With the new members, the BRICS account for 40% of the world's population. Another 23 nations have applied for membership.

The next vote will take place in early October 2024 in Kazan, Russia. Existing member nations voted unanimously in support of Russia presiding over the next meeting.[30] As challenging as it might be to get Brazil, Russia, India, China, and South Africa on the same legal footing to support an international currency, not to mention their competing global ambitions, the subject is already on the table. The stewards of the world's current reserve currency can only sit by idly gloating while they try.

WEAPONIZING THE DOLLAR

In early 2022, following the Russian invasion of Ukraine, US-led Western sanctions froze nearly half of Russia's foreign currency reserves. They also removed major Russian banks from SWIFT, the international network banks use to facilitate payments.

Later in the same year, the US imposed restrictions on exports of semiconductor technology to China. Shirley Ze Yu, a senior visiting fellow at the London School of Economics, told Al Jazeera, "As the US weaponizes the dollar in the Russian and Iran sanctions, there is increasing desire by other developing countries to seek alternative currencies for trade, investment, and reserves, as well as developing alternative multilateral clearance systems outside of SWIFT."

Further, Yu notes, as the US Federal Reserve has raised interest rates in recent years, "developing countries have widely suffered from paying higher interests on their dollar debt and battling the exchange rate impact from a strong dollar. The interest to borrow in local currencies or other currencies is strongly motivated by economic considerations."[31]

The "BRICS [are] not anti-West. We are not in competition," South Africa's BRICS ambassador, Anil Sooklal, said after playing host to the August meeting. "Nor are we against the dollar. But what we are against is the continued dominance of the dollar in terms of global financial interactions."[32]

"The US dollar served its purpose since the end of WWII and became the major foreign exchange reserve currency," Brazilian economist Ricardo C. Amaral forecast a decade ago. But, he suggests more forcefully, "the days of the U.S. dollar playing that special role . . . has reached the end of the line . . . [and] today that system is very sick."[33]

"The US supplied the Allies in WWII and got paid in gold." The Mida Gold Group helps us with an historical review:

> After the war, countries linked their currencies to the US dollar, which was linked to gold. The Gold Standard ended completely in 1971, but the US dollar's reserve status remained. Today more than 61% of all foreign bank reserves are denominated in US dollars. Nearly 40% of the world's debt is in US dollars. **Reserve currency** status has both benefits and drawbacks. The benefits are lower exchange rate risk and greater buying power, and the drawbacks are artificially low-interest rates that can spur asset bubbles. Since 1450 there have been six major world reserve currency periods. Portugal (1450–1530), Spain (1530–1640), Netherlands (1640–1720), France (1720–1815), Great Britain (1815–1920), and the United States from 1921 to today. If you notice the average currency span is 94 years. The US dollar presently has been the world's reserve currency for roughly 99 years.[34]

If something isn't done to restore confidence in the dollar, says the legendary investment biker Jim Rogers, it will "lead to a huge decline in the standard of living of U.S. citizens like nothing we've seen in nearly a century."[35] Bill Gross, the world biggest bond investor, has advised all his clients that if they had just one investment idea, it should be an investment in a non-dollar, non-euro currency.[36]

WHAT IF WE'RE WRONG?

We've been exploring the "facts of life," the deep current unseen, uncharted, and misunderstood. Amid all the noise and distractions of "politics," who talks about the hidden causes—the megapolitics—of public policy decisions?

Why does the US favor low interest rates over high ones? Why does it favor deficits over surpluses? Why did it abandon the successful (over 18 decades) discipline of a gold-backed dollar in favor of worthless "paper" money?

Why did the US launch unnecessary wars with Iraq and Afghanistan? And now, why does the US government back Israel and not Palestine?

Why does it back the Ukraine and not Russia?

You will say that it aims to do the "right" thing; but how does it know what is right?

We could return to these and other aggravating questions over and over again. For now, we address a more pressing investment concern: what if we're wrong?

A MORE PRESSING CONCERN

The primary trend for investors turned around in two moves. First, bonds topped out in July 2020. Then, stocks reached their apogee at the end of the following year. We urged investors to move to MSM—maximum safety mode—while we awaited a crisis.

Deflation was the immediate threat, not inflation. Higher interest rates would cause financing problems, we believed. Another shoe was bound to drop—a penny loafer of a big company suddenly unable to pay its bills, a steel-toed government debt auction going "no bid," a fast-moving Nike crash in the stock market.

This crisis, we figured, would cause the Fed to panic, to "pivot," lowering its key lending rate, while letting inflation rip.

But what happened? So far, the bond market did as expected—with the sharpest selloff in bond prices (along with the steepest increase in yields) ever seen. When the Fed began raising rates, in February 2022, its key lending rate was actually more than 5% *below* zero. Now, it's more than 5% above zero in nominal terms, and inflation adjusted (depending on which measure you use) it's about 1% or 2% positive.

The 10-year Treasury yield, on average through 2020, was under 1%. Now, it's four times as high. Interest rates have come down recently. But they haven't gone anywhere near the all-time lows of 2020. Inflation rates have fallen, too, as expected.

THE GOOD OLE DAYS

As we began the update of this edition, stocks had behaved more or less as we thought they would. The market sold off in 2022. Then, after losing almost 8,000 points, in September 2023 the Dow stabilized. But then, for no apparent reason, it recovered—led by a manic performance of the big techs, including a bubble-like enthusiasm for AI.

Then, out of the blue—unprovoked—the Fed appeared to "pivot." No crisis. No panic. And no real reason to drop the fight against inflation; after all, core inflation is still about twice the Fed's 2% target.

Was it a "pivot error," as we have suggested? Or was the Fed trying to help the Biden team win re-election by giving the system a little holiday cheer?

We don't know. But investors believe the good ole days are back. Matthew Fox explained a chart of the week in late 2023 for Yahoo!Finance's *Markets Insider*:

> The long-term bull market in stocks is alive and well after the Dow hit a record high this week. The US stock market has been in a secular bull market since 2013, when it broke out of a 13-year sideways consolidation range that began at the peak of the 2000 dot-com bubble.
>
> Bank of America highlighted the long-term nature of the Dow in its chart, as the index is typically marked by long periods of sideways consolidation, which is then followed by long-term breakouts to the upside. The firm expects that the long-term upside trend for stocks will continue.[37]

What was going on? Was the low of September 2022 just another opportunity to "buy the dip?" Is the bull market that began in August 1980 still intact, with an even higher high still ahead?

Who knows? But we'd be careful about coming to a conclusion too soon. While stocks are up, they're still below the highs set two years ago when measured in gold or adjusted for inflation.

The lower rates of inflation we're seeing do not mean that the Fed has won its fight with rising prices. Consumer prices are still going up; just not as fast. And inflation is probably ebbing largely because the economy is slowing, not because the economy is getting more color in its cheeks.

RUNNING ON AIR

"Dere's dem dat's smart ... an' dere's dem dat's good," said Uncle Remus. Many young people today can't even identify Uncle Remus.

Some of their elders might want to arrest you for quoting him in the original dialect. But the man was a genius.

When we were young, we were a lot smarter. But as the years go by, many of the things we thought were smart don't seem so smart anymore. And now we realize that no matter how smart we think we are, we are never quite smart enough. We think stocks are going up, we think we can build a better world in Mesopotamia, we think we can tell the person down the street how to discipline their children or decorate their house. But what do we know?

It is easier to be smart than to be good; that's why there are so many smart people, and so few good ones. Smart people get elected to high office. They run major corporations. They write editorials for the newspaper. Pity the poor good people; they go to parties and have nothing to say that is not mocking and cynical. Others talk about their smart deals, their smart ideas, their smart plans and successes. People crowd around them; a smart person grows taller as they speak. The good person shrinks.

But in economics and investing, it is virtue, not brainpower, that really pays off. "All the world is moral," said Emerson. It is moral in the sense that if you are careless enough to step on a hoe, the handle will hit you in the face.

One generation takes the virtuous path. The next is likely to slip off, honoring the old virtues in speech, but not in act. The oldest generation of Americans remembers the Great Depression. They borrowed reluctantly, saved eagerly, and made the United States the greatest power on earth. Their children still talked their parents' talk, but didn't mind walking off in a different direction when the wind was at their backs. And their grandchildren? The newest generation seems to have no regard whatsoever for the virtues of their grandparents or the futures of their grandchildren. They disregard the wisdom of the dead and load up the unborn with debt.

The end of the empire may be near or far. We don't know. It seems nearer now. Washington will probably not be sacked any time soon. But the imperial money—the dollar—is in danger, you'll likely agree. America's central bankers not only fail to protect it, they invite the barbarians to destroy it . . . slowly. And in perpetuity.

It is as if the police had not only gone on strike but also started holding up liquor stores and mugging pedestrians. Because the central bank won't protect your wealth, you'll have to do it yourself. How? In the old-fashioned way—by packing heat, holding reserves of your own. Traditionally, what the central banks hold in reserve is gold.

Mr. James Surowiecki wrote a wise and moronic piece on gold in the *New Yorker*. His wisdom is centered on the insight that neither gold nor paper money are true wealth, but only relative measures, subject to adjustment.

"Gold or not, we're always just running on air," he wrote. "You can't be rich unless everyone agrees you're rich."[38]

In other words, there is no law that guarantees gold at $450 an ounce. It might just as well be priced at $266 an ounce, as it was when George W. Bush took office for the first time. Since then, a man who counted his wealth in Krugerrands has become 200% richer.

But gold wasn't born yesterday, or four years ago. Mr. Surowiecki noticed that the metal has a past, just as it has a present. He turned his head around and looked back a quarter of a century. The yellow metal was not a great way to preserve wealth during that period, he notes. As a result, he sees no difference between a paper dollar and a gold doubloon, or between a bull market in gold and a bubble in technology shares.

"In the end, our trust in gold is no different from our trust in a piece of paper with 'one dollar' written on it," he believes. And when you buy gold, "you're buying into a collective hallucination—exactly what those dot-com investors did in the late nineties."[39]

Pity he did not bother to look back a little further. This is the moronic part. Although Mr. Surowiecki looked at a bit of gold's past, he did not see enough of it. Both gold and paper dollars have histories, but gold has far more. Both gold and dollars have a future. But, and this is the important part, gold is likely to have more of that, too.

The expression, "as rich as Croesus," is of ancient origin. The king of historic Lydia is remembered, even today, for his great wealth. Croesus was not rich because he had stacks of dollar bills. Instead, he measured his richness in gold. No one says "as poor as Croesus." We have also heard the expression, "not worth a Continental," referring to America's paper money during the Revolutionary War era. We have never heard the expression, "not worth a Krugerrand."

Likewise, when Jesus said, "Render unto Caesar that which is Caesar's," he referred to a denarius, a coin of gold or silver, not a paper currency. The coin had Caesar's image on it, just as today's US money has a picture of Lincoln, Washington, or Jackson on it. Dead presidents were golden back then. Even today, a gold denarius is still about as valuable as it was when Caesar conquered Gaul. America's dead presidents, whose images are printed in green ink on special paper, lose 2% to 5% of their purchasing power every year. What do you think they will be worth 2,000 years from now?

A few years before Jesus, Crassus, who had made his fortune on real estate speculation in Rome, decided to put together an army to hustle the east. Alas, such projects almost always meet with disaster; the attempt by Crassus was no exception. He was captured by the Parthians and was put to death in an unusually cruel and costly way. He did not end his days with paper money stuffed down his throat, and certainly not dollar bills. No, they poured molten gold down his gullet—or so the story has it.

EVERYTHING THAT EVER HAS BEEN

Gold has a long history. And during its history, many was the time that humans were tempted to replace it with other forms of money—which they believed would be more convenient, more modern, and most importantly, more accommodating. Gold is hard to find and hard to bring up out of the earth. By its nature, the quantity of gold is always limited.

Paper money, by contrast, offers irresistible possibilities. The list of bright paper rivals is long and colorful. You will find hundreds of examples, from assignats to zlotys, and from imperial purple to beer suds brown. But the story of paper money is short and predictable. Since the invention of the printing press, a new paper dollar or franc can be brought out at negligible cost. Nor does it cost much to increase the money supply by a factor of 10 or 100—simply add zeros. It may seem obvious, but adding zeros does not add value.

Still, the attraction of being able to get something for nothing has always been too great to resist. That is what makes goldbugs so irritating: They are always pointing it out. Even worse, they seem to enjoy saying "There ain't no such thing as a free lunch," which comes as a big disappointment to most people.

Once people were able to create money at virtually no expense, no one ever resisted doing it to excess. No paper currency has ever held its value for very long. Most are ruined within a few years. Some take longer. Even the world's two most successful paper currencies—the US dollar and the British pound—have each lost more than 95% of their value in the past century, which is especially remarkable because both were linked by law and custom to gold for most of those years. For the dollar, the final link to gold was severed only 34 years ago.

Some paper currencies are destroyed almost absentmindedly. Others are ruined intentionally. But all go away eventually. By contrast, every gold coin that was ever struck is still valuable today; most have more real value than when they first came out of the mint.

Central bankers reported in early 2005 that 70% of them were increasing their reserves of euros. As for the world's erstwhile and present reserve currency, the dollar, they seemed to have, not growing reserves, but growing reservations. We also have reservations about the dollar. Whatever it is worth today or tomorrow, we are sure it will have less worth eventually. That it is not regarded as worthless already is remarkable. The average dollar is nothing more than electronic information. It exists thanks only to the ability of digital technology to keep track of it. Relatively few dollars ever make it to paper, and many of them end up in the pockets of Russian drug dealers and African politicians. Most dollars in most people's accounts are not even graced with the image of a dead president; when the end comes, they won't even be useful for starting fires.

It is imperial vanity that keeps the dollar in business. And it is vanity that will make it worthless. Economists want money they can control. Central bankers want money they can debase. And politicians want money they might get their mug on.

The trouble with gold is that it turns its back on world improvers, empire builders, and do-gooders. It is money that no central bank promotes and none destroys. It is money that exists only in a tangible form, a real metal—a number on the periodic table. "Gold goes up and down, just like other kinds of money," say economists. Which is true. "You can protect yourself from inflation in other ways," say the speculators. True again. "Gold pays no dividends or interest," say the investors. True.

Nor will gold cure baldness or add inches to your most private part. Even as money, gold may not be perfect. But it is better money than anything else.

Gold was around millions of years before the US dollar was invented. It will probably be around a billion years after. This longevity is not in itself a great recommendation. It is like buying a suit that will last longer than you do; there is no point to it. But the reason for gold's longevity is also the reason for its great virtue as money: It is inert; it yields neither to technology nor to vanity.

The world improvers will always be with us. They will spend more than they have, boss other people around, and generally make the world a worse place to live. They will offer proposals like those of Thomas L. Friedman. The nice thing about gold is that it is so unresponsive. It neither laughs nor applauds. Gold is money that no central bank promotes and none destroys.

Paper money is a handy tool for world improvers. They use it like politicians use civil service jobs and generals use heavy bombers—to get their way. Whatever the vapid ideal du jour, it takes money to pursue it. Given enough money, the poor can be fed and housed. The middle classes can be given free medical care and low-cost loans for houses. The upper classes can be given contracts and favors. Enemies can be summoned up, bombed, and reconstructed. Bread, circuses, war—the imperial program costs money.

How to get more money for these great new programs, these marvelously worthwhile ideals, these fabulous public spectacles? Gold flatly refuses to cooperate. It doesn't even give a reason. Instead, it stays as mute and reticent as a dead man in front of a television. No matter how persuasive the advertising, the man is not going to go for it.

Paper money, however, barely needs encouragement. Start up the presses! Lower the interest rate! Relax reserve requirements and lending standards! Sell more bonds! Create more paper! Paper money is ready to go along with anything. Like George W. Bush, it never met a boondoggle it didn't like. Sooner or later, it ends up as worthless as the projects it was meant to pay for.

Gold is merely the subversive investor's way of protecting himself.

Is. Was. Will be again. If things remained the same, there would be no need for verb tenses. But things do not remain the same, they change.

After a long while of remaining the same, investors begin to under-price change. A speculator can make money by betting against the present tense. But not always, not when the present tense only came into being recently. For that case, investors still price things based on the past. But after a long spell, investors begin to believe that that which is will be forever. They make their bets on a false premise by underpricing risk, underpricing change, and overpricing stability.

Everything in life has a beginning, a middle, and an end. Each day that passes in which present trends do not come to an end brings us a day closer to the day when they will.

"Stability leads to instability," said economist Hyman Minsky.[40] The longer things remain stable, the more people become convinced that they will never change. As long as the camel's back doesn't break, why not heap more straw on it?

We know the past tense—how America's empire of debt was built. What we don't know is the future tense—how and when it will end. It is like our own death; we know it will happen, but we don't want to think about it. Still, it is the sort of thing you want to be prepared for all the time. A sensible person might not know the hour or the place of their demise, but they do not doubt that it is coming. If they are smart, they are ready for death any day of the week. So is a sensible investor ready for the day a great empire collapses. They don't know when it will happen. And the longer it doesn't happen, the more they believe it might never happen at all. But nature smiles neither on vacuums nor monopolies. Empires are a monopoly on force; they don't last forever. What is peculiar and promises to be entertaining about the US debt empire is that it is more absurd than most, which is to say it is less likely to last very long. That does not mean that the United States will disappear. But you should be prepared for a write-down of its debt and its dollar at any moment.

What more needs to be said?

THE COMPANY OF CIVILIZED

The empire of debt grows larger, more incompetent, and more corrupt, day after day. In the early winter months of 2024, its debt $34 trillion. The *New York Times*, using rudimentary math, forecast it would be $55 trillion within a decade.[41] And that's just the rough, published number. It'll take a new AI-powered algorithm to actually keep pace with its unfunded liabilities. Who's going to pay it all back?

Who actually cares?

The debt has to be financed and refinanced. Interest rates jumped after the 9% inflation reading of June 2022. With higher interest rates, the debt became a bigger burden. Interest payments on the debt crossed $1 trillion annually in October 2023.[42]

It was a cost of empire, but of an empire that was already past tense. In 2023, it paid for missiles built in 2017 or 2005. It paid for the circuses of the Russian election interference and the COVID panic—both long since forgotten. It paid for the fuel used to subdue the Iraqis or to kill Afghans—already distant memories. It will continue paying for those things until 2033 and beyond.

Time is the enemy now. The empire tries to move into the future. But the weight of the past holds it back. By 2023, the cost of the debt—for empire past—was greater than the current defense budget. Every dollar needed to kill a new enemy had to compete with a dollar needed to pay the interest on debt incurred to kill an old one.

The entire system is beholden to the past and afraid of the future. Like an old man, it takes its steps carefully and avoids drafts. America's economy was once the most competitive in the world. But now, rather than compete, openly and honestly, it tries to close the door, stifle trade, and block the competition; that is the meaning of the "trade wars" and of attempts to withhold vital technology from the Chinese. Rather than embrace new ideas and new policies, America sticks with geriatric politicians and the same worn-out programs that have brought it to where it is. Rather than engage in an open discussion, the elites try to cancel ideas, censor the internet, and eliminate free speech.

And there is no sign that this is going to get anything but worse. Despite what both Joe Biden and Donald Trump called "the greatest economy ever" the US still can't pay its current expenses. The debt increases. And so do the imperial imbroglios.

The new fiscal year begins in October. The first two months of 2024 were already disaster. The government received $678 billion in tax receipts. It paid out $1,059 billion (or $1.059 trillion) to support the arts, pay off cronies, kill Palestinians, and other worthy causes.

This leaves a deficit for the two months of $383 billion.[43] For every dollar the feds spent, roughly two are borrowed. And if they keep on like this, the total deficit will be over $2 trillion for the year.

Any fool could see that it was a mistake to continue spending so much money. And it is easy to dismiss the phenomenon as "politicians doing stupid things." But that would miss the point. The things that they are doing aren't stupid; they are just disastrous.

Everybody's got to play a role in the empire's final chapters. The "intelligent" thing to do would be to retreat. Imagine Hitler pulling his troops back across the Oder, rather than continuing a death match with the Soviet Union? Imagine Napoleon making haste to get his entire army, intact, back to the west bank of the Rhine rather than pursue his ill-fated attack on Russia? Suppose Roman troops had been recalled from Gaul, from Spain, and North Africa, to defend the homeland? How differently things might have turned out!

Imagine now, a new president, in his state of the union address: "It was fun having an empire. But we can't afford it anymore. As commander-in-chief, I've recalled all the troops from their foreign bases. And I've instructed Congress that I will veto any budget or other temporary spending bill that isn't fully covered by incoming revenue."

America could then take her place in the company of civilized nations.

Fortunately for history, but unhappily for many of its leading figures, the empire bug seems to worm its way into the hegemon's brain—and turn that person into an idiot.

So it was on December 13, 2023, that 87 members of the Senate—an overwhelming majority—voted to advance further across the frozen steppes. That is, they eagerly devoted more money, which they didn't have, to the military and its suppliers, who didn't need it, for programs that were basically suicidal.

The war in the Ukraine was winding down; America's proxy war fighters, the Ukrainians, were the clear losers. Israel and Hamas are at war and the conflict threatens a wider involvement of all the Anglo-Saxon nations. When debating "aid" the question never arises. They need less money, not more; it would encourage them to end the butchery as soon as possible.

Israel's program of mass murder and ethnic cleansing, backed by the US, though, served a greater purpose. Here we see the elegant hand of history, carefully arranging the pieces on the board. An especially powerful empire—such as Napoleon's France or the Third Reich—is not easily defeated. It sometimes needs more than just a single enemy. It took dozens of fierce and desperate tribes, from all around the empire, and internal enemies, too, to bring down ancient Rome. Napoleon's famous defeat at Waterloo, too, required the combined efforts of England, Prussia, the Netherlands, and other Germanic duchies. The Wehrmacht, meanwhile, faced off against Britain, France, the US, Australia, New Zealand, Canada, and several other nations. This then is the genius of America's unhedged support for the Israelis rather than for the Palestinians. It helps to pit the US—or more broadly, the European ascendancy that has been on the top of the world for the last 500 years—against almost everyone else on the planet.

Among the "everyone else," of course, is one that may be in position to match the US empire's firepower. By 2023, China's economy was already bigger than that of the US, with considerably more manufacturing capacity. China also had technological skills that were in many ways equal or superior to those of the US.

As we've seen, all bureaucracies tend toward entropy and incompetence. The bigger they are, and the older they are, the more ineffective they are likely to be. This is merely an aspect of the same phenomenon that happens with debt. Every dollar of debt service is a tribute paid to the past. The more debt you have, the less you have left over to finance the future. So too, the bigger, and older, your military establishment the more suitable it becomes for fighting the wars of the past. The skills of your senior officers, the weapons systems, the tactics—all are drilled and devoted to a decisive victory against a long-dead enemy.

And there's the money, too. The more of a defense budget that is earmarked for retired personnel, legacy weapons, and huge, expensive armaments from the last war, the less is left for battlefield improvisation and adaptation in the next one. America spends billions on ships and planes that were designed many years ago, built many years ago, and then upgraded and modernized, also, many years ago. These contraptions may be dinosaurs in the world of fast-moving electronic warfare. But they must be maintained and serviced—at a cost of billions more—until they are finally blown to bits by an unencumbered enemy.

The money system itself is little different. It is exposed to time in the same way. The first dollars that are "printed up" have as much value as the ones already in existence. But as the system ages, the dollars become less virile. Over time, as they accumulate, they gradually lose their mojo. Then, the government has to print more and more of them to have the same impact. That is, ultimately, the problem with the whole empire of debt scam. Both the empire and the debt are hollow and unstable. The empire expands in order to draw more resources unto itself. But because it produces no extra resources itself, it must take them from elsewhere, by hook or by crook. The fake money system attempts to cover up the absence of real money by providing an ersatz alternative. But then, as more and more of it is put into service, the less useful it becomes. And, finally, the pile of confusion, contradictions, and fraud on which the whole enterprise rests—the whole empire with its mountain of debt—implodes.

So, you see, the US empire is doomed. It is a victim of its past success, which shaped its attitudes, its economics, its debt, its politics, its pensée, its weapons, its conceits and military doctrines, and its available resources. Americans played their part—sometimes heroic, sometimes sordid—in building the empire. Now, older and less dynamic, they must play their parts in its decline.

You do not want to go to your grave after saying an unkind word to your mother. Neither do you want to wake up to a dollar bust with a pile of Treasury bonds and pieces of green paper.

There is never a good time to die. Nor is there a good time for a depression and monetary collapse. Still, death happens. Be prepared. Say something nice to your mother. Offer a bum a drink. And buy gold.

NOTES

INTRODUCTION: THE BUBBLE EMPIRE, REDUX

1. https://thehill.com/business/4301871-annual-interest-payments-on-us-debt-cross-1t-bloomberg/#:~:text=The%20estimated%20yearly%20amount%20the,recent%20analysis%20by%20Bloomberg%20found.
2. https://www.visualcapitalist.com/u-s-share-of-global-economy-over-time/.
3. https://www.statista.com/statistics/262962/countries-with-the-most-prisoners-per-100-000-inhabitants/.
4. https://en.wikipedia.org/wiki/List_of_countries_by_life_expectancy.
5. https://www.factcheck.org/2010/11/ask-factcheck-trip-to-mumbai/.
6. https://www.secretservice.gov/careers/paths#:~:text=The%20Secret%20Service%20employs%20approximately,professional%20and%20technical%20support%20personnel.
7. Claes G. Ryn, "Appetite for Destruction: Neoconservatives Have More in Common with French Revolutionaries Than American Traditionalists," American Conservative, January 19, 2004.
8. John Chuckman, "America's Imperial Wizard Visits Canada," December 6, 2004, http://www.countercurrents.org/us-chuckman061204.htm.
9. https://www.reuters.com/world/us/eight-quotes-by-about-former-louisiana-gov-edwin-edwards-2021-07-12/.

10. https://www.epi.org/publication/ceo-pay-in-2022/#:~:text=Using%20 the%20realized%20compensation%20measure%2C%20the%20 CEO%2Dto%2Dworker,%2C%201980s%2C%20or%20early%201990s.
11. https://home.treasury.gov/policy-issues/coronavirus/assistance-for-american-families-and-workers/economic-impact-payments.
12. Ramsay MacMullen, *Corruption and the Decline of Rome*, Yale University Press, 1990.
13. https://interestingliterature.com/2023/02/shooting-an-elephant-key-quotes/#.
14. https://en.wikipedia.org/wiki/The_End_of_History_and_the_Last _Man#:~:text=The%20End%20of%20History%20and%20the%20Last%20 Man%20is%20a,reached%20%22not%20just%20.

CHAPTER 1: DEAD MEN TALKING

1. Margaret Wilson Oliphant, *The Makers of Venice, Doges, Conquerors, Painters and Men of Letters*, Burt, 1897.
2. Ibid.
3. Edward Gibbon, *The Decline and Fall of the Roman Empire*, Everyman's Library, 1993.
4. See note 1.
5. Edmund Randolph, 1787 Constitutional Convention.
6. James Madison, "The Federalist No. 10: The Utility of the Union as a Safeguard Against Domestic Faction and Insurrection (continued)," *Daily Advertiser*, November 22, 1787.
7. https://www.nps.gov/articles/000/constitutionalconvention-september17 .htm.
8. Costantino Bresciani-Turoni, *The Economics of Inflation: A Study of Currency Depreciation in Post-War Germany*, Routledge, reprint ed., 2003.
9. Karl Theodor Helfferich, Das Geld, Adelphi English ed., 1927, p. 650.
10. See note 7.
11. http://chinese-school.netfirms.com/abacus-Sir-John-Templeton-interview.html.
12. Nassim Nicholas Taleb, *Fooled by Randomness: The Hidden Role of Chance in Life and in the Markets*, 2nd ed., Texere, 2004.
13. Ibid.
14. Ibid.
15. https://www.gao.gov/assets/aicpaben20041204.pdf, slide 10.
16. See note 8.

17. https://www.cnbc.com/2023/10/20/us-wraps-up-fiscal-year-with-a-budget-deficit-near-1point7-trillion.html#:~:text=Economy-,U.S.%20wraps%20up%20fiscal%20year%20with%20a,near%20%241.7%20trillion%2C%20up%2023%25&text=The%20federal%20government%20wound%20up,trillion%2C%20up%20about%20%24320%20billion.
18. https://www.bea.gov/news/2005/us-international-trade-goods-and-services-january-2005.
19. Ibid.
20. https://tradingeconomics.com/united-states/balance-of-trade#:~:text=Gap%20Below%20Forecasts-,The%20US%20trade%20gap%20narrowed%20to%20%2463.2%20billion%20in%20November,%240.7%20billion%20to%20%2426.2%20billion.
21. See note 8.
22. https://fred.stlouisfed.org/graph/?g=VtLo.
23. Ibid.
24. https://www.investopedia.com/articles/investing/040115/reasons-why-china-buys-us-treasury-bonds.asp.
25. https://www.marketplace.org/2023/08/21/china-japan-us-treasuries-debt/.
26. https://en.wikipedia.org/wiki/Exorbitant_privilege.
27. https://www.brainyquote.com/quotes/dick_cheney_564190.

CHAPTER 2: EMPIRES OF DIRT

1. Paul Ratchnevsky (Thomas Nivison Haining, trans.), *Genghis Khan: His Life and Legacy*, reprint ed., Blackwell, 1993.
2. https://www.smithsonianmag.com/smart-news/other-men-who-left-huge-genetic-legacies-likes-genghis-khan-180954052/#:~:text=Since%20a%202003%20study%20found,stood%20as%20an%20unparalleled%20accomplishment.
3. "Changing Perceptions of Genghis Khan in Mongolia: An Interview with Dr. Ts. Tsetsenbileg by Yuan Wang," *Harvard Asia Pacific Review*, http://hcs.harvard.edu/~hapr/winter00_millenium/Genghis.html.
4. http://khubilai.tripod.com/mongolia/id3.html.
5. http://en.wikipedia.org/wiki/Genghis_Khan.
6. Francis Fukuyama, *The End of History and the Last Man*, Free Press, 1992.
7. http://www.rain.org/~karpeles/armadadis.html.
8. http://www.angelfire.com/ok3/chester/maindir/armarda.htm.
9. Alfred Thayer Mahan, *The Influence of Sea Power upon History, 1660–1783*, Dover Publications, 1987.

CHAPTER 3: HOW EMPIRES WORK

1. Emily Eakin, "Ideas and Trends; All Roads Lead to D.C.," *New York Times*, March 31, 2002.
2. Robert Kaplan, *Warrior Politics: Why Leadership Demands a Pagan Ethos*, Vintage, 2003.
3. Roger Cohen, "Globalist: Rumsfeld's Blunt Style May Backfire in China," *International Herald Tribune*, June 11, 2005.
4. Paul Kennedy, "The Greatest Superpower Ever," *New Perspectives Quarterly*, Winter 2002.
5. Thomas Cahill, *How the Irish Saved Civilization*, Anchor, 1996.
6. Ibid.
7. Ibid.
8. Deepak Lal, *In Praise of Empires: Globalization and Order*, Palgrave Macmillan, 2004.
9. Ibid.
10. https://www.imf.org/external/pubs/ft/issues1/ (fig. 4).
11. https://data.worldbank.org/indicator/NY.GDP.MKTP.KD.ZG?end=2022&locations=CN&start=1990.
12. https://data.worldbank.org/indicator/NY.GDP.MKTP.KD.ZG?end=2022&locations=IN&start=1986.
13. Rudyard Kipling, "The White Man's Burden," McClures, 1899.
14. Stephen Howe, *Empire: A Very Short Introduction*, Oxford University Press, 2002.
15. Ramsay MacMullen, *Corruption and the Decline of Rome*, reprint ed., Yale University Press, 1990.
16. Ibid.
17. Ibid.
18. http://www.antiwar.com/justin/j112299.html.
19. Aristotle, *Politics*, Nuvison Publications, 2004.
20. John Perkins, *Confessions of an Economic Hit Man*, Berrett-Koehler Publishers, 2004.
21. Niall Ferguson, *Colossus: The Rise and Fall of the American Empire*, reprint ed., Penguin, 2005.
22. John Quincy Adams's Address, July 4, 1821.
23. https://www.pgpf.org/chart-archive/0053_defense-comparison.
24. https://www.aei.org/research-products/speech/in-defense-of-empires/.
25. Floyd Norris, "Floyd Norris: Will China Be Setting U.S. Rates?" *International Herald Tribune*, May 13, 2005.
26. Grandfather Economic Report Series, http://home.att.net/~mwhodges/debt.htm.
27. *China Daily*, http://www2.chinadaily.com.cn/english/doc/2004-12/15/content_400251.htm.
28. See note 19.

29. *CIA: The World Factbook*, http://www.odci.gov/cia/publications/factbook/geos/us.html#Econ.
30. Institute for International Economics, http://www.iie.com/publications/papers/paper.cfm?researchid526.
31. See note 23.
32. Niall Ferguson, "The End of Power: Without American Hegemony the World Would Likely Return to the Dark Ages," *Wall Street Journal*, June 21, 2004.

CHAPTER 4: AS WE GO MARCHING

1. John T. Flynn, *As We Go Marching*, reprint ed., Ayer Company, 1972.
2. Ibid.
3. Ibid.
4. Ibid.
5. Ibid.
6. Ibid.
7. Jose Ortega y Gasset, *The Revolt of the Masses*, reissue ed., W.W. Norton & Company, 1994, Chapter 7.
8. See note 1.
9. Ibid.
10. Ibid.
11. Ibid.
12. https://www.brainyquote.com/quotes/niccolo_machiavelli_394858.
13. Sol Bloom, Chairman of the House Foreign Relations Committee, 1926, to colleagues.
14. "Arming for Peace," *New York Times*, October 31, 1951, p. 27.
15. Finance and Development, http://www.worldbank.org/fandd/english/0696/articles/0100696.htm.
16. https://www.treasurydirect.gov/kids/history/history_1950-1980.htm.
17. Garet Garrett, in his pamphlet "Rise of Empire," 1952.
18. Ibid.
19. Garet Garrett, *The People's Pottage*, Truth Seeker Co. Inc., 1992.
20. Ibid.
21. Ibid.

CHAPTER 5: THE ROAD TO HELL

1. Malcolm Gladwell, *Blink: The Power of Thinking without Thinking*, Little Brown, 2005.
2. Ibid.

3. Ibid.

4. Ibid.

5. Warren Harding, Inaugural Address, 1921.

6. H. L. Mencken, 1880–1956.

7. Judge Learned Hand, speech at "I Am an American Day" ceremony in Central Park, 1944.

8. Sigmund Freud, William C. Bullitt, *Thomas Woodrow Wilson: A Psychological Study*, Transaction Publishers, 1999.

9. https://graceredeemer.com/omission-accomplished/.

10. Woodrow Wilson, Address to Congress Asking for a Declaration of War, April 2, 1917.

11. The Raab Collection, http://raabcollection.com/detail.aspx?cat50&subcat 534&man5344.

12. http://www.ieru.ugent.be/palo.html.

13. See note 9.

14. Ibid.

15. Adam Gopnik, "The Big One: Critics Rethink the War to End All Wars," *The New Yorker*, August 23, 2004.

16. Viscount Esher, 1852–1930.

17. Winston Churchill, MIT's "Mid-Century Convocation," April 1949.

18. Ibid.

19. See note 8.

20. See note 9.

21. Hew Strachan, *The First World War*, Viking, 2004.

22. https://www.theunion.com/opinion/columns/cynthia-hren-we-are-not-a-democracy/article_1fb31e75-f2b1-50ad-9e34-dcbe0050c313.html.

23. https://www.independent.org/news/article.asp?id=8691.

24. https://press-pubs.uchicago.edu/founders/documents/v1ch10s9.html.

25. See note 21.

26. Winston Churchill, letter to his wife, July 28, 1914.

27. Stefan Zweig, *The World of Yesterday*, Viking Press, 1970.

28. Randolph Bourne in his essay, "The State," http://www.bigeye.com/rbquotes.htm.

29. See note 21.

30. Ibid.

31. Ibid.

32. The International School of Toulhouse, http://194.3.120.243/humanities/ibhist/war/wwi/europe_1914/germany/germany_before_1914.htm.

33. See note 9.

34. John F. Kennedy, Inaugural Address, January 20, 1961.

35. Richard Nixon, Inaugural Address, January 20, 1973.

36. Thomas Fleming, *The Illusion of Victory: America in World War I*, Basic Books, 2003.

37. https://en.wikipedia.org/wiki/Soap_made_from_human_corpses#:~:text
=The%20soap%20rumor%20was%20thoroughly,allowing%20them%20
to%20cast%20doubt.
38. https://www.johndclare.net/peace_treaties3.htm.
39. https://en.wikipedia.org/wiki/Talk:Robert_M._La_Follette_Jr.
40. David Lloyd George, War Memoirs, 1934.
41. Ludwig von Mises Institute, http://www.mises.org/fullstory.aspx?control
5224&id574.
42. History News Network, http://hnn.us/articles/10108.html.
43. Edward Chancellor, *Devil Take the Hindmost: A History of Financial
Speculation*, reissue ed., Plume, 2000.
44. Rod Mickleburgh, "He Did the Best He Could That Day . . . He
Survived," The Memory Project, *Toronto Globe and Mail*, http://www.
theglobeandmail.com/special/memoryproject/features/fox.html.
45. https://content.time.com/time/subscriber/article/0,33009,1635833,
00.html.
46. https://anthonybergen.medium.com/a-paralyzed-presidency-woodrow-
wilson-s-hidden-health-crisis-5800f8fafb06.
47. https://en.wikipedia.org/wiki/Economic_history_of_World_War_I#:
~:text=The%20cost%20of%20the%20war,the%20rest%20came%20
from%20taxes.
48. See note 41.

CHAPTER 6: A GREAT DEPRESSION

1. John T. Flynn, *The Decline of the American Republic and How to Rebuild It*,
Devin-Adair Publishers, 1955.
2. https://academic.oup.com/book/27019/chapter-abstract/196269728?
redirectedFrom=fulltext.
3. Civil War Currency Facts, http://www.civil-war-token.com/civil-war-
currency-facts.htm.
4. The Ludwig von Mises Institute, http://www.mises.org/etexts/rootofevilb
.asp.
5. Ibid.
6. Representative Robert Adams, January 26, 1894.
7. See note 4.
8. President William H. Taft's Message to Congress, June 16, 1909.
9. Amendment XVI, 1913.
10. https://constitutioncenter.org/the-constitution/articles/article-i#article-
section-3.
11. Article V of the Constitution in its original form.
12. John Dickinson, June 7, 1787, Constitutional Convention.

13. James Madison, "The Federalist No. 63, The Senate (continued)," *Independent Journal,* March 1, 1788.
14. C. H. Hoebeke, "Democratizing the Constitution: The Failure of the Seventeenth Amendment," *Humanitas,* Volume IX, No. 2, 1996.
15. https://constitutioncenter.org/the-constitution/amendments/amendment-xv.
16. John Kenneth Galbraith, *A Short History of Financial Euphoria,* Penguin Books, 1990.
17. United States Constitution, Tenth Amendment.
18. Franklin Delano Roosevelt, "Fireside Chat," March 9, 1937.
19. Ibid.
20. See note 1.
21. https://cei.org/studies/ten-thousand-commandments-2023/#:~:text=Ten%20Thousand%20Commandments%20is%20the,the%20U.S.%20economy%20at%20large.
22. Ibid.
23. Ibid.
24. https://www.forbes.com/sites/waynecrews/2023/12/28/national-association-of-manufacturers-pegs-cost-of-regulation-at-3079-trillion/?sh=53e384f04544.
25. Ibid.
26. https://www.treasurydirect.gov/kids/history/history_ww2.htm#:~:text=1933%20%2D%20The%20U.S.%20debt%20reached,to%20more%20than%20%24258%20billion.
27. https://www.worldeconomics.com/grossdomesticproduct/debt-to-gdp-ratio/United%20States.aspx#:~:text=GDP%20in%20United%20States%20is,debt%20level%20is%20%2428%2C652%20Billion.
28. https://en.wikipedia.org/wiki/History_of_the_United_States_public_debt#:~:text=The%20public%20debt%20as%20a,a%20post%2Dwar%20economic%20expansion.
29. https://www.archives.gov/milestone-documents/president-dwight-d-eisenhowers-farewell-address.
30. Ibid.
31. https://www.infoplease.com/history/us/major-military-operations-since-world-war-ii#:~:text=Data%20collected%20by%20the%20Uppsala,%22one%2Dsided%22%20conflicts.
32. See note 29.
33. Ibid.
34. Ibid.

CHAPTER 7: McNAMARA'S WAR

1. Ken Hagler's Radio Weblog, Recitation of the Battle of Camerone, April 30, 2003.

2. *Le Figaro*, May 7, 2004.
3. Ibid.
4. Ibid.
5. William J. Duiker, "Ho Chi Minh," *Theia*, September 27, 2000.
6. Ibid.
7. Vo Nguyen Giap, "When a Nation Was Born," Vietnam News Agency, 2000.
8. Charles W. Eliot, The Congressional Record.
9. Oliver Cromwell, letter to the synod of the Church of Scotland, August 5, 1650.
10. Robert S. McNamara, James Blight, Robert Brigham, Thomas Biersteker, and Herbert Y. Schandler, *Argument Without End: In Search of Answers to the Vietnam Tragedy*, Public Affairs Press, 2000.
11. The infamous domino theory: "You have a row of dominoes set up; you knock over the first one, and what will happen to the last one is that it will go over very quickly," President Eisenhower, April 7, 1954.
12. Lyndon B. Johnson, speech, October 21, 1964.
13. Memorandum from the President's Special Assistant for National Security Affairs (Bundy) to President Johnson, en route from Saigon to Washington, February 7, 1965.
14. See note 10.
15. Lyndon B. Johnson, Public Papers, 1963–1964, p. 952.
16. Walter Heller Oral History, 1965, in the Johnson Library.
17. "Tell the Vietnamese they've got to draw in their horns or we're going to bomb them back into the Stone Age," General Curtis LeMay, May 1964.
18. See note 10.
19. Bruce Palmer, *The Twenty-five Year War: America's Military Role in Vietnam*, University Press of Kentucky, 2001.
20. See note 10.
21. Ibid.
22. Martin Luther King, speech, New York City, April 4, 1967.
23. Lyndon B. Johnson, conversation with McGeorge Bundy, May 27, 1964.
24. See note 10.

CHAPTER 8: TRICKY DICK

1. Richard Duncan, *The Dollar Crisis: Causes, Consequences, Cures*, John Wiley & Sons, 2003.
2. Gardner Ackley, memo to Lyndon B. Johnson, July 30, 1965.
3. Lyndon B. Johnson, State of the Union Address, January 12, 1966.
4. Joseph Califano, *The Triumph and Tragedy of Lyndon Johnson*, Touchstone Books, 1992.

5. Ibid.
6. Ibid.
7. Ibid.
8. The Columbia Electronic Encyclopedia, copyright © 2005, Columbia University Press.
9. https://www.visualcapitalist.com/purchasing-power-of-the-u-s-dollar-over-time/.

CHAPTER 9: AMERICAN MONEY

1. https://www.washingtonpost.com/archive/opinions/2004/05/02/grand-designs/00d2b743-9308-450a-b151-988d55ff9149/
2. Ibid.
3. Claes G. Ryn, "Appetite for Destruction: Neoconservatives Have More in Common with French Revolutionaries Than American Traditionalists," *American Conservative*, January 19, 2004.
4. https://www.deseret.com/2008/2/14/20070486/thomas-sowell-fascism-s-origin-and-past-allies-may-surprise-leftists.
5. https://www.investopedia.com/updates/adam-smith-wealth-of-nations/#:~:text=Smith%20introduced%20the%20concept%20that,free%20trade%2C%20domestically%20and%20abroad.
6. https://en.wikipedia.org/wiki/The_Use_of_Knowledge_in_Society#:~:text=Hayek%20argued%20that%20information%20is,than%20by%20a%20central%20authority.
7. George Gilder, *Wealth and Poverty*, Basic Books, 1981, https://manhattan.institute/book/wealth-and-poverty.
8. Ibid.
9. Ross MacKenzie, "The Reagan Legacy: He Led a Revolution. Will It Survive?" *Economist*, June 10, 2004.
10. Ronald Reagan, Inaugural Address, January 20, 1981.
11. Murray N. Rothbard, "Repudiating the National Debt," Ludwig von Mises Institute, posted Friday, January 16, 2004, http://www.mises.org/fullstory.aspx?control51423&id574.
12. Bonner and Wiggin, *Financial Reckoning Day: Surviving Today's Global Depression*, John Wiley and Sons, 2009.
13. Rod Martin, Thank You, President Bush: Reflections on the War on Terror, Defense of the Family, and Revival of the Economy. World Ahead Publishing, August 30, 2004.
14. Ibid.
15. https://www.csmonitor.com/USA/2024/0103/How-plagiarism-claims-fueled-Claudine-Gay-s-resignation.
16. https://ritholtz.com/1979/08/the-death-of-equities/.
17. Peter G. Peterson, *Running on Empty*, Picador, 2005.

18. Jude Wanniski, "A Chinese/Asian Currency Zone?" http://www.wanniski
.com/showarticle.asp?articleid54529.
19. https://www.mauldineconomics.com/frontlinethoughts/archive/2005/12.

CHAPTER 10: THE EMPIRE OF DEBT

1. David H. Levey and Stuart S. Brown, "The Overstretch Myth," *Foreign Affairs*, March/April 2005.
2. https://www.huffpost.com/entry/chinese-want-to-buy-the-b_b_144920
3. H. A. Scott Trask, "Perpetual Debt: From the British Empire to the American Hegemon," Ludwig von Mises Institute, posted January 27, 2004.
4. Thomas Jefferson to James Madison, September 6, 1789.
5. Ron Suskind, *The Price of Loyalty: George W. Bush, the White House, and the Education of Paul O'Neill*, Simon & Schuster, 2004.
6. Alan Greenspan at the Adam Smith Memorial Lecture, Kirkcaldy, Scotland, February 6, 2005.
7. George Orwell, "The Lion and the Unicorn: Socialism and the English Genius," essay, 1941.
8. James Surowiecki, *The Wisdom of Crowds*, Anchor, 2005.
9. F. A. Von Hayek, "The Pretence of Knowledge," Nobel Memorial Lecture, December 11, 1974.
10. Richard Duncan, "How Japan Financed Global Reflation," ANDONGKIM, May 20, 2005.
11. Ibid.
12. *Grant's Interest Rate Observer* vol. 23, no. 16 (August 12, 2005), Bank of the Yield Curve.
13. See note 1.
14. Ibid.
15. See note 10.
16. Ibid.
17. https://www.motherjones.com/politics/2005/01/what-could-go-wrong-2005/.
18. See note 10.
19. https://en.wikipedia.org/wiki/You%27ll_own_nothing_and_be_happy.

CHAPTER 11: MODERN IMPERIAL FINANCE

1. http://www.princeton.edu/pr/news/03/q2/0612-brain.htm.
2. "Dennis Kucinich on Free Trade" *On the Issues*, http://www.issues2000
.org/2004/Dennis_Kucinich_Free_Trade.htm.

3. Raymond Aron, *The Dawn of Universal History: Selected Essays from a Witness of the Twentieth Century,* Basic Books, 2003.
4. https://www.statista.com/statistics/246268/personal-savings-rate-in-the-united-states-by-month/.
5. https://fred.stlouisfed.org/series/W207RC1Q156SBEA.
6. https://www.cnbc.com/2023/01/07/2022-was-the-worst-ever-year-for-us-bonds-how-to-position-for-2023.html.
7. Alan Greenspan at the Adam Smith Memorial Lecture, Kirkcaldy, Scotland, February 6, 2005.
8. Robert McTeer, Dallas, 2001.
9. Edmund L. Andrews, "Greenspan Shifts View on Deficits," *New York Times,* March 16, 2004, section A, column 1, page 1.
10. http://www.census.gov/prod/www/abs/decennial.html.
11. https://www.ncbi.nlm.nih.gov/pmc/articles/PMC1930177/#:~:text=Talleyrand%20once%20remarked%20to%20Napoleon,allowing%20this%20pregnancy%20to%20continue.
12. See note 7.
13. Ibid.
14. Stephen Roach, "Global: Confession Time." Global Economic Forum, Morgan Stanley, February 7, 2005, http://www.morganstanley.com/GEFdata/digests/20050207-mon.html.
15. https://en.wikiquote.org/wiki/Joseph_Schumpeter.

CHAPTER 12: SOMETHING WICKED THIS WAY COMES

1. Thomas L. Friedman, "Outrage and Silence," *New York Times,* May 20, 2005.
2. Ibid.
3. https://www.youtube.com/watch?v=ZwFaSpca_3Q.
4. https://www.washingtonpost.com/archive/opinions/1997/09/19/the-end-of-an-era-of-bashing-government/05dcef35-2c4f-4e1c-8dd8-cc480f29a846/.
5. https://twitter.com/caitoz/status/1706103295822164433.
6. https://twitter.com/LeaderMcConnell/status/1704886396572315675.
7. https://www.whitehouse.gov/briefing-room/speeches-remarks/2023/09/19/remarks-by-president-biden-before-the-78th-session-of-the-united-nations-general-assembly-new-york-ny/.
8. https://www.nytimes.com/2023/09/15/opinion/ukraine-war-putin.html.
9. https://www.nato.int/cps/en/natohq/opinions_218172.htm.
10. https://www.commondreams.org/opinion/nato-chief-admits-expansion-behind-russian-invasion#:~:text=Oleksiy%20Arestovych%2C%20

former%20Advisor%20to,Ukraine%2C%20just%20many%20years%20later.

11. https://www.nytimes.com/2023/09/15/opinion/ukraine-war-putin.html.
12. Ibid.
13. Ibid.
14. Ibid.
15. Ibid.

CHAPTER 13: WELCOME TO SQUANDERVILLE

1. https://www.latimes.com/archives/la-xpm-2005-apr-03-fi-afford3-story.html.
2. https://www.economist.com/united-states/2008/11/20/the-end-of-the-affair.
3. David Streitfeld, "They're In—But Not Home Free," *Los Angeles Times* staff writer, April 2, 2005.
4. Ibid.
5. Ibid.
6. Joyce Cohen, "The Hunt: Becoming a Mogul, Slowly," *New York Times*, April 10, 2005, late edition—final, section 11, column 1, page 12.
7. Ibid.
8. Warren Buffett and Charlie Munger, Berkshire Hathaway shareholders meeting, April 30, 2005.
9. Jane Hodges, "Flipping Real Estate . . . Without Getting Burned," *Seattle Times*, May 3, 2005.
10. Ibid.
11. Ibid.
12. Testimony of Chairman Alan Greenspan, *Federal Reserve Board's Semiannual Monetary Policy Report to the Congress*. Before the Committee on Banking, Housing, and Urban Affairs, U.S. Senate, February 16, 2005.
13. Dan Ackman, "Retirement Doomsday," *Forbes*, May 4, 2005.
14. Alan Greenspan, at the Federal Reserve System's Fourth Annual Community Affairs Research Conference, Washington, DC, April 8, 2005.
15. https://www.economist.com/special-report/2004/06/17/mirror-mirror-on-the-wall.
16. Ibid.
17. Ibid.
18. https://nces.ed.gov/programs/digest/d10/tables/dt10_025.asp.
19. https://www.bls.gov/opub/btn/volume-1/pdf/a-comparison-of-25-years-of-consumer-expenditures-by-homeowners-and-renters.pdf.
20. https://www.fool.com/the-ascent/research/average-household-debt/#:~:text=American%20households%20carry%20a%20total,the%20second%20quarter%20of%202023.

21. https://thehill.com/business/4301871-annual-interest-payments-on-us-debt-cross-1t-bloomberg/.
22. https://www.nytimes.com/2007/08/05/books/review/Gross-t.html.
23. See note 12.
24. William Shakespeare, *The Tempest*, Act iii, Scene 2.

CHAPTER 14: KINGDOMS ARE OF CLAY

1. Peter Thal Larsen, "Goldman Pays the Price of Being Big," *Financial Times*, August 13, 2007.
2. Citigroup Inc., Q3 Earnings Call Transcript, October 16, 2008.
3. James Howard Kunstler, speech in Vancouver for SFU urban studies program, "Challenges to Cities and Agriculture from Peak Oil," January 24, 2008.
4. Economagic: Economic Time Series Page, http://www.economagic.com/em-cgi/data.exe/var/togdp-householdsectordebt.
5. https://www.treasurenet.com/threads/six-nobel-prizes-finance-article-from-vanity-fair-magazine.106612/.
6. Ibid.
7. Robert Plummer, "Madoff Millions Vanish into Thin Air," BBC News, December 15, 2008.
8. "Citigroup's Chuck Prince Stops Dancing," Wcomimportuser1, Time.com, November 4, 2007.
9. "Keep Your Shirt On," Economist.com, August 5, 2007.
10. Ron Chernow, *The House of Morgan: An American Banking Dynasty and the Rise of Modern Finance*, Grove Press, 2001.
11. Ibid.
12. Andrew Clark and Elana Schor, "Lehman Brothers Chief Executive Grilled by Congress over Compensation," Guardian.co.uk, October 6, 2008.
13. Roger Lowenstein, *When Genius Failed: The Rise and Fall of Long-Term Capital Management*, Random House, 2001.
14. Christine Harper, "Morgan Stanley Said to Be in Talks with China's CIC (update 2)," Bloomberg.com, September 18, 2008.
15. https://www.nbcnews.com/id/wbna26820117.
16. Ruth Gledhill, "The Archbishop of Canterbury Speaks in Support of Karl Marx," Times-Online, September 24, 2008.
17. Garrison Keillor, "Garrison Keillor: Where Were the Cops?" *International Herald Tribune*, September 25, 2008.
18. https://www.nbcnews.com/id/wbna26898632.
19. Luigi Zingales, "Why Paulson Is Wrong," September 21, 2008, https://cepr.org/voxeu/columns/why-paulson-wrong.
20. https://www.pbs.org/wgbh/pages/frontline/meltdown/etc/script.html.

21. HR 1424 Library of Congress.
22. Nathaniel C. Nash, "Let Banks Enter Securities Field, Greenspan Says," *New York Times*, November 19, 1987.
23. Andrew Balls, "Greenspan Relaxed About House Prices," *Financial Times*, May 21, 2005.
24. Jessica Holzer, "Greenspan Sees a Soft Landing," Forbes.com, October 26, 2006.
25. Speech by Chairman Ben S. Bernanke at the Federal Reserve Bank of Chicago's 43rd Annual Conference on Bank Structure and Competition, Chicago, May 17, 2007.
26. David Jackson, "Bush: U.S. Is Not Headed into a Recession," *USA Today*, February 28, 2008.
27. Michael M. Phillips and Greg Ip, "Henry Paulson Dismisses Mortgage Rescue Plans," Wall Street Journal Online, February 29, 2008.
28. Gabriel Madway, "Paulson: Subprime Mortgage Fallout 'largely contained'," MarketWatch, March 13, 2007.
29. "Bear Sterns CEO: No Liquidity Crisis for Firm," CNBC.
30. Stephen Labaton, "Agency's '04 Rule Let Banks Pile Up New Debt," *New York Times*, October 2, 2008.
31. Jeannine Aversa, "Bernanke: Fannie, Freddie in No Danger of Failing," USA Today, July 16, 2008.
32. George W. Bush, Speech to the Nation on Financial Crisis and Economic Recovery Plan, September 24, 2008.
33. Brian Wingfield and Josh Zumbrun, "The Paulson Plan: Bad News for the Bailout," Forbes.com, September, 23, 2008.
34. "Paulson Defends Federal Financial Rescue Effort" (transcript), NewsHour with Jim Lehrer, PBS, November 13, 2008.
35. Anton Antonowicz, "Barack Obama's Victory Changes the World," *The Mirror*, November 6, 2008.
36. "U.S. Elects President Obama," editorial, *The Guardian*, November 5, 2008.
37. https://content.time.com/time/specials/packages/article/0,28804, 1856381_1856380_1856376,00.html.
38. Bernard-Henri Levy, "Obama Arouses a Wild Yet Reasonable Hope," *Financial Times*, November 5, 2008.
39. Ibid.
40. https://www.dailyjournal.com/articles/289621-the-dream-deferred.
41. David Brooks, "Revolt of the Nihilists," *New York Times*, September 30, 2008.
42. Martin Wolf, "Congress Decides It Is Worth Risking Depression," *Financial Times*, September 30, 2008.
43. Murray N. Rothbard, America's Great Depression, 5th ed., The Ludwig von Mises Institute, 2000.
44. https://millercenter.org/the-presidency/presidential-speeches/october-2-1930-address-american-bankers-association.

45. See note 43.

46. Ibid.

47. Ibid.

48. Ibid.

49. Alex Kerr, *Dogs and Demons: Tales from the Dark Side of Japan*, Hill and Wang, 2001.

50. Ralph T. Foster, *Fiat Paper Money: The History and Evolution of Our Currency*, Foster Publishing, Coin and Stamp, 2008.

51. Remarks by Governor Ben S. Bernanke before the National Economists Club, Washington, DC, November 21, 2002.

52. "Les Bourses de Paris, Londres et Francfort clôturent en forte baisse," *Le Monde*, January 14, 2009.

53. http://www.rbz.co.zw/pdfs/2008%20MPS/AprilMPS2008.pdf.

54. The Crisis and the Policy Response. Remarks by Ben S. Bernanke, Chairman Board of Governors of the Federal Reserve System at the Stamp Lecture. London School of Economics. London, England. January 13, 2009

55. Joseph Tainter, *The Collapse of Complex Societies*, Cambridge University Press, 1988.

56. Ibid.

57. Giovanni Battista (Giambattista) Vico, Scienza Nuova (The New Science), 1725.

58. CNN Politics, "Commentary: Obama's Lofty Ideas Lack Specifics." http://edition.cnn.com/2009/POLITICS/01/08/campbell.brown.obama/.

59. "Do Asset Markets Really Provide Lifetime Buying Opportunities?" *The Gloom, Boom & Doom Report*, a publication of Mark Faber Limited, January 2009.

60. E. D. Hirsch, *The New Dictionary of Cultural Literacy*, 3rd ed., Houghton Mifflin Company, 2002.

61. *Thirty-Six Stratagems*, published in English by Harro von Senger, 1992, 2000.

62. "Bin Laden: Goal Is to Bankrupt U.S.," CNN.com. November 2, 2004.

CHAPTER 15: TURNING ARGENTINE

1. https://www.washingtonpost.com/business/2020/03/31/trump-democrats-coronavirus-infrastructure/.

2. https://www.heritage.org/poverty-and-inequality/report/the-war-poverty-after-50-years#:~:text=In%20his%20January%201964%20 State,trillion%20on%20anti%2Dpoverty%20programs. The totals in foreign aid to Ukraine and Israel have barely begun to be tabulated.

3. https://www.thirteen.org/wnet/supremecourt/capitalism/sources _document1.html.

4. https://en.wikipedia.org/wiki/Randolph_Bourne#:~:text=From%20 this%20essay%2C%20which%20was,authority%20and%20resources%20 during%20conflicts.
5. https://www.laphamsquarterly.org/contributors/mencken.
6. https://www.nytimes.com/2021/08/17/business/ppp-fraud-covid.html.
7. https://www.nbcnews.com/politics/justice-department/biggest-fraud-generation-looting-covid-relief-program-known-ppp-n1279664.
8. https://fortune.com/2020/09/24/coronavirus-stimulus-checks-mark-cuban-1000-dollars-a-month/.
9. https://www.trcp.org/2011/01/18/it-is-not-the-critic-who-counts/.
10. George Frisbie Hoar, *The Advocate of Peace*, American Peace Society, 1898.
11. https://openendedsocialstudies.org/2018/07/22/the-philippines-in-the-american-empire/.
12. https://www.washingtonpost.com/opinions/2020/07/10/biden-just-ate-trumps-populist-lunch/.
13. https://theweek.com/speedreads/926430/kanye-west-wants-marijuana-free-everyone-who-baby-million-dollars.
14. https://www.rogueeconomics.com/unpublished/the-2020-democratic-national-conventions-solution-to-americas-problems-is-more-government/.
15. https://www.goodreads.com/quotes/1182-never-interrupt-your-enemy-when-he-is-making-a-mistake.
16. https://www.google.com/search?q=milei+davos+speech&sourceid =chrome&ie=UTF-8.
17. Ibid.
18. Ibid.
19. https://mises.org/print/65325.
20. Ibid.

CHAPTER 16: GRAY SWANS

1. https://www.cnbc.com/2024/01/16/divide-between-political-elites-and-the-working-class-is-a-major-risk-allianz-ceo-says.html.
2. https://twitter.com/Snowden/status/1746299284075557177
3. James Dale Davidson and Lord William Rees-Mogg, *Plague of the Black Debt*, Agora Publishing, 1993.
4. https://en.wikipedia.org/wiki/High_Performance_Computing _Act_of_1991.
5. https://www.ntu.org/about.
6. https://www.newyorker.com/magazine/2009/06/29/angelos-ashes.

7. https://www.statista.com/statistics/262340/daily-time-spent-with-digital-media-according-to-us-consumsers/#:~:text=In%202021%2C%20adults%20in%20the,compared%20to%20the%20previous%20year.
8. https://companiesmarketcap.com/tech/tech-companies-ranked-by-pe-ratio/.
9. https://www.bonnerprivateresearch.com/p/when-the-heads-start-rolling
10. https://static.seekingalpha.com/uploads/sa_presentations/470/57470/original.pdf
11. https://www.bonnerprivateresearch.com/p/when-the-heads-start-rolling
12. Ibid.
13. Ibid.
14. Ibid.
15. https://www.investopedia.com/terms/g/grey-swan.asp.
16. Ibid.
17. https://en.wikipedia.org/wiki/Exorbitant_privilege.
18. https://en.wikipedia.org/wiki/Nixon_shock.
19. https://www.sandstoneam.com/insight/rise-of-the-petrodollar.
20. http://en.wikipedia.org/wiki/1973_oil_crisis.
21. http://www.imf.org/external/np/speeches/2006/032306a.htm.
22. http://www.cbsnews.com/8301-505123_162-57339831/the-30-year-bull-market-in-bonds-is-over/.
23. http://uk.reuters.com/article/2009/02/28/uk-berkshire-buffett-bubbles-sb-idUKTRE51R1Q720090228.
24. https://www.tehrantimes.com/economy-and-business/94459-iran-to-regularly-offer-crude-oil-on-bourse-next-year.
25. https://www.projectcensored.org/9-irans-new-oil-trade-system-challenges-us-currency/.
26. https://en.wikipedia.org/wiki/Iranian_oil_bourse.
27. https://www.aljazeera.com/economy/2023/8/22/can-brics-end-apartheid-against-the-global-south.
28. https://www.reuters.com/markets/currencies/what-is-brics-currency-could-one-be-adopted-2023-08-23/.
29. https://www.aljazeera.com/economy/2023/8/24/saudi-arabia-iran-to-join-brics-as-grouping-admits-six-new-members#:~:text=Argentina%2C%20Egypt%2C%20Ethiopia%2C%20Iran,starting%20point%20for%20BRICS%20cooperation.
30. https://www.aljazeera.com/economy/2023/8/24/saudi-arabia-iran-to-join-brics-as-grouping-admits-six-new-members#:~:text=Argentina%2C%20Egypt%2C%20Ethiopia%2C%20Iran,starting%20point%20for%20BRICS%20cooperation.
31. https://www.aljazeera.com/features/2023/8/24/can-brics-dethrone-the-us-dollar-itll-be-an-uphill-climb-experts-say.
32. Ibid.
33. http://www.charlierose.com/view/interview/11289.

34. https://www.midasgoldgroup.com/news/world-reserve-currencies-since-1450/#:~:text=Since%201450%20there%20have%20been,currency%20span%20is%2094%20years.
35. http://www.beeland.com/THE_DOWNWARD_SPIRAL.htm.
36. http://www.forbes.com/sites/afontevecchia/2011/08/30/pimcos-bill-gross-stay-out-of-euro-us-china-menage-a-trois/.
37. https://finance.yahoo.com/news/chart-day-long-term-bull-232601861.html#:~:text=The%20chart%20suggests%20to%20BofA;the%202000%20dot%2Dcom%20bubble.
38. James Surowiekci, "Why Gold," *New Yorker*, November 29, 2004.
39. Ibid.
40. https://www.edgarepeters.com/blog-2-2/the-financial-instability-minsky-regime.
41. https://www.nytimes.com/2024/02/07/business/us-national-debt-congressional-budget-office.html#:~:text=Congressional%20Budget%20Office%20projections%20released,spending%20cuts%20had%20slowed%20deficits.
42. https://thehill.com/business/4301871-annual-interest-payments-on-us-debt-cross-1t-bloomberg/#:~:text=The%20estimated%20yearly%20amount%20the,recent%20analysis%20by%20Bloomberg%20found.
43. https://www.crfb.org/press-releases/cbo-estimates-383-billion-deficit-first-two-months-fiscal-year#:~:text=CBO%20Estimates%20%24383%20Billion%20Deficit%20For%20First%20Two%20Months%20of%20Fiscal%20Year,-Dec%208%2C%202023&text=The%20United%20States%20borrowed%20%24383,from%20the%20Congressional%20Budget%20Office.

INDEX